LADIESORGENTLEMEN

To my wife, Barbara Cady,
a remarkable writer and editor
who has been the main inspiration
of my life since we married
two decades ago.
With love.

Text © 2005 Jean-Louis Ginibre
Copyright © 2005 Filipacchi Publishing USA, Inc.

First published in the United States of America by
Filipacchi Publishing
1633 Broadway
New York, NY 10019

Art Directors: Patricia Ryan and Michele Tessler
Proofreading: Jennifer Ditsler-Ladonne
Indexing: Cathy Dorsey

ISBN: 1-933231-04-1

Printed by Editoriale Bortolazzi-Stei, Verona - Italy

A
PICTORIAL
HISTORY
OF
**MALE
CROSS-DRESSING**
IN THE MOVIES

LADIESORGENTLEMEN

BY
**JEAN-LOUIS
GINIBRE**

FOREWORD BY
JOHN LITHGOW

EDITED BY
BARBARA CADY

filipacchi
publishing

LADIES**OR**GENTLEMEN

257

34

345

119

266

193

John Lithgow with Jane Curtin in the episode "I Enjoy Being a Dick" of the hit television series *3rd Rock From the Sun* (season 1995-96.)

FOREWORD

IN 1957, ON A HOT summer evening in Ohio, I appeared in a outdoor skit on the last night of Boy Scout Camp. I was 11 years old. The skit was a brief, hastily rehearsed version of the familiar tale of the villain, the hero, and the damsel-in-distress tied to the railroad tracks. I had been cast as the damsel-in-distress. I remember nothing of the preparations leading up to the performance, only the queasy fear that I was about to suffer catastrophic embarrassment and humiliation in front of hundreds of jeering boys.

What I do remember, in vivid detail, is the performance itself. From my first appearance, I created a sensation. A flowery tablecloth pinned around my waist was my skirt. A scout bandanna was my coquettish headscarf. A T-shirt and hiking boots completed the look. The shrieking crowd emboldened me to mince around in my makeshift drag. I squealed for mercy as the villain manhandled me and tied me to the tracks. Eagle Scout Larry Fogg, playing my hero, untied me, hoisted me aloft, lost his footing and collapsed with me on top of him. Gales of laughter showered down on us. I was probably the shyest boy at camp, but that night I was the number one in camp.

What made all those raucous boys laugh like that? I have been thinking about that question for years.

I am a character actor now. Since that night in Ohio, I have played more roles than I can count, on stage, on television, in films, even in a ballet. My distinguishing characteristics as an actor have been my versatility, my audacity, and a marked tendency toward excess. So perhaps it is not surprising that

BY JOHN LITHGOW

among my many roles there have been six in which I have worn women's clothing.

In three of these drag roles I was unabashedly looking for laughs, just like that 11-year-old at Boy Scout Camp. To this end, I have impersonated Margaret Thatcher on *Saturday Night Live*; I have crashed a women's group on *3rd Rock from the Sun*; and I have donned massive padding and a ballroom gown as Mabel Buntz, the School Nurse, in the New York City Ballet's *Carnival of the Animals*. These comic turns have taught me that nothing makes an audience laugh as readily as a man in a frock.

But the other three drag roles were something else again. In the last moments of Brian De Palma's *Raising Cain,* my character's split personality took on the shocking guise of a sinister, silent woman in a red suit, staring directly at the camera. Audiences screamed in horror. In the stage role of diplomat René Gallimard in David Henry Hwang's *M. Butterfly,* I transformed myself into a Kabuki Cio-Cio-San, complete with kimono, black wig and chalk makeup. Her ritual suicide with a sword is the heartbreaking final image of the play.

And then there is the most captivating part I've ever played. This was the transsexual former pro-football player Roberta Muldoon in the film based on John Irving's *The World According to Garp*. In both the novel and the film, Roberta is a remarkable creation—droll, wistful, melancholic, tragic. Her first appearance on screen is a comic encounter with Robin Williams' T.S. Garp. A few scenes later, she is overcome with sadness that she cannot have children. She becomes the strong, tender comforter of the Garp family as it suffers appalling tragedy. In her last appearance, Roberta is wailing with grief at the death of her beloved mentor, Garp's mother Jenny. For all of her eccentricities, Roberta Muldoon is a role that travels far beyond drag comedy.

So what have all these adventures taught me? That the sight of a man playing a woman can indeed be hilarious. But it can also be horrific. And it can be deeply moving. Switching genders is the most potent tool an actor has to startle an audience, whether his intent is to amuse, to frighten, or to move them. It is a mysterious weapon, and its power is derived from the darkest, most unknowable mystery: deep down, what is the opposite sex really like? For men and women, this basic question is a primary source of both titillation and anxiety. We carry this emotional baggage with us when we watch movies and plays. It's no wonder that we are so drawn to the sight of men in drag on screen: no matter what kind of movie they're in, they are exploding our fears.

Jean-Louis Ginibre has done us the immense favor of creating an encyclopedic record of men in drag on film. Pore through these pages and you will find stills from many performances you have seen, but many more will be new and fascinating to you. All of these actors have something in common with that skinny kid in 1957, camping it up in front of an audience of whooping Boy Scouts: they surprise, they disarm, and they entertain by playing tricks with our sense of ourselves. •

John Lithgow

INTRODUCTION BY JEAN-LOUIS GINIBRE

AS THE REMARKABLY versatile actor John Lithgow writes in his foreword to this book, nothing in the theatrical experience seems to guarantee a laugh like a man in a frock. In turn-of-the-century America, in fact, many vaudevillians did not consider their act complete unless they brought the house down with a drag routine complete with frilly skirts and flouncy ringlets. Female impersonation retained its stature as reliable comic relief with the invention of the "flickers" in the early 20th century, maintaining this status through the silent era all the way to the present. Therefore, when in 2000 the American Film Institute listed the 100 funniest movies, it came as no surprise to me that the gender-bending classics *Some Like It Hot* and *Tootsie* ranked number one and two respectively.

Since my teenage years in suburban Paris, I have been fascinated by jazz and film. So, like any enthusiast, I started collecting records, books, posters and movie stills relating to my favorite art forms. Later, in the early '70s, when I was editor-in-chief of a rather sophisticated men's magazine called *Lui,* I asked British collector and archivist John Kobal to prepare a couple of four-to-five-page, black-and-white features for us, one of them about female impersonation in the movies. When I saw how funny and intriguing the pictures John brought us were, we published the story. This article sharpened my awareness about cross-dressing in film and, in the following years, I kept an eye on the increasingly popular phenomenon, adding related memorabilia to my want list during my collector shopping sprees.

A decade later, after moving to the United States and working during most of the '80s for *The Hollywood Reporter*, I recognized just how many useful functions drag was providing the screenwriter and director: the entire story line or a simple plot device; a way for a character to hide from pursuers; a formula to facilitate an impersonation or a hoax; a technique for portraying cops undercover; a system for delivering a point of view and a means of showing the gay lifestyle when it first began to come out of the closet. Finally, there was the pleasure of discovering a well-known star out of character. (Think of Marlon Brando in pioneer dress and poke bonnet, of virile Robert Mitchum as a cowboy masquerading as a western belle and of Yul Brynner singing— and looking —like a torch singer.)

Going through my film books in these pre-Web years, I tried to establish a list of films that included cross-dressing scenes. The more I researched the subject matter, however, the more I discovered movies that were unknown to me: it became clear that female impersonation in movies was a much larger niche than I had originally thought. And an underexplored one that, if delved into, could be the theme of an interesting book. So with this idea in mind, I began to acquire pictures in earnest—in whatever city I happened to find myself.

GETTING CROSS-DRESSED FOR THEIR CLOSE UP. Top: Rod Steiger, *No Way to Treat a Lady* (1967, Paramount); bottom left: Mickey Rooney and makeup artist Emile Lavigne, *Babes on Broadway* (1941, MGM); bottom right: Bob Hope, *Casanova's Big Night* (1953, Paramount).

I started enrolling the help of my wife, Barbara, my step-daughter, Monica, in London, my son, Jean-Noël, in Paris and a handful of friends.

The essence of *Ladies or Gentlemen*—as its amusing photos make obvious—is entertainment. I do not mean to imply by this, however, that the book is unworthy of the attention of the film devotee. My aim through the years has been to produce a comprehensive and highly accurate piece of cinematic research with a mainly nonjudgmental approach. That is why you will find in these pages photos and synopses of masterpieces such as Lucchino Visconti's *The Damned,* of cult films like *The Rocky Horror Picture Show* and even of stinkers like Ed Wood's *Glen or Glenda*. Video has been a precious tool that allowed me to watch such movies along with films from all over the world that had been long ignored or forgotten. These sometimes grueling screenings revealed hundreds of errors in plot descriptions that, because they were available before only in text form, had gone undetected.

Aside from its entertainment value, *Ladies or Gentlemen* informs without taking itself too seriously. That is why you will not find herein a text about the history of male cross-dressing through the ages, nor an evaluation of the complex psychological meaning of female impersonation. For this, one can turn to Swiss psychologist Carl Jung's Anima Theory—the anima being the feminine side of the male personal unconscious—as well as about 100 books such as *Vested Interests: Cross-dressing and Cultural Anxiety* by Marjorie Garber (Routledge, 1992). And if you are curious to know more, please Google the word "cross-dressing": when I finished the book I did it and got 866,000 related items in just 0.22 seconds!

One of the challenges of *Ladies or Gentlemen* was to organize the book into chapters that would make sense. I decided to separate the repeaters, mostly comedians like Stan Laurel, Bob Hope or Jerry Lewis, from the one- or two-timers. This second group has been divided according to the reason why the actor in drag has disguised himself. Some chapters overlap, but I think that each of them will help you discover new films —a new film being one you have not yet seen—or will revive memories of those you have already enjoyed (or hated), and bring you, I hope, a lot of smiles. It is as simple as that. •

ACKNOWLEDGEMENTS

Many of the stills created to promote new film releases would have been destroyed or lost if national and private archives had not collected and preserved them. I am grateful to these organizations and forever indebted to the many individuals who have devoted their lives to the protection of movie memorabilia out of their sheer love of the art form. Many have not only been responsive to my research requests by giving me support, but have also suggested films and sources unknown to me and often helped me find the unfindable. Without their crucial help, *Ladies or Gentlemen* could not have come to fruition.

My gratitude goes first to André Chevailler, photograph curator of the Cinémathèque Suisse in Lausanne, and his associate Richard Szotyori, who have been generous with their time and extremely helpful when I was returning to this project after more or less long hiatuses.

Kudos are due to Robert Cushman, photograph curator and photo services director, Academy of Motion Pictures Art & Sciences, Margaret Herrick Library in Beverly Hills; Mary Corliss, former curator of the MoMA Film Stills Archive in New York; Elisabet Helge, photograph curator, Swedish Film Institute in Stockholm; and in Paris Catherine Ficat, former curator of the Cinémathèque Française's Photothèque, now known as the Iconocothèque of the Bibliothèque du Film (BiFi).

I must also pay special tribute to the incomparable Claire Brandt who maintains Eddie Brandt's Saturday Matinee's stills department in North Hollywood: she knows more about B-actors than most film historians, and has provided us with high quality photographic research for the last five years.

A heartfelt thank-you to my London-based step-daughter, Monica Cady Clements who, with or without Jason Moreland, was for some time my contact with the wonderful researchers and curators of the British Film Institute National Library, where Information Officer Tessa Forbes and Access Researcher Nina Harding have been extremely helpful in the last stage of this long journey.

My sincerest thanks to Wolfgang Theis and Peter Latta at the Stiftung Deutsches Kinemathek, Filmmuseum in Berlin; Janet Lorenz, National Film Information Service, Beverly Hills; Florence Rossier, archives Hachette Filipacchi Medias, Paris; Jorge de Cominges, Fotogramas, Barcelona; Juan Caño and Augustin de Tena, Hachette Filipacchi, Madrid; Yves Bougon, Hachette Fujingaho, Tokyo; Wolf Pazurek, Hachette Rusconi, Milan; Iwona el Tambouli and Kristof Demidowicz, Warsaw.

My gratitude goes also to Giorgio Rao who, in the late '90s, when I was too busy to pursue my research, offered help in his country, Italy. When I received the material gathered by Giorgio's deputy, Marco Rostagno, I went back to the project and decided to finish it, if only to not disappoint these two generous gentlemen.

At Hachette Filipacchi Media, people aware of the project have encouraged me to finish it. I appreciate the moral support and help given to me by Gérald de Roquemaurel, Jack Kliger, Philippe Guelton, John O'Connor and Catherine Flickinger. My deep appreciation goes to employees who have offered me their time, creativity and skills when I needed them: Karl Rozemeyer, *Premiere*'s international editor who has been a key photo researcher in the last four years; Len La Grua, unflappable staff

photographer and photo department manager; Dorothée Walliser, Filipacchi Publishing's publisher; Jean-Jacques Naudet, a photographic guru who has been a fan of this project for almost two decades; and three wonderful women who have been my administrative assistants during the last 18 years: the late Jacqueline O'Reilly, Sandy Hall and Rachelle Ryp have successively updated my increasingly hefty database without losing a word. Many thanks also to François Théry, the indispensable master of the screen grab, and the fully committed art directors Patricia Ryan and Michele Tessler who have contributed so much to the design of *Ladies or Gentlemen*. John Lithgow, who was my first choice for the book's foreword, delivered an insightful text that adds another dimension to this book. I thank him profusely. I also want to praise all the actors who, like John Lithgow, have agreed to don female clothing in one or several films: it is thanks to them that his book exists.

Among the other people who have been part of the creation of this book, I thank the late Dr. Leslie Dornfeld, a great friend and supporter; French publishers Michel Birnbaum and Marie-Françoise Audouard; Frédéric Rousselot from the CID, Paris; Louis Dreyfus; Jennifer Cady; Maureen McFadden, Renée Simone and Matt Severson; Richard W. Bann, Critt Davis, Ralph W. Judd, the late John Kobal, four collectors with whom I exchanged stills in the early '80s; and art directors Guillaume Bruneau and Ragnar Johnsen who worked on early prototypes of *Ladies or Gentlemen*, now a reality after numerous years of research, film screening, photo editing and writing as well as doubt, procrastination and publishers' rejections. •

SEVEN DRAG CLASSICS

Some Like It Hot

Tootsie

The Rocky Horror Picture Show

Comedies

La cage aux folles

Charley's Aunt

that pushed cross-dressing into the mainstream

Victor/Victoria

The Carry On Series

CHARLEY'S AUNT

The essential cross-dressing farce
that has circled the globe for a century

▶ **SYDNEY CHAPLIN**
CHARLEY'S AUNT (1925, Christie)
Directed by Scott Sidney.

▼ **CHARLES RUGGLES**
CHARLEY'S AUNT (1930, Columbia)
Directed by Al Christie.

CHARLEY'S AUNT, the quintessential cross-dressing farce, was written in 1890 by Brandon Thomas, who had been asked by the then-famous English comedian W.S. Penley to write something in which he could star. Its December 21, 1892 opening in London was a sensation, after which it ran for four record-breaking years. The play was exported first to Germany in 1893, and then to New York as a vehicle for stage star Etienne Girardot. Translated into many languages, *Charley's Aunt* eventually morphed into a global success—at one point 44 performances were running simultaneously throughout the world. Still popular with regional and college theaters, *Charley's Aunt* has also found a home on TV with productions starring Art Carney (1957), Danny LaRue (1970) and Charles Grodin (1983). The story line concerns young Charley Wykeham, an Oxford student who is hopelessly in love with one Amy Spettigue, and whose roommate, Jack Chesney, adores Amy's friend, Kitty Verdun. When Charley's aunt and benefactress, the mysterious Donna Lucia D'Alvadorez, fails to arrive from South America as expected, Charley and Jack are stuck for a chaperone for their dates. Distraught, the clever swains prevail upon Lord Fancourt Babberley to don a black ▶▶

dress, shawl and grey wig and pose as the Brazilian heiress. Trapped in an alien femininity, at no time does Lord Babberley attempt to even act like a woman. And yet his mask is never disturbed. To his amusement, however, he is pursued by both Jack's kindly widower father and Amy's guardian, the choleric barrister Stephen Spettigue. When the real Donna Lucia shows up towing a female ward with fond memories of her sole encounter with Lord Babberley, the amatory confusion increases exponentially. In the end, however, the impostor reveals himself and almost everybody lives happily ever after. *Charley's Aunt* has made its way to the movies about 20 times starting with a 1925 silent version starring Syd Chaplin, Charlie's brother, as the cross-dresser. Then, in the U.S., three other big screen adaptations were shot starring Charles Ruggles (1930), Jack Benny (1941) and Ray Bolger (1952). Filmed once in Sweden, England, Italy, Denmark, Austria and the Soviet Union, twice in Germany, Spain, Argentina and France, *Charley's Aunt* was always modified, sometimes conservatively, sometimes more liberally. According to the language of each country, Brandon Thomas' aunt became a "tante," a "zia," a "tia" or a "tyotya." In France, she even became a godmother in the two versions titled *La marraine de Charley*. But in whatever country she appears, it is never her last performance. Just wait. ●

◄ **ELIS ELLIS** CHARLEYS TANT (1926, Sweden) **Directed by Elis Ellis.**

▼ **PAUL KEMP** CHARLEYS TANTE (1934, Germany) **Directed by R.A. Stemmle with Erik Ode (left) and Albert Lieven (right).**

◄ **ERMINIO MACARIO** LA ZIA DI CARLO (1942, Italy) **Directed by Alfredo Guarini.**

► **LUCIEN BAROUX** LA MARRAINE DE CHARLEY (1935, France) **Directed by Pierre Colombier.**

▲ JACK
BENNY
CHARLEY'S
AUNT
(1942, Fox)
**Directed by
Archie Mayo
with Laird
Cregar (right).**

▶ ARTHUR
ASKEY
CHARLEY'S
BIG HEARTED
AUNT (1940,
England)
**Directed by
Walter Forde.**

▲ PEDRO QUARTUCCI
LA TIA DE CARLOS (1946, Argentina)
Directed by Leopoldo Torre Rios.

▶ DIRCH PASSER
CHARLEYS TANTE (1959, Denmark)
Directed by Poul Bang.

▲ ALFREDO BARBIERI
LA TIA DE CARLITOS (1953, Argentina)
Directed by Enrique Carreras.

▶ PETER ALEXANDER
CHARLEYS TANTE (1963, Austria)
Directed by Geza von Cziffra with Marlene Rahn and Erika Pulwer.

▲ FERNAND RAYNAUD
LA MARRAINE DE CHARLEY (1959, France)
Directed by Pierre Chevalier with Paul Preboist (left).

▲ **RAY BOLGER**
WHERE'S CHARLEY?
(1952, Warner)
Directed by David Butler.

◄ **CASSEN**
LA TIA DE CARLOS
EN MINIFALDA (1967, Spain)
Directed by Augusto Fenollar.

► **HEINZ RÜHMANN**
CHARLEYS TANTE
(1956, Germany)
Directed by Hans Quest.

▼ **PACO MARTINEZ
SORIA**
LA TIA DE CARLOS
(1980, Spain)
**Directed by Luis
Maria Delgado.**

▲ **ALEKSANDR KALYAGIN**
HELLO, I'M YOUR AUNT! (1975, USSR)
Directed by Victor Titov with Armen Djigarhanyan.

SOME LIKE IT HOT

Two dolled-up boys in the band make an all-girl orchestra swing

RIOTOUSLY FUNNY, this 1959 screwball comedy written by I.A.L. Diamond and Billy Wilder did not uncover new situations nor travel unknown paths. In fact, the idea of unemployed male musicians joining–in drag–an all-female band had been used before in France by director Richard Pottier in *Fanfare d'amour* (1935) and in Germany in *Fanfaren der Liebe* (1951) and its sequel *Fanfaren der Ehe* (1953). But what Paramount's *Some Like It Hot* lacked in pure originality was redeemed by a clever script inspired by '30s gangster films, superb casting and brilliant direction by farcemeister Wilder. The result is a hilarious 122-minute masterpiece that enjoys the well-deserved reputation of being one of the best comedies of all time. *Some Like It Hot*'s story starts in Chicago on February 14th, 1929, when saxophonist Joe (Tony Curtis) and bass player Jerry (Jack Lemmon) inadvertently witness the St. Valentine's Day Massacre in which Spats Columbo (George Raft) and his thugs wipe out

Toothpick Charlie (George E. Stone) and his gang. Fleeing town in a mad rush, they accept a job with the Sweet Sue all-girl orchestra and disguising themselves as women join the band on a Florida-bound train. Joe immediately falls for the group's singer, Sugar Kane Kowalczyk (Marilyn Monroe), a vulnerable and sexy babe of the sort wolfish Joe routinely victimizes. In their forced drag roles as Josephine and Daphné, Joe and Jerry go from feeling conventionally ▶▶

Top: Sweet Sue (Joan Shawlee, right) leads her Society Syncopators, which includes Josephine (Tony Curtis), Daphné (Jack Lemmon) and singer Sugar Kane (Marilyn Monroe).

Bottom: Tony Curtis and Marilyn Monroe.

Opposite: Saxophonist Josephine (Tony Curtis) and bass player Daphné (Jack Lemmon).

ridiculous to grudgingly sympathetic concerning the tribulations of their "fellow" female musicians. Finally, they attain a giddy state of sexual confusion that includes empathy for Sugar's dreams of true love. Joe, however, cannot resist trying to seduce her and dons another disguise, this time posing as a suave but impotent millionaire whose family owns an oil company. Meanwhile, Jerry, still masquerading as Daphné, is wooed by a genuinely eccentric heir named Osgood Fielding III (Joe E. Brown). After Joe follows Jerry/Daphné onto Osgood's yacht, it is Sugar who turns the tables and entices him, but then, back at the hotel as Josephine, he gives Sugar big-sisterly advice about his own caddish designs on her. The atmosphere of loony sexual ambiguity is slightly dispelled when the mob catches up with the two wayward witnesses and a chase begins during which, after a kiss, Sugar Kane realizes that Josephine is not only a man, but the man she has been looking for. It all concludes in Osgood's speedboat with Joe and Jerry confessing their true identities to their respective paramours. When Daphné reveals to Osgood that he is a man, the nonplussed millionaire utters simply: "Nobody's perfect." •

Top, left: Jack Lemmon rehearses with Billy Wilder.

Top, right: Jack Lemmon and Joe E. Brown between takes.

Center: Tony Curtis and Jack Lemmon wait for their next scene.

Bottom: Tony Curtis and Jack Lemmon welcome visitor Maurice Chevalier.

OTHER WELL-ORCHESTRATED FARCES

◀ **JULIEN CARETTE & FERNAND GRAVEY**
FANFARE D'AMOUR
("Fanfare of Love," 1935, Solar Films)

French precursor to *Some Like It Hot* directed by Richard Pottier ● Two friends, pianist Jean (**Fernand Gravey,** right) and bassist Pierre (**Julien Carette,** left), are jobless. Noticing that the fad of all-female orchestras is preventing them from working, they masquerade as women and get a gig with The Dutch Tulips. Dressed on stage as Batavian peasant girls and in contemporary outfits between jobs (**photo**), the boys are so credible in their gender reversal that nobody would notice if they were not falling in love: Jean with the bandleader Gaby (Betty Stockfeld), Pierre with cellist Poupette (Gaby Basset). To express their feelings, Jean and Pierre are forced to revert, when possible, to suits and ties in a series of increasingly arduous quick-changes. And when the owner of a Riviera hotel falls for the coquette that Jean becomes when in drag, a fight breaks out. Uncloaked, Jean and Pierre are embarrassed before being embraced by their forgiving flames.

▲ **DIETER BORSCHE & GEORG THOMALLA**
FANFARES OF LOVE
(German title "Fanfaren der Liebe," 1951)

German precursor to *Some Like It Hot* directed by Kurt Hoffmann ● Two unemployed musicians, Peter Schmidt (**Georg Thomalla,** center) and Hans Martens (**Dieter Borsche,** left), audition out of desperation for an all-women's band led by Lydia d'Estée. With the help of women's clothing, "Hansi" and "Petra" are on their way to a performance in Munich. Friction arises when the two men—who now live in drag on stage (**photo**) and off—both fall for the band's singer, Gaby (Ingeborg Egger). First out of the gate is Hans, who reverts to male garb and poses as a composer. Parrying, Peter asks Lydia d'Estée to look for his pal Hans who later appears as Petra's brother. Dressed as men, Hans and Peter go with singer Gaby and band member Sabine (Isle Petri), but they must provide an alibi when Gaby requests that Hansi and Petra join the foursome. All is resolved when Gaby, after seeing Hans remove his wig, reveals her affection for him while Peter realizes he loves Sabine.

▲ **GEORG THOMALLA & DIETER BORSCHE**
FANFARES OF MARRIAGE
(German title "Fanfaren der Ehe," 1953)

Unabashedly nutty sequel to *Fanfares of Love* directed by Hans Grimm ● Musicians Peter (**Georg Thomalla,** left) and Hans (**Dieter Borsche,** right) have married their band mates Sabine (Isle Petri) and Gabby (Ingeborg Egger). One couple had a boy, the other a girl and they all live together. When Peter and Hans cannot find a job, their wives sign on for a cruise with the Swing Girls, an all-female band. Hans and Peter agree to play Mr. Mom. Not very gifted at this job, the duo is fingered as incompetent by their irascible landlord. When a social worker comes to check on the toddlers' welfare, Hans and Peter flee with the kids. Joining their wives in Genoa where their cruiser is anchored, they smuggle the babies aboard, masquerade as two missing American female passengers and are promptly accused of murdering the babies. Thankfully, when the two women show up, the enigma is solved. From then on, the couples enjoy the cruise, listening to the fanfares of marriage.

VICTOR AND VICTORIA

Double cross-dressing comedy in which a woman pretends to be a man to play a woman

WRITTEN AND DIRECTED by Reinhold Schünzel, *Viktor und Viktoria* was shot in 1933 and released in the States in 1935 under the title *Victor and Victoria.* Schünzel, who was born in 1886 in Hamburg, shot this gender-bending classic just before Hitler's men started to take control of the German media. A box-office success, it opened the doors of Hollywood for Schünzel, a Jew who, seeing the writing on the wall, had left Germany two years after the film's debut. *Viktor und Viktoria* takes place in Weimar Berlin when two performers, both rejected at an audition, share solace in a meal together. Viktor Hempel (Hermann Thimig), an actor, shows Susanne Lohr (Renate Muller), a singer, a photograph of him as a female Spanish dancer. Explaining he has a cold, he asks her if she will substitute for him as the female impersonator in his vaudeville drag act. Susanne, in need of a job, agrees and is a hit. Landing a contract, she continues her masculine cross-dressing off-stage and commences a tour with Viktor as her manager. When in London, she meets debonair Robert (Adolf Wohlbruck) and coolly sexual Elinor (Hilde Hildebrand), stylish movers and shakers in the city's *haut-monde.* Complications multiply when Robert becomes attracted to "Viktor" and, discerning almost immediately her sexual identity, toys with the implicit gender assumptions of Susanne's adopted masculinity.

Nevertheless, like the true sophisticate he is, he seems comfortable with the gender bending, accepting the fact that Susanne is just as intoxicating when she is a young man as when she is a woman. Like *La cage aux folles* five decades later, *Viktor und Viktoria* became the subject of remakes and adaptations. In fact, Schünzel was the first to create an immediate French language facsimile with the help of director Roger Le Bon. Titled *Georges et Georgette,* it was shot in parallel on the same soundstage with Julien Carette and Meg Lemonnier playing the cross-dressing entertainers. When Reinhold Schünzel arrived in Los Angeles, he directed several films, including the musical *Balalaika* (1939) with Jeannette MacDonald, and later concentrated on acting . He died in 1954. ●

Opposite: Hermann Thimig in his drag act as Viktoria.

Above: Renate Muller (left) and Hermann Thimig (right) both as Viktor.

SONNIE HALE
FIRST A GIRL (1935, Gaumont)

British version of *Viktor und Viktoria* directed by Victor Saville ● On a rainy day, hopeful singer Elizabeth (**Jessie Matthews,** bottom photo, right) meets Shakespearian actor and female impersonator Victor (**Sonnie Hale,** bottom photo, left). He takes her home to dry her clothes and, when he realizes that his oncoming cold is making him lose his voice, asks Elizabeth to perform in his place. Reluctant at first to impersonate a man who plays a woman on stage, she finally accepts. After a year playing a man who sings, dances and dresses like a woman, Elizabeth, under the name of Victoria, becomes the toast of the continent. In Paris, she and Victor meet Princess Mironov (Anna Lee) and her walker, Robert (Griffith Jones), the latter becoming quickly suspicious of Victoria's gender. Invited by the princess to take a trip to Nice, a car breakdown forces the four to stay in a small inn where the three "men" must share a room. Victoria succeeds in hiding her real gender, but the next day at the beach Robert discovers the truth. He soon declares his love, with Victoria following suit. When she decides to leave the show, Victor, unfazed, replaces her in his old stage role of Victoria (**top photo**). Outfitted in her glamorous costumes, he becomes such a comical sensation that the princess falls head over heels for him.

▼ ROBERT PRESTON
VICTOR/VICTORIA (1982, MGM)

Genial remake of the German gender-bender directed by Blake Edwards ● In 1934 Paris, unemployed British singer Victoria Grant (**Julie Andrews,** left) and openly homosexual American entertainer Carol "Toddy" Todd (**Robert Preston**) meet in a brasserie and share their woes. Having been ejected from her hotel on that rainy night, Victoria spends the night at Toddy's. Next morning, her clothes having shrunk, Victoria borrows a male outfit left by one of his lovers. A bolt of creative lightning strikes Toddy when he sees Victoria suited as a man: she would entertain as a female impersonator from Poland named Count Victor Breszinski. The ploy works, and, managed by Toddy, Victoria becomes a major nightlife attraction. When Chicago gangster King Marshall (James Garner) goes to see the new sensation, he finds himself strangely attracted to him. Feeling suddenly insecure about his sexuality, King hides in Victor's hotel room and realizes that he is not a man. Relieved, King starts a romance with a delighted Victoria, a romance that must be kept a secret as King fears his business associates will think he is homosexual. The couple separates but Victoria is so unhappy that she decides to end the charade. One evening at the supper club where she performs, she arrives dressed as a woman and surprises Duke at his table. When Victoria is introduced, Toddy appears on stage squeezed into her Spanish dancer outfit (**bottom photo**) and sings her signature hit "The Shady Dame from Seville."

THE CARRY ON SERIES

The English troupe of merry pranksters that brought parody and cross-dressing to the Empire's masses

IN THE ANNALS of English humor—a particularly irreverent and often ribald species—a special place is reserved for the *Carry On* film series. This is not only because the smarmy and modestly produced comedies were a huge financial success, but also because, at the time, their characters held sway over the affection of Brits everywhere. The formula was a clever one: take some randy, resourceful working-class blokes, a couple of arrogant snobs, a few skimpily attired but strong-minded lasses and plunk them in situations where there are bound to be sexual innuendos, frequent male cross-dressing and lots of over-the-top fun. The key ingredient that elevated these movies above their music-hall origins was the continuity of the cast, which helped the actors perform better together with each passing movie. Produced by Peter Rogers and directed by Gerald Thomas, the initial hit, *Carry On Sergeant,* was first screened in 1958. Written by comedy genius Norman Hudis, it featured future repertory series members Charles Hawtrey, Kenneth Williams and Kenneth Connor, all of whom would play through

the years the same type of characters: Hawtrey the effeminate proto-dandy, Williams the flamboyant know-it-all and Connor the skittish hayseed. In 1959, tapped for *Carry On Nurse,* cheeky Joan Sims, mainly portraying sex-starved middle-aged women, and rotund Hattie Jacques, who would excel in the roles of authoritative hospital matrons, signed on as regulars. In 1960, the mercilessly funny prankster Sid James, whose suggestive laugh would become the series' trademark, signed on for the fourth film, *Carry On Constable.* Jim Dale, who would become ▶▶

▲ **KENNETH WILLIAMS & CHARLES HAWTREY**
CARRY ON CONSTABLE (1959, Anglo-Amalgamated)
Blast of well-policed comic irreverence directed by Gerald Thomas ● A flu epidemic is thinning London's police ranks and an urgent need for replacements prompts Sgt. Frank Wilkins (Sidney James) to hire new graduates from the Police Academy. Assigned to Wilkins' station is a trio of clueless cops: Constable Charlie Constable (Kenneth Connor), a tense man obsessed with astrology, jovial womanizer Tom Potter (Leslie Philips) and know-it-all Stanley Benson (**Kenneth Williams,** left). Timothy Gorse (**Charles Hawtrey,** center), an effeminate bloke who operates in a daze, joins them. During their first few days, Constable Constable breaks down the door of an apartment after hearing cries for help emanating from...a radio, while Benson and Gorse, having read in the paper that shoplifting is on the rise, offer help to a local emporium. Their borrowing of dowdy female garb from the women's department results in disaster after they are accused of stealing merchandise (**photo**). Thankfully, the new graduates luck into capturing a gang of thieves after a fierce struggle, thereby triggering the promotion of the understanding Sgt. Wilkins to the station's top post.

KENNETH CONNOR
CARRY ON
CABBY
(1963, Anglo-
Amalgamated)
**Bittersweet farce
about the battle
of the sexes directed
by Gerald Thomas** ●
Charlie Hawkins
(Sid James), owner of
Speedy Cabs, is a
crusty but endearing
workaholic. When he
does not show up
for his wedding
anniversary, his long-
suffering wife Peg
(Hattie Jacques)
decides to teach him a
lesson. Hiring a bunch
of sexy female drivers,
she discretely starts a
rival firm, Glamcabs,
which quickly steals a
sizeable market share
from Speedy. Charlie
and his partner, Ted
Watson (**Kenneth
Connor**), strike back
by sabotaging their
rival's taxis, but the
plan does not work, as
the women are always
finding men willing to
fix their cabs for free.
Deciding to ransack
the Glamcabs' office
after hours, Charlie
asks Ted to steal one
of the women's
uniforms so he can
open the door from
the inside. His
masquerade is
uncovered by the girls,
one of whom (**Amanda
Barrie**, left) makes him
sweat bullets by
revealing a bit of skin
(**photo**). When Charlie
realizes his wife is the
boss of the new
company, he walks out
on her. But when she
is held up after picking
up her payroll at the
bank, Charlie calls all
his cabbies who
surround the
kidnappers and deliver
them to the police.

27

►► the bumbling leading man of the series, appeared first in *Carry On Cabby* (1963), and for the riotous James Bond send-up, *Carry On Spying* (1964), busty blonde Barbara Windsor was hired. The last member of the core group was gentle giant Bernard Bresslaw who joined in 1965 for *Carry On Cowboy.* But the ensemble was by no means a closed society. Over some 20 years, the cream of British comics was enlisted, including Peter Butterworth, Terry Scott, Jack Douglas, Leslie Philips and Bernard Cribbins. Though harsh critics hoped the series would end with its two masterpieces written by Talbot Rothwell, *Carry On Screaming!* (1966), a spoof of the British horror films of the time, and *Carry On...Up The Khyber* (1968), a parody of the *Gunga Din* genre, Rogers and Thomas continued to grind out one *Carry On* after another at London's Pinewood, their "home" studio. After a long hiatus, in 1993, they resumed shooting for the last film, *Carry On Columbus,* starring Jim Dale in the eponymous role. But the fun was gone, as some of the cast had died in the interim. The series carries on, however, thanks to video and word of mouth as new generations of Brits discover the humorous heritage handed down by its top beer-and-skittles comics ●

▲ SID JAMES
CARRY ON...DON'T LOSE YOUR HEAD (1966, Rank)
Lowbrow Scarlet Pimpernel-like romp directed by Gerald Thomas
● Paris 1789: the revolution has begun. Near the Bastille nobles are routinely beheaded. Watching is the most dreaded man in France, Citizen Camembert (**Kenneth Williams,** left), Robespierre's chief of the secret police. He is assisted by Citizen Bidet (Peter Butterworth), who keeps a head count. Meanwhile, across the Channel, the English aristocrats continue to lead comfortable lives. That is until a couple of fops, Sir Rodney Ffing (**Sid James**) and Lord Darcy de Pue (Jim Dale) don disguises to audaciously snatch potential victims from the guillotine—including the unhinged Duc de Pomfrit (Charles Hawtrey). Sir Ffing, the mastermind, signs his abductions the Black Fingernail and ridicules Camembert incessantly, most notably when, disguised as a woman, he flirts with him (**photo**). After chasing the Black Fingernail to Calais and London, Camembert returns to his château where swordfights between his foot soldiers and the Brits result in bedlam—and a deadly failure for the Big Cheese and Bidet whose heads are harvested.

▶ BERNARD CRIBBINS
CARRY ON SPYING
(1964, Anglo-Amalgamated)
Hilarious send-up of the 007 movies directed by Gerald Thomas ● When the chief of BOSH (British Operational Security Headquarters) learns that a secret formula has been stolen by STENCH (Society for the Total Extinction of Non-Conforming Humans), he orders four agents-in-training to recover it: Desmond Simkins (Kenneth Williams), an inept but confident man; jittery Charlie Bind (Charles Hawtrey); bumbling Harold Crump (**Bernard Cribbins**) and balmy Daphne Honeybutt (**Barbara Windsor**, right). After meeting at Vienna's Café Mozart, the agents find the formula's thief who divulges the nickname of his boss, Fat Man, and his destination, Algiers. There, spotting Fat Man in the Casbah, agents Honeybutt and Crump costume themselves as exotic dancers and follow him into a bordello (**photo**). The ill-proportioned tart that Crumb has become turns Fat Man off, but Honeybutt attracts him, allowing the two to recoup the formula. Eventually, the Brits are taken to the STENCH underground offices where they set a time bomb to blow up the fortress. After escaping safely, they realize STENCH's headquarters are located under BOSH's: the destruction of both is unavoidable.

◀ PETER BUTTERWORTH
CARRY ON SCREAMING!
(1966, Anglo Amalgamated)
Astute debunking of the horror genre directed by Gerald Thomas ● After six women have disappeared from Hocombe Park, Detective Sgt. Sidney Bung (Harry H. Corbett) and Detective Constable Slowbotham (**Peter Butterworth**) investigate. First they visit the Bide-A-Wee Rest Home where they meet Dr. Orlando Watt (Kenneth Williams) who tells them he has been dead for years, but that through a regenerative process, he awakens from time to time. When his body dissolves in front of their eyes, the cops flee in panic. The doctor returns to his lab where his busty sister Virula (Fenella Fielding), through a vitrification process, transforms into shop-window mannequins women murdered by Odbodd (Tom Clegg), a monster of Watt's making. Unable to connect the gathered evidence, Bung baits a trap with a female—Constable Slobotham in drag (**photo**). When Odbodd abducts Slobotham, Bung finally deduces that something weird is happening at Dr. Watt's mansion. There he finds, along with Slobotham on the verge of being vitrified, the scientist, who falls into a tub full of petrifying brew. Curvaceous Virula becomes Sgt. Bung's maid.

▼ PETER BUTTERWORTH, TERRY SCOTT, CHARLES HAWTREY & ROY CASTLE
CARRY ON…UP THE KHYBER (1968, Rank)
Comedic gem about stiff upper lips and missing underpants directed by Gerald Thomas ● It is 1895 and the "devils in skirts" of the Third Foot and Mouth Regiment guard the Khyber Pass. The unit inspires fear among the natives because of their glorious tradition—wearing nothing under their skirts. When the Khasi of Kalabar (Kenneth Williams) learns from a photo that most of them sport underpants, he knows he can foment a rebellion—and possibly end British rule—if he shows the evidence to the Burpas, a tribe whose warriors would then no longer fear the "devils." Concerned, Gov. Sidney Ruff-Diamond (Sid James) sends Cpt. Keene (**Roy Castle**, far right) and Sgt. Maj. MacNutt (**Terry Scott**, second from left) to the Burpas' compound in order to retrieve the picture. Enrolling bumbling Pvt. Widdle (**Charles Hawtrey**, second from right) and a civilian (**Peter Butterworth**, left), they enter the fortress but are quickly jailed. Princess Jelhi (Angela Douglas), Kalabar's daughter, who has fallen for Cpt. Keene, gives them sacred female dancers costumes (**photo**) for escape purposes. Meanwhile, Kalabar orders an attack on the governor's compound. But Sir Ruff-Diamond ignores the assault and orders a formal dinner during which the mansion collapses around his guests. When the Burpas enter the compound, the governor stops the combat, lines up his troops and has them lift their skirts. The Burpas, seeing that the "devils" still have a lot to offer, retreat in panic while the governor and his friends return to their dinner.

▶ KENNETH COPE
CARRY ON MATRON (1971, Rank)
From-here-to-maternity low-brow goof directed by Gerald Thomas ● The high street value of prescription drugs prompts small-time sharper Sid Carter (Sid James) to plan a robbery at the Finisham Maternity Hospital. When he cases the place, his demeanor arouses the suspicions of the matron (Hattie Jacques), so he decides that his son Cyril (**Kenneth Cope**) would do the job better if disguised as a female nurse in training. The lad agrees to the scheme, which turns out to be dicey, as he becomes a sex magnet for the lecherous Dr. Prodd (Terry Scott). Fighting him off, Cyril inadvertently gives him a shot of anesthesia and must deliver triplets in an ambulance, an event prompting newspapers to lionize him. When he later trips on the stairs (**photo**), Nurse Ball (Barbara Windsor) sees something that reveals his gender. But no setback alters Sidney's plans—with his son's help, he dynamites the door of the hospital's drug supply room. Cornered by the matron, Sid raises a scandalous possibility: What if it were made public that the triplets were delivered by an impostor in drag? The matron cuts the bumbling burglars loose.

◄ **BERNARD BRESSLAW**
CARRY ON GIRLS
(1973, Rank)
Gleefully raunchy and relentlessly coarse farce directed by Gerald Thomas ● In the rainy seaside resort of Fircombe, Sidney Fiddler (Sid James) convinces the municipal council to let him organize a beauty contest to promote tourism. In need of a press agent, Sidney calls publicist Pete Potter (**Bernard Bresslaw**) who is excited at the prospect of joining a group of free-thinking birds. Soon Pete and two dozen beauties arrive in Fircombe. Sidney, who wants to publicize the event, thinks of leaking the rumor that one of the contestants is a transvestite to women's libber Augusta Prodworthy (June Whitfield). He also has a reluctant Pete prepped as a leggy babe (**photo**) by airhead Miss Easy Rider (**Barbara Windsor**, right). When Pete joins the girls for a group shot in the hotel lobby, Ms. Prodworthy and her anti-male group burst in to unmask the impersonator. As hoped for by Sidney, the local paper publishes a front-page story on Pete's unladylike exit. The day of the event, the filled-to-capacity Pier Theatre is the scene of a disaster engineered by the Prodworthy girls who pepper the bikinied contestants with itching and sneezing powders. The angry crowd turns on Sidney who escapes with the box-office cash—and Miss Easy Rider.

THE ROCKY HORROR PICTURE SHOW

Subversive rock 'n' roll revue that dragged bisexuality into the cultural spotlight

Above:
Susan
Sarandon as
Janet, Barry
Bostwick
as Brad and
Jonathan
Adams as
Dr. Von Scott.

Opposite:
Tim Curry as
Frank-N-Furter
and Richard
O'Brien as
Riff Raff.

ARGUABLY THE most popular campy cult film of all time, *The Rocky Horror Picture Show* (1975) is a rock 'n' roll homage to B-grade film genres as well as a salute to '70s hedonism. It concerns the deviant doings of the maniacal Dr. Frank-N-Furter (Tim Curry), a transvestite scientist on a spy mission from his planet Transsexual in the galaxy of Transylvania. Into his debauched world enter Brad Majors (Barry Bostwick) and Janet Weiss (Susan Sarandon), a super-straight, recently engaged couple on their way one stormy night to visit Dr. Everett Von Scott (Jonathan Adams), an old professor friend. When their car gets a flat, the two walk towards the lights of a Frankenstein-like castle. There Dr. Frank—a bi-sexual vision in garter belt, bustier and platform heels—is hosting a convention of fellow aliens. Attended by his sister/incest partner Magenta (Patricia Quinn) and his hunchback henchman Riff Raff

(Richard O'Brien, who created the original stage musical), the "Master" unveils Rocky Horror (Peter Hinwood), the *himbo* he has created to satisfy his sexual desires but who rejects him. Everyone then watches in shock as Dr. Frank murders super nasty biker Eddie (Meatloaf), an earlier failed experiment. Suddenly, Dr. Von Scott, who is looking for his nephew Eddie and who threatens to reveal Dr. Frank's devious plans, shows up. The over-sexed Master then lures Brad and Janet into bed and Janet, in pheromone heaven, seduces Rocky. Next the four perform a tush-twisting all drag revue. Reappearing in Transylvanian space gear, Magenta and Riff Raff wrest the mission from their boss by ray-gunning him and Rocky, who tried to rescue his maker. The musical tour de farce ends with the formerly innocent Brad and Janet unable to go back to their squeaky-clean existence. First produced in London by Michael White in

1973, the play was purchased for the U.S. by music impresario Lou Adler. With Jim Sharman and O'Brien directing, the Adler/White movie for 20th Century Fox featured, most importantly, the brilliant Tim Curry who is *The Rocky Horror Picture Show.* Born in 1946, in Cheshire, England, and a serious student of drama when approached for the part, Curry infused the role with a playful erotic ambiguity. A bomb at first, *The Rocky Horror Picture Show* soon became an underground smash, thanks to midnight screenings. As its young audiences became part of a familiar unnamed club, dressing in the costume of their favorite character, yelling out dialogue and singing the songs, interactive cinema was born. ●

TOOTSIE
One actor in drag takes one giant step for womankind

A CRACKERJACK COMEDY of female ambition and empowerment, *Tootsie* made cross-dressing a widely accepted phenomenon, thanks mainly to Dustin Hoffman's superb embodiment of the lead character. Written by Larry Gelbart, directed by Sydney Pollack and released in 1982 by Columbia, the film received 10 Academy Award nominations and became an instant classic. The story is centered around struggling actor and part-time waiter Michael Dorsey (Dustin Hoffman), who is unable to find work because of his irritating perfectionism—which his agent, George Fields (Sydney Pollack), reminds him has alienated every pro in the business. Needing $8,000 to help his whacked-out roommate, Jeff (Bill Murray), finance his new play, Michael dons a wig, a dress and a pair of specs and auditions for the part of a 30-plus woman on a daytime television soap opera. Unfortunately, he must step on the toes of his fragile actress-buddy, Sandy (Teri Garr), who wants the role for herself. Fortunately for him, he lands it. From this point on, Dorothy Michaels, Dorsey's alter ego, becomes an instant star who is always at odds with the show's director, Ron Carlisle (Dabney Coleman), over making the scripts more reflective of Dorothy's new distaff-oriented viewpoint. Meanwhile he/she gets involved in almost every sort of sexual mix-up imaginable. Not wanting to hurt Sandy's feelings by telling her he is television's latest sensation, Michael instead tries to soothe his longtime friend's insecurities by sleeping with her. She, in turn, does not understand why he is never around and begins to suspect that he is having an affair or is homosexual. Things get further out of hand when Dorsey—who is falling for Julie Nichols

(Jessica Lange), his costar and also his director's girl—must escape the clutches of both the show's aging male lead, John Van Horn (George Gaynes), and Julie's father, widower Les (Charles Durning). After getting chummy with Dorothy, Julie then begins to wonder if she might be a lesbian. Finally, the frustrated actor's double existence causes him to literally flip his wig—or rather remove it in front of the camera, thereby revealing his true identity. Ultimately Michael Dorsey ends up with his heart's desire. ●

Top: Dustin Hoffman (left), Dabney Coleman (center) and George Gaynes (right).

Bottom: Dustin Hoffman (left) and Charles Durning (right).

LA CAGE AUX FOLLES

A thriving franchise about love, bigotry and drag queens

IN 1973, WHEN comedian Jean Poiret started to rehearse *La cage aux folles,* a play he had written as a vehicle for Michel Serrault and himself, he could not have imagined he had created one of the most prolific franchises in the entertainment business. Hugely successful in Paris, the play became a film directed by Edouard Molinaro in 1975, and because it was a Franco-Italian production, Poiret allowed Ugo Tognazzi to replace him in the role of Renato. Serrault, who kept the plum part of drag diva Zaza Napoli that he had created on stage, was fortunate to embark on the adventure that followed—two cash-generating sequels. Then, in 1983, a musical composed by Jerry Herman became an enormous hit on Broadway and, basically, the rest is history. Sadly, in 1992, before director Mike Nichols started shooting a remake of the original film entitled *The Birdcage,* Poiret passed away. The play that had become such a record-breaking film almost two decades earlier is a good-natured cross-dressing comedy about political bigotry, family values and tolerance. It concerns Renato Baldi (Ugo Tognazzi) and Albin Mougeotte (Michel Serrault), two lovers who have been living together for 20 years. They own ▶▶

Above: Michel Galabru as representative Charrier (left) and Michel Serrault as Albin (right).

Left: Michel Serrault as Zaza Napoli.

Opposite: Michel Serrault as a tanned Marlene Dietrich in *La cage aux folles II* (1980).

a Saint-Tropez *boîte de nuit* called La cage aux folles where under the stage name of Zaza Napoli, Albin headlines the drag queens' show. Together the couple has raised Renato's son, Laurent (Remy Laurent), the tangible result of a one-night stand. One evening while his "mother" is on stage, Laurent informs his father he has decided to marry Andrea (Luisa Maneri), the daughter of representative Simon Charrier (Michel Galabru), who heads the Union for Moral Order. When Laurent adds that Mr. Charrier, his wife (Carmen Scarpitta) and Andrea are coming for dinner, Renato and Albin reluctantly agree and start remodeling their flamboyant flat above the club, transforming it into a monastery-like space. Conscious of appearances, Renato convinces Laurent's biological mother, Simone (Claire Maurier), to meet the Charriers, forcing an upset Albin to go into hiding. The next day, when the Charriers arrive, Simone has not yet shown up, so Albin dresses up in matronly drag to impersonate Laurent's mother. The charade crumbles bit by bit, notably when Albin's wig is displaced just as Simone introduces herself as Laurent's mother. Charrier realizes he is trapped in a homosexual environment and—noticing the paparazzi outside the club—a political Venus fly trap. That is when Albin, using his make-up skills, gives Charrier a new identity that allows him to escape anonymously. A few months later, Laurent and Andrea are married in a Saint-Tropez church by a priest whose precious concluding gesture leaves little doubt about his sexual orientation. ●

▼ MICHEL SERRAULT
LA CAGE AUX FOLLES II
(1980, United Artists)

Pleasant but uninspired sequel directed by Edouard Molinaro ● Longtime lovers Renato (Ugo Tognazzi) and Albin (**Michel Serrault**) have moved their show, *La cage aux folles,* to Casino Ruhl in Nice. Albin, starring under the name of Zaza Napoli, has decided that his new spectacle will be an homage to Marlene Dietrich's *The Blue Angel.* Upset that Renato thinks he is too old for the role, Albin goes to town dressed up as a woman and is picked up by a spy who uses him as a getaway cover. Inadvertently taking possession of a much sought after microfilm, Albin becomes part of an international imbroglio. To protect him against foreign agents, Renato takes him to Italy and, once at his mother's farm, suggests Albin costume himself as a female peasant (**photo**). *La signora* Baldi thinks her son could have married a better looking woman, but some less discriminating laborers are attracted by the flirtatious Albin, who wants to make Renato jealous. Eventually, bad and good spies discover the couple's hideout and the French authorities recoup the microfilm and apprehend the criminals. Renato and Albin gladly return home.

◄ **MICHEL SERRAULT**
LA CAGE AUX FOLLES III – THE WEDDING
(1985, Columbia)

Second sequel of a famous French comedic gem directed by Georges Lautner ●

Back at La cage aux folles in Saint-Tropez, Albin (**Michel Serrault**) and Renato (**Ugo Tognazzi,** bottom photo, left) rehearse a new *Queen of the Bees* production number (**photo**). The club, however, is in dire financial straits. Coincidentally, Albin's Scottish uncle dies and leaves him his fortune. But there is one condition: Albin must marry and father a child within 18 months. If not, the inheritance will go to a cousin, Mortimer (Saverio Vallone). Renato sees this as a solution to their economic woes, but Albin is unable to entertain the idea of sex with a woman. A *deus-ex-machina* arrives in the person of Cindy (Antonella Interlenghi), a pregnant girl who has been abandoned. She likes Albin's marriage proposal, but there is a fly in the ointment: Mortimer has fallen in love with her. At Albin's wedding—where he shows up in an over-the-top outfit— Renato strikes a deal with Mortimer: He can marry Cindy and become the sole heir— and then split the inheritance with Albin. An elated Mortimer replaces Albin who, equally jubilant, leaves on Renato's arm (**photo**).

Top: Michel Serrault (center) rehearses the "queen bee" number in *La cage aux folles III – The Wedding* (1985).

Left: Ugo Tognazzi (left) and Michel Serrault (right) in *La cage aux folles III: The Wedding* (1985).

39

THE BIRDCAGE

NATHAN LANE & GENE HACKMAN
THE BIRDCAGE
(1996, United Artists)

Slick and campier-than-camp remake of *La cage aux folles* directed by Mike Nichols ● Armand Goldman (**Robin Williams**) and Albert (**Nathan Lane**) live as husband and wife above their gay nightclub in Miami's South Beach area. Albert reigns as The Birdcage's drag diva while Armand runs the business. When Val (Dan Futterman), Armand's son from an isolated heterosexual encounter, arrives for a visit, he tells his father he is marrying Barbara Keeley (Calista Flockhart), daughter of Senator Kevin Keeley (**Gene Hackman**). Val elaborates that his future father-in-law is the politician who organized the hyper-conservative Coalition for Moral Order. Val's fiancée tells her parents that Armand's last name is Coleman—so as not to offend her anti-Semitic father. When the cofounder of the Coalition dies in the arms of a black prostitute, the Keeleys head for Miami. Val, meanwhile, begs Armand to tone down the flamboyantly appointed apartment and hide Albert. He also convinces his father to ask his biological mother Katherine (Christine Baranski) over for dinner with the Keeleys. Saddened, Albert disappears but when Katherine fails to show up on time, he bravely puts on a wig and a low-key dress and joins in the festivities. By the time Katherine arrives, Albert has won over the senator with "her" similar political convictions but Val has realized the sham must end. He unwigs Albert and confesses everything. The Keeleys want to leave precipitously, but reporters swarm the club. Albert comes to the rescue again, turning the senator into a blond siren (**photo, above right**) and helping everybody blend into the show's finale. At the nuptials, all is sunshine as Albert has regained his identity.

Barry Humphries

Danny LaRue

Arthur Lucan

SEVEN MASTERS OF

Divine

Charles
Busch

DISGUISE

Julian Eltinge

Female impersonators go to the movies

Akihiro
Murayama

JULIAN ELTINGE

Director Donald Crisp (left) and Julian Eltinge (center) relax with visitor Cecil B. DeMille between takes of *The Clever Mrs. Carfax* (1917, Paramount).

▲ THE CLEVER MRS. CARFAX (1917, Paramount)

Social satire about fortune hunting directed by Donald Crisp ● Under the nom de plume of Mrs. Carfax, Temple Trask (**Julian Eltinge**) writes a lovelorn column for a newspaper. While attending a college reunion, he reprises his popular drag act for his fellow alumni. When he gets back home, an old college chum challenges him to revive his female impersonation at a local restaurant. A bon vivant who is distrustful of a woman's wiles, Temple picks up the gauntlet, but once there, sees Helen Scott (Daisy Robinson) and succumbs to her charms. He notices, however, that con artist Adrian Graw (Noah Beery) has targeted Helen and her money. So Temple hatches his own scheme: assuming Mrs. Carfax's identity, he escorts his new love and her mother, Mary Keyes (Jennie Lee), on a steamer voyage in order to keep them out of Graw's clutches. But Graw doesn't fade away and Mrs. Carfax is forced to scuffle with him. After having him arrested by the police, Temple takes off his wig and welcomes Helen into his arms.

JULIAN ELTINGE, the most renowned female impersonator of the early 20th century, was born Julian Dalton in Newtonville, Massachusetts, in 1881. From the limelight of pre-World War I vaudeville, Eltinge moved on to the flickering glow of motion pictures and finally into the dusk of dubious nightclubs. His professional life began in 1893 when as a lark he dressed in drag for a revue of the Boston Cadets. He was further encouraged at the age of 17 when he showed up for cakewalk lessons at Mrs. Wyman's dance studio in 1898 and did a burlesque imitation of one of her students, which he transformed into a graceful dance. Discovering a knack for wearing female clothing more attractively than many women, Eltinge drew upon a good singing voice and a subtle physical grace to launch himself on the stage. He also relied on beautiful gowns and the aid of his devoted Japanese dresser, Shima. His first stage success came in 1904, when he appeared in Jerome Kern's musical comedy, *Mr. Wix of Wickham.* In 1906, the illusionist made his London bow at the Palace Theatre ▸▸

and four years later starred for the first time in the legitimate theater in *The Fascinating Widow.* The play was so profitable that its grateful producer opened the Eltinge Theater on New York's 42nd Street. This gesture seemed to reinforce what Eltinge's critics feared most—namely that the nation's manhood was going to hell in a wig. Hoping to parlay his stage fame into films, Eltinge moved to Hollywood where he capitalized on his cross-dressing talent in *The Countess Charming* and *The Clever Mrs. Carfax* (1917) and *The Widow's Might* (1918). Between engagements, the resolute bachelor—who sometimes went to bizarre lengths to highlight his masculinity—lived in his California ranch with his mother. He began touring vaudeville again in the early '20, having written some sketches for his Julian Eltinge Players, and added to his act sets designed by Erté. By 1931, when he appeared in the B talkie, *Maid to Order,* Eltinge's star had begun its descent, and by the late '30s he was begging the L.A. police to let him perform in drag at a club where, as the men in blue put it, "persons of questionable morals" assembled. Reduced to merely standing in proximity to his beautiful frocks, Julian Eltinge baffled his few remaining fans who ventured to seedy venues where he performed his still brilliant impersonations in a tuxedo. Eltinge died in 1941. ●

▼ JULIAN ELTINGE
THE COUNTESS CHARMING
(1917, Paramount)

High society comedy of revenge directed by Donald Crisp ● Socialite bachelor Stanley Jordan (**Julian Eltinge**) attends a benefit held at a posh country club. While romancing one of the guests, Betty Lovering (Florence Vidor), he inadvertently slights one Mrs. Vandergraft (Mabel Van Buren), a doyenne of the smart club set. When she blacklists the young man, he plans his revenge. Insinuating himself into the local beau monde as Countess Raffelski, he gets himself invited into the parlors of the upper crust toadies who have ostracized him as Stanley Jordan. He also makes off with their jewels and contributes them to their favorite charity–the Red Cross. When the alarmed victims unite and retain a detective, it comes to light that the popular Russian countess is dying. Betty rushes off to visit the ailing royal, who soon reveals that "she" is a he–and none other than the love of Betty's life. *(With **George Kuwa**, left, as butler Soto.)*

▲ MADAME BEHAVE (1925, Al Christie)
Low-key charmer directed by Scott Sidney ● Roommates Jack Mitchell (**Julian Eltinge**, second from right) and Dick Morgan (**David James**, far left) are unable to pay the rent to their prickly landlord, Henry Jasper (**Jack Duffy**, far right). By chance, they learn that Jasper is also suing Dick's uncle, Seth Morgan (**Lionel Belmore**, fourth from left), for wrecking his Rolls Royce. When testimony reveals in court that a Madame Brown has witnessed the accident, the judge postpones judg-ment to allow the lawyers to locate her. The defen-dants, knowing that a wife cannot testify against her husband, want to find her so one of them can marry her. Before the search begins, Dick con-vinces Jack to impersonate the missing witness. So disguised, Jack gets marriage offers from both Jasper and Morgan while falling in love with Mor-gan's ward, Gwen (**Ann Pennington**, third from left). When Madame Brown shows up, the judge throws the case out of court, allowing Jack to revert to his male persona and marry Gwen.

◄ JULIAN ELTINGE
AN ADVENTURESS
(1920, Fred J. Balshofer Productions)

Imaginary kingdom frivolous adventure directed by Fred J. Balshofer ● Jack Perry (**Julian Eltinge**), Dick Sayre (William Clifford) and Lyn Brook (Frederik KoVert) are a trio of Americans with a taste for adventure. Their search leads them to the imaginary European seaside country of Alpania, which is in the throes of civil war. Perry immediately gets in trouble with the monarchists who sentence him to death. After Brook bombs the prison where his friend is being held, Perry, disguising himself as Mamzelle Fedora (**photo**), wangles his way into the royalist circle of Prince Halbere (**Leo White,** left) and attracts the love of Zana (Virginia Rappe), an Alpanian courtier. Next, Brook disguises himself as Thelma, giving Perry time to relay the royalist plot to the republicans. When Perry is captured again, he decides to flee Alpania and, after seizing an airplane, escapes with Zana to the States. *(Shot in 1918 as* Watch on the Rhine, *released in 1920 as* An Adventuress *and re-released in 1922 with new footage as* The Isle of Love.*)*

◄ THE WIDOW'S MIGHT
(1918, Paramount)

Imbroglio about love and money directed by William C. de Mille ● New Yorker Dick Tavish (**Julian Eltinge**) suspects that millionaire Horace Hammer (Gustav von Seyffertitz) has duped him into the purchase of some western land. Dick goes to the resort where Hammer is vacationing and encounters calendar girl Irene Stuart (Florence Vidor) relaxing at the same spa with her aunt, Mrs. Pomfret. When Dick searches Hammer's room for incriminating papers, he is interrupted. Escaping through the bedroom of Irene's aunt, he surprises Mrs. Pomfret hiding her thinning hair with a wig. Dick decides to borrow one of her hairpieces and a cape, warning her that he will divulge her little vanity if she refuses to introduce him as Princess Martini at an upcoming party. As a flirtatious female royal (**photo**), Dick becomes the center of attention, which allows him to gather evidence implicating Hammer in the land deal. Finally, Dick happily proposes to Irene.

◄ MAID TO ORDER
(1931, Jesse Weil Productions)

Female-impersonator-vs.-smugglers comedy directed by Elmer Clifton ● Vaudeville artist **Julian Eltinge** (as himself, right) is enlisted by the police to capture a ring of smugglers who dump cut diamonds hidden in coffee cans onto the rooftop of a New York nightclub. After Scotland Yard arrests the European link of the gang, French singer Lotti Loncraine (**Jane Reid,** left), Eltinge impersonates her and takes a job as a chanteuse at the Big Apple club. *(Film currently classified as lost.)*

OLD MOTHER RILEY, Arthur Lucan's famous comic female character of the stage and screen, departed from British music hall tradition in that his screechy-voiced virago evoked humor clouded with a touch of darkness. Whether washerwoman, barkeep or fishmonger, she was always the underdog, shaking her scrawny fist at the world in defense of the downtrodden. Born in Sibsy, Lincolnshire, in 1885, Arthur Towle left home at age 14 to join the Musical Cliftons. On tour in Dublin, he realized he needed an Irish stage name and chose Lucan. During this time, he married 15-year-old Kitty McShane and the two eventually began performing together. For one sketch entitled "Bridget's Night Out," he put on women's clothing to create an old, lower-class Irish mother named O'Flynn, a character that gave birth to "Old Mother Riley." By the mid-'30s, the couple was England's biggest box-office draw, the politically progressive Lucan exploring the collective conscience of the middle class. The ►►

ARTHUR (aka Old Mother Riley) LUCAN

Opposite:
Old Mother Riley's Ghosts **(1941) directed by John Baxter.**

◀ OLD MOTHER RILEY'S CIRCUS
(1941, British National)

Directed by Thomas Bentley ● Back when Maggie O'Hara was a music hall star she married a man named George Riley. Now, many years later, she is known as Old Mother Riley (**Arthur Lucan**), and is reduced to working as an usherette. She finds a new job with Santley's Circus, but learns that to escape creditors its proprietor has disappeared. After masquerading as a countess (**photo**) with the help of the handsome ringmaster (**John Longden,** right), she takes over the leadership of the circus and discovers that Kitty (**Kitty McShane,** center), the knife thrower's partner, is her long-lost daughter. Under Mother Riley's guidance, the big top is so successful that Mr. Santley wants his circus back. The tenacious old dame fights him and discovers that her late husband was the original and rightful owner.

◀ OLD MOTHER RILEY IN PARIS
(1938, Butchers)

Directed by Oswald Mitchell ● When her fiancé, Joe, is transferred to Paris, Kitty Riley is so depressed that her mother takes her there. On the plane, a terrified Mother Riley requests a parachute and jumps out, landing in a French army maneuvers field. Arrested as a spy, she escapes and joins her daughter in Paris where they learn Joe has fallen for Madame Zero (Magda Kun). In a cabaret where the Rileys have followed the couple, Mother is asked to dance by an "apache" (**George Wolkowsky, photo**). The strenuous exercise leaves her with just enough energy to assault the seductress. During the donnybrook, photos of the Maginot Line fall from Madame's handbag, proving she is a spy. Awarded a Gallic decoration, Mother Riley returns to London a celebrity. *(Rereleased as* Old Mother Riley Catches a Quisling.*)*

◀ OLD MOTHER RILEY HEADMISTRESS
(1950, Harry Reynolds)

Directed by John Harlow ● Good news: Mother Riley has inherited the laundry where she toils daily. Bad news: daughter Kitty, a music teacher, has been fired from St. Mildred's. Mother Riley finds a solution: she mortgages the laundry, buys the school and becomes its headmistress. One day, she gets a £15,000 offer to sell. When she discovers the speculators want to buy her property to resell it to a railway company that plans to run their trains through it, she refuses (**photo**). After the thugs set fire to the premises, Mother Riley learns the railroad has changed its route and now wants it to go through the laundry. She cleverly agrees to sell the school to the crooks for £20,000 and the laundry to the railroad for £40,000. *(With **Cyril Smith,** right.)*

▶▶ breadth and depth of his morality-tinged humor—plus the comic appeal of his specific body language—opened the way for the *Old Mother Riley* series. The 15 movies, produced between 1937 and 1952, were, unfortunately, unevenly scripted. Also, while Lucan was playing the part of a woman about his own age, Kitty was 35 when the first comedy was shot and she became progressively less credible playing an attractive young daughter. In the mid-'50s the last of the series was released in the States under the title *My Son the Vampire,* probably because costar Bela Lugosi was in and McShane was out. Successful as entertainers, Lucan and McShane led a volatile life, with Kitty indulging in extramarital affairs. After tiring of his wife's infidelities and fiscal irresponsibility, the unassuming actor declared bankruptcy. Now estranged, he continued to tour throughout England. He died in 1954 of a heart attack in his dressing room while waiting to go onstage. Kitty McShane passed away 10 years later. ●

◀ARTHUR LUCAN
OLD MOTHER RILEY IN SOCIETY (1940, British National)

Directed by John Baxter ● To hear daughter Kitty sing at a local theatre, Mother Riley hides in the star trap. Accidentally catapulted into the air, she lands on stage, causing the leading lady to walk out. Seizing the opportunity, the washerwoman pushes her daughter onto center stage. Arts patron Tony Morgan (John Stuart) follows Kitty backstage where Mother Riley introduces herself as her dresser. When Kitty and Tony end up marrying, Mother Riley works at the Morgan mansion as Kitty's maid. Realizing her demeanor puzzles Lady Morgan (**Ruth Maitland,** left), Mother Riley flees. After Kitty reveals the truth to her husband, he forgives her and Mother Riley is welcomed back at Lord and Lady Morgan's.

◀OLD MOTHER RILEY'S JUNGLE TREASURE
(1951, Renown Pictures)

Directed by Maclean Rogers ● In the junk shop where she works and lives with daughter Kitty, Mother Riley has nocturnal visions of a friendly ghost who introduces himself as the notorious pirate Henry Morgan (Sebastian Cabot). The ectoplasm tells her the map of his fabled treasure is in a secret compartment of her bed. After finding the document, Mother Riley organizes an expedition funded by her boss, and charters a plane that crash-lands on an island. After days of searching that include encounters with hostile flora and fauna, the motley group finds the loot. But instead of leaving the isle a rich woman, Mother Riley gets an offer from the natives (**photo**) that she simply can't refuse–to be their queen.

◀OLD MOTHER RILEY M.P.
(1939, Butchers)

Directed by Oswald Mitchell ● Neighbors and daughter Kitty encourage Mother Riley to run for parliament against Mr. Wicker (Henry Longhurst), a real estate tycoon. To finance her campaign, Mother Riley auctions her furniture and gets help from her tenant, Archie (**Patrick Ludlow,** right), an artist who is painting her portrait so she can look "as fresh as a magnolia." When the populist washerwoman gets elected, she is so vocal at Parliament about the right of Brits to be employed that she is named Minister of Strange Affairs. As such, she forces the emperor of Rocavia to pay his country's debt to the Crown–a sum that will fund her social programs.

▲ ARTHUR LUCAN
OLD MOTHER RILEY MEETS
THE VAMPIRE
(aka "My Son the Vampire," 1952,
Fernwood-Worldwide Entertainment)
**Last film of the series directed by John
Gilling** ● Baron Von Housen (**Bela Lugosi,
right**), a wacky London scientist with a taste for

human blood, plans to take over the world with
the help of his robot named Mark I, which has
been accidentally shipped to Mother Riley's
(**Arthur Lucan**) grocery shop. Using radar control, Von Housen orders Mark I to come to his
mansion. The robot obeys, bringing with him
the putty-nosed Mother Riley and a lot of trouble for his master. Now a cleaning lady for Von

Housen, she discovers a prisoner at the mansion, Julia Loretti (Maria Mercedes), who
refuses to reveal to the mad inventor and his
thugs the location of a map leading to a large
deposit of uranium needed to feed the robot.
After disabling Mark I, Mother Riley frees Julia,
chases the limousine of fugitive Von Housen on
a motorcycle and helps attain his arrest.

AKIHIRO MARUYAMA

◀ BLACK LIZARD
(Japanese title "Kurotokage,"
1968, Shochiku)

Bizarre meditation on greed and passion directed by Kinji Fukasaku ● A tall, spectacular bloom of a woman nicknamed Black Lizard (**Akihiro Maruyama**) is the queen of Tokyo's criminal underground. For some time, she has coveted the Star of Egypt, a flawless diamond owned by a local jeweler (Junya Usami). To obtain the precious stone, she kidnaps the shopkeeper's daughter, Sanaya (Kikko Matsuoka), and holds her for ransom. The merchant, who wants to get his child back and at the same time keep the stone, hires private detective Akechi (**Isao Kimura,** right), who is no match for Black Lizard. The underworld ruler, however, falls for and seduces Akechi in an emotional entanglement that triggers her downfall. The conclusion takes place on Black Lizard's private island where she stores not only her ill-gotten treasures, but also the embalmed bodies of earlier sexual partners.

▲ BLACK ROSE MANSION
(Japanese title "Kuro-bara no yakata,"
1969, Chimera)

Melodramatic oddity about unattainable love directed by Kinji Fukasaku ● Enigmatic Ryuko (**Akihiro Maruyama**) performs nightly at the Black Rose Mansion, an exclusive men's club where she sings melancholic torch songs and carries a black rose that, she tells admirers, will turn red when she meets her true love. Her magnetism enthralls the Mansion's audience and the fact that three of her former lovers successively burst onto the scene to passionately claim her as theirs only deepens her mystery. The club's owner, wealthy Kyohei (Eitaro Ozawa), is so mesmerized by Ryuko that he falls hard for her. When his estranged son Wataru (**Masakazu Tamura,** right) returns home and learns of his father's dalliance, he shows hostility to Ryuko, but quickly falling under her spell (**photo**), convinces her to elope. After the femme fatale mentions that their lack of money is an obstacle, Wataru determines to remedy the problem. Unfortunately, the lucrative drug deal he participates in goes terribly wrong and the police shoot him. He is, however, able to reach Ryuko in time to flee in a speedboat. Just as the blood from his wounds turns her black rose red, Wataru dies in her arms.

AKIHIRO MARUYAMA is probably Japan's most famous female impersonator. Born in Nagasaki in 1935, Maruyama started his career as a transvestite singer in 1952, and in the mid-'60s became a theater star when he joined Tenjosajiki, Shuji Terayama's repertory company. It was around this time that Maruyama became the lover of poet, novelist and political activist Yukio Mishima who helped him get the female lead in *Black Lizard* (1968), a film for which he had written the screenplay. Her success in that dark melodrama made Maruyama the obvious choice for the femme fatale in *Black Rose Mansion* (1969), a second camp-noir movie directed by Kinji Fukasaku. Mishima's ritual suicide in 1970 did not end Maruyama's career. Au contraire: later adopting the stage name of Akihiro Miwa, Maruyama, at 70 remains a popular singer—favoring French *chansons*—on stage and television. He is also a theater actor, a voice-over specialist (he provided the voice for one of the characters in *Princess Mononoke*, Miyazaki's recent animated feature) and an author. ●

DANNY LARUE

OUR MISS FRED (1972, EMI)
Wartime farce filled with double-entendres directed by Bob Kellet ● At the tail end of WWII, British actor Fred Wimbush (**Danny LaRue,** far left) is sent to France. Entertaining the troops, he plays female roles under the name of Frederica, a ploy that allows him to get away safely when the Germans capture his unit. He then meets the severe Miss Flodden (**Lally Bowers,** far right) and her group of teenage schoolgirls who are hiding a shot-down RAF Squadron leader named Smallpiece (Lance Percival) in a barn. To protect him, they have abducted Officer Schmidt (**Walter Gottel,** center) for an eventual trade. To sever Small-piece's sexual attraction toward her, Frederica

reveals his true gender and agrees to help fight the Germans. Entering the enemy compound to steal medicine for the now sick Miss Flod-den, Frederica is surprised by General Brincker (Alfred Marks) who invites her to dinner. Dressed as a glamorous temptress (**photo at left**), he succeeds in fending Brincker off and escapes again. After joining a handful of French models in a fashion show, Fred and Smallpiece plan to steal a plane from an airfield near Calais. Pursued by the Germans, they only succeed in making off with a hot air balloon. They are nevertheless able to bring everyone safely back to London. After being congratulated by the authorities, Fred parachutes back into France to become a female spy.

A STAR OF THE ENGLISH variety theatre, Danny LaRue was hailed by no less than Noel Coward as the only female impersonator he had seen "who is not embarrassing." Born Daniel Patrick Carroll in Cork, Ireland, in 1927, he began his theatrical career after a stint in the Royal Navy. His transformation from Carroll to LaRue came in the '50s when he first appeared in female costume. Engagements at such London hot spots as Churchill's made him famous, and in 1964 he opened his own club in Hanover Square that became a celebrity hangout, where the occasional royal would show up to catch LaRue's glamorous and often risqué send-ups. In 1966, LaRue had the starring role in the musical *Come Spy With Me,* and two years later moved his *Queen Passionella and the Sleeping Beauty* from North London to the West End with great success. But despite the exposure, LaRue failed to make it big in the movies. His 1972 film *Our Miss Fred* was a disappointment but this misfire did not dim his popularity as television work and huge turnouts for his annual tours attest. Audiences continue to appreciate his adventurousness—starring in *Hello Dolly*, he became the first man to play a female role in a major musical. More than anyone in Britain, Danny LaRue has brought men in mascara into the mainstream. ●

BARRY (Dame Edna Everage) HUMPHRIES

BARRY HUMPHRIES' alter ego, Dame Edna Everage, began her career as a caricature of the middle-class Australian housewife in dribble-down socks, and has since morphed into a "megastar" who she herself asserts is one of the most popular and talented women in the world today. Dame Edna Everage is without a question one of today's most complex and funny comedic talents. Self-described as "an up-market Mother Teresa"— "I share and I care" is one of her several mottos—she looks anything but, with her oversized pale-violet '50s hairdo, jeweled harlequin glasses and sequined dresses tightly fitted to her generous six-foot-four frame. Humphries, who performed the character in 1955, while on ▶▶

THE ADVENTURES OF
BARRY McKENZIE
(1972, Longford)

Visually and verbally crude satire of Ozzies attitudes directed by Bruce Beresford ● A $2,000 inheritance will go to stereotypical Ozzie, Barry McKenzie (**Barry Crocker,** right), if he travels to Britain to "further the culture and tradition of the McKenzie dynasty." His amiable and hilarious Aunt Edna Everage (**Barry Humphries**) accompanies him. Reunited in London with old mate Curly (Paul Bertram), who has booked him in a local fleabag hotel, Barry's adventures include encounters with a staggering variety of wackos. Among them is Mr. Gort (Dennis Price), a victim of shell-shock who dashes about in boys' knickers begging to be caned, and a trio of hippies who hire him to perform an Australian folk song in a crowded underground club. His success there leads to a guest appearance on the live talk show *Midnight Oil* to speak about Australians in England. Barry brings along his chums and proves a point, after dropping his trousers and showing full frontal nudity. The audience's excitement triggers a fire that the Ozzies, having demonstrated their prodigious appetite for pints, extinguish with a shower of lager and urine. That is when Aunt Edna wisely decides it is time to bid the Brits cheerio. *(Based on a comic strip created by Barry Humphries and Nicholas Garland as published in* Private Eye.*)*

tour with an acting troupe from Down Under, was born in 1934 in a well-off Melbourne suburb, the first of four children to upwardly striving parents. When they sent the boy to the city's most prestigious school, his response to its conformity was rebelliousness. It was an attitude that would continue through his Dadaist activities in college and finally culminate in Edna, an anarchistic blend of jollity and spitefulness, probity and melancholy. Humphries as Aunt Edna appeared for the first time in film in Bruce Beresford's *The Adventures of Barry McKenzie* (1972), a corrosive satire of Australian mores, and its sequel *Barry McKenzie Holds His Own* (1975). By the end of the '80s, the Brits, howling at the advice she gave the Royal family, had practically adopted the high-voiced bird of paradise who threw her "possums" gladioli from the stage. She has sung at the Royal Albert Hall and has been immortalized in wax for Madame Tussaud's. After an unsuccessful attempt in the '70s to appeal to American theatergoers, she won them over in the '90s through a couple of wildly successful Broadway shows. Thanks to the clever marketing of Humphries, whose relationship with his female alter ego might seem surreal to those who do not understand his professional passion for creating fame for its own sake, Dame Edna's star looms ever brighter even as she parodies the self-absorption of celebrities while touting herself as one. ●

▼ BARRY HUMPHRIES
BARRY McKENZIE HOLDS HIS OWN
(1975, Roadshow)

Amiable buffoonery directed by Bruce Beresford
● On their way back to the land down under, the ale-swilling naïf Barry McKenzie (**Barry Crocker**, right) and his decorous Aunt Edna Everage (**Barry Humphries**), stop over in Paris. There, Edna is taken for the Queen of England by Count Eric Plasma (Donald Pleasence), culture minister of Transylvania, a country that has become communist. Plasma orders his operatives to snatch Edna and take her to his homeland as a tourist attraction. Secretly making his way back to England, Barry gains the support for a rescue attempt from the British Foreign Office and the Australian High Commission. The count, who has since learned Edna is not the royal sovereign, hooks her up to his blood-draining contraption. Just in the nick of time, however, Barry's twin, the Reverend Kevin (Barry Crocker also), holds up a cross made of beer cans in front of the count who promptly crumbles into a skeleton. When Barry and his aunt finally arrive in Sydney, the prime minister announces that Edna has been made a Dame.

▲ LES PATTERSON SAVES THE WORLD
(1987, Humpstead Productions Pty)

Excessively lowbrow Australian spy spoof directed by George Miller ● The day Sir Leslie Patterson (Barry Humphies), the bean-gorging Australian ambassador to the UN steps before the General Assembly, he dispels the gathering's torpor by breaking wind. The odoriferous explosion produces worldwide headlines and a fall from grace. Subsequently banished to the remote mid-eastern country of Abu Niviah, the nitwit arrives at his new post in the midst of a coup d'état engineered by Col. Godowni (Thaao Penghlis). In between two binges, Patterson learns that a French scientist, Dr. Charles Herpes (Henri Szeps), has developed an antidote to a virus that Godowni intends to spread around the globe via toilet seats manufactured by his factory. In the meantime, eccentric television star **Dame Edna Everage** (**Barry Humphries**), an undercover CIA operative, arrives with a koala bear named Colin (**photo**) hoping to convince Sir Patterson to prevent the epidemic and save the world. She helps him by giving Col. Godowni a replica of her bear that explodes while the dictator is in his helicopter.

▲ BARRY HUMPHRIES
NICHOLAS NICKLEBY (2002, United Artists)

Masterfully crafted Dickens family feast directed by Douglas McGrath

● In dire straits after his father's death, young Nicholas Nickleby (**Charlie Hunnam,** center) travels to London with his mother (Stella Gonet) and sister Kate (Romola Garai) to seek the help of Uncle Ralph (Christopher Plummer). Their rich relative refuses to give the monetary aid the noble lad had hoped for, offering instead a job in a godforsaken school in Yorkshire. Sickened by the brutality of its owners, Nicholas leaves one day with the headmaster's favorite scapegoat, cripple Smike (**Jamie Bell,** left). After taking up with a traveling theatrical troupe run by the generous Mr. Crummles (Nathan Lane) and his convivial wife (**Barry Humphries,** right), the two return to London only to learn that Uncle Ralph has insinuated Kate into the lecherous clutches of Sir Mulberry Hawk (Edward Fox). When Nicholas rescues his sister, his angry uncle has Smike kidnapped and then promises the hand of Nicholas' new love, Madeleine (Anne Hathaway), to Hawk in exchange for relieving her pauper father's debt. Uncle Ralph then suffers unexpected financial doom and, learning that Smike, now dead, was his son, hangs himself. Nicholas marries Madeleine and returns to the country home from whence he started his adventures.

DIVINE

▲ HAIRSPRAY (1987, New Line)

Bouncy bubble-coiffed satire of segregated times directed by John Waters ● It is the fabulous early '60s in Baltimore and *The Corny Collins Show*, a teen television dance program, is holding a competition for the crown of Miss Auto Show. Zaftig Tracy Turnblad (**Ricki Lake,** far left), who lives with her father (Jerry Stiller) and mega-proportioned mom (**Divine,** second from left), plots with her friend Penny (Leslie Ann Powers) to win the segregated show's contest. Tracy triumphs in a landslide and is invited by Corny Collins (Shawn Thompson) to audition for the show's regulars—much to the dismay of the stuck-up Amber von Tussle (**Colleen Fitzpatrick,** far right) and her mother (**Debbie Harry,** second from right). At the all-white audition, Tracy speaks out for integration, lures away Amber's beau and becomes a local sensation. Things heat up when Penny falls for Seaweed (Clayton Prince), son of the black DJ who hosts Corny's all-African-American program, and when Seaweed's little sister is denied entrance to the station's all-white preteen day. At the von Tussle's segregated amusement park, just as it looks like Tracy will edge out Amber for Miss Auto Show, a riot breaks out when Tracy proclaims her political views on camera. Taken to jail, she is released by the governor and easily unseats Amber from her throne. Baltimore now rocks to a racially mixed beat.

▶ PINK FLAMINGOS (1973, Saliva Films)

Trailer-trash midnight-cult-classic directed by John Waters ● Babs Johnson (**Divine**) squeezes her 300-plus-pounds into the skimpiest dresses and balances everything on stiletto heels. Living in a trailer among plastic pink flamingos, she has the reputation of being "the filthiest person in the world." This sits well with her weird family, which includes her aptly-named son Crackers (Danny Mills), her egg-obsessed Mama (Edith Massey) and cute young thing Cotton (Mary Vivian Pearce), who gets her jollies observing Cracker's bizarre sexual activities. But another family that considers itself the "world's filthiest," the Marbles, are less than thrilled. Raymond Marble (David Lochary) and his wife Connie (Mink Stole), after all, peddle heroin to children and kidnap young women, whom they have their butler, Channing, impregnate so they can sell the resulting babies. The contest begins when the Marbles send Babs a shriveled turd as a birthday present. As a result, Babs vows to kill them. At the birthday celebration, Mama, who spends her days in a playpen, weds the egg man and the guests devour the police squad that comes to raid the party—thanks to the Marbles' complaints. In retaliation, Babs and Crackers attempt to curse the Marbles' house by rubbing their bodies against everything in sight. Babs finds the women in the basement and watches as they castrate Channing. When the Marbles burn down the infamous trailer, Babs and Crackers kill their rivals—while reporters from the *Confidential* and *The Tattler* look on. To dot the "i" in disgusting, Babs picks up some poodle poop—and eats it.

PRAISED BY HIS mentor, king-of-trash film director John Waters, as "the most beautiful woman in the world," the 320-pound drag star Divine was one of the most outrageous screen personas in an era that regarded outrage as a virtue. Born Glenn Harris Milstead in 1945, and growing up in a Baltimore suburb, this only son of middle-class parents was so bullied by his classmates for his obesity that he took shelter in a dream life centered on idolizing female movie stars like Elizabeth Taylor. Milstead was recruited by high school buddy Waters for a series of 8 mm films in which the ballooning neophyte actor with the loud, husky voice debuted as a cross-dressing phenom. In 1972, Waters and Divine earned their cult status with the feature *Pink Flamingos.* After the two filmed the highly disturbing *Female Trouble* in 1974, Divine focused on his stage work, returning to the movies in 1981 with *Polyester,* a quasi-mainstream film costarring erstwhile matinee idol Tab Hunter. Seven years later Divine appeared in *Hairspray* in which he plays a genial mother and devoted housewife. Gentle and soft spoken beneath the vulgarity of his circus makeup and freakish costumes, "The Drag Queen of the Century," as *People* magazine dubbed him, was rather conventional in private life. But eventually depression, marijuana and overeating consumed Divine, who died of asphyxiation in 1988. •

▶ DIVINE

FEMALE TROUBLE
(1975, New Line)

Highly dispiriting comedic portrait of a headline-hungry criminal directed by John Waters ● In 1960, after running away from home, 300-pound teenager Dawn Davenport (**Divine**) heads up to Baltimore. En route, brutish Earl Peterson (Divine as a male) rapes her. From this mating a baby girl named Taffy is born. Dawn makes her living as a go-go girl and prostitute, and by 1968, has become a cat burglar. She also marries (**photo**) a hairdresser who introduces her to the pseudo-chic owners of a beauty salon, Donald (David Lochary) and Donna Dasher (Mary Vivian Pierce). The couple, exercising their theories on the connection between beauty and crime, brainwash Dawn with their loony ideas. Meanwhile, daughter Taffy (Mink Stole), now an angry teenager, wants to live with her biological father. Upon arrival, she is almost raped and kills her attacker, but Dawn could not care less. Now the guinea pig of the Dasher's crime-is-beauty experiment, Dawn gives a performance at the Theatre Club during which she works herself into a frenzy and shoots a gun into the audience. She gets the electric chair for murder and welcomes it, equating in her twisted mind the death penalty with an Oscar.

▶ POLYESTER (1981, New Line)

Dark but amusing soap-opera parody directed by John Waters ● The wealthy Fishpaws are the ultimate dysfunctional family. There is the toupee-wearing father, Elmer (David Samson), a pornographic film exhibitor carrying on an affair with his secretary; his glue-snorting son, Dexter (Ken King), who has an unusual shoe fetish prompting him to stomp on women's feet; his daughter Lulu (Mary Garlington) who dreams of being a go-go dancer; and Elmer's obese wife, Francine (**Divine**), a loving mate coping with the situation—barely. When Francine catches Elmer and his mistress in a motel room, learns that her daughter needs an abortion and that the courts have declared her son criminally insane, she succumbs to alcoholism. Then everything grows rosier for Francine when chain-bedecked hunk Todd Tomorrow (**Tab Hunter,** left) starts wooing her. The same night he seduces her, however, she discovers that he is in cahoots with her greedy mother, who is planning to bump her off, and that former husband Elmer also wants her dead. After all the evildoers are haphazardly eliminated, Francine finds some form of solace with the survivors, Dexter and Lulu, her miraculously rehabilitated children.

◄ **DIVINE**
LUST IN THE DUST
(1985, New World)
Laborious spaghetti western spoof directed by Paul Bartel ● While riding across the New Mexico desert on an exhausted mule, the obese Rosie Velez (**Divine**) is gang-raped by bandits led by Hard Case Williams (Geoffrey Lewis). After reducing the men to sexual dishrags, she is rescued by handsome buckaroo Abel Wood (Tab Hunter), who takes her to their common destination, Chili Verde. There, they meet hot-tempered saloon owner Margarita Ventura (Lainie Kazan), her body-guard Bernardo (Henry Silva) and her cleaning lady Big Ed (**Nedra Volz, photo,** right). The newcomers get the cold shoulder from the locals who have a secret: a stash of gold coins is hidden somewhere and everyone wants it. After several violent incidents reveal that Rosie and Margarita are slaves to their passion for sex and money, Abel learns they are long lost sisters, each of whom have half the treasure map tattooed on their rear end. Abel succeeds in matching the two fleshy documents and unearths the gold. Simultaneously, Hard Case, Rosie, Margarita and the local padre (Cesar Romero) show up at the site and kill each other off, leaving the clever cowpoke to ride off with the loot.

CHARLES BUSCH

SINCE THE EARLY '80s, Charles Busch has been the reigning playwright-actor and diva of gender-twisting entertainment. A genius at channeling the glamour gals of Hollywood's heyday, Busch strives not for the one-off character but for the mélange—mixing, for example, Greer Garson, Susan Hayward and Rosalind Russell. Born in 1954, Busch lived with his Aunt Lillian from the age of seven when his mother died. After studying drama at Northwestern, he began his impressive slate of theater credits by creating his own roles for New York's gay venues. Starting in 1986 in the East Village's Limbo Lounge, his *Vampire Lesbians of Sodom* became one of off-Broadway's longest running plays. A master at movie genre satire, Busch starred in the stage version of *Psycho Beach Party* (1987), a success that became a film released in 2000. He wrote more plays such as *The Lady in Question* (1989), a parody of WWII movies, and *Red Scare on Sunset* (1991), a melodramatic political spoof. Later, *The Allergist's Wife*, was nominated for a Tony and, in 2003, the film version of his *Die Mommie Die* won him a best performance award at Sundance. Playwright and impersonator extraordinaire, Busch earned critical acclaim as Nat Ginzburg, the cross-dressing inmate on HBO's series *Oz*. ●

◄ DIE MOMMIE DIE
(2003, Aviator Films)
Resolutely camp send-up of the '40s and '50s "women's films" directed by Mark Rucker ● Angela Arden (**Charles Busch**), once a popular songstress who performed in nightclubs with her sister Barbara, is now a retired celebrity living the Bel Air good life. Her velvet world, however, is a dark one, trapped as she is in a loveless marriage with her failing film producer husband, Sol Sussman (Phillip Baker Hall). The former star is also the mother of two warped children, dad-doting, mom-bashing Edith (Natasha Lyonne) and her brother, gay college washout Lance (Stark Sands). When Sol discovers Angela's affair with television has-been Tony Parker (Jason Priestley), he condemns her to a life without credit cards. Not one to take orders, Angela helps Sol out during one of his bouts of constipation with a deadly arsenic-laced suppository. Suspecting foul play in their father's death, Edith and Lance–both of whom Tony has seduced–trick their mother into taking an acid trip. Shockingly, Angela reveals that she is really Barbara, the less talented of the two sisters who, years earlier, had murdered Angela out of envy. This is obviously the reason "Angela" could never make a comeback. It is for this–and not the fact that Sol is still alive and she is guilty of attempted murder–that the diva is led out of her lavish estate in handcuffs.

▲ PSYCHO BEACH PARTY
(2000, Strand Releasing)
Clever parody of the '60s beach party and slasher genres directed by Robert Lee King ● Florence Forest (Lauren Ambrose), who lives with her mom (**Beth Broderick,** left) and foreign exchange student Lars (Matt Keeslar), is the victim of a multiple personality disorder. One day, her nerdy friend Berdine (Danni Wheeler) discovers that the girl in the car next to theirs has had her throat slashed. Police Captain Monica Stark (**Charles Busch**) investigates, but there are few clues. When Florence begins hanging out at Malibu beach, she asks teen idol the Great Kanaka (Thomas Gibson) to teach her to surf. He agrees after she makes a naughty pass at him during one of her blackouts in which she calls herself Ann Bowman. Dubbed "Chicklet" by the surfer dudes, she has other blackouts that coincide with other murders. Enter Capt. Stark again– and the star of the group's favorite horror films, Bettina (Kimberly Davies). After the big luau, Lars admits to Florence that he is the psychotic killer. Cured, she hooks up with StarCat (Nicholas Brendon), the handsome psych major that helped her recover her sanity.

WHEN DRAG WAS QUEEN

The slapstick stars of the silent screen

Roscoe "Fatty" Arbuckle

Larry Semon

Fred Mace

Syd Chaplin

Charlie Chaplin

Lupino Lane

Charlie Murray

Bobby Vernon

Chester Conklin

MACK SENNETT
& HIS "LAUGH FACTORY"

KEYSTONE, the first movie company designed solely for producing comedies, was founded by a lanky Canadian named Mack Sennett who, between 1913 and 1917, churned out a spate of short, fast-paced silent films that not only made audiences around the world roar but helped shape a fledgling medium soon responsible for transforming the way people viewed society. At his "laugh factory," he created a form of slapstick influenced by France's Pathé comedies and his own experience in burlesque. His studio was a lively environment where the genial but sometimes blunt Sennett encouraged every kind of inventive input—from improvised gags to the inclusion of newsreel footage. He also gave some of America's greatest comedians their real start—huge talents like Charlie Chaplin, Mabel Normand, Roscoe Arbuckle, Ben Turpin and Carole Lombard. Born in Danville, Quebec, in 1980, Michael (Mikall) Sinnott was 17 when his parents moved to Connecticut. Toiling as a ironworker and a boilermaker, the

strapping youngster started as an extra at D.W. Griffith's Biograph Studios in 1908. It was there that he progressed from walk-ons to lead roles opposite such actresses as Mabel Normand, with whom the eternal bachelor would have an on-again-off-again relationship. After branching out into writing and directing, he partnered with Adam Kessel and Charles Bauman, former bookmakers who financed his Keystone venture. Actual production began in Edendale, California, on August 28, 1912. The next year in its short comedies,

the studio featured a new recruit, Roscoe "Fatty" Arbuckle and a band of zany actors soon nicknamed the Keystone Kops, who tooled around in—and smashed into—every form of conveyance imaginable during their madcap chases. Though he always retained this Keystone trademark, Sennett began to move to a more sophisticated format that required better scripts and extensive editing. To help out, directors Clarence Badger and Eddie Cline were brought in and sex was added to the mix via the Bathing Beauties. ▶▶

▲ **MACK SENNETT & FRED MACE**
THE SLEUTH'S LAST STAND (1913, Keystone)
Spilt-reel comedy directed by Mack Sennett ● A pair of half-wit detectives (**Mack Sennett,** center left; **Fred Mace,** center right) clumsily investigate a case that leads them to a reservation where they dress as Indian squaws in order not to look too conspicuous (**photo**).

At 35, Sennett joined Griffith and Thomas Ince in the Triangle Film Corporation for which he teamed Gloria Swanson and Bobby Vernon in several comic features, including *The Sultan's Wife* (1917). When Griffith and Ince abandoned Triangle, he continued working under the banner of Mack Sennett Comedies. During the early '20s, he made a star of Ben Turpin, for whom he produced several parodies such as *The Shriek of Araby* (1923) and, in 1923, he hired baby-faced Harry Langdon. When the talkies arrived, Sennett moved to cash-strapped Educational, trying laboriously to adapt his style to the new medium. There, he produced six two-reelers showcasing a young Bing Crosby and several shorts featuring W.C. Fields, including *The Dentist* (1932). In 1932, Sennett coproduced and directed the tragically unfunny *Hypnotized* starring black-faced comedians Moran and Mack. It was such a flop that he declared bankruptcy in 1933 and, in essence, was forced to retire at age 55. He spent the rest of his life revered by the public and the industry—in 1937 he received an honorary Oscar—but remained basically unemployed. He passed away in Woodland Hills, California, in 1960 at age 80. ●

◀ BOTHWELL BROWNE
YANKEE DOODLE IN BERLIN
(1919, Mack Sennett-Sol Lesser)

WWI anti-German spy farce directed by F. Richard Jones ● Air Force Captain Bob White (**Bothwell Browne**) is sent to Germany to steal strategic plans. With his copilot (Charles Lynn), he lands behind enemy lines and dresses as a woman to better infiltrate the high command. "She" first meets Von Hindenburg (**Bert Roach**, far right) who falls for her. Soon, it is Crown Prince Freddie (**Mal St. Clair**, far left) and Kaiser Wilhelm (**Ford Sterling**, center). Bob makes the three men jealous of each other, a ploy that works to his advantage: he lures the kaiser to his room and, after an exotic dance (**photo, opposite**), passes along documents from the monarch's secret files to the American front via his copilot. Meanwhile, the crown prince, who has witnessed the dance from under the bed, tattles to the kaiserin (**Eva Thatcher**, second from left). Interrupting a romantic interlude, she pounds on the kaiser and, in front of his brain trust, removes Bob's wig (**photo, left**). His cover blown, he escapes just as a massive Allied assault is launched. Thanks to the stolen information, the Germans retreat.

▲ NICK COGLEY
LOVE, LOOT & CRASH (1915, Keystone-Mutual)

One-reel comedy directed by Mack Sennett ● Harold (**Charley Chase**) and his girlfriend Dora (Dora Rogers) plan to elope. Coincidentally, the signal they work out is the same as that of a pair of robbers planning to burglarize Dora's family house. As a consequence, one of the thieves, who had been masquerading as a female cook in ringlets and a Gibson girl get up (**Nick Cogley**) is "abducted" by Harold on a motorcycle (**photo**) while the other picks up Dora, assuming she is his cross-dressing partner. A chase ensues involving the Keystone Kops.

▲ CHARLIE MURRAY
THE GREAT VACUUM ROBBERY (1915, Sennett-Triangle)

Two-reel comedy directed by Harry Williams & Clarence Badger ● Two robbers (Edgar Kennedy and Louise Fazenda) use a vacuum cleaner to remove cash from a bank vault. To track the clever thieves down, the police hire two dull-bulb private investigators (**Charlie Murray** and **Slim Summerville**)—the first one dressed in drag (**photo**)—in order to trace the culprits to a resort hotel. From here, the chase takes on a frenzied pace as the sleuths, chasing the suspects in and out of rooms and up and onto roofs, finally close the net.

▶ TONY O'SULLIVAN
ARE WAITRESSES SAFE?
(1917, Mack Sennett-Paramount)

Two-reel comedy directed by Victor Heerman ● Proving that love is blind, waitress Louise (Louise Fazenda) is engaged to Ralph (Ben Turpin). She quits this unrewarding job to take a housekeeper position at a wealthy family's mansion. When her bosses leave for a weekend, she uses the house to give a party for her fiancé, Ralph; a close buddy (Glenn Cavender), a generously endowed lady (**Tony O'Sullivan**) and a few friends. Dressed in the family's best clothes, the group has a ball until a burglar (Slim Summerville) and his thugs break in. After a fistfight that attracts the police, the bad guys flee. But when Louise, her chums and the cops hear a noise at the door, they switch off the lights to better surprise the returning burglars. Unfortunately, it is the family that, coming back early, gets a beating. *(With **Wayland Trask**, left.)*

▶ NEAL BURNS
HIS HIDDEN PURPOSE
(1918, Mack Sennett-Paramount)

Two-reel comedy directed by Eddie Cline & Clarence Badger ● Walrus (**Chester Conklin,** second from right), a plainclothes cop, is smitten with a young lady (**Marie Prevost,** far left) whose father (**Gene Rogers,** far right) has given him her hand in marriage. Marie's actual boyfriend (**Neal Burns,** second from left), in order to continue to see her in spite of her parents' interdiction, dons widow's weeds. At the same time, a convict (Cliff Bowes) who has escaped from prison in order to settle a score with Walrus, also disguises himself as a woman. A great confusion ensues (**photo**) during which a gunfight erupts. Arrested, Walrus goes to jail and Marie gets her beau.

▶ FRED MACE
THE CURE THAT FAILED
(1913, Mack Sennett-Mutual)

Split-reel comedy probably directed by Mack Sennett ● In an attempt to help a friend (**Ford Sterling,** left) stop drinking, a man (**Fred Mace**) disguises himself as a woman (**photo**) and makes his chum believe they have married during one of his benders. After accepting the charade, the drunkard, when sober, realizes that his "new bride" is his buddy. In order to get even, he decides to simulate a suicide. After pouring red ink on his shirt, he shoots himself with a fake gun and falls on the bed. The masquerade ends when the police arrest both pranksters.

HARRY DEPP

WHEN HE WORKED for Mack Sennett between 1916 and 1917, Harry Depp was often cast for the parts requiring female impersonation, the prime example of this talent being *His Widow's Might* (1917) with Monte Banks. Never the film's star, always the supporting actor bringing a new twist to the plot, the *dragmeister* moved to Universal where he did more (but not exclusively) cross-dressing. At Al Christie's studio, he starred with Elinor Field in the two-reel situational comedy *Girl in the Box* (1918) and shared the bill with the comely Fay Tincher in *Rowdy Ann*. Depp continued to work during the silent era, sharing the cross-dressing honors with George K. Arthur in the Columbia feature film *When the Wife's Away* (1926). When the talkies came, the St. Louis-born actor (1883) moved on to become a successful agent. He died in Hollywood in 1957. •

► A LOVE CASE
(1917, Triangle)
One-reel comedy directed by Harry Kernan with Dale Fuller (far left), Harry Depp (center) and Lilian Biron (far right).

▲ THEIR HUSBAND
(1917, Mack Sennett-Triangle)
One-reel comedy—unidentified director—with Jack Dillon (far left), Alatia Marton (second from left), Harry Depp (second from right).

◄ SKIRT STRATEGY
(1917, Mack Sennett-Triangle)
One-reel comedy directed by Charles Avery with Grace Lane (second from left on the floor) and Harry Depp (far right).

▼ HIS WIDOW'S MIGHT
(1917, Mack Sennett-Triangle)
One-reel comedy directed by Henry Kernan with Mario Bianchi (aka Monte Banks, left).

▶ FRED MACE
MABEL'S
ADVENTURES
(1912, Keystone)

Split-reel comedy directed by Mack Sennett ● Mabel (**Mabel Normand,** second from right), dressed as a boy, goes to a vaudeville show in which Fred (**Fred Mace,** center) performs as the Queen of Burlesque. During his number he throws a stolen pearl necklace to his partner (**Ford Sterling,** second from left) who deftly makes it slip into one of Mabel's pockets. After realizing that she has gone home with the jewels, Fred and the whole troupe, still in their costumes, chase her through woods and, finally, into a river (**photo**).

▲ BOBBY VERNON
THE SULTAN'S
WIFE (1917, Mack
Sennett-Mutual)

Two-reel comedy directed by Clarence Badger ● While spending their summer vacation in India, sailor Bobby (**Bobby Vernon**) and his girlfriend Gloria (**Gloria Swanson,** hidden under the carpet) meet a rajah who invites them to his palatial compound. Smitten with Gloria, he decides that she would make a lovely addition to his harem and separates the couple by force. When she is ordered to dress in sheer clothes and perform a sensual dance, Gloria and Bobby reunite just in time to trade outfits and almost outwit the wily rajah (**photo**). Fortunately, their Great Dane Teddy comes to the rescue just in time.

▲ BILLY BEVAN & EDDIE QUILLAN
THE BULLFIGHTER
(1927, Mack Sennett-Pathé)
Two-reel comedy directed by Earl Rodney ● The legal guardian of a young girl (**Madeline Hurlock,** right) wants her to marry his son. Not

knowing the pretender and forecasting the worst, she flees. During her quest for freedom, she meets a charming young man (**Eddie Quillan,** center) and one of his friends (**Billy Bevan,** left). Forced to impersonate country girls, one of the buddies attracts the attention of a rube (Andy

Clyde) while the other romances the adorable fugitive. When a bull threatens them, the amorous lad lets his pal play the part of the torero—bravely but cautiously (**photo**). The girl is relieved when she learns that the enamored lad is her guardian's son.

▲ CHARLIE MURRAY
COURTING TROUBLE
(1932, Mack Sennett-Paramount)
Two-reel comedy directed by Leslie Pearce, with Matt MacHugh.

ROSCOE "FATTY" ARBUCKLE

ROSCOE ARBUCKLE, known as Fatty by the public and as Roscoe by his friends, was one of the greatest triple-threat talents in the early days of silent cinema. Comic actor, writer and director, he was immediately recognizable for his boyish demeanor and despite his considerable girth, his amazing physical agility. Born in 1887 in Kansas but brought to California as a child, the roly-poly teenager performed in carnivals before moving on to burlesque. In 1913, he was picked up by Mack Sennett to join Keystone's impressive roster of comedians. There, he starred occasionally with Charlie Chaplin and often with comic star Mabel Normand. By 1914, Sennett had given him some latitude as a writer and director, but in 1917 producer Joseph Schenck lured him away, giving him full creative control in a series of short comedies distributed by Paramount. In his initial two-reeler for Schenck, *The Butcher Boy*, Arbuckle introduced Buster Keaton to the world. The slapstick partnership the two men formed from 1917 to 1919 was to launch the poker-faced ▶▶

▲ MISS FATTY'S SEASIDE LOVERS (1915, Keystone)

One-reel comedy directed by Roscoe Arbuckle
● Mr. Finnegan, a mothball magnate, and his wife arrive at the Breakers Hotel, an elegant seaside resort. In tow is their flirtatious daughter, Miss Fatty (**Fatty Arbuckle**), a vision-in-the-round with her mismatched outfits, bee-stung lips and marcelled hair. The buxom heiress is not unattractive, however, for an eager trio of gold-digging would-be suitors (Harold Lloyd, Joe Bordeau and Edgar Kennedy) plunge into the sea to rescue her, after she is caught by the tide, with little appreciation from the spoiled brat.

◀ FATTY ARBUCKLE
PEEPING PETE
(1913, Mack Sennett-Triangle)

Split-reel directed by Mack Sennett ● While his overweight spouse (**Fatty Arbuckle,** second from left) toils at doing the laundry, cowboy Pete (Mack Sennett) spies on his neighbor's wife through a hole he has drilled in the fence that separates their houses. When the jealous husband (Ford Sterling) discovers Pete peeping, he confronts him with a gun. Pete, who is also armed, defends himself, initiating a chase through the village during which several volleys are shot at random. In order to stop a potential double murder, Pete's wife warns the sheriff and the villagers unite to search for the rivals (**photo**). They finally find them fraternizing over a bottle of Scotch.

◀ THE BUTCHER BOY
(1917, Joe Schenck-Paramount)

Two-reel comedy directed by Roscoe Arbuckle ● A general store owner has three problems: the customers, the help and his daughter Amanda (**Josephine Stevens,** left). His patrons, like loony Buster (Buster Keaton), are highly demanding; his employees, like Slim, the chief clerk (Al St. John), and Fatty (**Fatty Arbuckle**), the butcher boy, are undisciplined; and his teenage girl toys with the tender feelings that Slim and Fatty have for her. Their rivalry explodes when Amanda tells Fatty that Slim wants to marry her. Suddenly, all hell breaks loose in the store. When the dust has settled, the irate father sends Amanda to a nearby boarding school for girls. But naughty Fatty shows up at the institution as Amanda's ungainly Cousin Candy (**photo**) and tells the principal she might want to enroll. Welcomed for the night, Fatty is upset when he realizes that Slim has already been able to sneak into the boarding school. But thwarting Slim's plan to abduct Amanda, he takes her to a nearby preacher and marries her.

▶ REBECCA'S WEDDING DAY (1914, Mack Sennett-Mutual) **One-reel comedy directed by George Nichols.**

◀ THE SKY PIRATE
(1914, Keystone)

One-reel comedy directed by Eddie Dillon and Roscoe Arbuckle ● The kidnapping of a young heiress (**Fatty Arbuckle**) by a daring bandit in an airplane triggers a chase involving the Keystone Kops. To escape, the heiress extracts herself from her seat and dives into a river. The plane and its pilot—as well as the cops and their cars—follow suit. An epic mêlée ensues during which the kidnapper is arrested.

▶▶ funnyman's career with small jewels such as *Fatty at Coney Island* (1917) and *Good Night Nurse* (1918). In 1920, under the aegis of Jesse L. Lasky, Arbuckle began to star in feature films, such as *Brewster's Millions,* mingling seriousness and light comedy. At the zenith of his popularity, Arbuckle was felled in 1921 by a shocking event in San Francisco at one of his over-the-top drinking bashes. One of the attendees, an actress named Virginia Rappe, died soon after experiencing a ruptured bladder. The 300-pound host was arrested for rape and manslaughter and after two hung jury trials, was acquitted in a third. It made no difference to his public, however, which was appalled by the accusations of sexual misconduct aimed at their cherubic-faced idol. Arbuckle's career having collapsed, he directed a few short comedies anonymously for his nephew and former sidekick, Al St. John and under the pseudonym of William Goodrich for comedians Lupino Lane and Lloyd Hamilton. In 1932, Vitaphone hired him to reprise his acting and two short talkies were shot, the first being *Hey Pop,* which once again featured his talents as a female impersonator. Fate, unfortunately, prevented a comeback: Roscoe "Fatty" Arbuckle died at 46 of a massive coronary. ●

◄ FATTY ARBUCKLE
GOODNIGHT, NURSE
(1918, Joe Schenck-Paramount)

Two-reel comedy directed by Roscoe Arbuckle ● When Fatty comes home drunk with an organ grinder and his monkey, his wife hauls him to a hospital that advertises a cure for alcoholism through an operation. Meeting a surgeon (Buster Keaton) whose scrubs are covered with bloodstains, Fatty (**Roscoe Arbuckle**) resists the procedure but loses consciousness after he is administered ether. When he wakes up, he wants to get out—fast. Wriggling into a uniform of one of the off-duty nurses (**photo**), he fools the staff until the rotund owner of the white outfit, seeing it on Fatty, rips it off. Now in his underwear, he escapes chased by the surgeon and a couple of orderlies. Running down a dirt road, he joins a group of overweight joggers—all of them 200 pounds minimum—engaged in a race. Fatty easily wins and…awakens from the surgery.

► FATTY AT CONEY ISLAND
(1917, Joe Schenck-Paramount)

Two-reel comedy directed by Roscoe Arbuckle ● While Buster (Buster Keaton) watches a parade at Coney Island with girlfriend Alice (**Alice Mann**, right), Fatty (**Roscoe Arbuckle**) evades his wife's surveillance at the beach in order to freely ogle the bathing beauties. Fickle Alice, who has ditched Buster for Al (Al St. John), discards Al for Fatty. When everybody meets at the bathhouse, Fatty, unable to rent a male swimming suit big enough for him, borrows a matronly female one and steals a wig (**photo**). Meeting Fatty on a bench, Al starts to flirt with her until a laughing Buster removes Fatty's wig with a fishing rod. An acrobatic fight in the sea between Al and Fatty lands them in jail. In the meantime, Buster has reunited with Alice and they walk away serenely.

► HEY POP (1932, Vitaphone)

Two-reel comedy directed by Alf Goulding ● Little Billy (**Billy Hayes**, right), who has fled the orphanage where his mother has abandoned him, takes refuge in the kitchen of a restaurant. There, he meets a sympathetic cook (**Fatty Arbuckle**) who, after hiding him from the cops, and being fired for it, takes him home. Penniless for a few days, the good man finds ingenious ways to feed Billy, one of which is a food fight. On the verge of being arrested, the cook dresses as a woman, conceals Billy in a floral-decorated baby carriage (**photo**) and unwittingly wins first prize in a children's parade. But just as the cook starts to enjoy the moment, he is unmasked when his dress is accidentally ripped off. Billy, sadly, is returned to the orphanage.

WALLACE BEERY
(aka Sweedie)

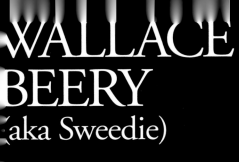

ALTHOUGH HE IS most remembered for the gruff-and-rough characterizations of his later years and the Academy Award he received in 1931 for his acting in the gritty classic *The Champ,* Wallace Beery's early cinematic work was in female impersonation. In mid-1914 he started shooting a series of short subjects for Essanay in which he played Sweedie, a funny-faced immigrant maid from Sweden. Most of the 40 one-reel films Beery shot in full drag until 1915, from *Sweedie the Swatter* to *Sweedie in Vaudeville,* have unfortunately disappeared. The burly actor was born in 1885 in Kansas City, Missouri. He entered the world of entertainment as an elephant trainer and eventually found himself at Mack Sennett's Keystone Studios where he made *Teddy at the Throttle* (1916) costarring Gloria Swanson, who he eloped with the following year. When talkies arrived, Beery found the perfect sullen mate in Marie Dressler—with whom he made the unforgettable *Min and Bill* (1930) and *Tugboat Annie* (1933)—and became a towering figure in films such as *Grand Hotel* (1932) and *Viva Villa!* (1934). He passed away in 1949. •

CHARLIE & SYD CHAPLIN

CHARLES CHAPLIN'S half-brother, Sydney, was born in Capetown, South Africa, in 1885; Charlie was born in London four years later in 1889. Raised in the slums of England's capital, these sons of an alcoholic father shared a childhood of deprivation, dancing in the streets for coins to help support the family. It was Syd who, while touring with Fred Karno's music-hall group, first made a name in show business. He introduced his sibling to the producer in 1908, which resulted in a job for Charlie. Six years later, when Charlie was leaving Keystone for greener pastures, he repaid the kindness by suggesting to Mack Sennett that he start making films with Syd. The fruit of that relationship was a hobo-like character named Gussle who, wearing a shrunken waistcoat, a smashed felt hat and an upward-curling moustache, appeared in a string of one and two-reelers. When Gussle showed signs of fatigue at the box-office, Syd switched to handling

his brother's burgeoning business affairs, gaining for him lucrative contracts with Mutual and First National while keeping his foot in the entertainment world with small parts in Charlie's films. Known for his spot-on takeoffs of movie divas at Hollywood's chic parties, Syd landed the lead in a 1925 production of *Charley's Aunt,* followed the same year by *Man on the Box,* and in 1926, *Oh! What a Nurse!* These three movies, in which he cross-dresses amusingly, provided the perfect coda for a comedian who lacked a clear identity. Continuing to concentrate on his brother's finances, Syd retired later in comfort in the south of France. Of the ▸▸

▲ CHARLES CHAPLIN
A WOMAN (1915, Keystone)

Two-reel comedy directed by Charles Chaplin ● In the park, the Tramp (**Charlie Chaplin**) meets two skirt-chasers in separate encounters. One of them (**Charles Insley,** left) has gone off to chase an attractive young flirt, leaving his wife and daughter Edna (**Edna Purviance**) dozing on a bench. The other gentleman (**Billy Armstrong,** right), Edna's fiancé, is convinced that the coquette has fallen for him. The tramp further confuses the situation when he accepts the wife's invitation for tea at their home. When the skirt chasers show up, they recognize him so the tramp is forced to flee into a bedroom. There, he locates his ticket to freedom: a stylish woman's suit and furs. After shaving off his mustache, he proceeds to entrance the two men (**photo**), reigniting their competitive male instincts. The rival is forced to leave, but when the father slyly kisses the edge of the tramp's long dress, it slides off revealing the beauty's real gender. Furious, he kicks out the impersonator.

two half-brothers, Charles, obviously, is the one who made it big artistically. His creation, that scruffy but dignified character known as the tramp, remains recognized around the world as the empathetic symbol of the struggling downtrodden. But though the plight of the mustachioed vagabond with the penguin-like walk is tinged with sadness, the bowler-hatted hobo always evokes laughter, responding as he does to the most dismal situations with a cheery gumption. By the time he was 21, Chaplin was a headliner in London's music halls and went on an American tour with Fred Karno's troupe. Mack Sennett saw him perform and signed him to his fledgling company, Keystone. Soon Chaplin was writing and directing, and like other clowns of early cinema, used cross-dressing as a comedic device before developing his famous baggy-panted personae. The character debuted fully formed in the Essanay Film Company's 1915 release, *The Tramp*. It made many more appearances in subsequent two-reelers and later in features he financed and controlled himself, such as *The Gold Rush* (1925), *City Lights* (1931), *Modern Times* (1936) and *The Great Dictator* (1940), in which, for the first time, he had a speaking role. Eventually, as his leftist views were publicized, his popularity waned. In 1952, he left the United States and vowed to never come back. But he returned in 1972 to receive an honorary Academy Award for lifetime achievement. Hollywood finally acknowledged the master of pantomime to be one of the most influential filmmakers in the history of the medium. Sir Charles Spencer Chaplin died in Switzerland in 1977 at age 88. Syd had died before him in France in 1965 at age 80. ●

◄ **CHARLES CHAPLIN**
THE MASQUERADER
(1914, Keystone)
One-reel comedy directed by Charles Chaplin ● At the Keystone Studio's gate, actor Charles Chaplin is picked up by a director (**Charles Murray,** left) and sent to a dressing room that he shares with cherubic farceur Fatty Arbuckle. After Chaplin has transformed himself into his tramp character, he goes to the set where, missing a cue, he ruins a take and throws the shooting into chaos. Furious, the director fires him. The day after, ravishing Señorita Chapelino (**Chaplin** in drag) shows up at the studio. Her beauty enthralls the director who, after making goo-goo eyes at the coquette (**photo**), accompanies her to the dressing room. When the director comes back to bring her to the set, Chaplin has reverted to his Tramp outfit, thinking that by incarnating a woman, he had proven he was a good actor. Realizing he has been duped, the director fires him—again.

◄ **CHARLES CHAPLIN**
A BUSY DAY (1914, Keystone)
Split-reel comedy directed by Charles Chaplin ● While attending the harbor festival in San Pedro, California, a lady (**Charlie Chaplin**) surprises her husband (Mack Swain) flirting with a cute young girl. The jealous wife confronts her spouse, creating a ruckus that, after attracting the police, ends up in the ocean.

◀ **SYD CHAPLIN**
OH! WHAT A NURSE!
(1926, Warner)
Lively Darryl Zanuck script directed by Charles Reisner ● While on his way to work on a ferry, cub reporter Jerry Clark (**Syd Chaplin**) saves the life of a drowning woman but falls overboard himself. Rescued by the crew of a speeding boat, Jerry meets Capt. Ladye Kirby (Matthew Betz), a cross-dressing rum smuggler known as the Veiled Runner. The captain forces him to don widow's weeds to confuse prohibition officers in hot pursuit. Back at the

office in the same garb, Jerry is asked by his boss to masquerade as the former female letters-to-the-lovelorn columnist and visit a girl upset by a recent piece of advice she got. Upon arrival, Jerry realizes that the troubled lady, June Harrison (**Patsy Ruth Miller,** right), is the woman whose life he saved on the ferry. When June's uncle (David Torrence) wants to gain her inheritance by marrying her off to a fortune hunter, Jerry poses as a nurse (**photo**) to gain access to a ship where she is being held prisoner. Fighting off thugs, he winds up winning June for himself.

▲ **SYD CHAPLIN**
THE MAN ON THE BOX (1925, Warner)
Easygoing espionage silliness directed by Charles Reisner ● Rich young bachelor Bob Warburton (**Syd Chaplin**) has invested a large sum of money in an invention that will revolutionize helicopter technology. At a reception given by Colonel Annesley (E.J. Ratcliffe), an old friend who has the secret plans hidden in his safe, he learns that Count Karaloff (Charles Gerrard) intends to steal the precious documents. To thwart this notorious foreign agent's scheme, Bob dresses as a maid—complete with sturdy undergarments and marcelled hair (**photo**)—has the spies arrested and, in addition, marries Betty (Alice Calhoun), the colonel's charming daughter.

► **FREDERICK KOVERT**
THE REEL VIRGINIAN
(aka "The West Virginian," 1924, Mack Sennett-Pathé)
Two-reel comedy directed by Reggie Morris & Ed Kennedy ● In order to impress local teacher Alice (Alice Day), cowboy Rodney St. Clair (**Ben Turpin**, right) decides to foil the predations of a gang of cattle rustlers. In the meantime, his Uncle Lorimer brings back from the big city a stunning mail-order bride, Mlle. Sans Souci and suggests a double wedding. But before the ceremony, Rodney becomes so smitten with the beautiful Sans Souci (**photo**) that he tells Alice he cannot marry her. When the guests—who include the rustlers—learn the news, they are so furious that they decide to shoot Rodney. Mlle. Sans Souci tells them he should be hanged instead. This diversion gives her the opportunity to call the sheriff, who quickly rounds up the bandits. Then, removing her wig, the Frenchwoman reveals that she is a male detective (**Frederick KoVert**), much to the embarrassment of everyone. Later, an understanding Alice agrees to become the bride of a repentant Rodney.

BEN TURPIN

BEN TURPIN, who had his most valuable comic asset—his crossed eyes—insured by Lloyds of London, was the silent screen's master of the preposterous visual gag. If sources agree about his real first name, Bernard, and his birthplace, New Orleans, they disagree on the date. Some mention as early as 1869, others 1874, or as late as 1886. What is certain is that Turpin started his career in burlesque, tried unsuccessfully to earn a living in film as soon as 1909, and after returning to the boards, reappeared on screen in 1914 as a foil to Wallace Beery in his cross-dressing farcical series *Sweedie*. In 1915, Turpin was one of Charlie Chaplin's partners in his first film made for the Chicago-based Essanay Studios, *His New Job*. The same year, Turpin followed Chaplin to California to work with him in *A Night Out* and stayed there hoping for more opportunities. It was the legendary Mack Sennett who in 1917 would give Turpin a decade of full employment and make him famous. For the pioneering producer, the pint-size comic made an impressive number of two-reelers, the best of them being a series of parodies in which, improbable as playboy Rodney St. Clair, he was a hilarious example of misplaced vanity and social clumsiness. Two of these buffooneries are still available

today: *The Shriek of Araby* (1923), in which he is a not-so-suave Rudolph Valentino, and *Three Foolish Weeks* (1924) in which he apes insufferable womanizer Erich von Stroheim's character from *Foolish Wives*. When sound finally arrived in film, the thrifty Turpin had enough money to survive his shrinking stardom. Nevertheless he made cameo appearances from time to time, his last one being in Laurel and Hardy's *Saps at Sea* in 1940. That same year, Ben Turpin passed away, the victim of a heart attack. ●

▲ **BEN TURPIN**
SHERIFF NELL'S TUSSLE
(1918, Mack Sennett-Paramount)
Two-reel comedy directed by William Campbell & Hampton Del Ruth ● Fearless Nell (**Polly Moran,** right) has married and replaced the cowardly Ben (**Ben Turpin**) as Triggerville's sheriff. When two shady cowpokes appear after crossing the desert, Nell senses that trouble is in the air. After learning that the law woman is proud of the city's library, the pair organizes a benefit during which Nell entertains her compatriots with the help of her spineless husband (**photo**). While the festivities are in progress, the crafty duo tries to rob the distant bank. But, having smelled a rat, the clever Nell, with the help of her hubby, thwarts the heist and restores law and order in her neck of the West.

◀ **BEN TURPIN**
HE LOOKED CROOKED
(aka "Why Ben Bolted,"
1917, Mutual-Vogue)
Two-reel comedy directed by Robin Williamson ● On April Fool's Day, car dealer Arthur Bean offers a job to hobo Timothy Hay (**Ben Turpin**). As a joke, Bean sends Timothy in a huge box to paramour Fannie Poppit with a note describing the contents as a "loof lirpa." Fannie's maid, Etta Fish, opens the present, discovers Timothy and falls for him. Planning to introduce her heartthrob as her sister Hetty so Arthur's gift will not reach Fannie, Etta gives him some of her clothes (**photo**). Meanwhile, Timothy calls a handsome friend to replace him in the box, promising money and an heiress. Surprised by the "loof lirpa," but attracted by his looks, Fannie takes him, her maid and Hetty to a ballroom. There, Hetty gets drunk and all hell breaks loose when Fannie realizes Hetty is a man. Fortunately, boyfriend Arthur shows up, explaining to Fannie that "loof lirpa" is April fool spelled backwards.

◀ **BEN TURPIN**
A HAREM'S KNIGHT
(1926, Mack Sennett-Pathé)
Two-reel comedy directed by Gil Pratt ● When French aviator Lt. Dubarry (Danny O'Shea) abducts Manda (Madeline Hurlock), the princess of Barbaria, the rajah offers 25,000 rupees for her safe return. Meanwhile, in a dark street, Lt. Dubarry assails Rodney St.Clair (**Ben Turpin**), a man of great elegance, and forces him to trade his evening clothes with Manda's Hindu dancing girl costume. Confused with the princess, St. Clair is arrested and brought to the rajah who, after spanking her, realizes she is wearing a moustache and throws her out (**photo**). Arrested for passionately kissing Lt. Dubarry while still dressed as a man, Manda escapes and sneaks into St. Clair's apartment. They exchange clothes again and in the process St. Clair falls for her. When the rajah shows up to get Manda back, St. Clair engages him in a duel. As he is on the verge of losing, Dubarry enters and overpowers the rajah and his men. Manda disappoints St. Clair when she follows the aviator, but Petunia (**Louise Carver,** far left), the rajah's homely sister, drugs St. Clair's drink, hoping to finally discover what love is. *(With Dave Morris, right.)*

MACK SENNETT STARTED Keystone Studios in 1912 with quick-action comedies that delighted a public hungry for laughs. But before the clever filmmaker and his crew of gagmen, acrobats and comics, a couple of actors dominated the field of cinematic humor.

JOHN BUNNY. Circus performer and classic melodrama actor, John Bunny was America's first real movie star. Born in 1863 in Manhattan, after years on the stage he developed a keen enthusiasm for "the flickers." In fact, according to several sources, he canceled a lucrative theatrical contract with the Shuberts to make a film for Vitagraph Studios for free. In 1911 at 48—a rather advanced age for a debut in film—the rotund comedian made his first, entitled *Doctor Cupid*, and under the direction of Ned Finley, appeared in drag in *The Leading Lady* (**photo**). Often paired with British actress Flora Finch in films that came to be known as *The Bunnyfinches,* Bunny often played the harmlessly mischievous husband whose wife always forgives in the end. Known all over the globe, he passed away in 1915, at age 51.

MAX LINDER. An influence on Charlie Chaplin, French actor Gabriel Maximilien Leuvielle is remembered for his boulevardier personae

Above: If Charlie Chaplin acknowledged Max Linder as one of his mentors, Mack Sennett also admitted that the French pre-WWI comedies showed a unique flair for slapstick that influenced him too. Director Ferdinand Zecca, one of the pioneers of this era, did not neglect to use cross-dressing as a comedic device, notably in 1912's *Dranem steno-dactylographe.*

Left: John Bunny in *The Leading Lady* (1911, Vitagraph).

and his ingenious sight gags. Born in 1883, he made his first movie in 1905 and, upon signing with Pathé, adopted the *nom de cinéma* of Max Linder. Humorously, the Pathé comedies almost always starred Linder's first name in their simplistic titles—*Max Takes a Bath* and *Max and His Dog*—and as they made their way around the world, turned him into an international star. In *Le duel de Max* (1912), he disguises himself as a woman to seduce the boyfriend of a girl he lusts after (top left). If Max Linder's career was not ended by his experience as a driver during World War I, it set him up for long periods of depression. However he was able to continue acting, making three movies for Essanay in 1917. In 1925, the year his last film, *King of the Circus,* was released, he and his 19-year-old wife died in a suicide pact.

MORE SILENT STARS IN DRAG

▲ GEORGE WALSH
I'LL SAY SO (1918, Fox)

Feature film about a patriotic flat-footed man directed by Raoul Walsh ● On the eve of WWI, Bill Durham (**George Walsh**) is rejected by the draft because of his flat feet. He decides, however, to serve his country to the best of his abilities, and in the interim falls in love with Barbara Knowles (Regina Quinn). He later learns that Barbara, an orphan, lives with her legal guardian, August Meyers (William Bailey), a man who, he discovers, is a German spy trying to foment a revolution south of the border. From New Mexico, Bill involves himself with Pancho Villa's band and soon discourages the *bandidos* from following through with the German plan. Back in New York, Meyers the spy has decided to marry off Barbara to one of his cohorts, Carl Vogel. Fortunately, Bill stops the proceedings and steps forward as the groom. *(This film, directed by George's brother, Raoul Walsh, is considered lost. The scene in which he appears in drag exists only in photos such as this one.)*

▶ LARRY SEMON
THE GOWN SHOP (1923, Vitagraph)

Two-reel comedy directed by Larry Semon ● A salesman in a haute-couture shop, Larry (**Larry Semon**) falls for salesgirl Kathleen (Kathleen Myers). Unfortunately, the owner (Oliver Hardy) also fancies the young beauty. Flirting outrageously with her, he upsets not only Larry but infuriates his wife. Also angry is the head of the pressing department who is equally smitten with Kathleen. When he chases Larry all over the store throwing burning irons at him, Larry hides in the models' dressing room and exits disguised as a frizzy-haired woman (**photo**). After the doorman unwittingly pulls off Larry's dress, the shop's proprietor catches him, but Kathleen stops her bellicose boss and leaves the place forever with an elated Larry.

▶ HENRY BERGMAN
THE RINK (1916, Mutual)

Two-reel comedy directed by Charles Chaplin ● Edna (Edna Purviance) lives with her father (**James T. Kelley**); Charlie (**Charlie Chaplin**) works as a waiter at a restaurant nearby. When Edna's father shows up for lunch, he invites the massive Mrs. Stout (**Henry Bergman** in drag) to join him. Charlie, unable to carve a chicken, creates a ruckus but deflects the blame. Meeting Edna on his lunch break, Charlie introduces himself as Sir Cecil Selzer and Edna invites him to a party she is giving at a roller skating rink. Coincidentally, Edna's father invites Mrs. Stout while one of Edna's friends invites her equally massive husband, Mr. Stout (**Eric Campbell**). At the party, Sir Cecil enjoys the embarrassment of Mr. and Mrs. Stout who were hoping to stray. After falling on Mrs. Stout, Charlie escapes her husband's rage thanks to his acrobatic aplomb. Now pandemonium on wheels, the party disbands. The cops arrive but Sir Cecil skates away.

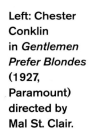

◀ CHESTER CONKLIN

Right: Chester Conklin in an unidentified silent short subject with Bud Jamison (left).

Left: Chester Conklin in *Gentlemen Prefer Blondes* (1927, Paramount) directed by Mal St. Clair.

▶ WILLIAM GILLESPIE
CHASING THE CHASER
(1925, Hal Roach)

One-reel comedy directed by Stan Laurel ● The wife of womanizer Gilroy is welcomed by an attractive secretary when she visits the office of a private investigator. After asking to see the detective, the female employee removes her wig, uncovering the bald dome of a man (**William Gillespie, top photos**). The private eye suggests a plan to catch her rapscallion of a husband red-handed. That afternoon, when Gilroy (**James Finlayson, bottom photo**, left) comes home, he is pleased to discover a new maid—who is none other than the embosomed gumshoe. Learning that his wife has gone downtown and not knowing that she is observing the scene, he comes on to the pretty servant. When Gilroy tries to kiss the maid, she blows a whistle, a signal to call the jealous wife. Embarrassed and repentant, Gilroy offers words of contrition, but when he realizes he has been entrapped by a man, he grabs a carbine and chases the detective from his home.

▶ BOBBY VERNON
BRIGHT LIGHTS
(1924, Al Christie)

Two-reel comedy directed by Walter Graham ● To get even with two pretty girls who have mercilessly made fun of him, Lem (**Bobby Vernon**) follow them to the elegant nightclub where they perform a dancing act. Dressed as a rube, he rushes out onto the dance floor, embarrassing the girls with his antics. Ejected by the manager, Lem makes several returns disguised in different outfits, and in spite of surveillance, dons one of the dancers' outfits and joins the girls in their performance. His improvised choreography triggers hilarity in the audience, but when he trips, his wig falls off (**photo**). The police notice the incident and the chase is on. Exiting the club, he enters a departing cab and forces the passenger to trade clothes with him. The police arrest the wrong man in a tutu while Lem escapes in a tuxedo.

▶ FRANKLIN PANGBORN
MY FRIEND FROM INDIA
(1927, Pathé)

Farce low in budget and high in yawns directed by E. Mason Hopper ● Charles (Ben Hendricks, Jr.) has a problem: his aunt is threatening to disinherit him if he doesn't introduce her to the Hindu prince he has been talking about. Meanwhile, William Valentine (**Franklin Pangborn**), a well-off gentleman, falls in love with a girl named Bernice (Elinor Fair) during an encounter so brief that he fails to get her address. To locate her, William looks for a fortuneteller at an Asian fair where soon-to-be-disinherited Charles is looking for a Hindu prince, real or false. When the police raid the place during a lottery, the two men flee together. After a hectic night, Charles asks William if he could impersonate the prince. All is well until a fakir (Tom Dugan) and his valet show up. Not to be recognized, William then dresses as a woman (**photo**), is forced to flirt with Judge Belmore (Tom Ricketts) and plays the "mirror trick" with Charles' Aunt (**Jeannette Loff,** right). A pair of nosy cops interrupts the scheme, but William is nevertheless a happy man when he realizes that Bernice is Charles' sister.

▶ LUPINO LANE
ONLY ME
(1929, Educational)

Two-reel comedy directed by Henry W. George ● A seriously inebriated gentleman in a top hat (**Lupino Lane**) asks a cab driver to take him to the Palace Theater without realizing it is across the street. Once there he buys a ticket for the matinee from a clerk who looks just like him. Inside the theater, everyone looks like him: a rowdy kid up to no good, the bandleader, the flutist, the master of ceremonies, five members of a singing group, the Spanish juggler and the strong man. In fact, the dead ringers perform all the vaudeville acts, including, during a tragic scene, a mother and her baby! Even the cutesy singer with ringlets, long dress and pouting mouth (**photo**) is his double! No mystery here, as all the parts in this film are played by Lupino Lane. *(Two-reeler inspired by Buster Keaton's* The Playhouse.*)*

SEND IN THE CLOWNS

High-jinx in high heels

Bob Hope

Totò

Buster Keaton

Bert Wheeler & Robert Woolsey

Harold Lloyd

Fernandel

Joe E. Brown

Jerry Lewis

Red Skelton

Harry Langdon

The Ritz Brothers

Louis de Funès

Monty Python

Bud Abbott & Lou Costello

Stan Laurel & Oliver Hardy

BUD ABBOTT & LOU COSTELLO

WHEN AMERICA was bereft of cheer during the dark days of WWII, the comedy team of Bud Abbott and Lou Costello arrived to fill the need. Their 1941 films, *Buck Privates* and *In the Navy,* immediately made them huge stars, roles they enjoyed throughout the '40s. More interested in slapstick gags and verbal routines than in character development, the duo's popular dynamic relied upon the contrast between their opposite personalities: the lovable, chubby Lou was forever at the mercy of his bullying, acid-tongued partner, always playing patsy to Bud, the slender, laconic straight man who came up with the outlandishly grand schemes—all of which had a payoff only for him.

Both comics were born in New Jersey: William "Bud" Abbott in 1895, with circus performers for parents; Francis "Lou" Cristillo in 1906, in a family that encouraged his athletic ambitions.

The pair came together in 1931, when Bud was asked to substitute as Lou's ailing straight man in his vaudeville act. After years ▶▶

LOU COSTELLO
LOST IN A HAREM (1944, MGM)

Cartoonish and campy escapade directed by Charles Reisner ● Singer Hazel Moon (Marilyn Maxwell) and illusionists Pete (**Bud Abbott,** left) and Harvey (**Lou Costello)** are stranded in the imaginary middle-eastern country of Barabeeha. Jailed after a brawl, they are approached by Prince Ramo (John Conte) who offers to arrange their escape on the condition that they help him recover his throne, which has been usurped by his Uncle Nimativ (Douglass Dumbrille). The trio enters the palace to steal the two hypnotic cats-eye rings that are forcing everyone into submission. Fascinated by Hazel, Nimativ plans to make her his 38th spouse, a decision that infuriates Teema (Lottie Harrison), the harem's chief wife. To create confusion, Harvey borrows Teema's clothes while Pete masquerades as Nimativ **(photo).** Chaos ensues, but when Harvey and Pete obtain the rings, they hypnotize the tyrant into abdication. Ramo then gets his throne back, asks Hazel to become his (only) wife and helps the boys get back home.

on the boards, they arrived in Hollywood in 1940, bringing some comic relief to *One Night in the Tropics*, a musical film starring tenor Allan Jones. In 1941, they starred in *Buck Privates*, their first blockbuster, after which they began their own Thursday evening radio program and made the first of their famous scare comedies, *Hold that Ghost*. By the end of 1942, Abbott and Costello had starred in eight box office smashes and by 1945—the year the classic *Who's on First* double-talk bit debuted in *The Naughty Nineties*— they began demanding special treatment from their studio, Universal, as well as a percentage of their films' profits. Although Costello played the more sympathetic of the two, it was actually he who commenced to drive a wedge in the partnership by asking for 60 percent of the team's earnings. When their films started to show box-office weakness, they moved on to television and a high-rated comedy program. But in 1957, the fun had drained from their performances, and a year after their final movie, *Dance with Me, Henry*, they split with no small rancor. Lou Costello died of a heart attack in 1959, at age 53, Bud Abbott after two strokes in 1974, at age 79. ●

◄ **BUD ABBOTT**
LITTLE GIANT
(1946, Universal)
Country-mouse-meets-city-rat comedy directed by William A. Seiter ● Docile bumpkin Benny Miller (**Lou Costello**) takes a sales course by mail, and landing a job selling vacuum cleaners in Los Angeles, leaves farm and fiancée (Elena Verdugo). He is so inept that the general manager, Tom Chandler (**Bud Abbott**), fires him. Re-hired by the firm's Stockton branch, his supervisor there (**Bud Abbott** also) makes fun of his boss, Mr. Chandler, a cousin he describes as a "double-crossing skunk" and proudly shows Benny a portrait of his grandmother (**Bud Abbott** also, **photo**). Benny soon becomes the butt of mind-reading jokes and begins to think he is a psychic. The gag backfires, however, when his sales soar. Mr. Chandler, guilty of embezzlement, believes the hype and uses his wife to find out the extent of Benny's clairvoyance. But Benny's girl suspects there is someone else and he heads back to the farm. There, the company's president delivers the news: the manager's filching has been exposed and Benny has been promoted.

◄ **LOU COSTELLO**
ABBOTT AND COSTELLO
MEET THE KEYSTONE
KOPS (1955, Universal)
Amusing evocation of silent filmmaking directed by Charles Lamont ● In 1912 New York, Harry (**Bud Abbott**, left) and Willie (**Lou Costello**) are convinced by hustler Joe Gorman (Fred Clark) to invest $5,000 in a Hollywood motion picture studio he doesn't own. When Gorman disappears, Harry and Willie realize they have been conned. The boys head for Los Angeles to get their money back but, by an unexpected twist of fate, they are hired by Amalgamated Pictures as stuntmen. Their first job has Willie in drag (**photo**) doubling for the studio's female star, Leota Van Cleef (Lynn Bari). The scene is a dangerous airplane sequence devised by director Sergei Toumanov —who is actually Gorman—to eliminate Harry and Willie. But with the help of Mack Sennett's squirrely Keystone Kops, the villains are brought to justice.

◄ LOU COSTELLO
ABBOTT AND COSTELLO MEET THE KILLER (1949, Universal)

Entertaining parody of Universal's classic horror films directed by Charles T. Barton ● In a swank resort where Casey (**Bud Abbott,** second from left) works as the hotel detective and Freddie (**Lou Costello,** second from right) as a bellhop, a celebrated criminal lawyer is killed. The murder is pinned on Freddie who, with the help of Casey, decides to clear his name and find the real culprit. The suspects are numerous—including the towering Swami Talpur (**Boris Karloff**)—and the dead bodies pile up quickly. To investigate without being recognized, Freddie adopts a hotel maid's uniform (**photo**). When it looks like the night concierge (**Percy Helton,** center) might see through the disguise, Casey and maid Freddie organize a card game with two corpses (**Morgan Farley** and **Vincent Renno**) to throw him off course. Finally, Freddie unmasks the killer.

◄ LOU COSTELLO
MEXICAN HAYRIDE (1948, Universal)

Sporadically funny south-of-the-border farce directed by Charles T. Barton ● After being swindled, Iowa halfwit Joe Bascom (**Lou Costello**) trails Harry Lambert (Bud Abbott), the hustler who has bamboozled him, to Mexico. After a few days, Joe stumbles onto Harry who is trying to concoct a silver mine scam. Again, Harry ensnares Joe, makes him the spokesman of the phony company and gets him to give a speech extolling Mexico's abundant mineral resources. The mimeographed stocks sell well until two American detectives (Tom Powers and Pat Costello) arrest the boys. Joe escapes and, suited up as an itinerant female food vendor (**photo**), tries to flee the country. Unfortunately, the two cops, who already have Harry in custody, spot him. When the gullible investors get their pesos back, no charges are pressed and Joe and Harry go back to the States, free to start a new life.

◄ LOU COSTELLO
HERE COME THE CO-EDS (1945, Universal)

Above average madcap ride directed by Jean Yarbrough ● Slats McCarthy (**Bud Abbott,** right), his sister Molly (Martha O'Driscoll) and his buddy Oliver Krackenbush (**Lou Costello**) are taxi dancers at the Miramar Ballroom. Always inventing publicity stunts, Slats plants an article about his sister's long-term goal of attending stuffy Bixby College. Reading the newspaper, Bixby's liberal dean, Larry Benson (Donald Cook), offers her a scholarship and hires Slats and Oliver as caretakers. Unfortunately, Mr. Kirkland (Charles Dingle), the school's mortgage holder, threatens to foreclose if Benson does not expel Molly. To save the institution, Slats and Oliver devise a plan to raise $20,000: they bet 20-to-1 on a basketball game pitting Bixby against Carlton. But hedging his bet, bookie Honest Dan (Joe Kirk) replaces the Carlton team with a group of rough female pros. When all of the ringers have been kayoed, Oliver—led to think that due to head trauma he is Daisy Dimple (**photo**), the best female player in the world—takes the floor with the Bixby team. Ultimately losing the game, he nicks Honest Dan's bankroll and saves Molly's alma mater.

JOE E. BROWN

WITH HIS moon-crater mouth and mischievous eyes, the almost forgotten Joe E. Brown was a major movie star in the '30s and a celebrity for the rest of his life. His comedy, which usually involved a mixture of pathos and laughs, struck his audiences as genuine and generous-hearted, probably because he was usually cast as the amiable underdog. The rubber-faced performer offered a physical comedic approach that often involved difficult moves and offbeat dancing and that appealed strongly to children and family audiences. Born in Holgate, Ohio in 1892, Joe Evans Brown credited his agility to his early start as a circus acrobat at age nine and to his years in semi-pro baseball. These experiences made him an all-around athlete, a fact that is reflected, for example, by his timid-florist-turned-track-and-field-star part in *Local Boy Makes Good* (1931). Joe E. Brown made his Broadway bow in *Jim Jam Jems* (1920) and developed his confident stage presence touring across the country. While in Los Angeles, ▶▶

◀ A MIDSUMMER NIGHT'S DREAM
(1935, Warner)

Shakespeare lavishly transposed to film by Max Reinhardt and Michael Curtiz ● While Duke of Athens Theseus is planning to wed Queen of the Amazons Hippolyta, he realizes that his court is rife with romance. Lysander (Dick Powell) and Hermia (Olivia de Havilland) are in love. But her father wants her to marry Demetrius (Ross Alexander), who pines for her but is the object of Helena's (Jean Muir) affections. Disobeying her father, Hermia plans to marry Lysander in the woods where the lovers discover a fairy kingdom ruled by King Oberon (Victor Jory) and Queen Titania (Anita Louise). Puck (Mickey Rooney), a mischievous elf, administers to the newcomers a magic potion that makes Lysander and Demetrius fall for Helena. After an acting troupe arrives in the woods to rehearse, Puck transforms its leading man, Bottom (**James Cagney,** right), into a donkey and makes Titania fall for him. When Puck reverses the spell, Bottom becomes human again and everyone goes back to Athens to attend the wedding of the duke, who gives Lysander Hermia's hand. The entertainers arrive and present to the court a comedic love story in which Bottoms is smitten by a large-grinned girl named Thisby, played by simpleton Flute (**Joe E. Brown**).

▲ SHUT MY BIG MOUTH
(1942, Columbia)

High-grade western send-up directed by Charles T. Barton ● Wellington Holmes (**Joe E. Brown**), a horticulturist going west, inadvertently foils a stagecoach holdup perpetrated by highwayman Buckskin Bill (**Victor Jory,** right). Because of his perceived courage, Wellington is named marshal of Big Bluff, a town held in thrall by the gunslinger. But he is not thrilled, knowing he will eventually have a showdown with Buckskin Bill. When he learns that the bandit treats women with courtesy, Wellington disguises himself as a lady named Henrietta, and taking the next eastbound stagecoach, meets fellow passenger Conchita Montoya (Adele Mara), a charming heiress. Unfortunately, the trip is interrupted by another holdup by Buckskin Bill who, ever the perfect gentleman, accompanies the ladies to the Montoya Ranch. Smitten with Henrietta, the robber dances with her all night (**photo**). Later, Wellington conjures up enough testosterone to capture Buckskin Bill, sweep Conchita off her feet and rededicate himself to his goal of "beautifying the West with flowers."

he made his film debut in the 1928 silent feature *Crooks Can't Win*. In 1930, the talkie *Hold Everything*, directed by Roy Del Ruth, made him an immediate star and prompted Warner Bros. to give him a long-term contract. A string of hits followed, many of them involving the big-grinned comedian as a wrestler, boxer, cyclist or football player. In 1935, Max Reinhardt directed him in Shakespeare's *A Midsummer Night's Dream*. His role as Flute, a man forced to impersonate a woman, was a great dramatic challenge that increased his box office draw. In 1941, Brown made the mistake of ending his contract with Warner to become a free agent. His films for RKO, MGM and Republic are somewhat inferior, except for the hilarious Columbia western *Shut My Big Mouth* (1942). When World War II took the life of his son, Donald, Brown spent energetic years entertaining the troops. But after 1945, Bob Hope and other younger comedians had replaced him in the minds of movie audiences. In 1959, however, the then 66-year-old was tapped for the Billy Wilder classic *Some Like It Hot* in which he played the part of airhead millionaire Osgood Fielding, who falls in love with Jack Lemmon's cross-dressing alter-ego, Daphné. Joe E. Brown died at 81 in July 1973, the victim of a stroke. •

▼ JOE E. BROWN
FIT FOR A KING (1937, RKO)
Love-beats-a-throne comedy directed by Edward Sedgwick ● Naïve cub reporter Virgil Jones (**Joe E. Brown**) is assigned to cover a recent attempt on the life of Archduke Julio (Harry Davenport), an exiled nobleman from a tiny European monarchy. On the boat to France, Virgil meets Briggs (**Paul Kelly,** left), a rival who constantly scoops him. In Paris, his boss sends him to Vichy where the Archduke is scheduled to introduce the rightful heir to the throne, Crown Princess Helen (Helen Mack), whom he has located in the States. In the meantime, Virgil meets a compatriot, Jane Hamilton, who shows signs of interest in him. To spy on the Archduke, Virgil frocks up as a hotel maid (**photo**) but is recognized by Briggs. He takes refuge in a room that happens to be Princess Helen's and realizes that she and Jane Hamilton are the same person. But before he can call his paper, Briggs has already broken the story. After a series of adventures during which Virgil discovers that Prime Minister Strunsky plans to eliminate both the Archduke and the Princess, the unlucky reporter finally nails a big scoop. He then marries the blue-blooded Jane, who has decided to choose love over a throne.

▲ JOE E. BROWN & GUS SHILLING
CHATTERBOX (1943, Republic)
Flat-footed pseudo-western directed by Joseph Santley ● Rex Vane (**Joe E. Brown**), a cowboy radio star who is a fake, goes Hollywood. At his first press appearance, he falls off his horse and is rescued by hillbilly Judy Boggs (Judy Canova) with whom he quickly falls in love. Despite the embarrassment and the adverse publicity triggered by the incident, Rex suggests marriage to Judy but, before accepting his proposal, she asks to meet Rex's mother. Because she is dead, Rex decides to impersonate his dear old mom. He does so credibly until Gillie (**Gus Schilling,** right), a screenwriter, does it too, creating a prickly enigma for Judy and celebrity reporter Carol Forest (**Rosemary Lane,** center). Ridiculed one more time, Rex redeems himself when he courageously handles an accident during a scene involving a mountain cabin about to be dynamited.

◀ **JOE E. BROWN**
THE DARING YOUNG MAN
(1942, Columbia)
Action-packed comedic escapade directed by Frank R. Strayer ● During WWII, Jonathan Peckinpah (Joe E. Brown), nerdy owner of a New York air conditioning company, tries to enlist. Found unfit to serve, he takes up bowling to get in shape. Conman Sam Long (William Wright) tells him he could make him a champion, so Jonathan agrees to try, not knowing that the bowling balls he uses are equipped with a short wave radio control that allows Sam to direct their trajectory. Attracting naive gamblers, the scam is a success until Nazi spies discover that their coded messages are being disrupted by Sam's swindle. Meanwhile, Jonathan's grandmother (**Joe E. Brown**) has left her retirement home to live at the Plaza and has bought a new wardrobe—including a chic evening gown (**photo**). But this is nothing compared to Jonathan's personal tribulations. Abducted by foreign agents, beaten by unhappy bettors and suspected by the FBI, he nevertheless has the conspirators arrested. A national hero, he proudly joins the army.

▼ WHEN'S YOUR BIRTHDAY? (1937, RKO)
Formulaic shaggy dog comedy directed by Harry Beaumont ● At the Acropolis nightclub, gambler James Reagan (Minor Watson) dares busboy Dustin Willoughby (**Joe E. Brown**), a passionate astrologer, to predict the outcome of a dog race. After learning the canines' birthdates, Dustin picks the winner. Convinced that Dustin can help his business, Reagan asks his aide, Lefty (**Frank Jenks,** left), to bring him to his table. Dustin thinks that Reagan is mad at him and avoids Lefty by dressing as a coquettish chorus girl (**photo**). Later hired as a fortuneteller at a carnival, he soon becomes the show's main attraction. But when he falls for assistant Jerry Grant (Marian Marsh), their jealous boss fires him. Learning Dustin's whereabouts, Reagan installs the astrologer in his offices to extract predictions from him. After a mix-up involving a foreign boxer brought in by Reagan for a major bout, he realizes the soothsayer has more chances to win than the pro. Forced to fight, Dustin wins the bout—and the girl.

FERNANDEL

◀ TRICOCHE AND CACOLET
(French title "Tricoche et Cacolet,"
1938, Emile Natan Productions)
French farce about wives and lovers, mistresses and detectives directed by Pierre Colombier ● Two idle boulevardiers, Tricoche (**Fernandel**) and Cacolet (Frédéric Duvallès), decide to partner in an investigation agency. They fight a lot but they quickly capitalize on Tricoche's talent for impersonating all sorts of people–a fireman one day or a rent collector the next. His most daring attempt, however, proves to be his transformation into a peroxide blonde (**photo**). One day, banker Van der Pouf (Saturnin Fabre) hires Cacolet to watch his wife Bernardine (Elvire Popesco) whom he suspects of having an affair. Concurrently, Bernardine asks Tricoche to stake out her husband and his mistress, Fanny (Ginette Leclerc). During their respective investigations, they discover that Turkish Prince Oscar Pacha (Sylvio de Pedrelli) is crazy about both Fanny and Bernardine. To set matters straight, the detectives convince Bernardine to go back to her husband while they facilitate the romance between Fanny and the prince– only after Tricoche has been sensually rewarded by the future princess.

▲ LAVARÈDE'S NICKEL
(French title "Les cinq sous de
Lavarède," 1938, Gray Films)
Around the world in 80 days, French style, directed by Maurice Cammage ● Armand Lavarède (**Fernandel**) is an armchair traveler known for his extravagant fabrications. One day, he learns that to collect his cousin's bequest, he must take a trip around the world in less than 100 days with only five pennies in his pocket– money, the rules stipulate, he can't even spend. Sir Murlington (Jean Dax), who roots for him, and Mr. Bouvreuil (Marcel Vallée), who wants him to fail, closely watch him while Murlington's daughter, a British beauty named Miss Aurette (Josette Day), assists him. Starting as a stowaway on the *Normandie*, Armand later uses all types of transportation to progress from place to place and employs some imaginative disguises–including masquerading as a bayadeer (**center in photo above**) in Calcutta to escape the ardor of a maharanee. Moving from scrape to scrape, the lucky globetrotter reaches Paris on time, inherits his deceased relative's 30 million francs and marries his blonde angel.

FERNANDEL, the comedian who made millions of fans roll in the aisles, was one of Europe's most beloved stars. His wide, horse-like mouth crammed with large white teeth made his appearance quirky and unforgettable. His perfect diction, tinged with a strong Provençal accent, was particularly endearing to Parisian audiences. In addition, his contagious laughter saved some mediocre vehicles from the abyss. In short, Fernand Joseph Désiré Contandin was a versatile actor in total control of his abilities. Born in Marseille in 1903, this son of part-time vaudevillians hit the boards at age five. Seven years later, he joined the ranks of the *tourlourous*—singers who practiced the *comique troupier*-style, dressing in military uniforms and singing humorous refrains about army life. The timing of Fernand Sined—then his stage pseudonym—was impeccable: France had entered another war with its eastern neighbors. Unfortunately, the competition killed his aspirations and he settled for a clerical job in a bank. Several banks later, in 1922, he accepted an offer from a Nice music hall: under the name of Fernandel, his career—one that encompasses 153 films ▶▶

▶ **FERNANDEL**
A DOG'S LIFE
(French title "Une vie de chien,"
1941, Optimax Films)
**Comedy about reincarnation and
treachery directed by Maurice Cammage** ● Gustave Bourdillon (**Fernandel**) hopelessly loves Emilie (Josseline
Gaël), the wife of Mr. Calumet, principal
of the small high school where he is a
teacher. When her husband dies, Emilie
has a problem: on the day of the funeral
she is supposed to take an exam to
qualify for a better academic position.
She asks Gustave to dress as a woman
(**photo**) and impersonate her, with the
promise that if he successfully completes the charade she will marry him.
After the wedding the merry ex-widow,
who believes in the reincarnation of human beings into animals, is convinced
that her new dog, Médor, is none other
than her late husband—albeit a four-
legged version. Fortunately, after several comical incidents, she realizes her
mistake and she and Gustave finally find
happiness.

▶ **ADHEMAR**
(French title "Adhémar ou le jouet de
la fatalité," 1951, Indusfilms)
**Story of a man too funny for his own
good directed by Fernandel** ● Adhémar
Pomme (**Fernandel**) cracks everybody
up—even when he does not want to. It is
a major drawback for a man who yearns
for a serious career. His close friend
Tisale (Andrex), who sympathizes with
his frustrations, is always finding new
jobs for him, such as theater prompter or
mortician. But Pomme is fired from every
job for unintentionally triggering hilarity,
even during the saddest of circum-
stances. Adhémar is finally hired by Lady
Braconfield (**Marguerite Pierry,** right), a
rich woman who has refused to smile
since the death of her husband, for the
specific purpose of making her laugh.
This apparently easy mission proves to
be impossible: all his pranks, including a
genial attempt at cross-dressing as a
Spanish dancer (**photo**), fail miserably,
leaving Lady Braconfield still disconso-
late—and a sourpuss.

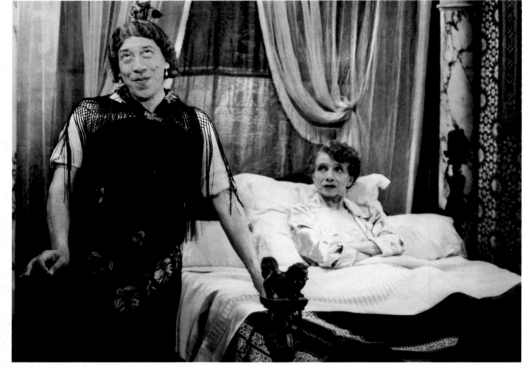

▶ IRMA LA VOYANTE
("Irma the Clairvoyant," 1947)
**One-reel musical film directed by
Antoine Toe** ● In this short, Fernandel
sings a half-dozen amusing *chansons*,
including his hit "La caissière du grand
café" and "Irma la voyante" in which he
masquerades as the ditty's soothsayer.

▲ FERNANDEL
PARIS HOLIDAY (French title "A Paris tous les deux," 1958, United Artists)

Two major comedians lost in a minor-league Franco-American comedy directed by Gerd Oswald ● French comic Fernydel (**Fernandel**) is coming home after a tour of the States. He befriends American comedian Bob Hunter (**Bob Hope**) who is travelling to Paris to purchase the rights of a play. Author Serge Vitry (**Preston Sturges**) warns him it is an exposé of a counterfeiting ring. This news excites Bob who wants to star in a drama. Leaving Vitry with a copy of the manuscript, he is soon arrested: Vitry has been murdered and Bob is the last person who saw him alive. Informed by the *Sûreté* that the forgers will eliminate everyone who possesses a copy of the play, Bob survives several attempts on his life with Fernydel's assistance, but tricked by gang moll Zara (**Anita Eckberg**), he is committed to a bogus mental hospital. Disguised as a frumpish matron (**top photo**), Fernydel tries to free Bob but fails at first (**right photo**). He succeeds later with the help of a helicopter. When the police round up the bad guys, Bob and Fernydel are decorated by the president of the Republic.

►► and more than 1,000 stage appearances—took off. Most of his early parts are in military comedies, which were very much in favor on the eve of WWII—classics such as *Les gaîtés de l'escadron* (1932), *Un de la Légion* (1936) and *Ignace* (1937). When superb wordsmith Marcel Pagnol cast him in the role of a dim-witted farmhand in *Angèle* (1934) and of a naïve knife-grinder in *Regain* (*Harvest,* 1937), the comedian proved he could embrace serious roles that projected deep emotion. With Pagnol doubling as director, Fernandel starred in *Le Schpountz* (*Heartbeat,* 1939) and *La fille du puisatier* (*The Well-digger's Daughter,* 1940). Subsequently, he played a pathetic hunchback in Pagnol's *Naïs* (1945). Fernandel became an international star when he agreed to portrait Don Camillo, the priest of a small Italian village who is constantly bickering with Peppone (Gino Cervi), its communist mayor: *The Little World of Don Camillo* (1951) was such a triumph in Europe that during the next 20 years it was followed by five sequels, the last one shot in 1969. In 1970, Fernandel began production of a sixth, but after a few weeks, he was sidelined by pleurisy and returned home for some rest. Early in 1971, at age 67, he died in his avenue Foch apartment, surrounded by his wife and children. ●

LOUIS DE FUNÈS

LA FOLIE DES GRANDEURS
("Delusions of Grandeur,"
1971, Gaumont)

Period farce of betrayal and power lust directed by Gérard Oury ● In 17th-century Spain, the king, under pressure from the queen (Karin Schubert), fires corrupt Prime Minister Don Salluste (**Louis de Funès**). Salluste plots a diabolical comeback with two trump cards: a hidden treasure and a loyal but slow-witted valet, Blaze (Yves Montand), who is in love with the queen. After coming out of hiding dressed as a dueña and flaunting a gigantic wig (**photo above**), Salluste demands Blaze's help. Abducting his cousin Don

Cesar, he sells him to Saharan slave owners and forces Blaze to impersonate the nobleman. Introduced as a conquistador returning from the Americas, Blaze (alias Don Cesar) thwarts an attempt on the lives of the royal couple, which earns him the prime minister's job. Now masquerading as his valet, Salluste plans to take advantage of the developing romance between Blaze and the queen to gain his power back. But Don Cesar reappears unexpectedly at the court, looking for revenge. Blaze sides with him to outwit his abusive master and a fuming Salluste is sent to the Sahara for life. Upon arrival, however, he starts scheming retaliation.

Opposite: On the set of *La folie des grandeurs* (1971), director Gérard Oury helps Louis de Funès shave closely for his next drag scene.

IN THE MID-'60s, when a 50-year-old hyperactive elf became France's leading box-office draw, he had already appeared in more than 100 films. His name, Louis de Funès, was familiar to audiences used to seeing the little balding man in supporting roles for such celebrated actors as Fernandel and Jean Gabin. Often employed as comic relief in dismal clunkers, De Funès hit it big in 1964's *Le gendarme de Saint-Tropez.* As conniving Sgt. Ludovic Cruchot, a man as obsequious with his superiors as he is high-handed with his subalterns, he embodied the famous resort's top cop in five sequels. From that point on, 50-year-old De Funès' career skyrocketed through a string of movies that made him a high-caliber star in Europe. The son of Spanish immigrants, he was born in Courbevoie, near Paris, in 1914. After high school, he eked out a living thanks to a dozen unrewarding jobs and in the early '40s, survived as a bar pianist in the Pigalle district. De Funès started his acting career as an extra in 1945, but it was not until age 47 that he enjoyed his first success in the theater. In *Oscar,* he perfectly incarnated an industrialist always eager to cheat friends, foes and ▶▶

► LOUIS DE FUNÈS
LE GENDARME DE SAINT-TROPEZ (1964, SNC)

First in a series of hit comedies directed by Jean Girault ● Transferred to Saint-Tropez, where the rich enjoy sunny topless beaches by day and glitzy hotspots by night, *gendarme* Ludovic Cruchot (**Louis de Funès**) arrives in town resolute about fighting the vacationers' indecent behavior. His daughter Nicole (Geneviève Grad), bedazzled by the surroundings and her success with the local playboys, pretends to be the daughter of a yachtsman. She even convinces a boyfriend to borrow her supposed father's sports car. The joyride ends in a crash that Sgt. Cruchot investigates. When he realizes his daughter is involved, he engineers a cover up, coincidentally discovering a gang of art thieves. Undercover at a stakeout, Cruchot attracts an Arab prince (**Jacques Famery,** left), who thinks the sergeant is a desirable woman (**photo**). Cruchot proceeds to round up the swindlers and receive hearty congratulations from his bosses.

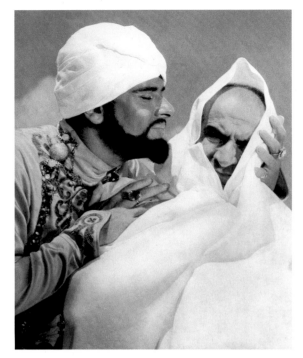

► LE GENDARME ET LES EXTRA-TERRESTRES (1979, SNC)

Penultimate episode of a six-film series directed by Jean Girault ● When hyperventilating Sgt. Ludovic Cruchot (**Louis de Funès**) sees a flying saucer, he assumes that extraterrestrials have landed near super chic Saint-Tropez. His boss, Adjutant Gerber (Michel Galabru) is skeptical, as are his brigade's bumbling *gendarmes*. Later, Cruchot discovers that the extraterrestrials are "replicants" and therefore capable of adopting the features of real humans. Confused, Cruchot physically assails Gerber, thinking he is from outer space. He is sent to a nuthouse, but escapes by disguising himself as a nun (**photo**) to investigate. The irascible Cruchot scores big with his superiors when he builds a copy of the flying saucer to destabilize the extraterrestrials. His triumph is celebrated with a parade attended by officials looking suspiciously other-worldly.

► THE WING OR THE LEG
(French title "L'Aile ou la cuisse", 1976, UGC)

Pleasantly highly charged culinary satire directed by Claude Zidi ● Charles Duchemin (**Louis de Funès**), a highly respected food critic and gourmet book publisher, is so well known that when he reviews a restaurant he is forced to use disguises in order not to be recognized (**photo**). His foremost nemesis is Mr. Tricatel (Julien Guiomar), a fast-food entrepreneur whose critics fault him with dishonoring France and the excellence of its culinary traditions. During a televised debate, Duchemin ridicules Tricatel and soon after, proud of his performance, prepares for the festivities celebrating his entrance into the Académie Française, the eminent group of the 40 most important living people in France. Everything is wonderful for the new academician until he realizes that Tricatel is catering the reception organized to honor him!

◄ LE GENDARME ET LES GENDARMETTES (1982, SNC)

Last installment in a comedy series directed by Jean Girault ● Adj. Gerber (Michel Galabru) and Sgt. Cruchot (**Louis de Funès**) move to a new office and reluctantly welcome four female police auxiliaries in training: Christine, Isabelle, Marianne and Macumba. Unfortunately, just when the colonel (Jacques François) informs Gerber that the interior minister plans to visit the *gendarmerie,* Isabelle and Marianne are abducted. Gerber and Cruchot panic, and when the two remaining auxiliaries are also kidnapped, Cruchot decides to adopt the uniform of a *gendarmette* (**photo**), hoping to be abducted. His wish is fulfilled as he is carried off to a yacht anchored in Saint-Tropez' bay. There he meets the brains of the operation and learns that each *gendarmette* has a number engraved on her bracelet. Together the four bracelets form a code allowing foreign agents to access the plans of the French XZ missile that are on the *gendarmerie's* computer. Cruchot and his men thwart the scheme and rescue the women.

▶▶ the government. This role was instrumental in his winning the lead in the film *Pouic-Pouic* (1963), in which he portrayed an irascible businessman. He was hilarious in this part and his constant irritability became a trademark that De Funès milked not only in the *"Gendarme"* series, but also in the cinematic version of his beloved *Oscar* (1967) and a clutter of big budget productions helmed by Gérard Oury: *Le corniaud (The Sucker,* 1965), *La grande vadrouille (Don't Look Now,* 1966), *La folie des grandeurs (Delusions of Grandeur,* 1971) and *The Mad Adventures of Rabbi Jacob* (1973). In these movies, he brought to life high-octane, treacherous men adept at negotiating the labyrinths of venality and deceit. In 1975, "Fufu," as his fans called him, was sidelined by a heart attack and took a three-year hiatus in his Loire valley's 365-window castle. In his triumphant comeback, *L'aile ou la cuisse (The Wing or the Leg,* 1976), he portrayed a supercilious food critic. Several films later, De Funès died. On that day, in January 1983, France lost its favorite comedian, a 5' 4" gimlet-eyed actor who had made them laugh riotously with his caricatures of motor-mouthed braggarts, impatient cranksters and abject cowards. ●

BOB HOPE

WITH A FLAIR for timing, topical humor and repartee, Bob Hope was the master of the impromptu quip. A genius monologist backed by a large team of talented gag writers, he enjoyed an unprecedented run of popularity and became one of America's most successful and beloved entertainers. Hope also became one of Hollywood's wealthiest, thanks to wise investments in oil wells and local real estate. In his more popular films, the likeable and not unattractive comedian usually played a clever though misguided wiseacre with an unfounded, nervous bravado and an eye for the ladies. Born in Eltham, England, in 1903, Hope moved with his family to Cleveland, Ohio, in 1907. At age 10 he won a Chaplin imitation contest, and at 17 partnered with Lloyd Durbin in a vaudeville comedy and dance act. He eventually went solo on Broadway in 1928, earning ▶▶

▲ THE ROAD TO RIO
(1947, Paramount)

Fifth "Road" adventure, 1947's box-office champ, directed by Norman Z. McLeod ● Musicians "Hot Lips" Barton (**Bob Hope**) and "Scat" Sweeney (**Bing Crosby,** left) stow away on an ocean liner en route to Rio de Janeiro. On board, they meet Lucia Maria (Dorothy Lamour), a knockout prone to mood swings. Intrigued, they realize that her Aunt Catherine (Gale Sondergaard), who wants to force her to marry a man she does not love, has hypnotized her. Upon their arrival, the boys find a gig in a club with the Weire Brothers, a trio of frenzied musicians who pretend to speak English, and discover that Lucia Maria's wedding is imminent. They crash the reception in disguise—Scat as a pirate, Hot Lips as Carmen Miranda—and perform a terrific song-and-dance routine to the great amusement of the guests (**photo**). After the buddies halt the ceremony, Lucia Maria inexplicably falls for Hot Lips. Flabbergasted because he always gets the girl, Scat investigates and soon discovers by watching though a keyhole that his wily pal is using hypnotism to win her over.

▶ THE ROAD TO MOROCCO
(1942, Paramount)

Third—and best—episode of the celebrated series directed by David Butler ● Two long-time chums, Jeff (Bing Crosby) and Orville (Bob Hope), constantly try to take advantage of each other. But when they are on the verge of following their basest instincts, Orville's Aunt Lucy (also **Bob Hope**)—a moralistic spinster who interferes in the form of a ghost—substitutes for the pals' conscience. When Jeff and Orville survive a shipwreck and land in Morocco, however, Aunt Lucy cannot prevent Jeff from selling Orville to a slave trader for a paltry $200. Remorseful, Jeff decides to save his buddy from a life of abject servitude. But when he finds him in a luxurious palace pampered by Princess Shalimar (Dorothy Lamour), who has purchased Orville to marry him, Jeff decides to turn the tables and seduce her by using a powerful weapon, the song "Moonlight Becomes You." But Sheik Kassim (Anthony Quinn), who also wants Shalimar, will stop at nothing to get her. Fortunately, the resourceful duo brings Kassim and a rival potentate to the brink of war and bow out in time to save their lives.

Opposite: Bob Hope with visitor Jack Benny on the set of *The Road to Morocco* (1942).

extra income shooting two-reelers for Vitaphone. After he landed a major part in the Broadway musical *Roberta* in 1933, Paramount cast him in *The Big Broadcast of 1938* in which he performed with Shirley Ross what was to become his lifelong theme song, "Thanks for the Memories." Now working on Pepsodent's radio show alongside such celebrated comedians as Jack Benny and Fred Allen, Hope had his next big break the following year with his first film hit, *The Cat and the Canary,* which featured the vivacious Paulette Goddard. In 1940, Paramount released the first of its *"Road"* pictures, *Road to Singapore.* In all seven of these big box-office moneymakers, Hope costarred with Dorothy Lamour, a veteran of South Seas movies, and renowned crooner Bing Crosby. The series showcased Hope as a mildly idiotic savant who could never keep up with Crosby's flimflam maneuvers nor understand why Lamour never fell for him. In his solo films, when he ▶▶

◀ BOB HOPE
THE LEMON DROP KID
(1950, Paramount)

Cat-and-mouse gangster comedy directed by Sidney Lanfield ● Sidney Milburn (**Bob Hope**), also known as the Lemon Drop Kid, is a fast-talking race-track tout who gives Moose Moran (Fred Clark) a tip that costs the gangster $10,000. Moran tells the Kid he has until Christmas to make good on the bet. To raise the money, the Kid opens a women's retirement home as a front for licensing bogus street corner Santa Clauses. Unfortunately, Oxford Charlie (Lloyd Nolan) muscles in on the racket and takes over the home. To sneak in without being spotted, the Kid dresses up as a spunky matron, (**photo**) and after conversing with two charming residents (**Hazel Boyne,** right, and **Ida Moore,** left), cleverly devises a subterfuge that lands the gangsters in jail.

◀ NOTHING BUT THE TRUTH
(1941, Paramount)

Dazzling truth-and-consequences comedy directed by Elliott Nugent ● In Miami Beach, compulsive liar Steve Bennett (**Bob Hope**) bets wealthy stockbroker T.T. Ralston (Edward Arnold) $10,000 that he can tell the truth, and nothing but the truth, for the next 24 hours. He is staked by Gwen Saunders (Paulette Goddard), T.T.'s niece, who hopes to double the $10,000 in charity money she has collected. Invited to spend an evening with T.T.'s family and friends on a luxury houseboat, Steve uses clever double-talk to deflect the questions designed to trick him into lying. At night, when T.T. and his associates confiscate his clothes to make sure he cannot leave the boat, Steve borrows a marabou-trimmed negligé from a guest (**Helen Vinson,** right) so he can sneak into Gwen's cabin. After a day of surmounting challenging obstacles by not telling a lie—but not telling the truth either—Steve wins his bet and Gwen's heart.

◀ HERE COME THE GIRLS
(1953, Paramount)

Period musical comedy directed by Claude Binyon ● Chorus boy and Broadway hopeful Stanley Snodgrass (**Bob Hope**) is fired from *Here Come the Girls*—starring dancer Irene Bailey (**Arlene Dahl,** right) and crooner Alen Trent (Tony Martin)—and returns to the family's coal delivery business. At the theater, Jack the Slasher (Robert Strauss), a psychopath smitten with Irene, attempts to kill Trent. Producer Harry Fraser (Fred Clark) knows that the Slasher will carve up the beauty's male co-stars, so he offers Stanley the show's starring role. Stanley jumps at the chance, especially since he and his father (**Millard Mitchell,** left) have been toiling in a laundry as washer women (**photo**). The cops catch the madman before he knifes Stanley, so Fraser fires the now useless decoy. When the lunatic escapes, Stanley comes back. This time, the killer, disguised as a clown, chases him all over the stage. After he is arrested, Fraser rewards Stanley with a bit part—albeit a ridiculous one—in the show.

▲ CASANOVA'S BIG NIGHT
(1954, Paramount)

Cheerful costume comedy directed by Norman Z. McLeod ● In 18th-century Parma, Pippo Popolino (**Bob Hope**), an apprentice tailor, impersonates Casanova in order to seduce a gorgeous widow, Francesca Bruni (**Joan Fontaine,** left). Casanova's creditors force Pippo to continue the charade when Duchess di Castelbello (Hope Emerson) offers him 10,000 ducats to come to Venice to test the faithfulness of her son's fiancée, Dona Elena (Audrey Dalton). The cowardly Pippo accepts only when widow Bruni proposes to accompany him. After several goofy attempts to fulfill his mission, Pippo, touched by Elena's candor, purposefully cools his ardor. In the meantime, Francesca falls for Pippo and together—as Baron and Baroness of Cordovia (**photo**)—they crash a ball organized by the cunning Doge of Venice (Arnold Moss). Pippo, hiding in his decolletage a petticoat that is crucial to defusing the Doge's evil-doings, derails a conspiracy to start a war with Genoa.

occasionally stopped playing characters that were basically Bob Hope and branched out into different parts—such as in *Sorrowful Jones* (1949)—his public grew impatient. Notable exceptions during the peak of his career were blockbusters like *The Paleface* (1948) with Jane Russell, *Fancy Pants* (1950) with Lucille Ball and his poignant role in *The Seven Little Foys* (1955). A weekly presence on NBC radio from 1937 to 1956, Hope expanded his television exposure in the mid-'50s. America also knew him as a tireless, patriotic trooper who devoted his Christmases during WWII and the Korean War to entertaining U.S. troops abroad and continued to do so during the Vietnam and Persian wars. The Presidential Medal of Freedom, many kudos for his humanitarian work and five special Academy Awards remain a testament to the adoration of his public and the respect of the entertainment industry and his adopted homeland. Bob Hope died at age 100 in 2003. ●

▼ BOB HOPE
THE PRINCESS AND THE PIRATE
(1944, RKO)

Seven Seas period comedy directed by David Butler ● It is the year 1700. After setting sail for America hoping to find receptive audiences, British comedian Sylvester The Great (**Bob Hope**) is terrified when a cutthroat pirate band led by the Hook (Victor McLaglen) boards the ship. To hide from the bloodthirsty rogues, the cowardly Sylvester dresses as a snaggle-toothed gypsy woman. But even as a harmless soothsayer, he annoys the Hook, who makes him walk the plank. Sylvester is saved by Featherhead (**Walter Brennan, right**), a dimwit who knows the comedian is in disguise (**photo**) and helps him escape in a dinghy. But before disembarking the galleon, Sylvester finds the courage to save an attractive young passenger, Margaret (Virginia Mayo), from an assault. On the island where they land, evil governor La Roche (Walter Slezak) recognizes Margaret as Princess Maria, abducts her and asks for a fabulous ransom. Again against type, the comedian shows extraordinary courage—especially when Margaret's father comes to the rescue with an imposing armada.

▶ BOB HOPE
THEY GOT ME COVERED
(1943, RKO)

Screwball espionage intrigue directed by David Butler ● Robert Kittredge (**Bob Hope**), an amazingly incompetent foreign correspondent based in Moscow, is fired from the Amalgamated News Agency for failing to file one of the biggest stories of World War II—Hitler's invasion of the USSR. While in Washington visiting his girlfriend, stenographer Christine Hill (Dorothy Lamour), he chances upon a fabulous scoop when he learns that an Axis network of Washington D.C.-based spies are planning the destruction of America's major urban centers. His disjointed investigation leads him to an Arabian-style club, Café Moresque, where he is drugged by German operative Otto Fauscheim (Otto Preminger), and later to a flower shop where he is captured by Italian spook Baldanacco (Eduardo Cianelli). Held prisoner in the beauty salon that the saboteurs use as a command center, Kittredge gives enemy agents their comeuppance, but only after using several ingenious disguises, including posing as a salon client in a sheet and a Veronica Lake-style wig (**photo**).

BUSTER KEATON

▲ OUR HOSPITALITY
(1923, Joseph Schenck-Metro)

Comedy of manners rich in gags and thrills directed by Buster Keaton & John Blystone ● In 1830s-New York, Willie McKay (**Buster Keaton**) learns that he is the sole heir of a Kentucky estate. Although his aunt warns him that his family is involved in a murderous feud with the Canfields, Willie travels south to claim his property. During the eventful train trip he meets a maiden named Virginia (Nathalie Talmadge) who, upon arrival in Rockville invites him to dinner at her family home. Overhearing a conversation plotting his murder, Willie realizes he is at the Canfields, but is relieved to learn that the rules of Southern hospitality prevent them from gunning down a guest while under their roof. In the morning, he boards a train in Virginia's garb (**photo**), jumps on a horse when his disguise is revealed and flees with the clan in hot pursuit. To protect him, Virginia joins the chase, which leads to a waterfall. Courageously, Willie rescues Virginia from drowning, after which a kindly parson (Monte Collins) helps the couple back to the Canfields. When the patriarch returns, he realizes that the reverend has married Willie and Virginia, putting a de facto end to a longstanding feud.

▶ THE PLAYHOUSE (1921, First National)

Astounding one-man show directed by Buster Keaton & Eddie Cline ● Buster Keaton's Opera House presents Buster Keaton's Minstrels. From the orchestra conductor to the stage hand, from the performers to the audience members, male or female, old or young, upper class or lower class, everyone looks surprisingly like Buster Keaton. In fact, it is the master comedian playing all the parts himself in this extravagantly inventive one-man show.

Opposite: Wardrobe test for MGM.

ONE OF THE most inventive comics of the "flickers," Joseph Francis Keaton learned early on that the biggest laugh came when he didn't. In his work, no matter what heartbreak or hurdle life presented, "the Great Stone Face" confronted it with dignified determination, allowing only a grim stare or the occasional twitch of an eyebrow to signal any reaction. Born in 1895 in Piqua, Kansas, Buster spent his early years in the family act. Only 5' 5" and dressed like his father, the little trooper was such an acrobatic virtuoso that it was suspected he was a midget. At age 21, Buster headed to New York for a solo career, acting in films for the first time as a supporting player for comedian Fatty Arbuckle. After 15 short comedies with the rotund star, Keaton followed him to Los Angeles where he acquired a deep understanding of camera gadgetry and its possible applications to his art. When Arbuckle was offered a million-dollar contract by Paramount, Keaton convinced producer Joe Schenck to give him unprecedented autonomy in his own ▶▶

▲ BUSTER KEATON & UNIDENTIFIED ACTORS IN DRAG
DOUGHBOYS (1930, MGM)

Second—and best—Keaton talkie directed by Edward Sedgwick ● During WWI, upper-class gent Elmer Stuyvesant (**Buster Keaton**, top center) is enamored with a salesgirl, Mary (Sally Eilers), who ignores him because he has not joined the army. When his German chauffeur (Arnold Korff) tells him he plans to enlist, the swell looks for a new driver. He then confuses a recruiting station for an employment agency and is quickly inducted in the service. After several weeks of boot camp, Elmer realizes that Mary has joined the army in the entertainment division. When they meet in France, Mary warms up to Elmer, but a misunderstanding concerning a French girl alienates her again. Elmer's pal, Cliff Nescopeck (Cliff Edwards), however, enrolls him in Mary's song and dance show. Joining a less-than-graceful all-male drag ensemble, Elmer is partnered with an energetic dancer for an astounding finale (**photo**). Later, muddied by trench fighting, Elmer volunteers to capture a German soldier and is surprised to meet his ex-chauffeur—who had enlisted on the other side—and a half-dozen of his compatriots willing to surrender. As a result of this "exploit," Mary falls into Elmer's arms when they meet on the battlefield.

▲ THE HOLLYWOOD REVUE OF 1929 (1929, MGM)

No-plot, all-star musical extravaganza directed by Charles Reisner ● In this feature film made to promote the talking, singing and dancing MGM stars at the dawn of the soundtrack era, King Neptune and eight tantalizing mermaids witness the antics of an Egyptian belly dancer (**Buster Keaton**) who has emerged from a giant shell that quickly sinks into the ocean. With exotic music, amusing pharaonic postures and seductive swirls and spiral motions, the impassible comedian exploits his voluble body language to produce an effervescent sketch.

▲ HIS EX MARKS THE SPOT (1940, Columbia)

Two-reel comedy directed by Jules White ● Buster (**Buster Keaton**) is modeling his wife Dorothy's (**Dorothy Appleby**, left) dress so she can hem it (**photo**). Plagued by financial troubles because of his alimony payments, Buster invites his ex-spouse and her boyfriend to move in with him and his second wife. After Dorothy sets the place ablaze with a cigarette, the obnoxious guests have a fight. Dorothy insists they leave but Buster demands they get married. With Dorothy holding a gun aimed at the infernal couple during the ceremony, the solution to Buster's alimony problem is found.

▼ BUSTER KEATON
SIDEWALKS OF NEW YORK
(1931, MGM)

Minor vehicle for the star's talent directed by Jules White & Zion Myers ● Millionaire Homer Harmon (**Buster Keaton**), who owns several East Side slums, pays a visit to the neighborhood. His arrival in a limousine creates such a ruckus that a tenant, Margie (Anita Page), joins in the scuffle to protect her kid brother, Clipper (Norman Philips). For Homer, it is love at first sight, and to win Margie over he decides to reform the tough boy. He first builds a gym for the street urchins, but Clipper convinces his buddies to boycott the place. Again trying to ingratiate himself with the rebellious children, he stages a two-act play. In the first, *The Duke and the Dancer* (**bottom photo**), his assistant Pogle (**Cliff Edwards**, right) plays a nobleman who has a crush on a gypsy maiden impersonated by Homer. In the second act, *Bad Habits Don't Pay*, the millionaire is supposed to play his own daughter, but the performance is cancelled when Clipper, who in the past has helped local mobster Butch (**Frank Rowan**, below left), refuses to kill Homer-the-reformer. Butch decides to do it himself and confronts Homer, still in his second act female outfit (**photo below**). Fortunately, Clipper and his friends, who have finally seen the light, rescue him. Margie and Homer embrace.

▶▶ films. Subsequently, he wrote, codirected and acted in a series of two-reelers, among them *The Playhouse* (1921), a funny piece loaded with ingenious special effects. In 1923, Schenck allowed the comedian to write and direct feature-length films, the first being *Our Hospitality* (1923). Now immensely popular, Keaton sustained his genius in *Sherlock, Jr.* (1924), *The Navigator* (1924) and *The General* (1927). All were amazing due to the spectacular stunts performed by Keaton himself and the superb timing of his sight gags. In the late '20s, he made a disastrous move by signing with MGM. Even though his first movie, *The Cameraman* (1928), was a quality comedy, his following talkies such as *Doughboys* (1932) and *Sidewalks of New York* (1932) show that his magic was fading. In 1933, MGM failed to renew his contract. At the end of 1934, the jobless actor agreed to return to two-reel comedies. At Educational, his 14 cheaply made shorts were unremarkable, including Mack Sennett's *The Timid Young Man* (1935). After a stint in a psychiatric hospital in 1937, Keaton went back again to two-reelers at Columbia. There, in the face of lame and hopeless material, he did his best. After 10 films, the studio dropped him and he was forced to work as a gag writer and a character actor in second-rate features. His supporting role in Chaplin's *Limelight* (1951) restored his reputation, however, and he survived to experience a second recognition of his genius. Buster Keaton died a legend in 1966 at age 70. ●

HARRY LANGDON

◀ THE SEA SQUAWK
(1925, Mack Sennett-Pathé)
Precision-tooled caper comedy directed by Harry Edwards ● On a ship sailing to the States, Black David (**William McCall,** left), a jewel thief who has just stolen a million dollar ruby, shares a cabin with Harry (**Harry Langdon**), an inoffensive passenger in a skirt and tam. When the police search the boat, Black David forces his cabin mate to swallow the stone. After the cops' departure, Harry escapes the super-thief's surveillance, knowing that he will try by any means to get the gem back. Dressed as a woman in a crinoline and blonde curly wig, Harry feels more secure during a masked ball–until Black David recognizes him (**photo**). A chaotic chase takes the two through the boat's galleys until Black David is arrested. That is when a pretty foreign passenger reveals that Harry has swallowed a fake stone and that the real one has always been in her possession.

▲ HIS FIRST FLAME
(1927, Mack Sennett-Pathé)
Deft but low-key comic fable directed by Harry Edwards ● Harry Howels (**Harry Langdon**) tells his uncle Amos (**Vernon Dent,** right), a battalion chief fireman, that he is getting married. Instead of congratulating him, Amos, a notorious woman hater, warns his nephew that the girl is only after his money. Perplexed, Harry aimlessly walks the streets, eventually meeting a couple pushing a baby buggy. He tries to befriend them but soon realizes that they are shop-lifters. When the police chase them, the woman shoves Harry into a building hallway and steals his clothes, leaving hers behind. Forced to don her skirt, ill-fitting blouse and feathered hat, Harry returns to the fire station where his uncle greets him with: "And I thought college would make a man of you!" (**photo**)

PART OF THE most celebrated quartet of early 20th-century American comedy, which included Charlie Chaplin, Harold Lloyd and Buster Keaton, Harry Langdon played the innocent young man who found it difficult to cope with the complexities of adulthood. With his cherubic face, he excelled as a sympathetic and rather silly character continually beset by life's daily problems. Born in 1884 in Council Bluffs, Iowa, to Salvation Army officers, Langdon ran away at age 13 to join the circus, and later toured on the vaudeville circuit for many years. Unlike most other comic stars of the silent era, Langdon failed to receive a film offer until he was 39, when Mack Sennett signed him to his studio's roster. His restrained style did not blend well with the breakneck pacing of Sennett's comedies but, luckily, he met a writer there who understood his artistic personae—Frank Capra. Langdon's best shorts at the studio were *The Sea Squawk* (1924) and *Saturday* ▶▶

Afternoon (1925) in which he played a henpecked husband, a part that mirrored his private life. After three years at Sennett's fun factory, he left for a better package offered by First National, taking his team, including Capra, with him. After four hits in 1926—*Tramp, Tramp, Tramp, The Strong Man, Long Pants* and *His First Flame*—Langdon, having convinced himself he could direct, fired Capra. It was a grave mistake: after declaring bankruptcy in 1931, his career sank rapidly. Hal Roach tried to resurrect him for the talkies, but the producer found it impossible to deal with the highly-strung former star who was beginning at his advanced age to look rather weird playing a babe-in-the-woods. Langdon labored during the '30s at Columbia's short-subject department but it was in features such as *Hallelujah, I'm a Bum* (1933) with Al Jolson that he seemed to come into his own again. At the end of the decade, he returned to Hal Roach's operation as a character actor and a writer for Laurel and Hardy and then he moved on to Monogram where his efforts continued to seem out of synch with his age. Cinematic history, nevertheless, views him as a truly original genius. Sadly, when he suffered a cerebral hemorrhage in 1944, his comeback dreams died with him. •

◀THE CHASER
(1928, First National)

Likeable but barely funny comedy directed by Harry Langdon ● Because Harry (**Harry Langdon**) often spends hours after work with friends, his nagging bride (Gladys McConnell) thinks he is a skirt chaser and asks for divorce. During separation hearings, the judge, hoping to engineer reconciliation, sentences Harry to take over his wife's household duties for 30 days. Chafing at the humiliation, Harry dons an apron and dust-skirt and proceeds to do the chores (**photo**). A second mortification comes when the ice-man, assuming he is a woman, kisses him square on the mouth. Harry feels he has lost his manhood and runs amok: deciding to commit suicide, he writes a goodbye note and drinks some poison. Soon after, his wife shows up with girlfriends, but Harry is nowhere to be found. Reading the note, she begins searching for him. The poison, how-ever, only induced sleep and Harry's buddy (Bud Jamison) finds him snoring in a field. The two pay a visit to a nearby camping park where, after mesmerizing several beauties that find him irresistible, Harry realizes that he has won back his "lost" manhood. Back home, his wife curls up lovingly in his arms when she sees him.

◀DOUBLE TROUBLE
(1941, Monogram)

Modestly amusing trifle directed by William West ● Mr. Whitmore, owner of a bean cannery, has agreed to welcome a pair of British war refugees. Upon their arrival, the family is surprised that the expected teenage brothers are middle-aged men, Bert (**Harry Langdon**) and Alf Prattle (Charles Rogers). In spite of his disappointment, Mr. Whitmore takes them home and gives them a job at his factory. When advertising director Spanky Marshall (George O'Brien) shoots a new canned food campaign that includes a diamond bracelet worth $100,000, a sabo-teur throws the jewelry in the trash. Bert finds it but, unaware of its value, puts it in an emp-ty can on the assembly line, hoping the girl he likes will see it. Distracted, she misses the bracelet and it gets canned, joining thousand of other containers. Learning it has probably been delivered to a sailors' bar on the water-front, the two dress as maids with Bert forced to flirt embarrassingly with the regu-lars (**photo**) in order to check every can in the place. When he succeeds in finding the right one, the brothers are welcomed again at the Whitmores for the duration of the war.

**Opposite: Harry Langdon in *Skirt Shy*
(1929) directed by Charles Rogers.**

STAN LAUREL & OLIVER HARDY

UNDOUBTEDLY the best comedy team of the silent and sound screen is that of Stan Laurel and Oliver Hardy. In an amazing output of over 100 movies, they kept their fans breathless with laughter, using a surefire formula of dignity-deflating slapstick and sight gags built around a bad situation gone worse. Through maelstroms of custard pies, they won universal appeal by creating two arguing friends who remained friends nevertheless; flawed but empathetic characters with whom their audience could identify. The bowler-hatted twosome also developed endearing mannerisms, such as Ollie's tie fiddling and Stan's head scratching, which became trademarks that never failed to bring a smile. "The boys," as they were called by their peers, could also deliver when dressed as girls, as the guffaws produced by Laurel's disguise in *That's My Wife* (1929) prove. When sound arrived, their voices, luckily suiting their physical appearance, allowed them to easily adapt to the new medium. The skinny one—and the brains behind the team—was Laurel, a Brit born Arthur Stanley Jefferson in 1890 in Ulverston, Lancashire. At age 20, he joined Fred Karno's stage troupe and became Charlie Chaplin's ▶▶

▲ STAN LAUREL
DUCK SOUP
(1927, Hal Roach-Pathé)

Two-reel comedy directed by Fred L. Guiol ● Unshaven **Oliver Hardy,** and clean-shaven **Stan Laurel,** are seated on a Los Angeles park bench. In the paper, Ollie reads that forest rangers are looking for help fighting fires started in the hills by two vagrants. When they see the head ranger approaching, the pals, weary of any kind of uni-formed authority, scram. They find shelter in a mansion owned by big game hunter Col. Buck-shot, who has just left for a long African safari after having put his home on the rental market. Stan and Ollie start to relax when the bell rings. Guessing it is potential tenants, Ollie impersonates the owner and asks Stan to masquerade as the maid (**photos**). The charade works perfectly: Lord and Lady Plumtree decide to lease the man-sion. Asking for a short delay, Ollie and Stan start pilfering the house's contents, but just when they are ready to leave, Col. Buckshot, who has forgot-ten his bow and arrows, shows up. Pandemonium erupts and, when the head ranger recognizes Laurel in drag, he arrests him and sends the duo to the fire's frontline. *(Film considered lost until a copy surfaced in a European film museum in 1974. Duck Soup is the first film in which Laurel and Hardy worked as a team with equal billing.)*

▶ STAN LAUREL & OLIVER HARDY
THEIR PURPLE MOMENT
(1928, Hal Roach)

Two-reel comedy directed by James Parrott ● On payday, **Stan Laurel** is able to hide another three dollars from his wife behind a family portrait. But **Oliver Hardy** is caught trying to squirrel away some of his pay by his equally domineering spouse. When the husbands get permission to go to the bowling alley, Stan removes his money from its hid-ing place and goes directly to the Pink Pup Café with his pal. There, chivalrous Ollie offers assistance to two flappers whose dates have left them to pay the bill. Ordering steaks and enjoying a floorshow featuring a troupe of midgets performing a choco-late-soldier dance, everybody has a swell time until Laurel realizes that his wife has substituted worth-less cigar coupons for his dollar bills. Panicked, Stan and Ollie try to leave on the sly, but they are drawn into a kitchen food fight that involves the wait-ers, the chef and their own wives. *(Biographer John McCabe indicates that Stan Laurel's ending for the film was shot but never used: "As originally con-ceived, the boys were to flee their wives in the café, stumble into the midgets' dressing room, hastily put on some of their costumes and walk out of the café on their knees." The still shown here was taken dur-ing the filming of this ending, which the studio re-placed with a food fight.)*

▶ STAN LAUREL (SANS HARDY)

THE SLEUTH (1925, Joe Rock-Standard)

Two-reel comedy directed by Harry Sweet ● The first client of neophyte private investigator Webster Dingle (**Stan Laurel**) is a young lady who has doubts about her husband's fidelity. To observe the suspect, Webster disguises himself as a woman and shows up as the new maid (**top photos**). Impressed, the husband (**Glen Cavender,** right) starts to flirt with the coquette to the great amusement of his wife. But the fun evaporates when Webster realizes that the philanderer has not only a lover but also a plan to get rid of his wife in order to seize her properties. When three thugs show up to help steal some official papers, Webster is involved in a room-to-room pursuit and to stop everybody, disguises himself again this time as a languorous vamp (**bottom right photo**), creating much confusion. (*Film shot before Stan Laurel teamed with Oliver Hardy.*)

▶ STAN LAUREL

SUGAR DADDIES (1927, Hal Roach)

Two-reel comedy directed by Fred L. Guiol ● After a rough night, millionaire Cyrus Brittle (James Finlayson) learns from his butler **Oliver Hardy** that during his carousing he got married and that the woman and her threatening brother are waiting downstairs. Brittle, guessing that the trio intends to shake him down, calls his lawyer **Stan Laurel** for help. When they demand $50,000 to have the mistake corrected, Brittle hides out in a seaside hotel with his butler and his lawyer but is soon identified and forced to leave precipitously. To help in the escape, Stan impersonates a lady wearing a long, ballooning cape under which Brittle, supporting the weight of his attorney on his shoulders (**photo**), hides in front of the "victim" (**Charlotte Mineau,** second from left), her daughter (**Edna Marion,** center) and her brother (**Noah Young,** left) who chase them into a fun house.

▶ STAN LAUREL

THAT'S MY WIFE (1929, Hal Roach)

Two-reel comedy directed by Lloyd French ● When **Oliver Hardy** (center) refuses to give in to his wife's ultimatum that their permanent houseguest, **Stan Laurel**, leave or she leaves, she walks out. It is bad timing because Ollie's rich Uncle Bernal (**William Courtwright,** left) arrives almost immediately after to seal Ollie's marital bliss with a generous inheritance. Panicked, Ollie begs Stan to sub for his spouse, a masquerade that unravels when the three go out to the Pink Pup Café for dinner. Stan is a passably fetching flapper, but when a waiter steals the necklace of a lady at the next table and slips it down the back of Stan's gown, he and Ollie must go through considerable gyrations on the dance floor to shake it out. Finally catching on, Uncle Bernal exits in disgust (**photo**), vowing to leave his money to a dog and cat hospital.

▼ STAN LAUREL
WHY GIRLS LOVE SAILORS
(1927, Hal Roach)

Two-reel comedy directed by Fred L. Guiol ● A tough sea captain (Malcolm Waite) falls for Nelly (Viola Richard), the girlfriend of young gob Willie (**Stan Laurel**). Forcing her to accompany him on his ship, he sequesters her in his cabin. To liberate Nelly, Willie needs to get past imposing petty officer Leggitt (**Oliver Hardy**), but arm-twisting not being his forte, he disguises himself as a curly-haired miss. When Leggitt sees this fatal beauty, he melts at the possibility of stealing a kiss (**photo**). In the meantime, the captain's jealous wife (Anita Garvin) shows up unexpectedly and gives a good hiding to her womanizing mate. Taking advantage of the commotion, Willie disembarks with his sweetie in tow. *(This film was assumed lost for years until a copy was found at the French Cinémathèque and screened in 1971.)*

▲ STAN LAUREL
ANOTHER FINE MESS (1930, Hal Roach)

Three-reel remake of *Duck Soup* directed by James Parrott ● Col. Buckshot (**James Finlayson,** center) has decided to lease his palatial home while he goes on a big game hunting trip. **Stan Laurel** and **Oliver Hardy,** meanwhile, are chased into the cellar by a policeman and cannot get out. Later, they overhear upstairs that the butler and maid are preparing to leave for the weekend. The prospective renters, newlyweds Lord (Charles Gerrard) and Lady Plumtree (Thelma Todd), then arrive to look over the house, with Ollie posing as the absent colonel. When Lady Plumtree inquires about domestic help, Stan is forced to play the maid, Agnes. Matters come to a head when Col. Buckshot returns and, discovering the charade, goes ape (**photo**). He summons the authorities, who pursue the boys dressed in tandem as a horse-like creature through a tunnel, resulting in the cops being left in their underwear and the animal splitting in half.

►► understudy. When everybody went back to England, after the group's second U.S. tour, Laurel stayed in the States and for more than 10 years acted in dozens hilarious shorts before being signed up by Hal Roach in 1926. Oliver "Babe" Hardy—the rotund one—was born Norvell Hardy in 1892 in Harlem, Georgia. After running away to use his soprano voice in a traveling minstrel show, he moved to Jacksonville, Florida, where he acted in some King Bee comedies. He spent several years playing second fiddle to other talented comics, finally landing at Roach Studios where starting in 1926 he appeared in several comedies with Charley Chase. It was in 1927 with *Duck Soup* that the duo finally worked as a team with equal billing. From that time on, their style developed naturally through 90 films shot for Hal Roach, the best being short subjects such as *The Battle of the Century* (1927), *Two Tars* (1928), *The Music Box* (1932)—for which they won an Oscar—and feature films such as *Sons of The Desert* (1933), *Tit for Tat* (1935) and *Way Out West* (1937). When they left Roach for MGM and Fox, the studio system drained the laughter from their movies. Hal Roach Jr. planned television specials for them in the '50s, but before filming started, Stan Laurel had a stroke. Oliver Hardy died in 1957 during his longtime partner's recovery, but Stan Laurel went on to become revered as a living comedy icon. He died in 1965. ●

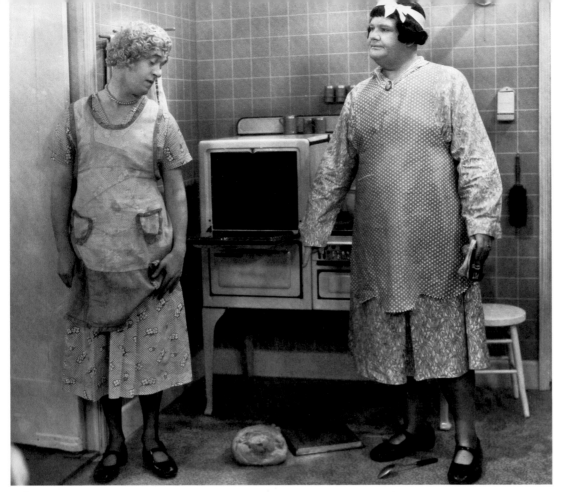

◀ STAN LAUREL & OLIVER HARDY
TWICE TWO
(1933, Hal Roach)

Two-reel comedy directed by James Parrott ● Brain specialist Dr. Oliver Hardy is assisted by switchboard operator Stan Laurel. Each has married the other's sister and this is the night the two couples have planned to celebrate their mutual first anniversary. Mrs. Laurel (**Oliver Hardy,** right) has decided to prepare a special dinner at home and Mrs. Hardy (**Stan Laurel,** left) has offered to help (**photo**). Alas, the two women are as clumsy as their husbands. It starts with the anniversary cake landing on Mrs. Laurel's head and ends with the replacement cake winding up in her face. In between, Mr. Hardy rips his pants when he opens the door, Mrs. Hardy and Mrs. Laurel bicker constantly, tempers flare and what was supposed to be a pleasant evening collapses miserably.

◀ STAN LAUREL
THE DANCING MASTERS
(1943, Fox)

Dismal attempt at reconnecting with the duo's genius directed by Mal St. Clair ● Owners of the Arthur Hurry's School of Dancing, Oliver Hardy teaches advanced students while **Stan Laurel,** decked out in sequined tutu and floral crown, takes care of beginners (**photo**). Unfortunately, they are on the verge of bankruptcy. When a certain Dr. Jasper makes them an offer they can't refuse, Ollie insures Stan for $10,000 should his partner break a leg. In the meantime, their favorite pupil, Trudy Harlan (Trudy Marshall), would like her father, who owns an armament factory, to test the invisible ray machine invented by her boyfriend Grant (Bob Bailey). Posing as Prof. Findash Gorp, Stan brings Grant's machine to Mr. Harlan and successfully operates it before it blows up. To build another, the devious Ollie thinks of using the insurance money and takes Stan to Coney Island. But, alas, it is he himself who falls from the roller coaster and breaks a leg. Meanwhile, Mr. Harlan has recognized the value of Grant's invention and has decided to finance it.

▲ STAN LAUREL
JITTERBUGS (1943, Fox)

Rootin'-tootin' action comedy directed by Mal St. Clair ● On their way to a gig, **Stan Laurel** and **Oliver Hardy,** sole musicians of the Original Zoot Suit Band, are stranded in the desert. Chester Wright (Bob Bailey), a flimflam artist who sells pills that allegedly turn water into gasoline, rescues them. Credulous, Stan and Ollie agree to peddle the miracle product at a carnival during their jitterbug music show. The pills sell briskly but the crowd soon discovers they are bogus and demands a refund. Impersonating a police detective, Chester "arrests" the duo and flees with them. When Chester learns that the mother of his paramour, Susan (Vivian Blaine), has been defrauded in a $10,000 land deal by con men who own a showboat in New Orleans, he decides to trail the thieves. Fond of Susan, Stan and Ollie agree to be part of Chester's pursuit. Ollie's impersonation of rich Texan Colonel Bixby, along with Stan's disguise as Susan's rich aunt, Ms. Cartwright (**photo**), are so convincing that they are able to retrieve the cash from the swindlers who, realizing they have been conned, lock up the twosome in the showboat's boiler.

JERRY LEWIS

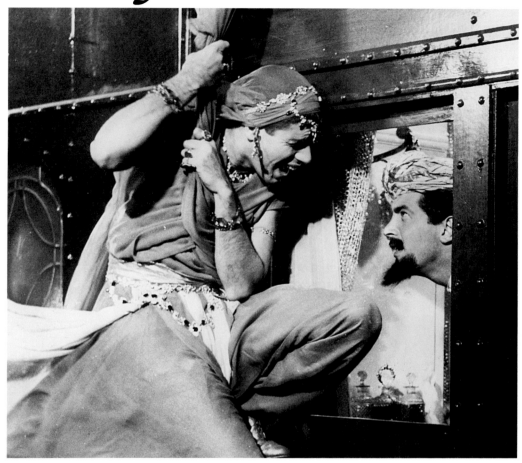

◀ AT WAR WITH THE ARMY
(1950, Paramount)

Not-so-funny visit to military schmuckdom directed by Hal Walker ● In a training camp during World War II, Sgt. Puccinelli (Dean Martin) romances the ladies while his friend, Pfc. Korwin (**Jerry Lewis**), is assigned to kitchen details. Together, they write a song, but on the evening Puccinelli is supposed to record it, he forgets the score on his desk. Korwin decides to bring him the music but can not get a pass, so he borrows female clothing from a U.S.O. van to leave the base surreptitiously. At the bar where he ends up, his curves captivate Sgt. McVey (**Mike Kellin,** left). McVey's interest grows as Korwin serenades him with a rendition of "Tonda Wonda Hoy" before delivering the chart to the bandleader (Dick Stabile). When the demo disc is engraved, it is back to the barracks where Korwin's antics and Puccinelli's womanizing drive Capt. Caldwell nuts. But the fun is soon over when the outfit is sent overseas to fight the enemy.

▲ MONEY FROM HOME
(1953, Paramount)

Runyonesque racetrack comedy directed by George Marshall ● During Prohibition, Honey Talk Nelson (**Dean Martin,** right), a horse-track gambler who has had a 126-day losing streak, is unable to settle his debt with bookmaker Jumbo Schneider. The racketeer tells him he will forgo the debt if Honey Talk fixes the next Tarrytown Steeplechase. Desperate, the gambler asks his cousin, assistant veterinarian Virgil Hokum (**Jerry Lewis**), to accompany him to Maryland, hoping he will drug My Sheeba, the horse Schneider wants eliminated. The dim-bulb agrees but before leaving New York, regrets it: Honey Talk has gambled away the train money. Fortunately, Sheik Poojah (Romo Vincent) and his entourage are also boarding the train, giving Honey Talk the idea of masquerading as members of the group. Dressed as a courtier, Honey Talk croons for the Poojah's wives while Virgil, pretending to be part of the harem, is forced to perform his own version of Salome's *Dance of the Seven Veils* before jumping from the train (**photo**) to escape the sheik's sexual advances. Virgil unexpectedly wins the big race while Honey Talk loses his heart to My Sheeba's pretty owner (Marjie Millar).

IN THE '50s, rubber-faced, whiney-voiced Jerry Lewis turned silliness into a comedic form that appealed to both the young and the young at heart. Usually loud and given to the most unbridled buffoonery, he could also project a sympathy-generating naïveté. Born Joseph Levitch in Newark, New Jersey in 1926, he spent his early years as part of his parents' Borscht Belt act, setting out on his own by age 17. In 1945, while playing at the Glass Hat Club in Manhattan, he met a fellow performer who was to change his life: baritone crooner Dean Martin. The two developed an act where, while Martin warbled a song, Lewis would continually interrupt him with various bits of foolishness. The singing-and-seltzer-bottle team became official in 1946 at Atlantic City's Club 500 and the rest, as they say, is show business history. After playing the famed Copacabana in 1948, they were signed for a seven-movie contract by producer Hal Wallis. Their first film, *My Friend Irma* (1949) was released the same year NBC introduced their Monday night radio program *The Martin and Lewis Show.* The pair proceeded to star in 16 films together, including *At War With the Army* (1950) and *Scared Stiff* (1952), in which Lewis does hilarious drag impersonations. When the ▶▶

▶ JERRY LEWIS
THE PATSY (1964, Paramount)

Tenuous satire of Hollywood mores directed by Jerry Lewis ● When famous comedian Wally Brandford dies in a plane crash, his devastated management team meets for the last time. Producer Caryl Ferguson (Everett Sloane) and writer Chick Wymore (Phil Harris) lament the fact they are now going to have to work independently. Director Morgan Heywood (Peter Lorre) comes up with the idea of replacing Brandford with somebody—anybody— and teaching him everything they learned from their deceased boss. After transforming childish bellboy Stanley Belt (Jerry Lewis) into a star, they have him record a single. At the session, the backup singers are a trio of unattractive vocalists (all **Jerry Lewis, photos**) whose whiney voices contribute to the failure of the enterprise. After disastrous gigs, Stanley's handlers realize their patsy has no talent. But when Stanley is simply himself on his first appearance on *The Ed Sullivan Show,* he is propelled to stardom.

▶ THE LADIES MAN (1960, Paramount)

Ingenious and pleasantly maudlin comedy directed by Jerry Lewis ● On graduation day, valedictorian Herbert J. Heebert (Jerry Lewis) is enthusiastic about proposing to his childhood sweetheart. Crushed when he catches her kissing her new beau, Herbert tells his weeping mother (also **Jerry Lewis, photo**) he will remain a bachelor forever. Looking for employment in Los Angeles, Herbert accepts a job as a houseboy in an all-female house for would-be entertainers. Herbert cleans and repairs everything, delivers the mail, answers the door and wrecks furniture. Soon, the unhandy man becomes indispensable, doubling as an acting coach. But feeling taken for granted, he quits. Fay (Pat Stanley), the only one who has empathy for him, tells the boarders to show Herbert that they care about and respect him. Finally having what he has always wanted, the ladies man happily stays.

▶ THREE ON A COUCH
(1966, Columbia)

Improbable quick-change romantic comedy directed by Jerry Lewis ● Chris Pride (**Jerry Lewis**) is invited to paint a mural in Paris. He plans to bring his wife-to-be, psychiatrist Liz Acord (Janet Leigh). Unfortunately, she has among her patients three man-haters who could not cope in her absence. When Liz tells Chris she cannot go, he decides to cure them himself by impersonating three men who would reconcile them with the male gender. For Anna Jacque (Gila Golan), he is cowboy; for Susan Manning (Mary Ann Mobley), he becomes a jogger; for entomologist Mary-Lou Mauve (**Leslie Parrish,** bottom left photo, right), he dresses as a dowdy woman named Heather (**photo**). In a red wig and misses-size gown, he praises his cousin Rutherford, another bug enthusiast and arranges a meeting. At the rendezvous Chris impersonates Rutherford and cures Mary-Lou. Liz' three patients convince her to take the Paris sabbatical.

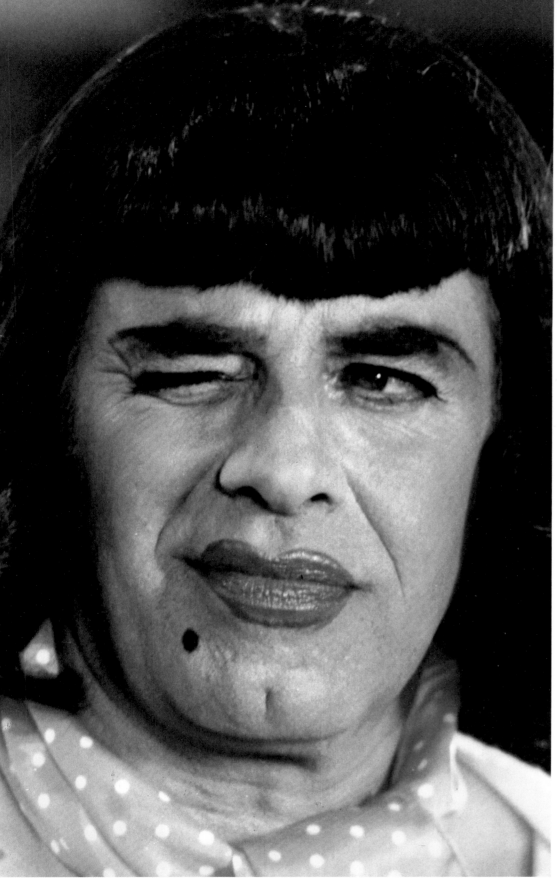

▲ JERRY LEWIS
HARDLY WORKING (1981, Fox)

Amusing job-hunting comedy directed by Jerry Lewis ● Bo Hopper (Jerry Lewis), an out-of-work clown, moves to Florida to live with his sister (Susan Oliver). In order to survive, he must find a job but unfortunately his clumsiness repeatedly produces more pink slips than wages. Whether a gas station attendant, a clerk in a mirror factory, a cook in a Teppan-style Japanese restaurant or a bartender in a strip joint, all his endeavors end disastrously. When he joins the Postal Service as a letter carrier, accident-prone Bo seems to have finally found his niche in society. But even delivering mail elicits some surprises: for instance, when asking for directions from a middle-aged lady (also **Jerry Lewis, photo**) on her way to a tennis club, Bo is puzzled when she asks if he ever "fools around." But life becomes sweet for the luck-impaired clown when he meets Millie (Deanna Lund), his boss's daughter.

two split up in 1957 after a heavily publicized feud, Lewis compared it to a painful divorce but went on to make some 30 more films sharing top billing with no one. His best efforts— *The Geisha Boy* (1958), *Cinderfella* (1960) and *The Disorderly Orderly* (1964)—were directed by Frank Tashlin. But soon, Jerry Lewis decided to take full control of his artistry by becoming his own producer, and more significantly, his own director. *The Bellboy* (1960), *The Ladies Man* (1961) and *The Nutty Professor* (1963) demonstrated his cinematic flair and gave him the status of a major filmmaker, at least in France. Unfortunately, the nebbish, childlike and accident-prone character created by Lewis did not age well. Now almost middle-aged, his antics generated neither sympathy nor spontaneous laughs. Sharing his time between personal appearances in his annual Muscular Dystrophy Marathon and making films that declined in both quality and box-office returns, he seemed to become somewhat bitter. But when Martin Scorsese offered him the possibility of reinventing himself in the critical hit *The King of Comedy* (1983) costarring Robert De Niro, Lewis did so. He eventually reconciled publicly with Dean Martin in 1989 and since then has appeared on stage, in film and television regularly, garnering increasing appreciation for his large and infectiously humorous body of work. ●

HAROLD LLOYD

◄ MOVIE CRAZY (1932, Paramount)
Tale of a wannabe leading man turned comedian directed by Clyde Bruckman ● Kansas hick Harold Hall (**Harold Lloyd**), hoping to become a romantic lead in the flickers, arrives at the Los Angeles train station where a location shoot is in progress. He is immediately hired as an extra but his clumsiness ruins take after take. One day, during a torrential rain, Harold helps a charming girl, Mary Sears (**Constance Cummings,** left), raise the top of her convertible, but in the process destroys it. Intrigued by the bungler, Mary invites him home and lets him wear one of her high fashion sailor outfits (**photo**) while her maid dries his clothes. Harold does not realize that Mary is a famous actress and falls for her. Mary's other suitor, an alcoholic leading man, picks a fight with Harold at the studio. Their scuffle leads them to a set—the hold of a ship—where a movie is being shot. The director, knocked unconscious, cannot stop the action, so Harold's pratfalls and missed punches are filmed. Seeing the footage, the studio offers Harold a long-term contract as a comic.

▲ SAFETY LAST! (1923, Hal Roach-Pathé)
Unforgettable metaphor about '20s upward mobility directed by Fred Newmeyer & Sam Taylor ● Harold (**Harold Lloyd**), who has moved to the big city to find fortune so he can marry sweetheart Mildred (Mildred Davis), works in a department store. He uses many subterfuges to make his chronic lateness unnoticed—like hiding inside a woman's outfit so an unsuspecting coworker can sneak him into the store as a mannequin (**photo**). Harold makes only $15 a week but his letters lead Mildred to believe that he is making more. When she shows up one day, Harold realizes that he needs to become rich quickly. Overhearing his boss suggest a $1,000 reward to the person who will create publicity for his emporium, Harold offers $500 to his steeplejack roommate Bill (Bill Strother) to scale the walls of the building to attract a crowd. The day of the event, however, Bill eludes a cop with whom he'd had a brush and Harold is forced to do the climbing himself. After fighting vertigo, avoiding falls and thwarting many perils, he reaches the top where Mildred is waiting.

MASTER OF THE thrill sequence that evoked shrieks alternating with laughs, Harold Lloyd was the most popular comedian of the late '20s. Recognizable by his black oversized horn rims and his straw hat, he represented a young man of optimism and mettle capable of keeping his eye on the goal—whether a career or the girl of his dreams—all the while executing split-timed gags. Born in Burchard, Nebraska, in 1893, he followed his father after his parents' divorce to San Diego where he made his show business debut in touring stock companies. After moving to Los Angeles, the five-dollar-a-day extra met ambitious coworker Hal Roach who was starting his own production company, Rolin Comedies, and offered his new friend a starring role in a series of one-reel farces. The character they invented, Willie Work, did not, and Lloyd joined Mack Sennett's studio. When he returned to Roach, the two created a Chaplin-inspired character, Lonesome Luke, the star of about 100 one-reel comedies between 1916 and 1917. In the last part of 1917, the pair developed a third character, a bespectacled every man who became wildly popular with American audiences. In 1920, while having a publicity photo taken, a fake bomb Lloyd was using to light a cigarette exploded, resulting in the loss of his right thumb and forefinger. The accident did not deter him from continuing to do his own stunts and to successfully tackle longer pictures, the first one being the five-reel feature *A Sailor-Made Man.* A few years later came his most emblematic film, *Safety Last!* (1923), in which ▶▶

"the human fly"—so nicknamed for Lloyd's penchant for comedy in high places—finds himself on the side of a tall building dangling from the hands of its giant clock. That same year, the comedian set up his own production company, financing hit films such as *Girl Shy* (1924), *The Freshman* (1925) and *Speedy* (1928). His first talkie was the enormously successful *Welcome Danger* (1929), initially filmed as a silent film and later reshot with sound and dialogue. Pictures like *Movie Crazy* (1932) and *The Milky Way* (1935) pleased both critics and audiences, but the failure of *Professor Beware* (1938)

pushed Lloyd to retirement. Through the years, by producing and controlling the rights to his pictures, he accumulated a huge fortune and had nothing left to prove. But in 1945, flattered by the fact that then-wonder boy Preston Sturges had written an unsolicited script for him, he agreed to star in *The Sin of Harold Diddlebock*. Unfortunately, the movie misfired and Lloyd left the spotlight for good. His sunset years were spent with his wife Mildred and his granddaughter Suzanne at Greenacres, his palatial Beverly Hills estate. In 1971, he died at age 77. ●

▼ ASK FATHER
(1919, Rolin Film Company)
One-reel comedy directed by Hal Roach ● A young man (**Harold Lloyd**), head over heels in love with a coquettish girl, goes to the offices of her father, the busiest businessman in town, to ask for her hand in marriage. Ejected by underlings (**Snub Pollard** and **Bud Jamison,** third and fourth from left), he stubbornly insists. Noticing a costume store on the same floor, he rents a female suit with diaphanous veils and, mincing about, is able to engage the workaholic man into conversation just when his rolled up pants, sliding to the floor, reveal the deception. The switchboard girl (**Bebe Daniels,** center left), who notices the comings and goings, compassionately softens the young man's falls by tossing a pillow under his behind. Expelled again, he even scales the side of the building, to no avail. Renting a suit of armor, he comes back again just to learn that the girl he was in love with has eloped with another suitor. Looking at the adorable receptionist, he asks her how busy her father is and happily hears he had passed away.

Opposite: Snub Pollard (kneeling) and Harold Lloyd (third from right) in *Kicked Out* (1918, Rolin Film Company), directed by Alf Goulding.

MONTY PYTHON

THE BRITISH COMEDY group known as Monty Python's Flying Circus drew fame from its outrageously silly television series, which became a classic parody of the medium itself, and from its equally irreverent movies, which generated no small degree of controversy. Consisting of five writer-performers—Englishmen John Cleese (b. 1939), Graham Chapman (1941-89), Terry Jones (b.1942), Eric Idle (b.1943), Michael Palin (b.1943), and one American, film animator-director Terry Gilliam (b.1940)—Monty Python grew out of Cleese's suggestion that he and his writing partner, Chapman, work together with another team, Palin and Jones. After Idle, who was soon asked to join in, recruited Gilliam, the six then proposed the idea of a comedy series to the BBC. The Flying Circus name allegedly originated with a network executive while the group itself decided on adding Monty and Python. This guaranteed that the content of their shows would be anybody's guess—which was exactly their aim. Though talented humorists in their own right, the group also drew on the revolutionary inventiveness of Britain's then popular comedy programs, such as the stage revue *Beyond the Fringe* and radio's *The Goon Show.* It was also influenced by Gilliam's free-wheeling graphics that as links between the program's segments were so Dadaist that a fixed structure was abandoned in favor of a surrealistic stream-of-consciousness flow. Skits with a beginning, middle and end or those reliance on a strong punch line were eventually discarded—though running gags and characters became ▶▶

▲ **TERRY JONES, MICHAEL PALIN, & ERIC IDLE**
MONTY PYTHON'S THE MEANING OF LIFE (1983, Universal)
Loosely connected montage of corrosive vignettes directed by Terry Jones ● In a British hospital, two careless pediatricians (John Cleese, Graham Chapman) deliver a baby in a traumatic way for the mother and, no doubt, the child. Then, an Irishman tells his some 50 children that, now jobless, he needs to sell them for science projects. His wife (**Terry Jones** in drag, top photo) agrees and everyone performs a song-and-dance routine around the theme "sperm is not to be wasted" while a sanctimonious protestant man (Graham Chap-

man) explains to his unfulfilled wife (**Eric Idle**, bottom right photo) how proud he is to have sexual self-control. Next, in a typical English public school, master John Cleese gives a very graphic classroom lesson in procreation using his wife as his partner. Later, the indifference of officers toward their men during a ferocious battle with Zulus exemplifies the privileges of society's upper strata. Even the Grim Reaper seems to hold no terror when he appears at a country house dinner party, and after trying to explain his identity to the six disbelieving guests (all Monty Python with **Michael Palin** and **Eric Idle** in drag, bottom photos), hauls them off to the afterlife. The conclusion is clear: life is nothing else than one giant, twisted hoot.

Opposite: Terry Jones, Graham Chapman and a friend play "Find the Fish" in *Monty Python's The Meaning of Life.*

Hilarious anthology of Monty Python's television skits directed by Ian MacNaughton ● *"Hell's Grannies" sketch.* London has become a beleaguered city. An ugly form of violence is afoot, stalking the seamier segments of the town's populace. Gangs of old ladies (**Eric Idle, John Cleese, Michael Palin, Graham Chapman,** in drag) are assaulting defenseless young toughs, with no respect for race, color, creed or sex. Occasionally riding motorcycles when they are not taking their afternoon tea, the innocuous but vicious crones' favorite targets are layabouts and the occasional telephone booth (**photo**).

a staple. The result was a sort of visual and mental merry-go-round, the show's riskiness often going far beyond its mirthful mayhem. For with Monty Python there would be no institutions like the church or the royal family that would be safe from their wacky lampoons. In addition, underlying the group's deliriousness, there was an intellectual bedrock and a penchant for the bawdy, if not outright vulgarity. Appropriately, their first show aired on a Sunday—October 5, 1969—as a fill-in for a cancelled religious program. After the second series, Monty Python's first feature film, *And Now for Something Completely Different*, a compilation of their best television efforts to date, was assembled. Thanks to its release in the U.S. and the airing of their shows on PBS, the Pythons became popular among Americans. Cleese left the group after the fourth season to star in his own television series, *Fawlty Towers.* He came back in 1975 for *Monty Python and the Holy Grail,* a demented feature about the trials King Arthur and his knights must endure in their search of the mythical goblet. The sextet's third movie, *Monty Python's Life of Brian*

▲ **JOHN CLEESE**
MONTY PYTHON AT THE
HOLLYWOOD BOWL (1982, Handmade)
Directed by Terry Hughes.

(1979), brought out a storm of vitriol. Critics saw in its portrayal of a people mistaking an oafish young man for the messiah—whom they crucify—as a sacrilegious attack on Christ. In 1983, *Monty Python's The Meaning of Life,* which took comedic pot shots at just about everything, was released. By this time, the team was disbanded, allowing the six funnymen to pursue solo careers. But it is their identity as a group and the aggregate of their loony sketches – ranging from the revolting and priapic to the fatuous and absurd—that insure Monty Python an exalted status in the pantheon of wit. ●

◄ **GRAHAM CHAPMAN**
THE SECRET
POLICEMAN'S OTHER
BALL (1982, Amnesty)
**Directed by Julian Temple
and Roger Graef with
Tim Taylor (left)
and John Bird (center).**

▼ **ERIC IDLE
& MICHAEL PALIN**
MONTY PYTHON LIVE
AT THE HOLLYWOOD
BOWL (1982, Paramount)
Directed by Terry Hughes.

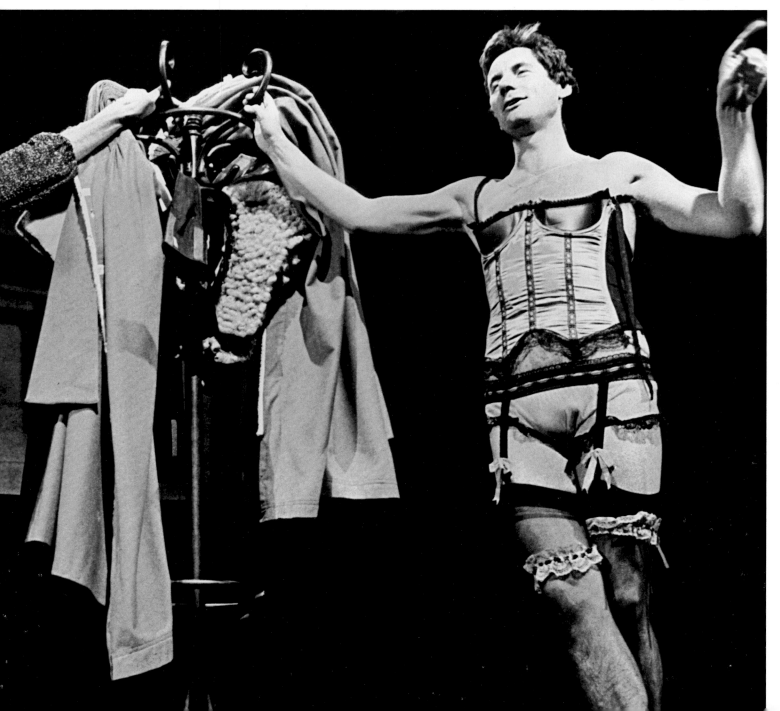

THE RITZ BROTHERS

THE RITZ BROTHERS
KENTUCKY MOONSHINE (1938, Fox)
Musical send-up of '30s country radio directed by David Butler ● After hearing that a popular radio show is looking to book a country act, the out-of-work **Ritz Brothers** go to Kentucky, disguise themselves as bumpkins and get an audition with the program's star, Jerry Wade (**Tony Martin,** right). Completely taken in, Wade brings them to New York where, after bollixing up all kinds of situations, they are unmasked. The show's sponsor, however, is impressed by the audience's enthusiastic reception to the brothers' skits—including a hysterical spoof of *Snow White and the Seven Dwarfs* with **Harry Ritz** as the Wicked Queen and Jimmy Ritz as the huntsman (**photo above**). They are so entertaining that the Sunshine Soap sponsor lets them close the show dressed as hillbilly waitresses (**photo at left**), singing backup for the urban Jerry Wade, and even extends their contract.

IN A CAREER that spanned six decades, the Ritz Brothers successfully combined music, comedy and split-second timing in a frenetic and unique style. Their specialties were wildly-paced, rather demented comic relief songs and sketches, outlandish costumes and inventive impersonations of famous movie stars, such as their roller-skating takeoffs of Boris Karloff, Peter Lorre and Charles Laughton in 1937's *One in a Million* and their hilarious imitation of the Andrews Sisters while dressed in Carmen Miranda-like outfits in *Argentine Nights* (1940). Born in Newark, New Jersey, Al (1901), Jimmy (1904) and Harry (1907) were the sons of Max Joachim, an immigrant from Austria who encouraged his boys to pursue careers in vaudeville. In 1925, they finally teamed up as The Collegians in a Coney Island nightclub act sporting baggy pants, gigantic bow ties and straw hats. An immediate hit, the trio, which was clearly dominated by Harry, performed in several of Broadway impresario Earl Carroll's *Vanities* before they ▶▶

made a two-reel comedy, *Hotel Anchovy* in 1934. The Ritzes were then spotted by 20th Century Fox director Sidney Lanfield who gave them their first feature film exposure in the musical comedy *Sing, Baby, Sing* (1936). The public reaction was so favorable that Darryl Zanuck offered them a long-term contract. After several successful films—including *Life Begins at College* (1937)—the trio was loaned out to Sam Goldwyn to be part of the all-star *Goldwyn Follies* (1938). The film was a flop and, when they returned to Fox, the studio cast them in what the three felt were B movies. After a vigorous protest, in 1939 they finally obtained a good script, a spoof of Alexandre Dumas' *The Three Musketeers,* as well as a topnotch director, Allan Dwan. The following year, they were forced by Zanuck to star in *The Gorilla*, a murder-mystery they forecast would be a box office bomb, but which remains one of their most famous films. Their move to Universal resulted in even lower budgets and, after *Never a Dull Moment* (1943), the Ritz Brothers returned to nightclubs, most of the time swank venues they continued to pack for years. In 1965, Al died from a heart attack, an event that devastated Harry and Jimmy. In their remaining 20 years working together, the duo continued to bring their zany brand of humor to television and to occasional movie cameos, as in *Won Ton Ton, the Dog Who Saved Hollywood* (1976). Jimmy passed away in 1985, Harry the following year. ●

▲ **HARRY RITZ**
LIFE BEGINS IN COLLEGE (1937, Fox)
Broadly appealing football romp directed by William A. Seiter ● Students in their seventh year at Lombardy College, the Ritz Brothers (**Jimmy, Harry** and **Al**) are members of the football team. But when they play, they have the lamentable tendency to score points for the opposing team. Fortunately, the students appreciate their song-and-dance rou-tines. At the annual Get Acquainted Dance, the brothers perform "The Rumba Goes Collegiate" with Harry in a co-ed outfit (**photo**). Later, during a crucial game against Midwestern, the boys sneak onto the field and incur penalties that drive Lombardy to their own six-yard line. A few minutes before the end, however, Harry, in a stupendous moment of impossible luck, catches his own pass and scores the winning touchdown.

▶ HARRY RITZ
ON THE AVENUE (1937, Fox)

Classy and amusing Irving Berlin musical directed by Roy Del Ruth ● Actress-singer Mona Merrick (**Alice Faye,** left) deeply offends socialite Mimi Caraway (Madeleine Carroll) by spoofing her mannerisms in a Broadway musical called *On the Avenue*. When the show's author and male star Gary Blake (Dick Powell) begins a romance with the heiress, Mona makes the satire more biting. Mimi, who blames Gary, buys the show from its producer and enrolls the Ritz Brothers to ridicule one of Mona's big numbers, *Let's Go Slumming on Park Avenue*—with **Harry Ritz** in Mona's signature polka dot blouse and flamboyantly bowed hat (**photo**). In addition, she arranges for 400 people to walk out on Gary's first song. Eventually, Mimi decides to marry a pompous explorer (Alan Mowbray) but, before the ceremony, Mona confesses to her that the nastier spoofing was her idea, not Gary's. Surprised by this revelation, Mimi jumps into the taxi where Gary waits to take her to City Hall—and wedded bliss.

▶ THE RITZ BROTHERS
THE GOLDWYN FOLLIES
(1938, United Artists)

Song-and-dance showstoppers directed by George Marshall ● The films of producer Oliver Merlin (Adolphe Menjou) have lost mass appeal. On location for his new motion picture *The Forgotten Dance,* he hires a simple country girl, Hazel Dawes (Andrea Leeds), to advise him on improving the movie's "human" aspects. Hazel moves to Hollywood and the shooting resumes, blending the diverse talents of a Russian ballerina (Vera Zorina), a suave ventriloquist (Edgar Bergen) and the Met's American Ballet. Oliver falls for Hazel, before the **Ritz Brothers— Al, Harry,** and **Jimmy**—emerge from a Venetian canal as singing mermaids (**photo**). In the meantime, in a local hamburger joint, Hazel discovers tenor Danny Beecher (Kenny Baker), who has enough "humanity" in him to take over the male lead of *The Forgotten Dance,* and, to Oliver's polite distress, steal her heart.

▶ THE RITZ BROTHERS
STRAIGHT, PLACE & SHOW (1938, Fox)

Gag-infested horseplay directed by David Butler ● **Al, Harry** and **Jimmy Ritz,** proud owners of the Wild West Pony Ride, place a $10 bet on a horse called Playboy and collect $3,000. Enthusiastic about the galloper, they put down more money every time he enters a race—but on each occasion they lose their investment. When Playboy's owner donates him to the Ritzes' pony ride, the trio soon discovers that the horse is a great jumper and scrape together enough money to pay the Southbury's steeplechase entry fee. Learning that three Russian jockeys, the Borukoffs, plan to use dirty tricks to win the race, the Ritz Brothers ask a friend to replace Harry as Playboy's jockey. They then succeed in locking up the Borukoffs and, after stealing their outfits, ride so badly that Playboy wins the derby, making them very rich. (**Photo** *at right from a musical number that did not make the film's final cut.*)

◄ **THE RITZ BROTHERS**
YOU CAN'T HAVE EVERYTHING
(1937, Fox)

Formulaic but endearing musical comedy directed by Norman Taurog ● Judith Poe Wells (Alice Faye), a novice at both playwriting and singing, meets musical theatre director George Macrae (Don Ameche) in a restaurant where she is performing for a free meal. Charmed by Judith's voice—and to help her financially—George options her very serious stage play *North Wind*. While rehearsing *Sunny Days,* his new Broadway show featuring the Ritz Brothers, he realizes that Judith would be the ideal female lead and sends the brothers to the YMCA where she resides. There, the no-men-allowed policy forces **Al, Harry** and **Jimmy** to disguise as scrubwomen (**photo**). When George eventually transforms *North Wind* into a lavish musical, Judith becomes the toast of Broadway.

► **JIMMY & AL RITZ**
HI 'YA CHUM (1943, Universal)

Indefatigable Hollywood-here-we-come farce directed by Harold Young ● The Merry Madcaps (The Ritz Brothers) are performing a skit in which **Jimmy** and **Al** are clumsy ballerinas whose butchered pas de deux greatly upsets **Harry,** their irascible Russian ballet master (**photo**). Not surprisingly, their number is a total dud but, undiscouraged, they announce they are going to Hollywood "in a big limousine" to become film stars. Two appealing singers from the show, Susan (Jane Frazee) and Madge (June Clyde) ask the Madcaps to let them tag along. The boys are reluctant, as the limo is really a Model-T Ford, but they finally say yes. When the clunker breaks down in a California ghost town and there is no money for repairs, the three accept jobs as cooks in a diner. Thanks to a wealthy businessman (Robert Paige) who is wooing Susan, the eatery becomes a success. Some jealous locals try to muscle in, but the ex-ballerinas prevail.

◄ **THE RITZ BROTHERS**
ARGENTINE NIGHTS (1940, Universal)

Exotic musical farce directed by Albert S. Rogell ● Talent agents **Al, Harry** and **Jimmy Ritz** book a gig at an Argentine resort for their clients, the all-female band of Bonnie Brooks (Constance Moore) and the vocal trio of Maxine, Patty and Laverne Andrews (The Andrews Sisters). Penniless one and all, the brothers and their clients embark on a Buenos Aires-bound liner. To pay for their fare, Bonnie Brooks and the girls perform in the ship's dining room, replacing the missing regular band detained by the Andrews Sisters in one of the cabins. When the Andrews Sisters are called on stage, Al, Harry and Jimmy appear instead, impersonating them in Carmen Miranda costumes while lip-synching one of their hits, "Rhumboogie" (**photo**). After disembarking, the entire troupe realizes that the Argentine resort is only a small hacienda. Not discouraged, the Ritz Brothers transform the property into a dude ranch.

RED SKELTON

▲ BATHING BEAUTY
(1944, MGM)

Pleasurable romantico-aquatic comedy directed by George Sidney ● In Los Angeles, athletic beauty Caroline Brooks (Esther Williams) and redheaded composer Steve Elliott (**Red Skelton**) get married. Both have pledged to abandon their profession–she as a swimming instructor, he as a popular songwriter–to start a new life together. When stage producer George Adams (**Basil Rathbone, top photo,** right) learns the news, he is apoplectic, as Steve had previously agreed to write original songs for an aquatic ballet. To derail the marriage, George asks an aspiring actress (**Jean Porter, top photo,** left) to claim that Steve is her husband and the father of her three kids. Feeling betrayed, Caroline resumes her old

job at all-girl Victoria College. Steve follows her and, thanks to an oversight in the college charter, is able to enroll as a student. In spite of Caroline's anger and the efforts of the faculty to expel him, Steve refuses to give up hope of getting her back, frequently enduring humiliating situations. When hiding in his wife's closet, for example, he dons her suit and hat in order to escape an attack dog poised outside; and later, to satisfy academic requirements, he attends in a tutu a dance class of a severe teacher (**Ann Codee, bottom photo,** right), making unintentional goofs that cause more than a few giggles among his fellow ballerinas. Finally discovering the truth, Caroline happily reunites with Steve, who promises George that he will write the songs for his ballet on the condition that Caroline stars in it.

Opposite: Wardrobe man Morris Brown laces Red Skelton into a ballerina's costume for a sequence of Bathing Beauty (1944, MGM).

A CLOWN'S clown, Red Skelton was a master of multiple comic identities. In a career that stretched over 70 years—if one counts his busking on the street to support his family at age seven—he created on radio, and later on television the famous Clem Kadiddle-hopper, Freddie the Freeloader, Willie Lump Lump and the Mean Widdle Kid. Dough-faced with two huge dimples, he also arguably portrayed the best drunk there ever was. Born Richard Skelton in 1913, in Vincennes, Indiana, the posthumous son of a grocer, Skelton paid his dues in an astounding variety of ways. Beginning at age 10 as a newsboy to help his mother support his two brothers and himself, he then became a gofer for *Doc Lewis's Patent Medicine Show* where he sang in blackface and perfected his pratfall. He moved on to circus rings and showboat venues, next to burlesque and vaudeville. When RKO cast him in *Having Wonderful Time* (1938) and the film flatlined, he would wait several years for his big break. It came when Mickey Rooney, ▶▶

◄ RED SKELTON
NEPTUNE'S DAUGHTER
(1949, MGM)

Breezily aquatic fun comedy directed by Edward Buzzell ● Eve Barrett (**Esther Williams**, center), a successful bathing suit designer, fights off the advances of suave South American polo player Jose O'Rourke (Ricardo Montalban). Meanwhile, her dim-witted sister Betty (**Betty Garrett**, right) falls for bland masseur Jack Spratt (**Red Skelton**), whom she assumes is the polo star. This case of mistaken identity proves to be pleasant for both but rather dangerous for Jack when gangsters want him to fix a game. To hide from them, he slips into a swimsuit fashion show (**photo**), hoping he will go unnoticed among much prettier models. He is quickly unmasked, but when the bad guys realize they have the wrong man, they abduct the real Jose to prevent him from playing in the upcoming match. Betty, however, is still convinced that Jack is Jose and forces him to join the South American team. In a remarkably unusual polo style, he scores a victory while Jose, freed by the police, is able to show up on time to claim not only the trophy but also Eve's heart.

◄ SEEING RED
(1939, Warner)

First Red Skelton film, a two-reel musical comedy directed by Roy Mack ● Fired by his exasperated boss, Mr. Jones (**John Regen**, right), Red (**Red Skelton**) threatens to haunt him forever. Later on, in a nightclub where the old man goes with his wife to be entertained by acts such as the Merry Macs vocal quartet, Mr. Jones sees Red everywhere: he is the doorman, the hat check boy, the maitre d', the waiter and the presenter. Troubled by Red's apparent ubiquity, Mr. Jones can't believe his eyes when he realizes that his wife has morphed into his former employee (**photo**).

Opposite: Test photos for an unidentified Red Skelton project.

who had seen Skelton perform at President Franklin Roosevelt's birthdays, touted him to Louis B. Mayer. His starring role in MGM's *Whistling in the Dark* (1941) brought him national attention, as did the debut of his NBC radio program, *The Red Skelton Show*. He costarred with Esther Williams in one of his funniest roles, playing a female ballet student in *Bathing Beauty* (1944), and made some reasonably successful movies under the influence of Buster Keaton, *A Southern Yankee* (1948) being one himself. *The Fuller Brush Man* (1948) was also a hit but it sadly coincided with a diagnosis of leukemia for his son, who would die 10 years later. In 1949, he costarred again with Williams in *Neptune's Daughter*, hilarious once again in a drag skit. Television's *The Red Skelton Show* lasted two decades with Skelton capping off his years in show business by signing several multi-million dollar deals in succession with various Las Vegas casinos. In 1990, at the age of 80, the clown who was also a success in selling his paintings of them, played to a full house at Carnegie Hall. Richard "Red" Skelton died in Rancho Mirage, California, in 1997. •

TOTÒ

IN FEBRUARY 1998, Italy kicked off a yearlong posthumous celebration honoring the 100th birthday of its best-loved comedian, the inimitable Totò. A national institution, Antonio Vincenzo Stefano Clemente—the illegitimate son of Giuseppe de Curtis, the son of a marquis who did not want his progeny to marry Totò's commoner mother—was born in Naples, the site of many of his films. A volunteer in WWI, he began to frequent theatre milieus in 1919, and after having the pleasure of witnessing his mother's marriage to his biological father after the death of the marquis in 1921, he followed his parents to Rome. Slowly, the voluble comedian rose to popularity in the '20s, playing humorous roles in music halls. He made his film debut as a Chaplin-inspired-tramp named Totò in *Fermo con le mani* (1936), but it took 10 more years for his cinematic career to take off. For two decades, starting in 1947, he starred back-to-back in almost 100 movies. Some of his more famous include Vittorio De Sica's *L'oro di Napoli (The Gold of Naples,* 1954), Mario Monicelli's *I soliti ignoti (Big Deal on Madonna Street,* 1958) and Pier Paolo Pasolini's *Uccellacci e uccellini (The Hawks and Sparrows,* 1966). Totò's style, elegant in its timing, was firmly rooted in the broad gestures of his native region and relied heavily on verbal brilliance, adroit physicality and facial flexibility. It was a rare combination and one that earned him a much-deserved place next to other comic geniuses like Chaplin, Keaton and Fernandel with whom he partnered in Christian-Jaque's *La legge e legge (The Law Is the Law,* 1958). When Totò died of a heart attack in 1967 at age 69, Italy went into mourning. ●

▲ FIGARO QUA, FIGARO LA
(1950, Golden Films)
Farcical version of a classic tale directed by Carlo Ludovico Bragaglia ● In Seville, the Count of Almaviva (Gianni Agus) decides to help his barber Figaro (**Totò**) pay a steep fine levied because his shop was illegally opened on Sunday. In exchange, the count asks Figaro to help him conquer the heart of the governor's daughter, Rosina (Isa Barziza). The obstacle is not the girl, but her father, who has promised her to the head of his police force, Don Alonso (**Renato Rascel,** left). The evening before the marriage, Figaro puts on a show at the end of which a wedding will be performed. During the spectacle, which is attended by the governor, Figaro trades outfits with Rosina and replaces her at Don Alonso's side (**photo**). Meanwhile on stage she and Count Almaviva are substituted for the comedians who were supposed to enact the ceremony. By the time the governor realizes that his daughter is now married to Almaviva, Figaro has disappeared. He is arrested at his shop the following Sunday but the newlyweds have him freed.

▶ TOTÒ THE CON MAN
(Italian title "Totòtruffa '62," 1961, D.D.L.)
Unabashedly contrived farce directed by Camillo Mastrocinque ● Music-hall performer Antonio Lo Ruffo (**Totò**) has become a scam artist in order to send his daughter Diana (Estella Blain) to boarding school. He makes a decent living but knows that Police Commissioner Malvasia (Ernesto Calindri) is set on catching him. In fact, when Antonio impersonates a woman (**photo**) trying to con Cavalier Terlizzi (Luigi Pavese), Malvasia is not amused. Meantime, during a school trip, Diana, who thinks her father is an ambassador, meets Franco Malvasia (Geronimo Meynier), the commissioner's son, and falls for him. Looking for a job, Franco comes upon the advertisement of an employment agency that, it turns out, is a fictitious operation devised by Antonio to collect enrollment fees. When he realizes he has conned the commissioner's son, Antonio does everything in his power to find him a real job. The reception of some unexpected inheritance money allows him to give back the ill-earned gains to his victims and come clean with his old adversary.

◀ TOTÒ
TOTÒ DIABOLICUS
(1962, Titanus-Buffardi)

***Kind Hearts and Coronets* Italian-style comedy directed by Steno ●** With the body of Marquis Galeazzo di Torrealta (Totò) a note is found from his murderer signed Diabolicus. His four siblings, now his heirs, immediately make the suspect list. They are Scipione (Totò), a fascist ex-general; Carlo (Totò), an absent-minded surgeon; Baroness Laudomia (**Totò** in drag, **photo**), a widow on the lookout for a young husband; and Monsignor Antonino (Totò), who has an airtight alibi. After the first three are murdered, the cleric renounces the bequest and gives it to the marquis' illegitimate son, Pasquale Buoncuore (Totò), who had been in jail at the time of his father's death. The mystery unravels when it is discovered that Diabolicus is, in fact, the marquis, a spendthrift who has iced Antonino and stolen his clothing to impersonate him. More goes awry and Pasquale, the illegitimate son, is left to enjoy his good fortune.

▶ FEAR AND ARENA
(Italian title "Fifa e Arena," 1948, CDI)

Blood-and-sand broad comedy directed by Steno ● In a village near Naples, Nicolino Capece (**Totò**) works in the pharmacy of his Aunt Marta who has developed a youth serum. In order to promote it, she books an advertisement in the *Gazetta di Napoli*. Unfortunately, the printer mistakenly switches the photo of Nicolino used in the ad with that of an escapee from a facility for the criminally insane. Nicolino, now chased by the police, dresses up as a female flight attendant (**photo**) and manages to board a plane to Seville. Waiting for him is a felon named Cast (**Mario Castellani,** right) who saw the newspaper and plans to partner with him in a nefarious scheme: Cast wants Nicolino to court wealthy American Patricia Cotton (Isa Barzizza) and, once married, kill her for her money. While trying to avoid Cast, Nicolino puts on a matador's outfit and is forced to participate in a bullfight. Thanks to a few flashy moves, he becomes an instant celebrity under the nickname of Nicolete, evocative of legendary torero Manolete.

◀ TOTÒ SEXY (1963, Cinex-Incei)
Comedy of frustrated behind-the-bars dreams directed by Mario Amendola ● Two itinerant musicians, Mimi Cocco (**Erminio Macario**, left) and Nini Cantachiaro (**Totò**), charged with contraband, are incarcerated. They are dressed in typical prison garb, save Mimi, who wearing white gloves continues his role as Nini's domestic—always ready to serve coffee after his idol's siesta. When Nini dreams, he speaks of love aloud and awakens the desires of his cellmates who begin to complain. But Mimi does not tolerate any criticism of his friend: after all, he tells them, Nini and he have performed their act in Paris, London and Berlin's nightclubs. To prove the point, the duo, borrowing wigs and female attire, re-enacts a sketch in which they used to dress up as women (**photo**). When their career floundered, confirms Nini, they tried to make some quick liras by smuggling Swiss chocolate into Italy. After recounting their adventures, Nini gladly goes back to sleep, his dreams populated by numerous beautiful women.

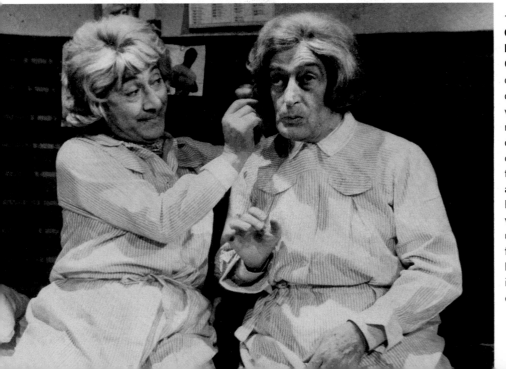

◀ **TOTÒ**
TOTÒ AGAINST
THE FOUR
(Italian title "Totò
contro i quattro," 1963,
Titanus-Buffardi)
**Winningly funny police
farce directed by Steno**
● A bad day begins for
police Commissioner
Antonio Saracino (Totò)
when he learns that his
car has been stolen.
Later, he is summoned to
the home of wealthy
commendatore Lancetti
(Mario Castellani), a
victim of blackmail. In the
afternoon, a self-styled
private eye named
Lamazza (Erminio Macario)
denounces suspicious
goings-on he has
observed outside a
secluded villa. When
Saracino and Lamazza
dress as painters to raid
the place, they find
a film crew shooting a
horror movie. At night, to
solve the blackmail case,
Saracino disguises
himself as a prostitute
(**photo**) and working the
streets of Villa Borghese,
catches the blackmailer—
the *commendatore's*
parasitic nephew. After
having investigated these
cases, Commissioner
Saracino gets his stolen
vehicle back from a
priest, Don Amilcare
(Aldo Fabrizi), but
not the names of the
thieves, who have been
absolved by the open-
minded man of God.

BERT WHEELER & ROBERT WOOLSEY

LESS POPULAR with critics than with audiences in their time, Bert Wheeler and Robert Woolsey starred in 21 happy-go-lucky features that were so successful they managed to keep their studio afloat during the Depression. Not unlike other comedy partners such as Laurel and Hardy and Abbott and Costello, they exploited their physical and psychological differences. Wheeler was a loveable shrimp with wavy hair, a choirboy face and a voice to match. Born in Patterson, New Jersey, in 1895, he was a master jokester who also excelled at visual humor. His major entry into show business was a vaudeville act with his wife Betty. Woolsey, in contrast, was the bespectacled Oxford don type. A native son of Oakland, California, who was born in 1889, he worked as a jockey in his teens. But when an accident sidelined him, he too turned to show business, his big break coming via leading roles in a Gilbert and Sullivan troupe. In 1928, Florenz Ziegfeld paired Wheeler—who, with his wife, had been performing in the great impresario's *Folies* for four years—with the cigar-chomping Woolsey in the Broadway ▶▶

◄ BERT WHEELER
PEACH O'RENO (1931, RKO)

Broadly appealing divorce romp directed by William A. Seiter ● By day, Swift (**Robert Woolsey,** left) and Wattles (**Bert Wheeler**) run a quickie divorce service in Reno, Nevada. By night, their offices morph into a high-flying casino. Life is good for the two shysters until Crosby (Mitchell Harris), a threatening cowboy-like giant, shows up at the gambling joint in order to meet—and rub out—his wife's divorce lawyer. To stay alive, culprit Wattles dresses believably as an eye-full of a blonde (**photo**), a masquerade that abruptly ends when a waiter accidentally sets Wattles' wig on fire. Recognizing him, Crosby chases Wattles through the casino's rooms, shooting his revolver at random. Fortunately, in the middle of this mayhem, the police arrive to arrest Crosby—for a parking violation—enabling Swift and Wattles to revert to their lucrative divorce law practice.

▲ BERT WHEELER
THE CUCKOOS (1930, RKO)

Pleasantly silly musical comedy directed by Paul Sloane ● Bogus fortunetellers, Prof. Cunningham (Robert Woolsey) and his assistant Sparrow (**Bert Wheeler**) find themselves broke at a plush resort on the Mexican border. Nearby, a band of Gypsies maintain their camp. Among them is Anita (Dorothy Lee), a raven-haired beauty who swiftly enthralls Sparrow. But knife-thrower Julius (**Mitchell Lewis,** left), the green-eyed leader of the tribe, proves to be a prodigious obstacle. When fortune hunter Baron de Camp offers $10,000 to Julius to kidnap heiress Ruth Chester (June Clyde), who refuses to marry him, her Aunt Fannie hires the professor and Sparrow to find her niece. Trailing the kidnappers south of the border, the quack soothsayers insinuate themselves into the Romany's hideout. Finding some women's clothes, Sparrow masquerades as a tantalizing *chica* (**photo**) and leads Julius and his men into a bedroom where Cunningham conks them all unconscious. Later, with the help of aviator Billy Shannon, Ruth's real love, the professor overcomes the evil baron and frees the heiress while Sparrow liberates the lovelorn Anita from Julius' clutches.

production of *Rio Rita*. The two immediately jelled and Radio Pictures, which became RKO, soon signed them for its movie version with the two providing formulaic laughter relief. Although both professed problems with transitioning from performing before a receptive audience to working in front of a disinterested film crew, the following year their popularity allowed them to star in their own film, *Half Shot at Sunrise.* From 1931, beginning with *Cracked Nuts,* until 1935, the duo was on a cinematic roll, energetically singing, dancing and cracking jokes. Though cross-dressing was not the primary source of their appeal, several of their movies featured hilarious examples of their skills in skirts. In *Peach O'Reno* (1931), Wheeler disports himself as a glitzy, platinum-wigged blonde. Two years later in Columbia's *So This Is Africa*—the only film they did not make for RKO—Wheeler and Woolsey don matching leopard skin bras and skirts. After Woolsey's death in 1938, Wheeler continued to incorporate female impersonation into his stage act, playing an elderly lady who is sometimes ill-treated by her son. He never appeared in another feature film, however, but stayed on in the entertainment world, trying out various other partners and appearing in vaudeville, radio and television. He passed away in 1968. ●

▼ ROBERT WOOLSEY
GIRL CRAZY (1932, RKO)

Merry adaptation of a Gershwin musical directed by William A. Seiter ● Girl crazy Danny Churchill (Eddie Quillan) is sent by his father to Custersville, Arizona, to live the rough existence of a westerner. Danny decides to transform the village into a dude ranch complete with music, girls and gambling. Planning to manage the gaming concession, a friend from Chicago, Slick Foster (**Robert Woolsey,** far right), joins him, chauffeured by cabby Jimmy

Deegan (**Bert Wheeler,** second from right). The successful opening of Danny's Dude Ranch enrages a local thug, Lank Sanders (**Stanley Fields,** second from left), who announces that he intends to kill Slick and Jimmy. At one point, the terrorized pair masquerades as Anapolis Indians (from Indianapolis). Jimmy introduces himself to both Sanders and a real native (**High Eagle,** left) as Sitting Bull—and Slick as his Indian wife, Sitting Pretty (**photo**). The subterfuge is short-lived but Slick, using his hypnotic powers, is able to neutralize the triggerman.

▲ BERT WHEELER & ROBERT WOOLSEY
MUMMY'S BOYS (1936, RKO)

Weak pharaoh's-curse-whodunit directed by Fred Guiol ● New York ditch-diggers Stanley Wright (**Bert Wheeler,** second from left) and Aloysius Whittaker (**Robert Woolsey,** third from right) become excavators at an accursed Egyptian archeological site. Their role is to help Drs. Browning and Sterling revisit King Pharatime's tomb, the original opening of which had claimed nine victims. In Cairo, caught trying to seduce the wives of Sheik Haroun

Pasha (**Mitchell Lewis,** left), Stanley and Aloysius escape the prince's furor by disguising themselves as local beauties (**photo**). Later, in the Valley of the Kings, grim events scare members of the expedition into borderline hysteria. Finally, the pharaoh's tomb is located, allowing Stanley and Aloysius to open cavernous sanctuaries. When their only exit is sealed, they discover that Dr. Sterling (Moroni Olsen), a madman who had killed the previous explorers, was the engineer of the bogus curse. Overpowering the criminal, Stanley and Aloysius lock him up in a sarcophagus.

▲ BERT WHEELER & ROBERT WOOLSEY
SO THIS IS AFRICA (1933, Columbia)

Diverting tropical escapade with a twist directed by Eddie Cline ●
When a film studio needs to produce a blockbuster animal feature or go bust, it hires bogus lion tamers Alexander (**Robert Woolsey**, second from right) and Wilbur (**Bert Wheeler**, second from left). The company execs find their felines so decrepit that they will be perfect for the director, Ms. Johnson Martini (Esther Muir), who is afraid of wild animals. On location, the director sets her sights on Alexander while Wilbur comes upon a jungle creature, Tarzana (Raquel Torres), who belongs to a sexually active tribe. They are elated until they learn that when the native women become aroused they kill their mates after use. To avoid this fate, Alexander and Wilbur dress as tribes-women (**photo**). But though the duo blends with the group for a short time, they are quickly recaptured, this time by Amazonian men. When the boys are next seen, they are doing the laundry with infants strapped on their backs.

◄ BERT WHEELER
KENTUCKY KERNELS (1934, RKO)

Farcical hillbilly family feud film directed by George Stevens ●
Two down-on-their-luck vaudevillians, Elmer Doyle (Robert Woolsey) and Willie Dugan (**Bert Wheeler**), live in a shack while waiting for a gig. A string of events leads them to take into their care a manipulative "orphan" named Spanky Milford (George "Spanky" McFarland). While freezing in their shanty, Elmer and Willie are informed that Spanky is the heir to a Kentucky estate. Hoping to collect some cash by delivering the tyke to his folks, the comedians head south with their bait but are soon involved in a feud between two violent families, the Milfords and the Wakefields. When the only solution for the duo is to flee, even the drag trick used by Willie (**photo**) fails: he is unmasked by Col. Wakefield (**Noah Beery**, far right) and his son John (**William Pawley**, far left). Just when they are about to be shot by the Wakefields, a wire delivered to the colonel reveals that Spanky is not the estate's heir. The old man cancels the feud and allows the romance between his daughter (Mary Carlisle) and Willie to burgeon.

The Three Stooges

Charley Chase

Roscoe Karns

SKIRTS IN SHORTS

Ben Blue

Cliff Edwards

The kings of American short films flirt with frou-frou

Eddie Foy, Jr.

Leon Errol

El Brendel

CHARLEY CHASE

▶ BE YOUR AGE
(1926, Hal Roach-Pathé)
Two-reel comedy directed by Leo McCarey ● Charley (**Charley Chase**), an impoverished young paralegal whose family is in need of quick cash, learns from his boss that a wealthy old widow, Mrs. Schwarzkopple, wishes to remarry with a younger man. During a party, Charley charms Mrs. Schwarzkopple so much that she falls in love with him. But suddenly getting cold feet, he tries to ditch the enamored matron by donning the fringed cover of a nearby piano and, with a rose in his mouth to hide his moustache, joins the trio of Spanish dancers performing at the event (**photo**). After upsetting Mrs. Schwarzkopple's son Oswald (**Oliver Hardy**, foreground right), Charley's masquerade unravels when he mistakenly runs into a door while escaping. Ignoring the failed ruse, the sunny Mrs. Schwarzkopple calls for the preacher.

▶ CHASING HUSBANDS
(1928, Hal Roach-Pathé)
Two-reel comedy directed by James Parrott ● On a luxury liner, a lady asks a detective (**Edgar Kennedy,** left) to take a photo of her philandering husband (Kalla Pasha) in a compromising situation. The investigator asks his assistant, Charley (**Charley Chase**), to dress as a woman (**top photo**) and flirt with the rascal, a trick that works until he is forced to wear a swimsuit. With the aid of sponges, the detective pads out Charley's scrawny legs and flat rear end to make him more curvaceous. Unfortunately, he falls in the ocean and the sponges expand, making Charley look merely deformed (**bottom photo**). Next he stumbles into the gallivanting husband, a coincidence that enables the sleuth to take the scandalous photo. Awarded $500 by the divorce-minded wife, the private investigator gives Charley one dollar for his services. Upset, he grabs the remaining $499 and throws the bills in the air.

RESPECTED DURING the '20s and '30s in the close-knit world of comedy for his abilities as a comedian, screenwriter and director, Charley Chase never hit the show business heights enjoyed by such contemporaries as Charlie Chaplin or Harold Lloyd. Film analysts point to the fact that the performer lacked a distinctive physical appearance and a definitive routine to set him apart, but perhaps it was simply that his sheer versatility spread his talents too thin. Born Charles Parrott in Baltimore, Maryland, in 1893, he turned professional on the vaudeville stage while still in his teens. He found his career start at Mack Sennett's Keystone Studios where, renamed Charley Chase, he appeared with Chaplin in several one-reelers, among them *The Masquerader* (1914). ▶▶

The following year, under his birth name, he was assigned several comic short subjects to codirect—some with Roscoe "Fatty" Arbuckle. In 1921, Chase became production director at the recently created Hal Roach Studio, where he shepherded the early *Our Gang* comedies. In 1923, as a slick-haired, bespectacled and rather engaging young man, he resumed his career in front of the camera in a highly successful series of 10- to 20-minute films, some directed by him, others by a novice who later became a major filmmaker, Leo McCarey. From the mid-'20s through the late '30s, Chase enjoyed the most fruitful period of his career, sometimes directed by his brother James Parrott. Slim and dapper, Chase incarnated the hectored married man or the dashing playboy, who always seemed to get caught up in ridiculous situations out of his control. After 1929, when films ceased to be silent and Chase was still under contract with Roach, he continued to shoot two-reelers and was assigned a terrific role in Laurel and Hardy's feature-length film *Sons of the Desert*. But the word was out that Chase was drinking heavily. He left Hal Roach and took a job at Columbia where he wrote several short subjects, directed such comic stars as the Three Stooges and starred in his own comedies, the first being *The Grand Hooter* (1937). Shortly after acting in *His Bridal Fright* (1940), Charley Chase died at age 47 of a heart attack in Hollywood, the town he could never quite conquer. •

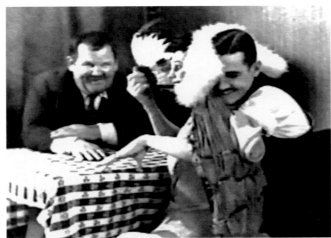

◄**CHARLEY CHASE**
FLUTTERING HEARTS
(1927, Hal Roach-Pathé)
Two-reel comedy directed by James Parrott ● Idle rich Charley (**Charley Chase**) is attracted to Martha but he learns that her father (William Burress) wants her to marry someone with ambition. To impress Martha's dad, Charley pretends to be penniless and succeeds in being hired as his chauffeur. Soon after, Charley's new boss receives a note signed "Big Bill," saying: "I have the compromising letter you wrote to my sister. Unless you pay me $10,000, I will turn it to the newspapers. Meet me at Joe's." Martha's father confides his predicament to Charley and asks him for help. Ever resourceful, Charley buys a life-size inflatable doll, brings it to Joe's and, after locating Big Bill (**Oliver Hardy,** left), uses his blow up "partner" to pique the bandit's interest (**photos**). With the doll's feet glued to his shoes, Charley performs a dazzling dance that titillates Big Bill immensely. Using the doll as a shield and moving as if he were her, Charley steals the letter and, after an epic battle, flees the place. Unfortunately, not understanding what he has gone through and why, Martha dumps him.

◄ **IN WALKED CHARLEY**
(1932, Hal Roach)
Two-reel comedy directed by Warren Doane ● Mr. Henderson (**Dell Henderson,** right) simulates insanity in order not to go on vacation with his family. Charley (**Charley Chase**), who works for a travel agency, does his best to convince his client not to cancel the trip. The madness engineered by the pseudo-crazy client forces Charley into several humiliating disguises, including trading his pants for a beaded lamp shade and pretending to be a woman, dancing with the manipulative man (**photo**).

◀ CHARLEY CHASE
YOUNG IRONSIDES
(1932, Hal Roach-Pathé)

Two-reel comedy directed by James Parrott ● Muriel (**Muriel Evans**), the daughter of a tissue paper tycoon, shocks her parents by entering the Ocean Beach Bathing Beauty Contest. To thwart her, they pay $1,000 to a man who calls himself Fearless (**Charley Chase**). On the train to California, Fearless, who does not know Muriel, meets the heiress and brags about his mission. At the competition, he falls into the ocean, loses his swimsuit and uses some detachable shirt collars for a skirt and pretends to be Miss Hamburg (**photo**). After Fearless asks his train-ride friend to replace Muriel in the pageant, the father is stunned to see his daughter is still a contestant. When the house dick charges Fearless with owing $1,000 in back rent, Muriel tells her dad she will compete if he does not pay the debt of the man she has fallen for.

◀ FOUR PARTS
(1934, Hal Roach-MGM)

Two-reel comedy directed by Charles Parrott and Eddie Dunn ● Thirty-something quadruplets, Eddie, Harry, Hal and Charlie (all played by Charley Chase), live with their charming mother (**Florence Roberts,** left). En route to work, Charlie fights with a pretty woman over a coin on the sidewalk. The woman, Betty (**Betty Mack**), takes a streetcar and is surprised when the conductor, a dead ringer for the man with whom she has just fought, blows her off. Puzzled, she encounters another Charlie look-alike in a policeman, who tells her to scram. Confounded, she loses it when she gets in a cab, only to find the driver another Charlie replica. When she asks him to take her to a doctor, he drops her at the office of Charlie, who is a dentist. To explain why she has been seeing so much of him, he invites her home where sister Charlotte (also **Charley Chase, photo**) drops by with a bag of cookies. Another set of quads appears after Charlie and Betty are wed.

◀ THE GRAND HOOTER
(1937, Columbia)

Two-reel comedy directed by Del Lord ● Charley (**Charley Chase**), a proud member of the Royal Order of the Hoot Howls, irritates his wife (**Peggy Stratford,** left) by his indefectible loyalty to his "brothers." A good hubby, however, Charley decides to take her on a second honeymoon, but at the hotel he puts himself in a compromising situation with the wife (**Nena Quartaro,** right) of a jealous man. He goes through panicking moments and tries to hide by improvising a feminine outfit out of a curtain (**photo**). Fortunately, everything ends well when the two men realize they both are members of the Hoot Howls.

THE THREE STOOGES

◀ CURLY HOWARD
MUTTS TO YOU
(1938, Columbia)

Two-reel comedy directed by Charley Chase ● Operators of the K-9 laundry store, the Three Stooges find what they assume is an abandoned baby on their doorstep and decide to take him home. When newspaper headlines reveal that an infant has been kidnapped, the boys get nervous and attempt to return the tiny tot to where they found him. To do it without being noticed, **Curly** disguises himself as an disheveled mother (**photo**). His outfit, however, seems suspicious to Officer O'Halloran (**Bud Jamison,** second from left), a cop patrolling the area. Panicking, Curly runs away with the policeman right behind him. But before any harm can be done, the parents reunite happily with their baby and ask the authorities to drop all charges.

▲ THE THREE STOOGES
POP GOES THE EASEL
(1935, Columbia)

Two-reel comedy directed by Del Lord ● The jobless Three Stooges agree they should show their willingness to work. In front of a hardware store, they grab three brooms and start to sweep the sidewalk in hopes of impressing the owner. Unfortunately, the man thinks they are stealing the brooms and calls a cop. A chase brings the trio and their pursuer into the Kraft College of Arts. There, dressed first as artists in smocks and floppy berets, they pretend to create inspired artworks. But when the policeman gets too close for comfort, **Larry, Moe** and **Curly** borrow some female outfits from the dance department (**photo**) and play a cat-and-mouse game. That done, changing back into painters garb, they succeed in fooling him once more. Clay-flinging erupts.

THE THREE STOOGES, to put it mildly, are not everybody's cup of tea. Their pig-bladder-wielding physical humor—wildly childish in its absence of nuance and logic—was probably best defended by the leader of the trio, Moe Howard: "It takes the old pratfall, a pie in the face, a good chase or a bop on the casaba to keep a laugh going," he said, describing the tactics of the enduring comic trio. And keep audiences laughing they did, through 24 years worth of some 190 two-reel lowbrow farces. Popular, though not overly so, during their productive years the threesome became an overnight sensation in the early '60s for a whole new generation of Americans, thanks to a glut of television exposure negotiated by Screen Gems. Suddenly—and unexpectedly—the hard working gut-busters were respectable and the object of a real cult that is still alive and well today.

The Stooges originated when Brooklyn-born Moe Howard (1897-1975) joined forces with rising vaudeville performer Ted Healy in 1923, later adding his brother Samuel "Shemp" Howard (1895-1955) and violin-playing funster Larry Fine (1902-1975) to what the act's leader labeled Ted Healy and His Stooges. When sound arrived, the four made the Fox feature *Soup to Nuts* (1930), but Shemp, attracted by the prospect of a solo ▶▶

career, left and was replaced by his younger brother, Jerry "Curly" Howard (1903-1952). But when the Stooges eventually split from Ted Healy, they developed, under the auspices of Columbia's short-subject comedy department, their collective image of klutzy misfits stuck in dead-end jobs and always at each other's throats. From 1934 to 1944, their two-reel films, directed mainly by slapstick veteran Del Lord, allowed them to perfect their individual personae—brash and in-your-face braggart Moe, spaced-out schlemiel Larry and boyishly inane airhead Curly. This weird hot-and-cold chemistry allowed them to produce their best work, which includes *Pop Goes the Easel* (1935), *Uncivil Warriors* (1935) and *Wee Wee Monsieur* (1938). The production values of these movies were even better than what Laurel and Hardy were getting from Hal Roach's Studio. But Harry Cohn, Columbia's feared boss, continued to lead the trio to believe with each successive contract negotiation that he was doing them a big favor when, in fact, their films were very profitable—and continue to be so today for Sony Pictures. In 1947, the Stooges' fortunes changed dramatically when Curly retired after a stroke. His brother Shemp, who had stepped in earlier to replace him, became a Stooge ▶▶

▼ CURLY HOWARD
UNCIVIL WARRIORS (1935, Columbia)

Two-reel comedy directed by Del Lord ● During the Civil War, northern agents 12 (**Larry Fine**, far right), 14 (**Moe Howard**, second from right) and 15 (**Curly Howard**, center) are ordered to pose as southern officers Duck, Dodge and Hyde. Their mission is to reach the mansion of Colonel Butts (**Bud Jamison**, left) and obtain information on the enemy's future moves. Every-thing seems to be going according to plan until a counter-intelligence officer (**Si Jenks**, second from left) starts asking questions. Telling 14 that he has just encountered his wife, 15 disguises himself as his loving mate, Mrs. Dodge (**photo**). When the officer adds that he has also met 14's father, 12 excuses himself and reappears masquerading as Dodge's dad (right). When finally he mentions that he has also seen his son, 14 brings back a cute black baby wrapped in a blanket.

▲ THE THREE STOOGES
WEE WEE MONSIEUR (1938, Columbia)

Two-reel comedy directed by Del Lord ● The Stooges, impecunious artists living in Paris, get into a fistfight with their landlord to whom they owe 10 months rent. Looking for help to go back to the States, they enroll unwillingly in the French Foreign Legion and are sent to North Africa. Their first mission is to free General Gorgonzola who has been kidnapped by a rebel sultan (Vernon Dent). Dressed as Santa Clauses, they sneak into the enemy's fortress. When the sultan, who wants to extract strategic information from the general, brings him to the harem, he asks the girls to dance for them. **Curly, Moe** and **Larry** join oafishly in the performance (**photo**), and after knocking out the sultan and his eunuch (**John Lester Johnson**, second from left), bring the general back to camp.

▼ LARRY FINE
HIGHER THAN A KITE (1943, Columbia)

Two-reel comedy directed by Del Lord ● The Stooges, who came to England hoping to join the RAF as pilots, have wound up as grease monkeys at the airport motor pool. After mutilating the colonel's automobile, they escape the officer's wrath by hiding in a sewer pipe, not realizing that it is a bomb headed for Germany. When the blockbuster lands unexploded on Marshall Bommel's (**Vernon Dent,** second from right) headquarters, **Moe** and **Curly** disguise themselves in German uniforms while **Larry** dresses as Carmen Miranda (**photo**). The lubricous Nazi starts courting Larry who steals some strategic plans that the marshall and his aide (**Dick Curtis,** far right) have been studying. The Stooges make a clean getaway.

▼ THE THREE STOOGES
NUTTY BUT NICE (1940, Columbia)

Two-reel comedy directed by Jules White ● Singing waiters at Ye Colonial Inn, the Stooges overhear two doctors conversing about the terminal sadness of one of their patients, a little girl whose father is missing. The boys ask the physicians if they can visit her and make her laugh. When **Larry, Moe** and **Curly** arrive at the hospital dressed as young girls in skirts with bows in their hair (**photo**), their antics fail to make the poor tyke even smile. To cure her malaise, the Stooges decide to find the father. While searching all over the city and bungling their investigation, by chance they find out that the man is a prisoner of thugs. After the trio frees him from the abductors, the little girl's face bursts out in a grin.

▲ LARRY FINE
ALL THE WORLD'S A STOOGE (1941, Columbia)

Two-reel comedy directed by Del Lord ● At the dawn of WWII, New York socialite Lotta Bullion (**Lelah Tyler**) convinces her husband, Ajax (**Emory Parnell**) to take home child refugees. When Mr. Bullion discovers the Stooges crouched in the back seat of his limousine, he gets the idea of transforming the trio into a girl, Mabel (**Larry**) and two boys: Frankie (**Curly,** second from right) and Johnnie (**Moe,** far right). He then introduces them as refugees to his wife, but her delight is short lived when the Stooges start displaying their natural misbehavior. At the party organized in their honor, they create such chaos that Mr. Bullion forces them out the window.

▲ CURLY HOWARD
MOVIE MANIACS (1936, Columbia)

Two-reel comedy directed by Del Lord ● In Hollywood, Fuller Rath (Bud Jamison), general manager of Carnation Pictures, is informed that three executives will be arriving to restructure the studio. When three aspiring actors—Moe, Larry and Curly—show up, they are mistaken for the East Coast suits and given full control over production. On stage 7, they create such pandemonium that director Cecil Z. Sweinhardt (Harry Semels) and his cast angrily quit. Without missing a beat, Moe takes over the helmer's job, **Larry** appropriates the leading man's part and **Curly** replaces the female star (**photo**), much to the bewilderment of the crew. The insanity ends when the honchos arrive. The boys get away by the skin of their teeth, unaware that a studio-owned lion is inside the car they have just borrowed.

◀ **CURLY HOWARD**
MATRI-PHONY (1942, Columbia)

Two-reel comedy directed by Harry Edwards ● When Emperor Octopus Grabus (**Vernon Dent,** bottom left) of Erysipelas decides to get married, he orders all redheads ages 18 to 22 to report to the palace. One of the potentials, Diana (Marjorie Deanne), is pursued by officers of the law and takes shelter in a pottery shop operated by Moedicus (**Moe,** top, right), Curlycue (**Curly,** bottom, right) and Larrycus (**Larry,** top, left). To protect the girl, Curlycue dresses as a not-too-ravishing redhead (**photo**) and goes to the palace with his buddies. The coquettish impersonator plays a game of hide-and-seek that whets the appetite of the tyrant. But the guards get wise to the disguise and take the trio into custody.

◀ **THE THREE STOOGES**
RHYTHM AND WEEP (1946, Columbia)

Two-reel comedy directed by Jules White ● Jobless musicians, the Three Stooges decide to jump from the roof of a New York skyscraper. There they meet three young female dancers with identically sad intentions. It could be the beginning of a beautiful friendship, but the two threesomes are too desperate to change their plans…until they discover on the same roof a jolly old man (Jack Norton) playing the piano. He introduces himself as Mr. Boyce, a millionaire casting a new Broadway show. After he offers parts to everyone, the Stooges and their companions forget about suicide and meet the day after in a rehearsal theatre. There, **Larry, Moe** and **Curly** present a routine dressed as overweight dancers (**photo**) and the girls perform a gracious ballet. After an army skit that has Mr. Boyce in stitches, he is so impressed that he doubles everybody's salary. But two muscle men from a nuthouse stop the proceedings and forcibly help Mr. Boyce make his exit.

◀ **CURLY HOWARD**
MICRO-PHONIES (1945, Columbia)

Two-reel comedy directed by Edward Bernds ● Handymen at a recording studio, the Stooges have fun when Curly, disguised as a woman, lip-synchs a song taped by a female singer. Mrs. Bixby (Symona Boniface), a radio sponsor, is so impressed by her voice, that she hires the trio to perform at a party. To repeat their act, the boys steal the demo copy left at the studio but Moe accidentally breaks it. Mrs. Bixby's daughter, Alicia (Christine McIntyre), recognizes the handymen and reveals that she is the singer on the demo. Now she wants to submit it to her mother anonymously and get a spot on her show. To get the Stooges out of trouble, she hides behind a curtain and sings live for **Curly,** who this time is dressed as a Spanish opera singer (**photo**). All seems to go well until a rival entertainer (**Gino Corrado,** far right) alerts the guests to the scam. The Stooges barely escape unscathed while Alicia's dream of singing on her mom's program is fulfilled.

◀ **THE THREE STOOGES**
SELF-MADE MAIDS (1950, Columbia)

Two-reel comedy directed by Jules White ● Artists Larry, Moe and Shemp fall for models Larraine (**Larry White,** left), Moella (**Moe Howard,** center) and Shempetta (**Shemp Howard,** right) and want to wed them. But obviously they need to ask for their hand in marriage. After the first encounter with the girls' father (Moe Howard also) turns into more of a collision than a meeting, the outraged dad returns to his apartment with very negative thoughts. It is only after a chase ending with a feet-tickling session that the boys get paternal consent. About a year later, three ugly babies are born: Larry, Moe and Shemp—juniors all.

▼ THE THREE STOOGES & BENNY RUBIN
BLUNDER BOYS (1955, Columbia)

Two-reel comedy directed by Jules White ● Feeling they are natural born detectives, Halliday (Moe), Tarraday (Larry) and St. Patrick's Day (Shemp) enroll in a criminology school from which they graduate with the lowest possible honors. Now ready for their first case, the bumbling trio is assigned to keeping tabs on the Eel (**Benny Rubin**), a mobster who operates in the guise of an old woman (**left photo**). The gumshoes spot the cross-dressing criminal at the Biltless Hotel but then loose track of him. Hunting through every room, they enter the women's Turkish bath and are forced to exit inconspicuously masquerading as female customers wearing turbans and robes (**right photo**). Too slippery for the three private investigators, the Eel escapes. Their dream shattered, Halliday, Tarraday and St. Patrick's Day become ditch-diggers, a job where every day is labor day.

▲ LARRY FINE
KNUTZY KNIGHTS (1954, Columbia)

Two-reel comedy directed by Jules White ● King Arthur (Vernon Dent) summons troubadours **Shemp, Larry** and **Moe.** Their mission: to entertain his daughter, Princess Elaine (Christine McIntyre), whose hand has been pledged to the Black Prince (Phil Van Zandt) but whose heart belongs to Cedric (Jacques O'Mahoney), the town's blacksmith. Unfortunately, the skit in which **Larry** plays the part of a lady (**photo**) who can't marry the man she loves prompts no laughs from the princess but only tears. When the boys later learn the prince's plan of killing the monarch after the wedding in order to take over the kingdom, they interfere and with the help of the muscular Cedric rout the forces of evil. Acknowledging his past mistake, King Arthur gives Elaine's hand to her beloved blacksmith.

▲ LARRY FINE
FIDDLER'S THREE (1948, Columbia)

Two-reel comedy directed by Jules White ● In Coleslaw-vania, King Cole (Vernon Dent) is entertained by three court fiddlers who act out nursery rhymes in which **Larry Fine** plays Little Miss Muffett (**photo**). When **Moe**, Larry and Shemp ask permission to marry the three handmaidens of Princess Alicia (Virginia Hunter), the King asks the Stooges to wait until his daughter marries Prince Galiant III of Rhododendron. Overhearing this plan, evil magician Mergatroyd (Phil Van Zandt), who wants to wed the fair lady in order to succeed King Cole, kidnaps her but promises he'll make the princess appear in his magic box in exchange for her hand. By pure luck, the Stooges locate and free Alicia. Taking her place in the magic box, they expose the magician for the fraud he is.

▶▶ bereft of grace but full of willingness to be Moe's passive victim: nobody has been slapped, poked, hit and yelled at as much as he on screen. He endured this abuse during 76 short subjects—from *Fright Night* (1947) to *Commotion in the Ocean* (released in 1956). When he died of a heart attack in 1955, mild-mannered Joe Besser took his spot in the trio. By then the farce factory directed by short-subjects department head Jules White had lost its luster. At the end of 1957, Columbia did not renew the Stooges' contract and Moe Howard, Larry Fine and Joe Besser became jobless. Moe and Larry planned to tour the country with an act built around their repertoire and hired hefty "Curly Joe" De Rita to replace Besser. But around that time their short comedies, now shown on television in all major markets, propelled them to fame. In 1959, Columbia, the studio that had canned them two years prior, offered to star them in a feature film, *Have Rocket Will Travel.* Other movies and personal appearances followed for more than a decade until Larry suffered a paralyzing stroke in January 1970, forcing the trio to retire. When Moe died in 1975, the Three Stooges' shin-kicking humor was finally laid to rest. ●

MORE KINGS
OF SHORTS

◄ GAYLORD PENDLETON
PIE A LA MAID (1938, Columbia)
Two-reel comedy directed by Del Lord ●
Waitress, Mary (Ann Doran) confuses Steve (**Charley Chase,** left) with a masher and throws a pie in his face. As a result, she is fired–and Steve is intrigued. The following day, as he consults foot specialist Dr. Kornbloom, he is surprised to discover that the physician's new secretary is none other than Mary. Smilingly, but with revenge for the pie incident on her mind, she invites Steve to come to her place that evening. In order to embarrass him, she asks her brother (**Gaylord Pendleton**) to disguise himself as her older sister and flirt with her guest. The trick works initially but soon Steve is on to the charade. While he tries to find a way to get even, the real masher, who has found Mary's address, interrupts him. Courageously assaulting the tough guy and neutralizing him, Steve is rewarded with a tender kiss from Mary.

► EDDIE FOY, JR.
DANCE, DUNCE, DANCE
(1945, Columbia)
Two-reel comedy directed by Jules White ● Eddie (**Eddie Foy, Jr.**) is an actor desperately trying to support his preteen daughter, his dog and himself. An attempt to get a job at Miracle Studios succeeds when Executive Producer B.O. Perkins (Jack Norton) agrees to see him. After Eddie arrives, he is surprised to see Perkins undressed and soon discovers that he has been confused with the executive's new masseur. Eddie quickly flees the office, takes refuge in the property room and disguising himself as a chorus girl (**photo**), gets involved in the shooting of a movie. Perkins, who is attending the filming, recognizes the actor and enjoys watching him dance with the girls so much that he signs him to a long-term contract on the spot.

► LEON ERROL
HOME WORK (1942, RKO)
Two-reel comedy directed by Ray D'Arcy ● Learning that a process server is waiting for him at the office, Leon (**Leon Errol**) stays at home. To remain incognito, he disguises himself as his own wife (**photo**), wearing her clothes and performing household chores. Regrettably, he is hassled by a vacuum cleaner salesman, a radio mechanic (**Tom Kennedy,** right) and finally, in spite of his masquerade, the process server himself.

◄ BEN BLUE
BRING 'EM BACK A WIFE (1933, Hal Roach)
Two-reel comedy directed by Del Lord with Billy Gilbert (right).

▲ IRVIN S. COBB
NOSED OUT
(1934, Hal Roach)
Two-reel comedy directed by Hal Yates with Benny Baker (left) and Frank Darien (right).

◄ ROSCOE KARNS
BLACK EYES AND BLUES
(1941, Columbia)
Two-reel comedy directed by Jules White with Don Beddoe (right).

► FRANK SULLY
KISS AND WAKE UP
(1942, Columbia)
Two-reel comedy directed by Jules White.

▲ EL BRENDEL
YUMPIN' YIMINY (1941, Columbia)
Two-reel comedy directed by Jules White with Fred Kelsey (left).

◄ CLIFF EDWARDS
STOP, SADIE, STOP
(1933, MGM)
Two-reel comedy written by Harry Sauber ● This short film, unfortunately never released and probably lost, is a parody of Lewis Milestone's 1932 tropical film *Rain*. In it, **Ted Healy** (left) reprises the part of puritanical missionary Rev. Davidson, played by Walter Huston, while **Cliff Edwards** spoofs in drag the role of loose woman Sadie Thompson, portrayed by Joan Crawford.

THE SHOW
...and so must tutus and tap shoes
MUST GO ON

◀ **FRED MACMURRAY**
SING YOU SINNERS
(1938, Paramount)

Bittersweet musical comedy directed by Wesley Ruggles ● The Depression Era Beebe brothers are as different as the times are hard. Wastrel Joe (Bing Crosby) has a taste for a "sure thing" while earnest David (**Fred MacMurray**) wants to save money and get married. Because of Joe's laziness, David provides for everyone, including his mother and his little brother Mike (Donald O'Connor). The only thing that keeps the family afloat is the brothers' singing trio. After forcing David to repeatedly postpone his marriage due to a series of hare-brained schemes, Joe goes to California to make good. When he wins at the racetrack, he buys a horse, rents a house and asks his mom and young brother to join him. Hopeful, David follows with his girlfriend only to learn they are to be evicted. The brothers fall back on their act, the high point of which is their rendition of Hoagy Carmichael's "Small Fry" with David as Granny (**photo**). But they are really hoping for Joe's horse, with neophyte Mike as jockey, to win the derby. After crooks pay Mike to throw the race, Uncle Gus comes in first anyhow. David rescues Joe and Mike from the race-fixers' beating and the trio returns to singing.

▲ **HARPO & CHICO MARX**
A NIGHT AT THE OPERA (1935, MGM)

Edge-of-madness burlesque directed by Sam Wood ● In Milan, nutty dealmaker Otis B. Driftwood (Groucho Marx) convinces social climber Mrs. Claypool (Margaret Dumont) to invest $200,000 in an opera company. Run by Herman Gottlieb (Sig Rumann), it headlines tenor Rodolfo Laspari (Walter King) and soprano Rosa Castaldi (Kitty Carlisle). Sailing to New York, Driftwood shares a cabin with stowaways—singer Ricardo Barone (Allan Jones), his agent Fiorello (**Chico Marx,** far right) and Laspari's ex-dresser, Tomaso (**Harpo Marx,** second from left). A dozen crewmembers join them and soon are pouring out of the room. On arrival, the stowaways take refuge in Driftwood's hotel room and learn that Laspari, enraged at having been rejected by Rosa, plans to use her understudy instead. Gottlieb fires Driftwood who along with Fiorello and Tomaso decides to sabotage the Met performance of Verdi's *Il trovatore*. After disabling the orchestra, destroying the set and confusing the cast by joining the chorus in drag (**photo**), they lock Laspari in a trunk. His lead missing, Gottlieb begs Ricardo to replace him and for Rosa to return. Two stars are born.

▶ WALLY VERNON
MOUNTAIN MUSIC (1937, Paramount)

Sweet and intermittently funny comedy directed by Robert Florey ● A victim of amnesia caused by a blow to the head, and then revived by water, Bob Burnside (Bob Burns) is wandering around Monotony, Arkansas, when he meets and falls for Mary Beamish (**Martha Raye,** right). Happy to have found a man who thinks she is attractive, the aspiring entertainer takes him to the annual Monotony Amateur Show where she does a song-and-dance number with her teacher, a male artist who performs in drag under the pseudonym of Odette Potts (**Wally Vernon**). Their comical interpretation of "Good Morning, Good Morning"—with the pair in matching outfits (**photo**)—is a rousing success. But when Bob is splashed with water, he fails to recognize Mary. Zigzagging between remembering and not remembering, Bob enlists Mary's help in saving the life of his brother (John Howard) who had been accused of killing him.

▶ MAXIE ROSENBLOOM, SHEMP HOWARD & BILLY GILBERT
TROUBLE CHASERS (1945, Monogram)

Anemically budgeted comedy directed by Lew Landers ● Taxi driver Tommy Young (Carlyle Blackwell, Jr.) is released from prison after serving time for a necklace robbery for which he claims he is innocent. Reuniting with his not-too-brainy pals, lousy boxer **Maxie Rosenbloom** (left of center), his manager **Billy Gilbert** (right of center) and his trainer **Shemp Howard** (center)—he finds that the real culprits have lost the jewelry and think that Billy Gilbert knows where it is hidden. The robbers intimidate Gilbert into revealing a secret he does not have until the notorious Goldie (Barbara Pepper) gives him the necklace she has stolen but that no fence wants to touch. A hangdog Billy informs Tommy who wants to frame the greaseballs to clear his name. At the Diamond Club, waiting for the cops to intervene, Maxie, Billy and Shemp, are forced to hide in a line of chorus girls, dancing heavy-footedly in full drag (**photo**). When the thugs are arrested, Tommy is exonerated and Billy gets the insurance company's reward.

▶ WALLY BROWN & ALAN CARNEY
RADIO STARS ON PARADE (1945, RKO)

Slapdash comedy about radio's golden days directed by Leslie Goodwins ● In early '40s-Hollywood, bumbling comedians Jerry Miles (**Wally Brown,** left) and Mike Strager (**Alan Carney,** center) become through no talent of their own managers of fledgling singer Sally Baker (Frances Langford). Miraculously they land her a job on bandleader Skinnay Ennis's radio show. While clumsily babysitting their future star, they become involved in the taping of several programs and wind up in the disguise segment of *Truth or Consequences.* **Ralph Edwards** (right), the show's host, asks one of them to impersonate a modern girl, the other an old maid. Mercilessly ridiculed by Edwards (**photo**), the buxom duo nevertheless succeeds in amusing the audience. Later, back in civvies, they witness the success of Sally Baker, still their only client.

◀ ARTHUR TREACHER, WALTER CATLETT & STERLING HOLLOWAY
STAR SPANGLED RHYTHM
(1942, Paramount)

All-star wartime fantasy directed by George Marshall ● Whenever sailor Jimmy Webster (Eddie Bracken) calls his father (Victor Moore), a gatekeeper at Paramount Studios, switchboard girl Polly (Betty Hutton) makes him proud of the old gent by inventing a string of promotions for him. After Polly, who is in love with Jimmy, learns that he and some naval buddies are in Los Angeles on leave, she forces his unassuming dad to impersonate the out-of-town studio überboss. Ensconcing him in the lot's head office, she leaves everybody bewildered. The stars come out when Jimmy's pop and Polly convince a lineup of big-time actors such as Bing Crosby, Bob Hope, Alan Ladd, Fred MacMurray, Franchot Tone and Rochester to put on an impromptu show for the sailors. One of the songs is a drag parody (**photo**) of the hit "A Sweater, a Sarong and a Peek-a-Boo Bang" with **Arthur Treacher** (as Paulette Goddard, left), **Walter Catlett** (as Dorothy Lamour, center) and **Sterling Holloway** (as Veronica Lake, right).

▶ JIMMY NERVO, CHARLIE NAUGHTON & JIMMY GOLD
OKAY FOR SOUND
(1937, Gainsborough)

Ensemble comedic madness directed by Marcel Varnel ● Mr. Goldberg (Fred Duprez), owner of a British movie studio, is looking for financial help. While he convinces a banker Mr. Rigby to bring some associates to his soundstages, one of his underlings hires a group of six eccentric street musicians, The Crazy Gang, as extras. Dressed as businessmen, the gang is taken for investors and surprised by Mr. Goldberg's deference. Next, they attend the shooting of *Okay for Sound* and after the filming of a 17th-century ballet scene disrupt the proceedings by having three from their group (**Jimmie Nervo**, left; **Charlie Naughton**, second from left; **Jimmy Gold**, right) dance in drag (**photo**) in a skit with **Teddy Knox** (second from right). Apoplectic, the director quits, but the gang finishes the movie just as the real investors show up. When their scenes are screened at the film's premiere, the public is so delirious that Mr. Goldberg gets Mr. Rigby's cash infusion. To reward the gang, Goldberg sends them back to the streets of London.

FROM BLACK FACE TO WHITE CHRISTMAS

▲ BING CROSBY
DIXIE (1942, Paramount)

Sanitized biography of Dan Emmett, insensitive inventor of the minstrel show directed by A. Edward Sutherland ● In New Orleans, before the Civil War, amateur singer Dan Emmett (**Bing Crosby**) and card cheat/musician Mr. Bones (Billy De Wolfe) try to eke out a living. After a fistfight in a restaurant over an unpaid bill, they go back to their boarding house with shiners. There the owner tells his tenants that he has gotten them a gig at the Maxwell Theatre. His daughter, Millie (Dorothy Lamour), suggests that to cover their black eyes they smear burnt cork on their faces and go on stage as "darkies." Emmet and Bones accept the idea, thereby creating the first minstrel show. Soon successful, Emmett writes all the music and lyrics for his revues in which he personally performs with the Virginia Minstrels, his blackfaced troupe of musicians and singers. He does not neglect comic relief, however, introducing drag skits (**photo**) that please his ever-growing audience and composes "Dixie," a song that becomes forever identified with the South.

▲ BING CROSBY & DANNY KAYE
WHITE CHRISTMAS (1954, Paramount)

Comedy weaving Irving Berlin tunes into a sentimental plotline directed by Michael Curtiz ● At the end of WWII, Private Phil Davis (**Danny Kaye**, right) and Captain Bob Wallace (**Bing Crosby**, left) become a hot song-and-dance team. Impressed by the singing talent of sisters Betty (Rosemary Clooney) and Judy (Vera-Ellen), the men befriend them. When the gals need to avoid the process server, Phil and Bob fill in for them, lip-synching one of their songs in impromptu drag (**photo**). The next gig for Betty and Judy being in a Vermont inn, Phil and Bob join them. There they learn that their former general (Dean Jagger) owns the establishment, which is being driven to bankruptcy by the lack of snow. Bob plans to do a plea on television for their old regiment to reunite at the inn for Christmas. But when Betty, who has fallen for him, hears—falsely—that he plans to broadcast the show for profit, she leaves. Upon seeing Bob's moving television appeal, however, she returns. More than a hundred soldiers arrive on the holiday with their wives for a celebration that includes a rendering of "White Christmas."

◄ **DENNIS PRICE**
CHARLEY MOON (1956, British Lion)
Overly sentimental musical comedy directed by Guy Hamilton ● In the army, country boy Charley Moon (**Max Bygraves,** seated) meets Harold Armytage (**Dennis Price,** far right), a would-be actor whose hamminess amuses him. When they are demobilized, Harold asks Charley to partner with him in a singing duo. Hired for a stage version of *Mother Goose,* Harold plays the eponymous part in a down-covered bird suit. Theatre director Monty Brass (Newton Blick) is so impressed by Charley's natural talent that he offers him a role costarring with Angel Dream (**Shirley Eaton,** center) in *Cinderella.* Charley accepts on the condition that Harold also be given a part in the production. Mr. Brass agrees but during a rehearsal Harold, who plays a lady in waiting (**photo**), has an argument with the director and is fired. Now alone, Charley gets the lead in a West-end version of *Golden Boy* and reaches star status. When he meets the still unsuccessful Harold, he his stunned to realize that his former partner is happier than he is. Charley then decides that he is through with the theatre and returns home to his waiting sweetheart.

▶ **OSCAR LEVANT & DAVID WAYNE**
THE I DON'T CARE GIRL (1953, Fox)
Musical faux-biography directed by Lloyd Bacon ● Producer George Jessel (himself) wants to make a movie about Eva Tanguay (Mitzi Gaynor), a forgotten show- business star of the early 20th century. To uncover the real woman she was underneath all the fluff, he asks two underlings to interview her contemporaries. They first meet song-and-dance man Eddie McCoy (**David Wayne,** right) who discovered her, then pianist Charlie Bennett (**Oscar Levant,** left) who introduced her to her husband, Larry Woods. Their conflicting testimonies agree only when it comes to their description—and the flashback reenactment of the outrageously anachronistic shows they performed with Eva. The productions includes a campily futuristic Florenz Ziegfield revue in which Eva plays the "I Don't Care Girl," while Charlie and Eddie impersonate hatchet-wielding decency league matrons (**photo**).

◄ **JAMES COCO**
THE WILD PARTY
(1975, American International)
Cautionary tale about fame's fragility directed by James Ivory ● In 1929 Hollywood, Jolly Grimm (**James Coco**), a rotund comic who headlined in early silent farces where he played all sorts of characters, from an oafish torero to a clownish 18th-century French noblewoman tormented by revolutionaries (**photo**), has been idle for five years. To reconquer fame, he throws a lavish party at his palatial mansion, Casa Alegria, to screen a new film he has written, produced and directed. Jolly's hopes are shattered when the guests deride the movie—a ridiculous attempt at mixing pathos and slapstick—as well as the acting talent of Jolly himself, who plays Father Jasper, a monk struggling with his faith. As the party degenerates into an orgy, the former star makes a drunken fool of himself after learning that his lover, Queenie (Raquel Welch), is having sex with a young actor (Perry King). Jolly's final performance is to shoot his beautiful innamorata to death.

◄**MAX DELYS & TANO CIMAROSA**
BREAD AND CHOCOLATE
(Italian title "Pane e Cioccolata,"
1973, Verona Productions)

Heartbreaking comedy about immigration and culture clash directed by Franco Brusati ● Nino Garofoli (**Nino Manfredi,** center) has left Naples to work as a waiter in Geneva. When the police catch him urinating in the street, Nino is fired. An industrialist offers him a job, unfortunately just before dying. Nino then moves to a migrant worker shelter where one evening he joins in a music show with chums Gigi (**Tano Cimarosa,** right) and Renzo (**Max Delys,** left) masquerading as singers Gigia and Rosina (**photo**). Still a fish out of water, Nino takes a job at a chicken farm where some illegal aliens toil for a Swiss-German family. He rejects this pitiable life and back in the city dyes his hair blond to fit in better. Ejected from a bar for cheering on the Italian team during a televised soccer match, he is deported. On the train, upon hearing his fellow Italians singing about sun, sea and laziness, he pulls the emergency cord and walks back into Switzerland.

▶ **DICK VAN DYKE**
THE COMIC (1969, Columbia)

Feeble homage to silent film clowns directed by Carl Reiner ● In the early '20s, vaudevillian Billy Bright (**Dick Van Dyke**) is hired by director Frank Powers (Cornel Wilde) to act in a string of slapstick shorts with leading lady Mary Gibson (Michele Lee). While developing a screen persona–a cross between Harry Langdon and Stan Laurel– Bright steals Mary away from Powers and rises to stardom with hits such as *Nothing but the Tooth.* Success allows him to form his own company but also brings its avatars: egotism and womanizing. On the set of a Civil War send-up where he plays an ingénue in full drag (**photo**), Bright is caught by his pregnant wife Mary kissing his partner. She forgives his indiscretion but ultimately leaves him on the night of his greatest triumph, the premiere of *Forget Me Not,* in which he has added pathos to his usual shtick. Depressed, but still full of himself, Bright rejects the talkies and, soon after, the industry rejects him. A broken man, he dies blaming his peers for his own self-destruction.

▶ **MICHEL SERRAULT**
THE KINGS OF GAGS (French title "Les rois du gag," 1985, Film 7)

Less than scintillating Gallic showbiz farce directed by Claude Zidi ● The star of a weekly television comedy, Gaëtan (**Michel Serrault**), decides to rejuvenate his show. He discovers two unknown comics, François (Thierry Lhermitte) and Paul (Gérard Jugnot), and hires them as writers and second bananas. Unfortunately, the pair comes up with the lamest of skits. In one, *The Tavern*, Gaëtan impersonates a female singer

(**photo**) whose beauty triggers a fight among pirates. Watching the performance is the most revered filmmaker alive, Robert Wellson (also Michel Serrault). Feeling a talented actor is hiding inside Gaëtan, he offers him the lead role in his next project. Shocked, Gaëtan drops his show and cuts loose his writers. But during the post-apocalyptic tale's shooting, Wellson realizes Gaëtan does not have enough gravitas. Fired, Gaëtan plans to commit suicide but François and Paul, who want their jobs back, dissuade him by rattling off a few fairly funny jokes.

▲ THE SHOW
OF SHOWS
(1929, Warner)
Plotless musical
revue directed by
John G. Adolfi in
which Willie Lightner
(ninth from left)
interprets "Singing
in the Bathtub"
joined by 16 bathing
beauties.

► IRISH EYES
ARE SMILING
(1944, Fox)
Sweetened biopic
of composer Ernest
Ball directed by
Gregory Ratoff with
June Haver (center)
as "Irish" O'Neill.

◄ PAPER LION
(1968, United
Artists)
Sports comedy
directed by Alex
March featuring
a chorus line
of football players.

◄ RANDY QUAID
KINGPIN (1996, Rysher Entertainment)

Lampoon of bowling-bums-on-a-bummer directed by Peter & Bobby Farrelly ● When tyro bowler Roy Munson (Woody Harrelson) beats veteran Ernie McCracken (Bill Murray) in a championship, Ernie hides his anger and encourages Roy to join in a hustle of some locals. The losers mangle Munson's arm in a ball return machine and the now crippled athlete spends the next 17 years eking out a living. He sees salvation in the talents of Amish bowler Ishmael (**Randy Quaid**) who must help his family fight their farm's foreclosure. After winning a jackpot, the two join female grifter Claudia (Vanessa Angel). En route to a tournament in Reno, Ishmael overhears Roy and Claudia making fun of him and going off on his own becomes a stripper in drag (**photo**) in a lap dancing bar. The trio reunites but things look dark when Ishmael injures his hand trying to punch out Ernie. Roy is forced to bowl with his prosthetic rubber hand against this old enemy and loses the final match. Afterwards, however, he gets a big check for endorsing condoms and gives most of it to Ishmael to rescue his farm.

▶ RICHARD PRYOR
JOJO DANCER, YOUR LIFE IS CALLING (1986, Columbia)

A death-is-easy-but-comedy-is-difficult film directed by Richard Pryor ● Jo Jo Dancer (**Richard Pryor**), a comedian at the peak of his fame, is hospitalized for burns incurred while free-basing. Delirious, he revisits his past in flashbacks, beginning with his upbringing in an Ohio brothel and his first gig at Club Shalimar in Cleveland. It was there that he began defining his irreverent style by impersonating his female costar (**photo**), stripper Satin Doll (Paula Kelly). Jo Jo's corrosive humor and his politically incorrect racial innuendos soon make him a smash in nightclubs, eventually opening the door to television and film. At the same time, the pressures of show business drive the insecure performer into the fast lane where alcohol, hard drugs and debauchery seem to solve all his problems. After reviewing 40 roller-coaster years, the comic decides to fight for his life and—thanking God—to savor his redemption.

◄ BILLY CRUDUP
STAGE BEAUTY (2004, Lions Gate)

Handsomely crafted tale of ambition, celebrity and gender confusion directed by Richard Eyre ● With the British theater dictating that only male actors can play women's roles, Edward "Ned" Kynaston (**Billy Crudup**) has become the Restoration's biggest female star. He has a charming female dresser, Maria Hughes (Claire Danes), who is secretly enamored as well as envious of him. Unbeknownst to Ned, she has been performing his famous role, Desdemona, at the Cockpit Tavern. King Charles II (Rupert Everett), meanwhile, is being goaded by his stage-struck mistress, Nell (Zoë Tapper), to allow women on the boards. When Ned insults Nell, the king rules that only women must play female roles. His career in shambles, Ned is reduced to appearing in lewd pub acts. Maria, now a stage star, tries to make him a man. Unfortunately Ned's haughtiness gets in the way, both then and when he is called upon to help her with her legitimate Desdemona debut. Still unsure of his sexuality, he nevertheless takes on the part of Othello, and with two hearts beating as one, the applause is deafening.

THE TOP BANANA BUNCH

Carmen Miranda and her tutti-frutti mimics

MICKEY ROONEY
BABES ON BROADWAY (1941, MGM)

Lets-put-on-a-show musical comedy directed by Busby Berkeley ● After being rebuffed by Broadway producer Thornton Reed (James Gleason), tyro entertainer Tommy Williams (**Mickey Rooney**) decides to create his own show by raising funds through a charity. He convinces the manager of the Dorman Street Settlement House, where would-be singer Penny Morris (Judy Garland) works, to endorse a Fourth of July block party to collect money for his production with the understanding is that the profits will allow the settlement house to send the children to the country for the summer. Not only is the party a hit, but Mr. Reed's assistant, Jonesy (Fay Bainter), is so impressed that she allows Tommy and the gang to use the long-closed Duchess Theatre to present their *Babes on Broadway* revue for her boss, whom she hopes will become its angel. The show opens with the number "Bombshell From Brazil" during which Tommy, outfitted as Carmen Miranda, sings "Mama iu quero" (**photo**). The musical looks doomed when a city inspector closes the theatre because it violates current fire laws. But fortunately Mr. Reed decides to bankroll Tommy and his talented teens, opening the show on the Great White Way.

Opposite: Carmen Miranda and Mickey Rooney on the set of *Babes on Broadway*, (1941, MGM).

▲ TOMMY TRINDER
FIDDLER'S THREE (1943, Ealing Studios)

British timeline-twisting fantasy directed by Harry Watt ● During World War II, two sailors on leave, Tommy (**Tommy Trinder**) and the Professor (Sonnie Hale), are bicycling in the English countryside when they have the occasion to save a Wren (Diana Decker) from a rape. A thunderstorm forces the trio to take refuge under the stone altar at Stonehenge where they are struck by lightning, which magically transports them back in time to ancient Rome. In the imperial palace, they impress Nero (**Francis L. Sullivan,** right) with their ability to predict the future. Later, Tommy impersonates a famous South American bombshell of the time, Lady Alvarez, charming the Roman ruler with her samba dancing (**photo**). Unfortunately, Nero's wife, Poppaea (**Frances Day,** center), desires Tommy's more masculine charms. When Nero discovers her lust, Tommy and his friends are thrown to the lions. At the last minute, they are saved by another stroke of lightning, which takes them back to Stonehenge.

◄ CURLY HOWARD
TIME OUT FOR RHYTHM (1941, Columbia)

Dinky musical comedy directed by Sidney Salkow ● Daniel Collins (Rudy Vallee) and Mike Armstrong (Richard Lane) run a successful talent agency thanks to Daniel's creativity. Everything is copacetic until Mike, who is in love with a modestly gifted singer named Frances Lewis (Rosemary Lane), asks Daniel to cast her as the star of the agency's new television show. Daniel has hired dancer Kitty Brown (Ann Miller) to headline the program and flatly refuses. An argument ensues, triggering the dissolution of the partnership. Later, when a movie mogul comes to town to hold auditions for Daniel's next revue, he is presented with a comic performance à la Brazil by the Three Stooges (**Larry Fine, Moe Howard** and **Curly Howard** dressed as Carmen Miranda, **photo**). Meantime, a backstage drama caused by the ambitions Frances unfolds, finally opening Mike's eyes to his inamorata's scheming nature. Mike and Daniel resume their partnership with a handshake while Kitty dances her way to stardom.

◄**MILTON BERLE**
ALWAYS LEAVE
THEM LAUGHING
(1949, Warner)
**Enjoyable but
conventional
showbusiness comedy
directed by Roy Del Ruth**
● Small-time comedian
Kip Cooper (**Milton
Berle**), notorious for
stealing other comics'
material, survives by
performing in various
dumpy Catskill venues.
One day, thanks to his
girlfriend Fay (Ruth
Roman), he is chosen to
replace the legendary
funnyman Eddie Egan
(Bert Lahr)—who has
had a heart attack—as the
star of a revue called *The
Wonder of It All* debuting
in Boston. In one of the
sketches, Kip cracks up
the audience with a
farcical impersonation of
Carmen Miranda (**photo**).
Unfortunately for the
hyped-up entertainer, a
few days before opening
on Broadway he is
informed that Egan has
recovered and will resume
his place in the show
when it hits New York.
Kip's misfortune turns
out to be a blessing
in disguise: he takes
his agent's advice
to find a style of
his own and becomes
a hit on television.

► GROUCHO MARX
COPACABANA (1947, United Artists)

Lame showbiz musical comedy directed by Alfred E. Green ● Lionel Devereaux (**Groucho Marx**), the small-time agent of Brazilian bombshell Carmen Navarro (Carmen Miranda), gets her an audition at the Copa. Owner Steve Hunt (Steve Cochran) hires her to perform in the main room, but he mentions to Lionel that he needs an additional act for the lounge–preferably a French *chanteuse*. Trying to maximize the opportunity, Lionel transforms Carmen into Mademoiselle Fifi with a *très chic* ensemble that reveals only her eyes and a repertoire of café *chansons*. Now that Carmen has both gigs, her evenings become quick-change marathons that run her down. So Lionel, in order to end the French act, pretends that the two women have had a fight and that Fifi has left. Steve, who was falling hard for her, calls the police and soon Lionel is accused of her murder. He tries to hide from the cops by borrowing one of Carmen's Brazilian costumes, but the disguise is too transparent. Arrested (**photo**), Lionel is freed by the police only when Carmen–by kissing every man present–convinces them that she is also Fifi.

► SASCHA BRASTOFF
WINGED VICTORY (1944, Fox)

Moving tribute to WWII U.S. airmen directed by George Cukor ● Ohio pals Pinky (Don Taylor), Frankie (Lon McCallister) and Allan (Mark Daniels) are elated to be inducted into the Air Force, but during the cadet's first night flight, two of the buddies are devastated by Frankie's plane crash. Upon graduating, gunner Pinky is happily assigned to the same bomber, *Winged Victory*, as his friend Allan. After a last evening in San Francisco with their women, the aviators join the fighting in the South Pacific. When a Christmas outdoor variety show is organized, **Sgt. Sascha Brastoff** (himself) impersonates Carmen Miranda dancing and lip-synching "Chica Chica Boom Chic" (**photo**). But sirens interrupt the show and the planes take off for combat. The *Winged Victory* crew returns with only one man injured, gunner Pinky who, upon landing, learns that his wife has given birth to a son. *(Another photo of the same film is shown in the chapter "Privates on Parade.")*

◄ JERRY LEWIS
SCARED STIFF (1952, Paramount)

Routine mix of comedy and terror directed by George Marshall ● Larry Todd (Dean Martin), a suave ladies man, and Myron Mertz (**Jerry Lewis**), a simpleton, are part of a duo performing in third-rate nightclubs. When Larry realizes that the chorus girl he is dating is a gangster's moll, he seriously fears for his life. So after a chance meeting with a young lady (Lizabeth Scott) who has just inherited a supposedly haunted castle on a Caribbean isle, Larry–and Myron, of course–sail with her to Cuba. On the boat, they stumble upon entertainer Carmelita Castinha (Carmen Miranda) who offers them a gig in Havana at El Caribe club. On opening night, Carmelita is so late that Myron is forced to impersonate the turbaned Brazilian bombshell, lip-synching to one of her records with disastrous but comical consequences (**photo**). After the gig, a scary visit to the castle reveals that the ghosts are the invention of a thief (William Ching), who wants for himself the gold buried there by previous owners.

▶ RICCARDO BILLI
ARRIVANO I NOSTRI
("The Cavalry Is Coming,"
1951, Excelsa Film)
**Modest but breezily entertaining
comedy directed by Mario Mat-
toli** ● Daughter of a debt-ridden
baron, Lisetta (Lisetta Nava) is in
love with Walter (Walter Chiari), a
student who works as a chauffeur
for Signore Garlandi (Carlo Rom-
ano). A shady businessman, Garlandi wants to marry Lisetta and
after acquiring her father's out-
standing notes gives him the alternative of convincing Lisetta to
marry him or of having his property
put on the block. Good daughter,

▶ DENIS QUILLEY
PRIVATES ON PARADE
(1984, Orion)
**Vivacious but unsubstantial song
and dance farce directed by
Michael Blakemore** ● Under the
supervision of Maj. Giles Flack (John
Cleese), a song-and-dance unit
based in war-torn Singapore in the
late '40s, is on tour entertaining
British troops. The group's artistic
director, Cpt. Terri Dennis (**Denis
Quilley**), loves to stage cross-dressing performances that his audiences
—puzzled natives and sex-deprived
soldiers—find impossible to compre-
hend. Dennis' favorites include an
imitation of Carmen Miranda
(**photo**), in which he sings accompanied by Sgt. Artwright (**Bruce
Payne**, left) and Bonny (**Joe Melia**,
right.) But when the troupe, which is
not without its share of interpersonal
gender-twisting dramas, is shipped
into an area held by Chinese communist guerrillas, tragedy strikes:
Sgt. Bishop (David Bamber), who
has made a deal with the Reds to
steal the Brits' munitions, kills Bonny
during a communist raid. Several
other performers are wounded
as well. When Movietone News
captures the troupe's homeward
journey, the commentary glorifies
them as "valiant" survivors. (Another
photo from the same film is shown
in the chapter "Privates on Parade.")

▶ BOB HOPE
THE ROAD TO RIO
(1947, Paramount)
Directed by Norman Z. McLeod ●
(Another photo of the film is shown
in the Bob Hope section.)

Lisetta agrees to wed the
scoundrel, but while attending a
party in her honor, she learns
that he has a mistress. To prevent
Lisetta from being sacrificed, Walter
joins forces with three vaudevillians
—among them Daniele (**Riccardo
Billi**), a Carmen Miranda-inspired
entertainer—and devises a plan
carried out with mixed results.
When all attempts have failed,
they miraculously find an expensive jewel that will allow the baron
to settle his debts. The four
buddies show up just before
Lisetta can say "I do," promptly
eject Garlandi and replace him
with an elated Walter.

▶ TED DANSON
THREE MEN AND A LITTLE LADY
(1990, Touchstone)
**Flighty sequel to a French film's remake
directed by Emile Ardolino** ● Three charming
bachelors, architect Peter (Tom Selleck), cartoonist Michael (Steve Guttenberg) and struggling actor Jack (**Ted Danson**), continue to bring
up as surrogate fathers adorable little Mary
(Robin Weisman). All is well until Mary's mother,
Sylvia (Nancy Travis), accepts a marriage
proposal and takes the five-year old with her to
London. While one of the bachelors, Jack, is off on
location shooting a film, the other doting "dads"
cross the Atlantic to bring mother and child back
home. Soon after, Jack abandons his ridiculous
role as a Carmen Miranda impersonator (**photo**)
and after interrupting the wedding ceremony
reunites the "family" of five—just before Peter
finally realizes that Sylvia is the woman of his life.

PRIVATES ON PARADE

Kiss the boys in the armed forces hello!

▲ BRUCE PAYNE, DENIS QUILLEY & JOE MELIA
PRIVATES ON PARADE (1984, Orion)

Breezy but insubstantial song and dance farce directed by Michael Blakemore ● Under the supervision of Maj. Giles Flack (John Cleese), a song-and-dance unit based in war-torn Singapore in the late '40s is on tour entertaining British troops. The group's artistic director, Captain Terri Dennis (**Denis Quilley,** center), loves to stage cross-dressing performances that his audiences—puzzled natives and sex-deprived soldiers—find incomprehensible. Dennis's favorites include an imitation of the Andrews Sisters (**photo**), in which he sings with Sgts. Artwright (**Bruce Payne,** left) and Bonny (**Joe Melia,** right). But when the carefree troupe, which is not without its share of interpersonal gender-twisting dramas, is shipped into an area held by Chinese guerrilas, tragedy strikes: Sgt. Bishop (David Bamber), who has made a deal with the Reds to steal the Brits' munitions, kills Bonny during an enemy raid. When Movietone News captures the performers' homeward journey, the commentary glorifies them as valiant survivors.

▶ ALAN HALE
THIS IS THE ARMY (1943, Warner)

Uncle Sam's "I Want You" musical directed by Michael Curtiz ● Jimmy Jones (Ronald Reagan), drafted into the service in 1942, is asked to produce a show to raise the patriotism of the general population. With the help of his father, Jerry Jones (George Murphy), who had the same assignment during World War I, Jimmy produces a lavish song-and-dance revue. Based on the flag-waving songs of Irving Berlin, *This Is the Army* features only male military personnel, with the female roles played by soldiers. A case in point is career sergeant McGhee (**Alan Hale**), whose performance in "Ladies of the Chorus" is highlighted by his clear aversion toward his powder blue dress and matching hat (**photo**). When the show ends its national tour in Washington, D.C., the cast washes off the greasepaint and ships off to battle. *(Based on two Irving Berlin shows: 1918's* Yip Yip Yaphank *and 1943's* This Is the Army.*)*

▲ HERBERT MUNDIN
EAST LYNNE ON THE
WESTERN FRONT
(1931, Gaumont)

Unapologetically lowbrow single-set farce directed by George Pearson ● In France, on a rainy day during World War I, a platoon of Brits who are billeted in an empty theatre try to make the best of a bad situation. Their ribald conversation leads to the idea of staging a play based on the classic English melodrama *East Lynne*. In need of a serious dose of fun, not one of the battle-hardened Tommies argues with what turns out to be the inspired casting of the main female part, Lady Isobel (**Herbert Mundin**, above **photo**, here shown with main man **Alf Goddard**). The melodrama is promptly transformed into burlesque where the belly laughs come more from the clumsy parading of stocky macho soldiers in frilly female garb than from the jokes full of army slang and Cockney accents.

▲ UNIDENTIFIED ACTORS IN DRAG
THE WOODEN HORSE (1950, British Lion)

Well-crafted account of a great escape directed by Jack Lee ● In the summer of 1943 at Stalag Luft III, POW John (Anthony Steel) has an idea: why not build a boxlike vaulting horse that will be placed in full view of the guards and while the officers are exercising during the day one man inside the horse will dig a tunnel? For months Peter (Leo Genn) and other volunteers excavate their way to freedom while to keep morale up Phil (Dave Tomlinson) organizes a drag revue using the dancing talents of a dozen prisoners ravaged by stage fright (**photo**). Finally, Peter and John escape and with the help of the Danish Resistance find liberty in Sweden.

▲ SIR JOHN MILLS
THE MIDSHIP MAID
(aka "Midshipmaid Gob,"
1933, Gaumont)

Cocktail of humor, music and love on a battleship directed by Albert de Courville ● Sir Percy Newbiggin (**Fred Kerr,** right) is sent to Malta to suggest drastic savings to the Royal Fleet. Accompanying him is his come-hither daughter Celia (Jessie Matthews). In their honor, an amateur concert is organized during which Midshipman Golightly (**John Mills**) performs an act dressed in a ballerina outfit much to the astonishment of Sir Percy (**photo**). The nobleman is even more shocked when he surprises Celia and Commander Ffosberry (Basil Sydney) embracing. He decides to report the incident to the First Lord of the Admiralty but learns that the ardent gentleman is none other than the First Lord's son. Consenting happily to his daughter's engagement, Sir Percy recommends leaving the Fleet's budget as it is.

◄ UNIDENTIFIED ACTORS IN DRAG

◄ UNIDENTIFIED ACTORS IN DRAG
GRAND ILLUSION (French title
"La grande illusion," 1937, Cinedis)
**Anti-war cinematic masterpiece directed by
Jean Renoir** ● In 1916, combat pilots Capitaine
de Boëldieu (Pierre Fresnay), a nobleman and
career soldier, and Lieutenant Maréchal (Jean
Gabin), a drafted mechanic, are shot down by the
Germans. As POWs, they strike up friendships
with men from all strata of society: a grouchy engi-
neer (Gaston Modot), a school teacher (Jean
Dasté), a comedian with a strong Parisian accent
called Traquet (Julien Carette), and a wealthy Jew
named Rosenthal (Marcel Dalio). All cooperate in

► MICHEL SIMON
TIRE AU FLANC
("The Malingerer," 1928, Néo Films)
**Realistically detailed comedy about
peacetime army life directed by Jean
Renoir** ● When poet Jean Dubois
d'Ombelle (Georges Pomiès) is drafted,
his loyal butler Joseph (**Michel Simon**)
volunteers to join the same regiment. The
victim of pranks at the hands of private
Muflot (Louis Zellas), Jean is sent to the
brig after being beaten by his tormentor.
He soon learns his fiancée Solange
(Jeanne Helbing) is having an affair with
Lt. Daumel. Fortunately, a visitor informs
him that Solange's younger sister, Lily
(Kinny Dorlay), is crazy about him. For the
annual regimental variety show, Jean
concocts an act in which he plays a faun
and his butler an overweight sylph
(**photo**). The number amuses Colonel
Brochard and his guests until impenitent
Muflot lights some panic-generating fire-
crackers. Furious, Jean catches the
culprit and gives him the punishment of
his life. The colonel, proud to see the
army has made a man of the poet, con-
gratulates Jean who happily marries Lily

digging an escape tunnel, hoping to rejoin their
bases. But although the war has woven a strong
bond between these men, they all know it is an illusion to believe that they will be friends forever:
their disparate social classes will ultimately prevent
their brotherhood from surviving the war. When
Rosenthal sends for theatre costumes from Paris
(**photo** above), one of the younger soldiers tries on
a wig and a dress and fascinates his comrades,
who become silent, as volumes are spoken about
life in captivity (center left **photo**). Later, the
French and English POWs organize a musical revue involving Traquet as the M.C. and presenting
several elaborately dressed male chorines (top left
photo). Upon learning that the occupied city of
Douaumont has been liberated by French troops,
Lt. Maréchal interrupts the show. The cast then
breaks into "La Marseillaise" to the furor of the
German guards. Unfortunately, before they can finish their tunnel, the prisoners are transferred to a
Gothic fortress administrated by disabled aristocrat Captain von Rauffenstein (Eric von Stroheim).
Later, Von Rauffenstein realizes that the bond tying
him to De Boëldieu, his social counterpart, does
not impair nationalist patriotism: to help Rosenthal
and Maréchal escape to Switzerland, De Boëldieu
sacrifices his life by forcing Von Rauffenstein to
shoot him to death.

◀**JACK SLATE, RED BUTTONS & HENRY SLATE**
WINGED VICTORY (1944, Fox)

Moving tribute to WWII U.S. airmen directed by George Cukor ● Ohio pals Pinky (Don Taylor), Frankie (Lon McCallister) and Allan (Mark Daniels) are elated to be inducted into the Air Force. Unfortunately, during the cadets' first night flight, Frankie's plane crashes. Upon graduating, gunner Pinky is assigned to the same bomber—*Winged Victory*—as Allan. After a last evening in San Francisco with their women, the aviators join the fighting in the South Pacific. When a variety spectacle is organized, three corporals—**Jack Slate** (left), **Red Buttons** (center) and **Henry Slate** (right)—masquerade as the Andrews Sisters in a hilariously choreographed version of "Pennsylvania Polka" (**photo**). But sirens interrupt the number and the planes take off for combat. The *Winged Victory* crew returns with one man injured, gunner Pinky who upon landing learns that his wife has given birth to a son.

◀**EDDIE FOY, JR. & BOB CROSBY**
ROOKIES ON PARADE (1941, Republic)

Barracks musical comedy directed by Joseph Santley ● Songwriters Cliff Dugan (**Eddie Foy, Jr**, left) and Duke Wilson (**Bob Crosby**, right) convince theatrical manager Augustus Moody (Sidney Blackmer) that they can compose a musical. Moody finds financing for the show, but Duke and Cliff are drafted. When Duke's fiancée, Lois (Ruth Terry), and her friend Kitty (Marie Wilson), show up at the base as entertainers, Kitty and Cliff become involved as Lois watches Duke becoming so disenchanted with his new life that he devises a scheme to produce a show for the army and share the profits with Moody. When the musical—in which Cliff and Duke appear in drag (**photo**)—begins to raise the troops' morale, Duke drops his business scheme. Lois, who overhears him expressing his change of mind, falls in love all over again.

▲ **WILLIAM BENDIX & DENNIS O'KEEFE**
ABROAD WITH TWO YANKS (1944, United Artists)

Down Under comic military escapade directed by Allan Dwan ● After fighting the Japanese in the Pacific, U.S. Marines Jeff Reardon (**Dennis O'Keefe**, far left) and Biff Koraski (**William Bendix**, second from left), plan to enjoy their furlough in Sydney. Biff is excited since he plans to meet Joyce Stuart (**Helen Walker**, far right), a young woman who wants to thank him for saving the life of Cyril North (**John Loder**, second from right), a family friend. When Jeff spots Joyce in the crowd upon their arrival, he pretends to be Biff and goes home with her. Later, aware of the misrepresentation, Biff wants revenge and sets off on a vicious series of tit-for-tats that culminate in the arrest of both Jeff and him by the MPs. Put in the brig, the two are coerced into volunteering for the Marine Follies in which they perform a song-and-dance number, "All I Need Is a Man," in drag (**right photo**). Using their costumes to bust out of prison, the rivals next crash a charity bazaar at Joyce's house, continuing their competition for the Aussie's heart (**left photo**). Unfortunately, she tells them that she has decided to marry Cyril. Gracious losers, the buddies wish the best to the betrothed and, dressed in their gowns, are escorted by the MPs to their cells.

JIMMY DURANTE
YOU'RE IN THE ARMY NOW
(1941, Warner)
Cheerful musical enlistment postcard directed by Lewis Seiler ● During WWII, a pair of vacuum cleaner salesmen, Breezy Jones (Phil Silvers) and Jeeper Smith (**Jimmy Durante**), go to the local Army recruiting station hoping to make a sale. Instead they inadvertently enlist. Almost immediately, Jeeper's zaniness gets on his sergeant's nerves and he is assigned to K.P. When spilled lemons cause his superior to fall, he chases Jeeper into the U.S.O. dressing room. Exiting as a blonde, Jeeper fools the sergeant (**Joe Sawyer,** left photo) into taking him for one of the female dancers preparing for the evening's show. Accidentally entering the stage, Jeeper rises to the occasion by aptly dancing with his *"Apache"* partner (**Anthony Caruso,** photo above). Later, Breezy and Jeeper use their salesmanship to help the amiable Capt. Radcliffe (Regis Toomey), who has been put in charge of converting the cavalry squadron into a tank unit. They succeed after creating some ruckus and in addition engineer the marriage of the captain to the colonel's daughter, Bliss (Jane Wyman).

▶ FRANK SINATRA, JULES MUNSHIN & GENE KELLY
ON THE TOWN (1949, MGM)

Dazzling musical tour de force directed by Gene Kelly & Stanley Donen ● How much fun can three American sailors cram into a one-day shore leave in Manhattan? Plenty—if they are all looking for Ms. Right. After a whirlwind tour of the Big Apple, Chip (**Frank Sinatra**, left), Ozzie (**Jules Munshin**, center) and Gabey (**Gene Kelly**, right) take the subway where they see a poster of Ivy Smith (Vera-Ellen), aka "Miss Turnstiles," and fall head over heels—especially Gabey. They instantly find her posing at the station stop for a photographer, but they lose her just as quickly and jump into a cab in pursuit. Their female driver, Brunhilde (Betty Garrett) is smitten with Chip and joins in the hunt, hoping to capture his heart. When the four follow a clue leading to the Museum of Natural History, an anthropologist, Claire (Ann Miller), catches Ozzie's eye. After he and Claire knock over a dinosaur skeleton, the police chase after the sailors, who decide to split up in their search. Gabey locates Ivy in a dance studio but, when the three couples start to paint the town she disappears again. Finding themselves at Coney Island with the cops in pursuit, Gabey, Chip and Ozzie insinuate themselves into the Rajah Bimmy's Oriental Extravaganza, transforming themselves into performing harem girls (**right photo**). Ivy, part of the troupe, reveals she was ashamed of her job as a hoochie coochie dancer and is reunited with Gabey. The women convince the police to drop charges and, with their boyfriends' leave at an end wistfully wave goodbye.

Opposite: Frank Sinatra between takes on the *On the Town* set.

◀ RAY WALSTON
SOUTH PACIFIC (1958, Fox)

Cinematic version of Rodgers & Hammerstein's musical hit directed by Josh Logan ● On a U.S.-occupied South Pacific isle during WWII, Navy nurse Nellie Forbush (**Mitzi Gaynor**, left) falls for Emile de Becque (Rossano Brazzi), a French plantation owner who gently tells her no one could fully replace his deceased wife. At the same time, Lt. Joseph Cable (John Kerr) falls in love with beautiful native girl Liat (France Nuyen), but won't commit to marriage either, angering her mother, Bloody Mary (Juanita Hall). At Thanksgiving, Nellie, in spite of a broken heart, sings "Honey Bun" for the homesick sailors. She is assisted by Luther Billis (**Ray Walston**), a smart-alecky Sea Bea dolled up as a female native complete with coconut shell-bra and grass wig (**photo**). Later, De Becque and Lt. Cable team up to locate a fleet of Japanese boats. Their mission, during which Cable is killed, saves many American lives. Upon return, the Frenchman finds Nellie taking care of his children. Marriage seems to be in the offing.

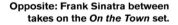

BUGLE CALL DRAG

As you wear! Gender goes on furlough

▲ TONY BILL
SOLDIER IN THE RAIN (1964, Allied Artists)

Melodramatic buddy comedy directed by Ralph Nelson ● In an army camp, wheeler-dealer Sgt. Eustis Clay (**Steve McQueen**, right) tries to convince Master Sgt. Maxwell Slaughter (Jackie Gleason) to start a business with him. Slaughter, who has a pleasant life, fears reentering the civilian world. When Eustis gets into a fistfight with two MPs, Slaughter comes to the rescue but collapses during the scuffle and is sent to the hospital. Eustis continues to dream of leaving the army and decides that a $1,000 first prize photography contest is his ticket out. Outfitting Pfc. Jerry Metzner (**Tony Bill**) as a female model in a plunging dress and mop wig, he is interrupted during the shoot by Lt. Magee (**Tom Poston**, second from left). With no time to explain the situation, Eustis is informed Slaughter's condition has worsened. He dashes through the rain to the hospital where he exchanges fantasies of future tropical vacations with Slaughter before he dies. Having finally found a home in "this stupid army," Eustis reenlists, while Pfc. Metzner, suspected of being a cross-dresser, reports for psychiatric treatment.

▶ CARY GRANT
I WAS A MALE WAR BRIDE (1949, Fox)

Witty comedy about love and red tape directed by Howard Hawks ● During a postwar mission in occupied Germany, French Army Captain Henri Rochard (**Cary Grant**) and American WAC Lieutenant Catherine Gates (Ann Sheridan) are given the same assignment: tracking down black marketeers. From the outset, they are at odds, quarreling and clashing over the pettiest of problems. But after some smooching in a haystack one pleasant afternoon their hostility morphs into love. Deciding to marry, they tie the knot just a few hours before Catherine is ordered home, and, most importantly, before they can consummate the marriage. Deciding to follow his wife to the States, Henri learns that the only way he can enter the country is through a Congressional Act governing war brides. Reluctant at first, he accepts Catherine's outrageous scheme: she borrows a female uniform, cuts the tail off a horse to create a wig and dresses Henri as a WAC, with skirt, lipstick and nylons (**photo**). The ruse works and not an instant too soon the lovers are sharing a cabin on a U.S. Navy ship bound for America.

Opposite: Cary Grant's wardrobe trial photo for *I Was a Male War Bride* (1949, Fox).

HAWKS-A556
CARY GRANT AS HENRI
Ch#9
EXT.DOCK-182-183-184-185
ON GANGPLANK-186
ON DECK-187
INT.CABIN-A-88-188
INT.CATHERINE'S CABIN-189
EXT.DECK-190-192-193
INT.NURSERY-191
EXT.UPPER DECK-194
INT.LIFE BOAT-194

W.C#1

◄ ROLAND TOUTAIN
THREE STRAYING ARTILLERYMEN
(French title "Trois artilleurs en vadrouille,"
1938, Vondas Films)

Sequel to a previous lowbrow hit directed by René Pujol ● Back for another reserve stint, Zéphitard (Pierre Larquey), Plume (Paul Azaïs) and Jacques Dancourt (**Roland Toutain**) are looking for laughs and a good time. Dancourt, however, unexpectedly falls for the colonel's daughter, Monique (**Gisèle Préville,** center). His chances of marrying the rich and beautiful girl are remote at best, Dancourt not being a wealthy enough suitor in her father's eyes. In order to propose to her, he sneaks into her boarding school dressed as a curly haired girl (**photo**), winning her heart and the envy of her schoolmates. In the end, the colonel realizes that opposing the marriage could have more unpleasant consequences than approving it and gives the young lovers his blessing.

◄ RAYMOND CORDY & NOËL-NOËL
MAM'ZELLE SPAHI (1934, Fox-France)

Saucy farce about musical beds and French dames directed by Max de Vaucorbeil ● Every night, the colonel (Saturnin Fabre) of a colonial regiment (the Spahis) tells his wife that he is participating in maneuvers. In fact, the rascal is with his mistress, sexy Aline (**Colette Darfeuil,** far left). Meanwhile, his daughter Nicole (Josette Day) is courted by Lt. Gilbert (Jean Rousselière), a ladies man who also has a hot ticket named Paulette (**Lynne Clevers,** far right). The two officers, unaware of the other's affair, have decided to break their respective liaisons. On the occasion of Nicole's engagement to Lt. Gilbert, the colonel's wife organizes a lavish party, leaving out Aline and Paulette. Miffed, the two take the uniforms of soldiers Perlot (**Raymond Cordy,** second from left) and Bréchu (**Noël-Noël,** second from right) and show up at the party to create havoc. The two Spahis have no other choice than to dress up in the girl's outfits (**photo**) and join the celebration. Fortunately, scandal is averted when Aline and Paulette accept checks from their former lovers aimed at softening the bite of rejection.

◄ FRÉDÉRIC DUVALLÈS
ONE OF THE CAVALRY (French title
"Une de la Cavalerie," 1938, BG Films)

Coarse and libidinous farce directed by Maurice Cammage ● Skirt-chaser Vigoulette (**Frédéric Duvallès**) plans to take advantage of a nine-day military training stint in Nice to escape the clutches of his henpecking wife Léonie (Suzanne Dehelly) and live it up. His buddy Poupardin (Félix Oudart), an inveterate wastrel, accompanies him for the fun of it. Quickly caught up in a cog of adventures with the local tarts, the two *amis* are unaware that Léonie, accompanied by Poupardin's daughter, have come to town to check on them. Disguised as a male soldier to enter the barracks, Léonie realizes that her husband is still out after curfew and replaces him during roll call. Meanwhile, in town, the rascal is having a good time in a bistro with some lovelies when his adjutant (**Pierre Darfeuil,** right) shows up. To avoid being recognized, he masquerades as a coquette (**photo**). In the end, everybody reconciles and Poupardin's daughter finds an attractive husband among the young officers.

ONE OF OUR AIRCRAFTS
IS MISSING
(1942, Anglo-Amalgamated)
Ode to Dutch Resistance directed by Michael Powell & Emeric Pressburger ● After raiding Stuttgart, Wellington bomber, *B for Bertie*, is shot down over Nazi-occupied Holland and the crew forced to bail out. They reunite after landing and are discovered by friendly children who take them to their village. To make sure they are not German spies posing as Brits, the schoolteacher (Pamela Brown) quizzes them. After proving their identity, they are welcomed by the burgemeister (Hay Petrie) and the parish priest (Peter Ustinov) and befriended by the population, who dress them as fellow countrymen. The one exception is navigator Frank Shelley (**Hugh Williams**), a former actor who is fitted out in traditional female Dutch garb (**photo**). Managing to avoid the occasional German patrol, the airmen are smuggled from village to village by freedom fighters. Critical to their fate is a female patriot who helps them escape in a small boat. Rescued by the British navy, the squadron reaches the coast and after a few weeks' rest is ready for a raid on Berlin.

▲ **MIKE MARSHALL**
DON'T LOOK NOW
(French title "La grande vadrouille,"
1966, Films Corona)
Hyperactive French Resistance farce directed by Gérard Oury ● In 1942, three flyers parachute to safety when their RAF bomber is gunned down over German-occupied Paris. The youngest airman, Alan McIntosh (**Mike Marshall),** lands safely on the roof of the Opera while inside irascible conductor Stanislas Lefort (Louis de Funès) rehearses the orchestra scheduled to perform that evening for Wermarcht officers. When Alan's parachute is found in Lefort's dressing room, the Germans suspect the maestro of having rescued the young Brit. Fearing arrest, Lefort flees with Alan who has been dressed up as a blond-braided country girl (**photo**) by the theatre's performers. The fugitives, joined by cowardly painter Achille Bouvet (Bourvil) and Alan's gap-toothed commander (Terry-Thomas), escape through Paris' sewage system while the third airman, Peter (Claudio Brook), takes a Burgundy-bound train. They all reunite in Beaune where a resourceful nun (Andréa Parisy) helps them cross the demarcation line to non-occupied France.

◄ HARVEY LEMBECK & TOM EWELL
BACK AT THE FRONT (1952, Universal)

Bill Maudlin's cartoon characters brought to life and directed by George Sherman ● Army reservists Joe (**Harvey Lembeck,** second from left) and Willie (**Tom Ewell,** second from right) are called to serve and, in order not to be sent to the Korean front, volunteer for duty in Japan. In Tokyo, they get into trouble in a bathhouse where, after easing them into a pool of perfumed water, two young girls are replaced by a pair of scrub boys. The G.I.s create a ruckus that brings the military police and after masquerading as geishas (**photo**), they barely escape. They also meet Eurasian Nida (Mari Blanchard) who introduces them to an armament smuggler, Johnny Redondo. His warm hospitality wins the soldiers' naïve cooperation in his nefarious plan to ship dynamite to North Korea. Unaware that they are being monitored by General Dixon (Barry Kelley), Willie and Joe derail the transfer of explosives, which results in Redondo's arrest. Hailed as heroes, the duo is sent back to the States with orders to never come back.

◄ JOHN SUTTON
& GEORGE MONTGOMERY
TEN GENTLEMEN FROM WEST POINT (1942, Fox)

Military tale of love and honor directed by Henry Hathaway ● In the early 1880s, two West Point cadets, aristocrat Howard Shelton (**John Sutton,** left) and woodsman Joe Dawson (**George Montgomery,** right), dislike each other from the outset. In addition, the interest in Joe's manly, less refined style showed by Howard's fiancée, Carolyn Bainbridge (Maureen O'Hara), exacerbates their antagonism. After several run-ins with the bombardiers—soldiers who train them—the cadets send their leader, obtuse Sgt. Scully (Ward Bond), a message proposing romantic encounters in the woods. When Scully and the bombardiers show up, each one is met by a cadet disguised as a Southern belle. Their faces hidden by lace mantillas, they lead the soldiers in a merry chase, eventually knocking them out one by one. Naturally, Howard picks a fight with Joe (**photo**) but they flee before being identified. Later, the 10 West Point gentlemen who have survived the grueling training gain the bombardiers' respect by using a strategic move that in the past had triggered the defeat of Indian Chief Tecumseh. Carolyn then drops Howard for Joe.

◄ ALFRED DRAYTON
& ROBERTSON HARE
WOMEN AREN'T ANGELS (1942, Pathé)

Endearing wartime farce directed by Lawrence Huntington ● Reservists Alfred Bandle (**Alfred Drayton,** left) and Wilmer Popday (**Robertson Hare,** right) run a music publishing firm in London while their wives, Thelma (Mary Hinton) and Elizabeth (Peggy Novack), are in the Auxiliary Territorial Service. The couples share a cottage and when their spouses are away the hubbies enjoy their freedom. One evening, they extricate a woman from a car crash, bring her in to spend the night and, the next morning, realize that their clothes, their cars and the lady are gone. After borrowing their wives' uniforms, Alfred and Wilbur hitchhike (**photo**) to join their reservists unit and spot the lady robber with two men driving toward a strategic bridge. Courageously, they prevent the trio from blowing it up. The day after, they read in the paper that that their wives have taken full credit for the arrest of the traitors.

◄**DANNY KAYE**
ON THE DOUBLE
(1961, Paramount)
Mistaken identity comedic yarn directed by Melville Shavelson ● Stationed in England in 1944, G.I. Ernie Williams (**Danny Kaye**) is identified by his superiors as a dead ringer for General Sir Mackenzie Smith, the architect of the imminent Normandy invasion. British intelligence officers ask the private to impersonate the general to confuse Nazi agents who want to assassinate him—without specifying that Williams will be risking his life. While Ernie fools Sgt. Bridget Stanhope (Diana Dors), the general's mistress, he is stunned to discover that as a German operative she is helping accomplices to whisk him (thinking he is MacKenzie Smith) off to Berlin. There, brutally questioned, Williams denies being Smith but finally feeds the enemy bogus information. Given a pistol to commit suicide, he uses it to escape and roams the streets of Berlin assuming diverse disguises, including that of a Marlene Dietrich-type singer (**photo**) in a cabaret infested with rowdy Wermarcht soldiers. Later, rallying England thanks to the involuntary help of a German plane, Ernie exposes as traitors a couple of high-ranking British officers.

▶ HARVEY LEMBECK
STALAG 17 (1957, Paramount)

Stirring tale of men at war behind barbed wire directed by Billy Wilder ● It is Christmas and the prisoners in Stalag 17 are celebrating in spite of fears about a spy in their midst. "Animal" Stosh (**Robert Strauss,** right), seriously tipsy, mistakes buddy Harry Shapiro (**Harvey Lembeck**)—dolled up as a blonde with straw hair—for his dream lover, movie star Betty Grable, and asks him for a whirl around the floor **(photo).** Later, Sergeant Sefton (William Holden), a cocky loner, becomes so suspect in the eyes of some men that they beat him brutally. Recovering in his bunk, he overhears Sgt. Price (Peter Graves) informing main guard Schultz (Sig Rumann), how pilot Lt. Dunbar (Don Taylor)—captured and tortured by the camp commandant (Otto Preminger)—had blown up an ammunitions train. Later, Sefton confronts Price in front of the other prisoners. His arguments have Price running from the barracks, only to draw fire from the tower guards.

▶ BRIAN DONLEVY
TWO YANKS IN TRINIDAD (1942, Columbia)

Scoundrels-turning-patriots comedy directed by Gregory Ratoff ● After an acrimonious feud, erstwhile partners in petty crime Timmy Reardon (Pat O'Brien) and Vince Barrows (**Brian Donlevy**) enlist separately in the Army and are sent to Trinidad. They bring with them their cocky attitude and some bad habits, the latter including a propensity for bribing their superiors—that fails to work with unbending Sgt. Valentine (Donald McBride). Their rivalry intensifies when they encounter attractive singer Pat Dare (**Janet Blair,** left) at a local dance club. Sentenced to serve time for cheating ruthlessly during war games, Vince decides to go AWOL and borrows an exotic female outfit from Pat **(photo).** The disguise doesn't fool Timmy, who after dancing with the feminized Vince, asks him back to camp. But, on their way to their barracks, Nazi sympathizers, who want to use the two soldiers' expertise in explosives to diffuse the mines surrounding Trinidad, abduct them. When Timmy and Vince learn that the Japanese have bombed Pearl Harbor, they sabotage the Nazi plans, eliminate the traitors and move up the ranks to sergeant.

◀ KENNETH CONNOR
WATCH YOUR STERN (1960, Rank)

"Carry On"-like comedy directed by Gerald Thomas ● The testing of a new torpedo, Captain David Foster's pet project (**Eric Barker,** left), fails. To modify it, U.S. Navy Commander Phillips borrows one of the two copies of its plan, while the other is kept on board for British specialists. Unfortunately, O/S Blissworth (**Kenneth Connor**) burns the plans by mistake and when Admiral Pettigrew decides to review them with scientist Agatha Potter (Hattie Jacques), Captain Foster and Lt. Commander Fanshawe (**Leslie Phillips,** right), in a panic, ask Blissworth to pose as Miss Potter and deliver bogus blueprints **(photo).** When the admiral, smitten with dolled up Blissworth, is warned that she is an impostor, she escapes and is picked up by a car driven by the U.S. commander, who is returning his copy. She exchanges her fake plans for the real ones and saves the day.

▶ NILS POPPE
SOLDAT BOM (1948, Sweden)

Swedish send-up of military heroism directed by Lars-Eric Kjellgren ● Unfit for military service, Tramalla's stationmaster Fabian Bom (**Nils Poppe**) finds a job at the infirmary's local base when beautiful Gabriella volunteers as a nurse. As Bom is closing up the station, he discovers a runaway, Agnes (Inga Landgre), and asks a friend to hire her as a maid. Meanwhile, Bom's pursuit of Gabriella is faring poorly and when her suitor, Lt. Fosberg (**Ake Jensen,** left), shows up to propose, Bom puts on a female nurse's uniform and tells him that a contagious disease has broken out **(photo).** When Bom's rumor spreading lands him in the slammer, Agnes begs him to escape to prevent an accident at Tramalla Station. After a motorcycle ride, Bom succeeds in aborting a train wreck and realizes that Agnes is the love of his life.

▼ WILLIAM TRACY & JOE SAWYER
AS YOU WERE! (1951, Lippert-Spartan Productions)

Nonsensical merry-go-romp directed by Fred L. Guiol ● When Col. Lockwood (Russell Hicks) meets ex-Sgt. Doubleday (**William Tracy,** left), who is gifted with a photographic memory, he urges him to reenlist. Doubleday is assigned to Camp Carver much to the exasperation of Sgt. Ames (**Joe Sawyer,** right). Having being driven crazy by the walking encyclopedia earlier in WWII, Ames tries to embarrass Doubleday but his efforts always backfire—notably when the duo is trapped in the camp's off-limits WAC compound. The empathetic Sgt. Peggy Harper (Sondra Rogers) provides the two with female uniforms (**photo**), preventing them from being caught. Sent as secretaries to Col. Lockwood, they pretend to have disguised themselves to conduct a security experiment against enemy infiltration. In the middle of a maneuver, the colonel dismisses the case against the pair when Doubleday explains the strategies used in victorious battles of the past.

▼ CLIFF NAZARRO & CHICK CHANDLER
SAILORS ON LEAVE (1941, Republic)

Broad pre-Pearl Harbor comedy directed by Albert S. Rogell ● Two sailors, Mike (**Cliff Nazarro,** left) and Swifty (**Chick Chandler,** center) tell their shipmates that pal Chuck Stephens (William Lundigan) will inherit $25,000 if he marries before he is 27 years old. Knowing Chuck mistrusts women, they take bets that it will not happen. The two gobs are confident they will win, but in order to prevent a bad surprise, they suggest to Chuck that he marry entertainer Linda Hall (**Shirley Ross,** right), aware that she hates sailors. When they get the inkling that, after a date that turned romantic Linda might fall in love with their buddy, Mike and Swifty dress up, respectively, as Chuck's ex-wife and aunt (**photo**), and try to dissuade her from pursuing any amorous liaison with him. In spite of their efforts, the couple gets hitched, but fortunately for the pranksters, a few minutes after the midnight deadline.

▶ BRIAN DEACON
THE TRIPLE ECHO
(aka "Soldier in Skirts," 1973, New Line)

Fate-driven wartime drama directed by Michael Apted ● In 1943 England, Alice (Glenda Jackson) is living unhappily on her farm as her husband has gone off to war. One day, she encounters Private Barton (**Brian Deacon**), who has lost his way, and invites him for tea. After a few days, she and Barton become lovers. Concerned that intruders might show up, Alice encourages Barton to wear women's clothing and tells the villagers that her sister Jill is visiting. Eventually, a thick-sculled M.P. Sergeant (Oliver Reed) turns up at her door. After a couple of visits, he asks Alice if he could invite Jill to the base's Christmas dance. Alice refuses, but Barton agrees. At the dance, the sergeant traps glamorous Jill in his room. When he realizes that Jill is a man, Barton—still dressed as Jill (**photo**)—returns to Alice's farm and prepares his departure. But the sergeant, knowing now that Barton is a deserter, shows up and arrests him with outrageous brutality. Taking a rifle, Alice aims at the sergeant but, surprisingly, shoots her lover to death.

◄ GEORGE BERNARD & BERT BERNARD
GOBS AND GALS
(1952, Republic)

Modestly amusing trifle directed by R.G. Springsteen ● Stationed in the South Seas, weathermen Sparks Johnson (**George Bernard,** second from left) and Salty Conners (**Bert Bernard,** far right) send off observation balloons with photos of their handsome commanding officer, Lt. Steve Smith (Robert Hutton). In return, they receive a huge amount of mail and gifts they sell to their buddies. When the unit gets back to the States, Lt. Smith is mobbed by a horde of female fans causing his fiancée Betty Lou (**Cathy Downs,** far left) to break their engagement. When her father, Senator Prentice (**Emory Parnell,** second from right), goes to Washington to discuss the Navy budget, Lt. Smith takes the same train with a locker full of reports showing the importance of his unit. Sparks and Salty, who have hidden their correspondence and money in the locker, go along and in order to retrieve the incriminating evidence incognito dress as two eccentrically charming women (**photo**). Thanks to the gobs' efforts, their past imposture remains a secret, the Navy keeps its budget, and after a group of Soviet spies is arrested, Lt. Smith and Betty Lou are reunited.

◄ KIERON MOORE & JOHN BAER
BIKINI PARADISE
(1967, Allied Artists)

Titillating and improbable postwar comedy directed by Gregg Tallas ● At the end of WWII, a teacher named Harriet Pembroke (Kay Walsh) has disappeared after escaping the Japanese. To find her, Navy Lt. Allison Fraser (**Kieron Moore,** left) and his aide Lt. Anthony Crane (**John Baer,** right), are sent to the Pacific. After a few days, they reach an island on which eight tantalizing girls, who have never seen a man before, capture them. Taken to the Amazons' leader, the officers realize that it is Ms. Pembroke herself. During a feast, she informs them that they will be used for reproductive purposes and then eliminated. Assigned to Rachel (Jeannette Scott) and Mata (Anna Brazzou), respectively, Fraser and Crane escape on their wedding night by disguising themselves as women (**photo**). After a second Naval search unit is told that Fraser and Crane have disappeared, the women remove the boat in which they were hoping to flee one day. Now trapped forever on the island, the two sailors resign themselves to their fate, hoping that they are creating a new paradise on earth.

McHALE'S NAVY JOINS THE AIR FORCE (1985, Universal)

Theatrical addition to the television series directed by Edward J. Montagne ● The son of a feared general, Lt. Harkness (Ted Bessell) has been shanghaied secretly to Vladivostok by the Soviets. After a series of zany events, hapless Navy Ensign Charles Parker (**Tim Conway**) is mistaken for the missing lieutenant. Negotiating a maze of wackiness, Parker finds himself in a jam when the general decides to visit his son, but he succeeds in hoodwinking him and the base colonel (**Henry Beckman,** left) into thinking he is a female nurse (**photo**). Still impersonating Harkness, Parker unwillingly dispatches planes on a mission that sinks a Japanese flotilla. Now a hero under his own name, Parker is honored at the White House and, when Harkness shows up after a plucky escape, nobody cares—even his father, the general.

▶ **DICK SHAWN**

WHAT DID YOU DO IN THE WAR, DADDY? (1966, U.A.)

Wacky WWII comedy directed by Blake Edwards ● As U.S. infantrymen surround a Sicilian village, the Italian garrison is watching a soccer game. At the end of the match, Capt. Oppo (**Sergio Fantoni,** right) agrees to surrender but on the condition the victors join them for a festival of wine, women and songs. By-the-book Capt. Cash (**Dick Shawn**) refuses, but Lt. Christian (James Coburn) convinces him to delay the surrender. The next morning, to make things seem kosher to General Bolt (Carroll O'Connor), commander of the nearby American forces, the hungover Italians and Americans join together in a fake battle. The Germans, suspecting resistance fighting, retake the village. The Italians and the Americans collude against their captors and, at one point, Capt. Cash poses as the female companion of Capt. Oppo disguised as a Wermarcht soldier (**photo**). When General Bolt arrives with his troops, the Italians and the Americans have forced the Germans to lay down arms, but the Italians refuse to surrender until the Americans give them a party.

▲ **MATT LEBLANC, DAVID BIRKIN, JAMES COSMO & EDDIE IZZARD**

ALL THE QUEEN'S MEN (2001, Atlantic Streamline)

Action farce with wigs and falsies directed by Stefan Ruzowitzky ● It is 1944 and OSS officer Stephen O'Rourke (**Matt LeBlanc,** left) has managed to get his hands on the Enigma typewriter, the secret German message-writing device. Escaping over the Italian hills, the American soon runs into the starchy British Col. Aiken (Edward Fox). Irritated by O'Rourke's hypermacho attitude, he tosses him into prison and smashes the Enigma. But when the brig's warden learns of the Yank's earlier renegade missions, he offers him his freedom if he can get another Enigma.

There is one big problem: every German soldier worth his Schnapps is at the front and women run the coding device factory. So O'Rourke and his crew—bookish decryption expert Johnny (**David Birkin,** second from left), English bureaucrat Archie (**James Cosmo,** second from right) and café drag performer Tony (**Eddie Izzard,** far right)—must round up some drab dresses and learn some feminine wiles. Once in enemy territory, the quartet finds its resistance contact, German librarian Romy (Nicolette Krebitz). They then succeed in infiltrating the plant, swiping another Enigma and, after rescuing the lovely librarian, escaping unscathed.

THE GANG THAT COULDN'T DRESS STRAIGHT

When scoundrels, spies and killers use female guise to gain the upper hand

◀ **LON CHANEY**
THE UNHOLY THREE
(1925, MGM)

Riveting tale of crime and redemption directed by Tod Browning ● Professor Echo (**Lon Chaney,** center) is a ventriloquist who performs in sideshows with strongman Hercules (**Victor McLaglen,** left), dwarf Tweedledee (**Harry Earles,** seated) and girlfriend/pickpocket Rosie O'Grady (Mae Bush). The three men open a bird store selling parrots that talk, thanks to Echo who runs the place dressed as one Granny O'Grady. The scam is simple: when a sold bird does not talk, Echo puts Tweedledee in baby clothes and wheels him in a carriage to the complaining customer. Then, while the midget memorizes the layout of the premises, Echo throws his voice again to make the parrot "talk." Later, the three burglarize the place. On Christmas Eve,

while Echo is busy, impatient Hercules and Tweedledee pull off a job at the Arlington residence, killing Mr. Arlington. This ruthlessness enrages Echo, but when a policeman (**Matthew Betz,** right) comes to the shop to question Granny O'Grady (**photo**), Echo is forced to lie to protect his disguise. After Tweedledee comes up with the idea of pinning the murder on Hector McDonald (Matt Moore), their naïve store clerk, Echo agrees, mainly because Rosie has fallen in love with Hector. On Christmas Day night the threesome abducts Rosie and takes refuge in a mountain cabin. Before Hector's trial, Rosie promises Echo she will always stay with him if he saves the clerk from the chair. Echo's testimony wins freedom for both the wrongly accused man and himself. After an ape dispatches Hercules and Tweedledee, Echo releases Rosie from her promise and goes back to the sideshow.

◀ **LON CHANEY**
THE UNHOLY THREE
(1930, MGM)

Talkie remake of Lon Chaney's silent hit directed by Jack Conway ● At the Old Fashioned Museum, Professor Echo (**Lon Chaney**) shares the program with strongman Hercules (John Linow) and dwarf Tweedledee (Harry Earles), while his girlfriend, Rosie O'Grady (Lila Lee), picks pockets. When a brawl prompts the police to close the carnival, the men open a bird shop that sells talking parrots to customers who do not realize the talking is done by ventriloquist Echo disguised as Granny O'Grady. If buyers complain about their bird's silence, Granny checks out the pet while Tweedledee, brought in a baby carriage, cases the house. On the eve of a heist, Echo realizes Rosie has fallen for the store's straight-laced sales clerk, Hector McDonald (Elliott Nugent) and, jealous, suspends the robbery. Hercules and the midget perpetrate it without him, steal a necklace and after killing someone hide the jewelry in Hector's apartment. The ploy works, but when the young man is arrested for the crime, Rosie begs Echo to save him. Disguised as Granny O'Grady, Echo takes the stand but, when harshly questioned by the prosecutor (**John Miljan,** right), he unintentionally reverts to his real voice and is unmasked. He is sentenced to a few years while Hector, who will marry Rosie with Echo's consent, is cleared. *(In the biopic* Man of a Thousand Faces, *James Cagney plays Lon Chaney and re-creates some of his roles, notably that of Granny O'Grady, see next page.)*

CAGNEY'S HOMAGE TO CHANEY

JAMES CAGNEY
MAN OF A THOUSAND
FACES (1957, Universal)

Engrossing chronicle of Lon Chaney's life and times directed by Joseph Pevney ● Born of deaf-mute parents, Lon Chaney (**James Cagney**) learns at an early age how to communicate through body language and facial expressions. At the turn of the century, the 17-year old gets a job at the local opera house as a stagehand and, after discovering the transformational power of makeup, becomes a versatile vaudeville mime. When he meets comely Cleva (Dorothy Malone), he falls in love and marries her, but their happiness is short-lived. Although she fears her future child will be afflicted by the same disability as Lon's parents, their son Creighton can fortunately hear and talk. But after trying to start her own career as a singer, Cleva eventually leaves Chaney and their son. When a judge puts the boy in a children's shelter until his father is able to raise him adequately, Chaney, upset but resolute to get his child back, moves to California where his art of disguise elevates him from simple extra to supporting actor. Financially secure, he resumes his life with Creighton, helped by close friend Hazel Bennett (Jane Greer). Through his taxing incarnations in *The Hunchback of Notre Dame* and *The Phantom of the Opera,* Chaney becomes a star of enormous proportion in '20s-Hollywood. Although overworked, he spends quality time in his mountain retreat with his compassionate new wife Hazel and his son. After eschewing sound, he stars in a talking remake of one of his most famous silent movies, *The Unholy Three,* in which he plays Echo, a scoundrel who dresses up as a larcenous granny (**right photo**). Like the 1925 film, the 1930 version is a huge success. Unfortunately, Chaney dies of lung cancer that very year, surrounded by his wife and son, who will later become B-movie star Lon Chaney, Jr.

Top photo: Lon Chaney (James Cagney) gives a comic impression of Mrs. Murgatroyd to amuse his son Creighton (Dennis Rush).

Bottom photo: During the shooting of *The Unholy Three,* ventriloquist Echo, played by Lon Chaney (James Cagney) and dressed up as Granny O'Grady, answers the questions of a suspicious policeman (Robert Forrest). Strongman Hercules, played originally by Victor McLaglen (here Charles Horvath) hides the face of midget Tweedledee, originally played by Harry Earles (here Billy Curtis).

Opposite: James Cagney as Lon Chaney in the role of ventriloquist Echo masquerading as Granny O'Grady.

▶ RICHARD LANE & EDWARD BROPHY
GIRL ON THE SPOT
(1946, Universal)

Musical crime-comedy directed by William Beaudine ● Gangster Weepie McGurk (**Richard Lane,** left) murders the owner of a club just before singer Kathy Lorenz (Lois Collier) shows up for an audition. McGurk, pretending to be the dead man, asks her to sing. Moved by her voice, he starts to weep but tells Kathy that his club is closed. Disappointed, Kathy goes to her father Popsy's restaurant—staffed only by singers of his once famous operetta troupe—just as her brother Leon announces he has found a backer for their Broadway version of *The Pirates of Penzance.* Journalist Rick Crane (Jess Barker) suspects that Kathy has iced the club owner until she identifies the new backer as the man who auditioned her in the first place. Weepie also recognizes Kathy and, fearing she could testify against him, decides to kill her. To avoid detection, he and side-kick Fingers Foley (**Edward Brophy,** right) show up at the premiere dressed as society matrons (**photo**). After sniffling at the beauty of the Gilbert and Sullivan songs, Weepie takes aim at Kathy, only to be stopped by Crane in the nick of time.

▶ RAIMU
THÉODORE & COMPANY
(French title "Théodore et Companie," 1933, Pathé-Natan)

Winning but amoral French bedroom farce directed by Pierre Colombier ● Jovially lazy Clodomir (**Raimu**) and his younger pal, the irrationally upbeat Théodore (Albert Préjean), devise small-time but ingenious scams that exploit the moral weaknesses—mainly sexual—of the '30s Parisian bourgeoisie. Among their prey is Théodore's uncle, Monsieur Chénérol (Alcover), a wealthy cheese whole-saler. When Chénérol learns that his wife Adrienne (Alice Field) has a lover, Théodore introduces his chubby relative to dancer Loulou (Germaine Auger), a sexy and frisky *demoiselle.* As an intermediary, Théodore gets some money from the *fromager.* Meanwhile Clodomir, an indefatigable transformation artist who is part of the con game, masquerades as Loulou's mother (**photo**). He thereby extracts more cash from the lusty uncle who later reconciles with his wife.

▼ VINCE BARNETT, FORREST TAYLOR & JOE DEVLIN
SWEETHEARTS OF THE U.S.A. (1944, Monogram)

Muddle-plotted wartime musical crime comedy directed by Lew Collins ● Patsy (**Una Merkel**, second from right), a klutzy air defense worker, whacks herself on the head with a hammer and dreams that she is out of work. In a club, she runs into an incompetent private investigator named Parky (**Parkyakarkus**, far right) who has inadvertently helped three robbers knock off a bank. Recognizing a soul mate in Parky, Patsy agrees to help him find the criminals. When bandleader Henry King convinces Parky to use his broken-down mansion as a nightclub for wartime workers, he realizes that the robbers occupy it. Air warden Patsy saves the day, however, when she captures the toughs who are dressed as matrons (**Vince Barnett**, left; **Forrest Taylor**, second from left; **Joe Devlin**; third from left) sneaking from the club. Rewarded by the police, she wakes up to find out that her hammer accident has helped the defense plant solve a major production problem.

▶ J. CARROLL NAISH
KING OF ALCATRAZ
(1939, Paramount)

Claustrophobic B-thriller directed by Robert Florey ● On the freighter *SS Escobar* en route to Panama, radio operators Ray Grayson (Lloyd Nolan) and Robert MacArthur (Robert Preston) are warned by the FBI that crime lord Steve Murkil has escaped from Alcatraz with the help of his gang. In order to check if the criminals are on board, Captain Glennon (**Harry Carey**, far right) conducts a passport inspection. Among the passengers is attractive Bonnie Larkin (**Virginia Dabney**, fourth from left) and her frail grandmother, Mrs. Farnsworth, who when asked for her papers (**photo**) draws a gun. The apparently harmless Mrs. Farnsworth is, in fact, escapee Steve Murkil (**J. Carroll Naish**) in drag. He and his cronies proceed to hijack the ship, but radio operator Grayson, in the middle of a dangerous situation, succeeds in sending out an S.O.S. that is heard by a passing ship.

◄ STURE LAGERWALL
LASSE-MAJA (1941, Sweden)
Romanticized life story of a Swedish Robin Hood directed by Gunnar Olsson ● In 19th-century Sweden, the young Lasse-Maja (**Sture Lagerwall**) is working in the kitchen of sheriff Holling. A manipulative man, Holling is trying to obtain the rights to a property where Lasse-Maja's girlfriend, Lena (Linae Linden), lives with her father. When Lasse-Maja's efforts to foil the sheriff's plans are discovered, Lena helps him and is jailed. The couple meets again when Lasse-Maja, who has become adept at female disguise (**photo**), is riding as a highwayman with sidekick Silver Jan (**Emil Fjellstrom,** left). When Lena convinces him to abandon his scheme for a holdup, the police suspect her involvement and lock her up once more. In a burst of high-mindedness, however, she refuses to leave with Lasse-Maja when he comes to help her escape. Later sentenced to life, the bandit remembers Lena's choice and makes the same decision. In an unforeseen development, Lasse-Maja is pardoned and, meeting up again with his love, vows to reform his roguish ways.

◄ DOM DELUISE
THE TWELVE CHAIRS
(1970, Crossbow)
Reworking of a famous '20s Russian novel directed by Mel Brooks ● In 1927, a former aristocrat, Ippolit Vorobyaninov (**Ron Moody,** left), learns from his dying mother-in-law that family jewels have been sewn into one of her twelve chairs to hide them from Bolshevik plundering. Father Foydor (**Dom DeLuise**), who has overheard the confidence, cuts his beard, dresses as a peasant woman and steals one of the chairs. Ippolit catches the thief (**photo**) but realizes the chair does not belong to the original set. When Ippolit makes the mistake of telling his secret to scoundrel Ostap Bender (Frank Langella), he is forced to partner with him to find the precious dozen. Their search leads to a Moscow museum, to a theatre and to a circus. They finally find the last chair in a communal house for railway employees who had discovered the jewels and used the loot to build their Recreation Center. Desperate to survive, Ippolit simulates an epilepsy attack in the street while Ostap collects change for his hospitalization. It works and the duo takes their show on the road.

BOB SIMMONS
THUNDERBALL
(1965, United Artists)

Fourth Connery-as-Bond adventure directed by Terence Young ● In a French village, a woman in widow's weeds attends the funeral of Jacques Boitier, a SPECTRE henchman, before being driven to a chateau. There, James Bond (**Sean Connery**) assaults her (**photo**) and during the fight removes her wig, revealing that "she" is Boitier himself (stunt coordinator **Bob Simmons**). After using his license to kill, 007 flees on a jet-propelled device amid a hail of bullets and jumps into more action when he is asked to thwart a last scheme devised by SPECTRE. After hijacking a NATO aircraft carrying nuclear warheads, the terrorist organization blackmails the world. In Nassau, Bond meets the brains behind the operation, Emilio Largo (Adolfo Celi), and French beauty Dominique (Claudine Auger). After multiple underwater battles, Bond gives Dominique the opportunity to kill Largo who was responsible for her brother's death.

▲ **LIONEL JEFFRIES**
BLUE MURDER AT ST. TRINIAN'S
(1957, British Lion)
**Second comedy based on Ronald Searle's cartoons directed by Frank
Launder ●** While St. Trinian's headmistress, Mrs. Fritton (Alastair Sim), is
in jail, the army is put in charge of the school's female students. Anxious to
win a UNESCO contest that offers a trip to Rome, the girls stage a heist of
the exam answers. Meanwhile, thief Joe Mangan (**Lionel Jeffries**), who has
robbed a stash of diamonds, seeks refuge at the school where his daughter is a senior. The girls, expecting a new headmistress, kidnap the woman
sent by the Ministry and force the crook to impersonate her. When, to the
amazement of all, the unscholarly St. Trinian's wins, Mangan sees his
chance to escape from England and hides the gems in a water polo ball.
Two dilapidated buses drive the unruly brats to Paris, Vienna and finally
Rome, where the water-polo match is to take place. During an incredibly
rough game, Mangan escapes with the ball (**photo**) but winds up being
chased by the girls—who know its contents—through Rome's historic sites.
When they catch him, they claim the insurance company's hefty reward.

▶ **OSKAR SIMA & THEO LINGEN**
MY AUNT—YOUR AUNT
(German title "Meine Tante—deine Tante,"
1956, Huble-Kahla)
**Parody of French bank heist film *Rififi* directed by Carl Boese
●** Small-time crook Tommy Schneider (Georg Thomalla) works as
a porter at a train station. When he spots two men standing near
a couple of suitcases, he offers to carry the luggage to their hotel.
Once there, Tommy realizes that the bags, full of feminine outfits,
do not belong to the men, Oscar Stargazer (**Oskar Sima,** left)
and Theo Muller (**Theo Lingen,** right), but to a singer named Lola.
Oscar and Theo are, in fact, two safecrackers who, inspired by
the suitcases' contents, decide to masquerade as women for
their next robbery. In drag, they rent an apartment situated above
a bank and start to plan the heist with Tommy's help. In spite of a
series of contretemps, the burglary is successful. But later, able
to locate the cracksmen in female attire, Tommy gets a reward
and a cleansed police record.

JEFF BRIDGES
THUNDERBOLT & LIGHTFOOT
(1974, United Artists)

Moving multi-faceted caper film directed by Michael Cimino ● Young drifter Lightfoot (**Jeff Bridges**) is attracted by Thunderbolt (**Clint Eastwood,** left), an astute man who robbed a government vault several years earlier. Unfortunately, the loot was lost, a version that Thunderbolt's partners in crime—violent war vet Red Leary (George Kennedy) and likable featherbrained Goody (Geoffrey Lewis)—do not believe. When the three men reunite, Lightfoot suggests they attempt the complex heist again. Each man is assigned a role, with Lightfoot's part consisting of adopting female attire (**photo**) to capture the guard's attention so the robbers can enter the fortress. The men execute the heist as planned but fail in their getaway: Goody is killed and Leary panics, severely beating Lightfoot in a rage. Escaping the police dragnet, Thunderbolt drives the gravely wounded Lightfoot to the old schoolhouse where the original loot was hidden and buys him his dream car. The two men, wandering along the Montana roads, enjoy the landscape until Lightfoot dies quietly, leaving Thunderbolt continue his lonely drifting.

GET CHARLIE TULLY
(aka "Ooh, You are Awful,"
1976, TBS)
Ribald farce of impersonation and disguise directed by Cliff Owen ● Likeable king of British conmen, Charlie Tully (**Dick Emery**) is determined to obtain the ill-gained loot his deceased partner in crime has stashed away in Switzerland. This entails tracking down four of his ex-mate's girlfriends whose tattooed behinds form the number of a Zurich bank account. To measure up to the challenge, Charlie enters the Police Women's Training College as Mandy and after a few days of strenuous instruction, during which his male attributes are painfully in the way (**photo**), he is ready to go after the *derrière*-marked beauties. Because each of the four lives in a different European city, and because gangsters have caught wind of Charlie's mission, he chases the women from London to Rome with the mafia on his tail. When he reaches the Eternal City, he tries to sell the Sistine Chapel to some credulous Americans. Finally, Charlie completes the combination and lays his hands on the money.

► MICHAEL ROBBINS
THE PINK PANTHER STRIKES
AGAIN (1976, United Artists)
Fourth episode of übergoofball Clouseau's adventures directed by Blake Edwards ● Driven over the brink by Clouseau, ex-Chief Inspector Dreyfus (Herbert Lom) escapes from a psychiatric asylum to plot revenge. After trying to kill Clouseau (**Peter Sellers,** left) in his Parisian apartment, Dreyfus realizes that once again his nemesis' dumb luck has protected him. Dreyfus then kidnaps Dr. Fassbender, the inventor of a death ray. This device at his command, Dreyfus threatens the world with total destruction. He will renounce his plan only if Clouseau is rubbed out. Investigating Fassbender's abduction, Clouseau follows the inventor's butler, Jarvis (**Michael Robbins**), to a gay club in London. There, surprising Clouseau with his performance as a female torch singer named Angela, Jarvis asks him to tango (**photo**) but before being able to squeal, he is done in by Dreyfus' goons. In the meantime, the international community has hired 26 assassins to eliminate the chief inspector. They all fail, without even being noticed by him. Later, learning where the death ray machine is located, Clouseau is able to destroy it and pulverize Dreyfus.

▲ VITTORIO GASSMAN
IL MATTATORE
("The Ham," 1963, Fair Films)
Hilarious portrait of an endearing conman directed by Dino Risi ● Gerardo Latini (**Vittorio Gassman**) is a flamboyant ham. Not on stage, for he is a failed actor, but in life. Known as The Artist, one day he masquerades as movie star Amedeo Nazzari, and on another day as a German Luftwaffe general. He even impersonates Greta Garbo—helped by a cloche hat, dark shades and a sophisticated cigarette holder (**photo**), and poses for paparazzi for money. Jailed for his swindling, when released he cannot stop himself from indulging his urge to abuse the credulity of people in spite of a strong plea from his family. In the end, Gerardo himself is the victim of a con game when he is arrested by a police commissioner who is none other than a disguised accomplice (Peppino De Filippo).

▲ HECTOR ELIZONDO
YOUNG DOCTORS IN LOVE (1982, Fox)

Silly parody of *General Hospital* **directed by Garry Marshall** ● At City Hospital, Dr. Prang (Dabney Coleman), the chief of surgery, welcomes new interns. As "the chief of busting balls," he is helped by a staff of kooky physicians, among them the nauseating lab director, Dr. Ludwig (Harry Dean Stanton) and an array of nurses dominated by the mousy Norine Sprockett (Pamela Reed). The interns, all equally diverse, include a midget, Dr. Cham-berlain (Gary Friedkin); a marriage-minded looker, Dr. Stephanie Brody (Sean Young); and a haughty surgeon-to-be, Dr. Simon August (Michael McKean). But the really unusual characters are a couple of patients, namely Angelo Bonnafetti (**Hector Elizondo**) and his dad (Titos Vandis), who are hiding in the facility disguised as daughter (**photo**) and father to evade a syndicate hit-man, the blundering Malamud (Michael Richards). In the end, Malamud dies by lighting a cigarette while in an oxygen tank, the two sanctuary seek-ers survive, and Stephanie marries Simon and moves to Beverly Hills.

▶ PETER FALK
HAPPY NEW YEAR (1987, Columbia)

Remake of a Claude Lelouch's jewel caper directed by John Avildsen ● Nick (**Peter Falk**), who has spent time in the slammer, moves to Palm Beach. To rob the Harry Winston store, he elaborates a scheme involving his becoming two different characters: wearing rubber masks, wigs and makeup, he plays a male octogenarian and his equally old sister (**photo**). Alternating visiting the shop, the two seniors gain the trust of manager Edward Sanders (**Tom Courtenay,** right). The evening of the heist, Nick returns to the store just after closing disguised as the old man, and with the alarm system still unarmed by the manager—who is hoping to close the sale—robs the place and passes the loot to his accomplice, Charlie (Charles Durning). Trapped inside by the time-lock door, Nick is arrested and sent back to prison. Fortunately, his love interest (Wendy Hughes) and Charlie remain loyal and, when Nick is released, the three fly off with the loot to Brazil.

▶ JEAN-PAUL BELMONDO
INCORRIGIBLE
(French title "L'incorrigible," 1975, Films Ariane)

Portrait of a charming loser directed by Philippe de Broca ● Swindler Victor Vauthier (**Jean-Paul Belmondo**) has a gift for impersonation. Out of jail, he joins his father figure, Camille (Julien Guiomar), in a trailer park. After meeting his parole officer, attractive Marie-Charlotte Pontalec (Geneviève Bujold), Victor nevertheless agrees to be the bait in a divorce case by impersonating a transvestite (**photo**) with disastrous results. Eventually, Marie-Charlotte falls for Victor and takes him to the city of Senlis' art museum where her father is curator. She shows him El Greco's *Pieta* and reveals how to bypass the alarm. When Victor recounts to Camille his evening with Marie-Charlotte, Camille decides to steal the painting. With Victor's reluctant help, he succeeds after a string of blunders. The government agrees to pay a ransom to get the masterpiece back, but after a series of twists and turns it is Marie-Charlotte who gets the cash.

◀ HARRY BELAFONTE
UPTOWN SATURDAY NIGHT
(1974, Warner)

Buddies-meet-the-mob comedy directed by Sidney Poitier ● Cabbie Wardell Franklin (**Bill Cosby,** right) convinces factory worker Steve Jackson (**Sidney Poitier,** far left) to paint the town. They venture into Madame Zenobia's, a gambling club, where gangsters suddenly arrive and steal everyone's valuables—including Steve's wallet that contains a winning lottery ticket. To retrieve it, Steve and Wardell try to enlist the services of detective Sharp-Eye Washington (Richard Pryor) and Congressman Lincoln (Roscoe Lee Browne). Failing, they are forced into the underworld where Geechie Dan Beauford (**Harry Belafonte**) reigns as the godfather. To enlist his trust, Wardell invents a story about a letter stashed in Steve's wallet that gives access to $300,000 in diamonds. The godfather goes to the Ebezener Picnic and confronts Silky Slim (Calvin Lockhart), the man behind the Zenobia heist. When the police arrive, Beauford, dressed as a woman (**photo**), escapes with the wallet. After a fight on a bridge, Steve dives into the river and gets his ticket back.

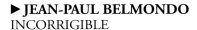

▶ ZAKES MOKAE
A RAGE IN HARLEM (1991, Miramax)

Action-packed movie based on a Chester Himes novel directed by Bill Duke ● During a robbery in Natchez, Mississippi, in 1956, Imabelle (Robin Givens) flees with the chest of gold stolen by her abusive boyfriend Slim (Badja Djola). In Harlem, where she plans to sell the loot to mobster Easy-Money (Danny Glover), she seduces Jackson (Forest Whitaker), a naïve accountant. When Slim shows up and gets back both the gold and the girl, a distraught Jackson asks his half-brother, hustler Goldy (Gregory Hines), to find her. Goldy enrolls the help of Big Kathy (**Zakes Mokae**), a flashy transvestite. Deadly confrontations lead to Easy-Money's office. But before he can buy the gold from Slim, cops Gravedigger (George Wallace) and Coffin Ed (Stack Pierce) burst onto the scene and waste Easy-Money. Slim then escapes with the cash, but Imabelle shoots him. To prove his trust, Jackson gives her the money just before he is arrested. Upon his release, Imabelle sends him the key to a Harlem train station box where he finds the cash. Giving it to his ecstatic half-brother, Jackson joins the Mississippi-bound Imabelle.

▶ PETER O'TOOLE
REBECCA'S DAUGHTERS (1992, Australma-Delta Film)

Merry swashbuckler fusing romance and thievery directed by Karl Francis ● In 1843, Anthony Raine (Paul Rhys), a soldier who gallantly served in India, returns to his late father's estate in Southern Wales. He soon realizes that he has thus become a member of the detested Whitman Turnpike Trust, a team of noblemen presided over by Lord Sarn (**Peter O'Toole**). A greedy boozer, Sarn is the uncle of Anthony's childhood sweetheart, Rhiannon (Joely Richardson), for whom Anthony still carries a torch. But Rhiannon holds him responsible —as a Trust fellow—for the tollgates that have been built everywhere to extort more money from destitute peasants. Inspired by a sermon, Anthony disguises himself as a masked avenger modeled on a biblical figure and is soon leading Rebecca's Daughters, warriors-in-petticoats who burn the tollgates. During a ball at which Lord Sarn masquerades as Queen Elizabeth (**photo**), Anthony reveals to Rhiannon that he is Rebecca. Chased by Sarn, he escapes, and a few days later learns that the British rulers, as a result of the Rebecca's Daughters uprising, have ended the policy of tollgate levies. Rhiannon and Anthony fall into each other's arms.

▲ JEREMY IRONS
AND NOW LADIES AND GENTLEMEN (2002, Paramount Classics)

Glossy tale of love and amnesia in picturesque locations directed by Claude Lelouch ● Valentin (Jeremy Irons) is an English jewel thief who uses charm and even female impersonation (**photo**) to pull off his heists. Jane Lester (Patricia Kaas) is a Parisian club chanteuse reeling from a love affair with a philandering trumpet player. Both are disenchanted jetsetters in search of a life. Valentin rents a yacht in Fécamp and sets sail for Southern horizons while Jane accepts a gig at Palais Jamal in Fez. When Valentin's sailboat crashes off the coast of Morocco, fate arranges for the two melancholic souls to meet in a clinic where they have both come to cure a minor form of amnesia: Valentin doesn't remember which places he has robbed, Jane often forgets her song lyrics. As Valentin and Jane head for the tomb of a local healer, they embark on a string of glamorous but dangerous adventures that will help them find recollections of their past and the excitement of a newborn love.

Cross-dressing shrinks?

PSYCHOPATHS IN SILK STOCKINGS

Analyze this!

◄ ROD STEIGER
NO WAY TO TREAT A LADY (1967, Paramount)

Portrait of a respect-craving serial killer directed by Jack Smight ● New York theatre owner Christopher Gill (**Rod Steiger**) uses his knowledge of costumes and makeup to hide his grisly crimes. As a plumber, a priest or a cop he strangles dowdy matrons. The serial killer's trademark is a mouth painted with lipstick on his victims' forehead. A publicity-seeking psychopath, Gill gets additional kicks by phoning in clues to the investigating detective, Morris Brummel (George Segal). At Joe Allen's, an actors' hangout, transvestite Sadie (Kim August) offers shelter to a weeping middle-aged female afraid of becoming the strangler's next target. The teary lady, who is Gill in drag (**photo**), finishes off the cross-dresser and marks his face with his signature lips. When Brummel cunningly pins on Gill a sixth murder he has not committed, the killer fears a copycat is trying to steal his thunder. Realizing later that the detective has lied to provoke him, Gill suits up in a caterer's outfit and enters the apartment of Brummel's girlfriend, Kate Palmer (Lee Remick), with the intention of strangling her. Fortunately, Brummel arrives in time to save her life. Gill, it turns out, hated his deceased actress mother so much that he exacted murderous revenge on frowzy women.

▲ LIONEL BARRYMORE
THE DEVIL DOLL (1936, MGM)

Horror classic directed by Tod Browning ● Paul Lavond (**Lionel Barrymore**), a former French banker who had served 17 years in Devil's Island penitentiary because of the trickery of his three partners, escapes. With him is Marcel (Henry B. Walthall), a near-death mad scientist who has invented a serum capable of shrinking people into tiny dolls that respond only to the will of their masters. Back in Paris, Lavond disguises himself as a likable old lady (**photo**) to escape a police search. Using the identity of Mme Mandelip, he looks for his daughter Lorraine (Maureen O'Sullivan) and learns that she grew up with hatred for her criminal father. More resolute than ever to exact revenge—and still masquerading as Mme Mandelip—Lavond opens a store and with the help of the scientist's widow, Malita (Rafaela Ottiano), sends out living dolls to kill Coulvet (**Robert Greig,** right) and the two other men who had wronged him. But before dying, the third man confesses the frame-up and establishes Lavond's innocence. The police discover the secret of the dolls and go to Mme Mandelip's shop but they arrive too late: an irate Malita has torched the place and died in the fire. Originally innocent, yet now a psychopath, Lavond disappears, knowing that his stolen money will be returned to Lorraine.

▶ **FRANK PUGLIA**
BULLDOG
DRUMMOND'S
REVENGE
(1937, Paramount)
Made-on-the-cheap murder-mystery directed by Louis King ● Capt. Hugh "Bulldog" Drummond (John Howard), an ex-British army officer who yearns for adventure, finds out that foreign agents plan to steal a cache of newly discovered hextonite, an explosive to be used in airborne bombs. When the inventor is murdered and the explosives disappear, Drummond investigates. The killer-thief, he soon discovers, is Draven Nogais (**Frank Puglia**), the inventor's assistant, who is traveling on the same train as Drummond disguised as a rather stylish woman. After a cat and mouse game that leads everybody to the Dover Ferry, Nogais is killed before he can set off the stolen explosives. That done, Drummond finally marries his fiancée, Phyllis (**Louise Campbell,** right).

◄ PHILIPPE NICAUD
COME DANCE WITH ME (French title "Voulez-vous danser avec moi?" 1959, Vidès Films)

Vixen-turned-sleuth comedy directed by Michel Boisrond ● When Hervé (Henri Vidal), Virginie Dandieu's (**Brigitte Bardot,** right) amorous dentist husband, is accused of killing dance instructor and notorious blackmailer Anita Florès (Dawn Adams), the curvaceous bride sets out to find the real villain. She goes undercover at the dance studio as a teacher and during her investigation baffles Police Commissioner Marchal (Paul Frankeur) with her seemingly innocent questions and irresistible charm. Thanks to her sheer stubbornness and some serendipitous mistakes, Virginie discovers that Daniel (**Philippe Nicaud**), a sexy young man who worked for Anita, is not only a transvestite performing at The Blue Fetish, a Parisian gay *boîte,* but also the lover of the late teacher's sole male heir. This connection eventually reveals Daniel as the psychopathic murderer.

◄ RAY WALSTON
CAPRICE (1967, Fox)

Industrial spying murder-mystery comedy directed by Frank Tashlin ● Patricia Fowler (**Doris Day,** right) is an industrial spy employed by a cosmetics firm, unofficially investigating the murder of her father, a CIA operative who had been on the trail of an international drug-smuggling ring. Helped by Interpol agent Christopher White (Richard Harris), she discovers that successful chemist Stuart Clancy (**Ray Walston**) is a fraud. Then she learns his mother-in-law, Madame Piasco, is the real creator of his inventive concoctions—most notably the water-repellent hairspray *Caprice.* Patricia eventually concludes that Clancy is also the head of the global narcotics ring, and most importantly, her father's killer. Feeling threatened, Clancy, dressed as a cleaning woman, tries to kill Patricia (**photo**), boasting that before shooting her dad he had disguised himself as a woman and almost seduced him. Fortunately for Patricia, Clancy slips on the staircase and falls to his death.

◄ ROSS MARTIN
EXPERIMENT IN TERROR (1962, Columbia)

Top-drawer thriller directed by Blake Edwards ● In San Francisco, bank teller Kelly Sherwood (Lee Remick) is assailed by a stranger who says he will kill her unless she steals $100,000 for him. Instead, Kelly calls the FBI and reaches Agent John Ripley (Glenn Ford) who encourages her to cooperate with her attacker while his team investigates. Learning the Bureau is involved, the extortionist frequently contacts Kelly, notably in the powder room of a restaurant where he shows up dressed up as an old woman (in costume and makeup trial **photos**). The thug then kidnaps her 17-year old sister, Toby (Stefanie Powers), and orders her to steal the money. Using Kelly as bait, Ripley discovers that the suspect is a killer named Red Lynch (**Ross Martin**). While his men free Toby, Ripley follows Kelly, who carries a stash of banknotes, to Candlestick Park. There, in the middle of a game's end crowd, Ripley extracts Kelly from the psychopath's clutches and guns him down.

▲ ALDO VALETTI, PAOLO BONACELLI & UMBERTO PAOLO QUINTAVALLE
SALO: THE 120 DAYS OF SODOM
(Italian title "Saló o le Centoventi Giornate di Sodoma," 1975, Alberto Grimaldi)

Hard-to-watch journey into De Sade's circles of hell directed by Pier Paolo Pasolini ● In the waning days of Mussolini's Italy, four rich and influential men—a banker (**Aldo Valetti,** left), a duke (**Paolo Bonacelli,** second from right), a magistrate (**Umberto Paolo Quintavalle,** far right), and a bishop (Giorgio Cataldi)—debauch themselves by rounding up attractive adolescents and subjecting them to a litany of tortures, cruel humiliations and orgiastic molestations. Behind the walls of a Garda Lake villa, the four wantons—who yearn to quench their sick thirst for absolute power and degrading sexual pleasures—follow to the letter the rituals set down by the Marquis de Sade and methodically put their young hostages through the legendary writer's circles of hell. In the circle of perversion, the victims hear the stories of one of the elegant old prostitutes involved in the debasing games, with several victims being put through what is being recounted. In the circle of feces, a banquet of excrement is eaten during which the magistrate marries one of the prisoners, a beautiful boy in a bridal gown. In the circle of blood, agonizing torments and amputations are savagely enacted. In the epilogue, three of the gentlemen perverts dressed as women (**photo**) are married to three of the guards in the courtyard. The violent abuse that follows is observed and enjoyed from above by the fourth.

▶ HELMUT BERGER
THE DAMNED
(Italian title "La caduta degli dei," 1969, Pegaso Films)

Mesmerizing study of Nazi corruption directed by Lucchino Visconti ● In February 1933, a powerful German industrialist, Joachim von Essenbeck, is celebrating his birthday with his family. The overly formal event is disrupted first by a scandalous transvestite performance by Joachim's grandson (**photo**), a troubled omnisexual named Martin (**Helmut Berger**), and second by the shocking news that the Reichstag is burning. The rise of the Nazi party triggers a vicious familial power struggle over the control of the von Essenbeck's steelworks and munitions factory. Martin's widowed mother, Sophie (Ingrid Thulin), pushes her lover, Friedrich Breckman (Dirk Bogarde), to kill the patriarch and take over the company. After June 1934's Night of the Long Knives, during which Hitler's goons eliminate much of the opposition by slaughtering the S.A.'s militia at a homosexual orgy, Martin takes his revenge on his mother—whom he hates with a passion—by seducing her. Dressed as a Nazi officer, an ominous incarnation of remorseless evil, Martin orders her to marry Breckman and then forces the couple to commit suicide.

▶ **CHRISTOPHER PLUMMER**
THE SILENT PARTNER
(1979, Embassy)

Suspenseful roller-coaster ride directed by Daryl Duke ● Low-key Mike Cullen (Elliott Gould) is a teller at a shopping mall branch of the First Bank of Toronto. One day, he stumbles across a plan to hold up the bank and guesses that the man in the Santa outfit is the robber. Filching a large portion of the day's take and hiding it in a lunch box, Cullen leaves the thief with a lot less loot than the newspapers claim. The culprit, a hardened criminal named Harry Reilke (**Christopher Plummer**), figures out who has spirited the missing cash. Enraged, he ransacks Cullen's apartment looking for the money—and bloody revenge. Terrified at first, Cullen progressively finds in himself the courage to play the game. After dating Elaine (Céline Lomez) and guessing she works for Reilke, Cullen is sickened when she is brutally iced in his apartment by the psychopath. He then tells the killer to show up in a disguise at the bank the day after to get the missing cash. In full makeup and a Chanel suit (**photo**), Reilke glides up to Cullen's window. When the teller rings the alarm, a stunned Reilke is instantly shot to death by a guard. After the commotion, Cullen asks coworker Julie Carver (Susannah York) to leave the country with him to start a new life.

◄ STEPHEN FORSYTH
HATCHET FOR THE HONEYMOON
(Italian title "Il rosso segno della follia,"
1969, Mercury Produzione)

Cheesy psycho-thriller directed by Mario Bava ●
In a luxurious Parisian estate, 30-year old cad John Harrington (**Stephen Forsyth**) runs the upscale fashion house specializing in weddings that his mother created in 1928. Married to a rich widow, Mildred (Laura Betti), John is mentally ill, his madness pushing him to murder women with a meat cleaver while in bridal dress. He first kills a honeymooning bride on a train, then executes several of his models, cremating their bodies in his greenhouse furnace. After Mildred refuses to divorce him, he decides to kill her but as he can't ask her to don wedding whites he dresses in them himself (**photo**). In the virginal outfit, John butchers his wife but Mildred's ghost starts to haunt him. Increasingly demented, he has a revealing flashback: when he was a child, he had killed his mother the day she remarried, a fact he had suppressed.

◄ DENNIS DUGAN
NIGHT CALL NURSES
(1972, New World)

Unthrilling sex thriller directed by Jonathan Kaplan ● In a Los Angeles psychiatric hospital, three shapely nurses—brunette Barbara (**Patricia T. Byrne,** left), blonde Janis (Alana Collins) and African-American Sandra (Millie Lawrence)—are in charge of the night shift. Routinely dealing with lunatics, they are helped by Kit (**Dennis Dugan**), an efficient orderly who dreams of becoming a head nurse. On their downtime, the women try to have fun. But Barbara, who attends group therapy sessions under the guidance of Dr. Bramlett (Clint Kimbrough), discovers that she is psychotic. When she finally sleeps with the psychiatrist, he tells her that she was only an experiment for him: he wanted to know if a normal person could be driven into a psychotic state just by being told that he or she is psychotic. At that very moment, a female nurse jumps into the room and kills Dr. Bramlett with an axe. A terrified Barbara discovers the murderess is Kit in drag (**photo**).

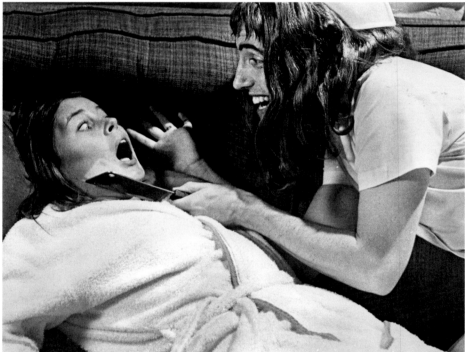

◄ GENE SIMMONS
NEVER TOO YOUNG TO DIE (1986, Paul Entertainment)

Tongue-in-cheek action-adventure schlock directed by Gil Bettman ● Power-hungry and leather-bound hermaphrodite Velvet Von Ragner (**Gene Simmons** of the rock group Kiss, **photo**) plans to poison Los Angeles' water supply with radioactive waste from Diablo Canyon. But government agent Drew Stargrove (former 007 impersonator George Lazenby) has commandeered the floppy disc designed to trigger the disaster. Executing him, Von Ragner and his biker thugs start to hunt down Stargrove's son, Lance (John Stamos), a clean-cut high school gymnast whom they think has the disc. With the technological help of his Asian roommate, Cliff (Peter Kwong), and his late father's assistant, Danja Deering (Vanity), he fights off Von Ragner's Mad-Max-type gang, and thanks to his superb physical condition acquired on a trampoline avoids multiple death traps. During his downtime, he falls for the curvaceous Danja. Eventually Von Ragner succeeds in obtaining the disc and after driving to the reservoir confronts Lance in a brutal face-off. The plucky hero sends the criminal to a precipitous death and stops the poisonous countdown.

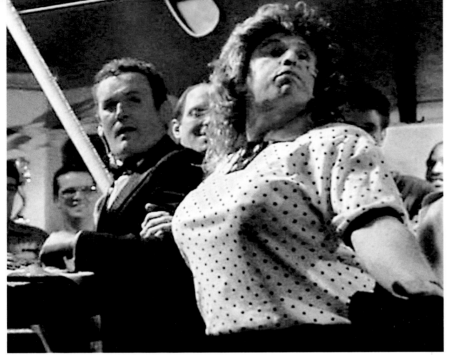

◀ GARY BUSEY
UNDER SIEGE (1992, Warner)
High-octane action thriller directed by Andrew Davis ●
On the *USS Missouri*'s last voyage, a surprise party is held by Commander Krill (**Gary Busey**) for Capt. Adams. During the dinner, featuring outside catering and a rock 'n' roll band, Krill vamps as a busty blonde (**photo**) but later bumps off the captain and joins bandleader and rogue CIA operative William Strannix (Tommy Lee Jones) and his caterers-turned-hijackers. They herd the crew into the forecastle except for one man, former Navy SEAL Casey Ryback (Steven Seagal), who works as the captain's cook as an end to a career full of medals—and one instance of insubordination. A martial arts specialist and a master in weaponry, the in-your-face Ryback derails the scheme of turncoat Krill and traitor Strannix, who want to seize the ship's 32 Tomahawk missiles for profit. Also a high-tech communication expert, Ryback succeeds in phoning Washington's war room and prevents Strannix's nuclear attack on Honolulu.

▶ JOHN LITHGOW
RAISING CAIN
(1992, Universal)
Psycho-thriller based on an unsettling plotline directed by Brian De Palma ● Child psychologist Carter Nix (John Lithgow), a perfect husband and father, has taken a sabbatical to better raise his daughter Amy. His wife Jenny (Lolita Davidovich) feels he is obsessed with their little girl when he suggests sending her to a Swiss school that investigates the mysteries of childrens' minds. Nix turns criminal when, encouraged by his evil brother Cain (John Lithgow also), he kills several women to steal their children. After drowning Jenny, Nix is recognized by Dr. Waldheim (Frances Sternhagen) who tells the police Nix has been the victim of his psychologist father's research and is probably a schizophrenic enacting multiple personalities—his imaginary brother Cain or his deceased father among others. But Jenny is alive and leads the authorities to Nix's hideout. There they find Amy but Nix escapes. In the park with Amy months after, Jenny fails to see the smiling woman observing them (**photo**).

▶ JAMES COBURN
THE LAST OF SHEILA (1973, Warner)
Labyrinthine murder-mystery directed by Herbert Ross ● Sheila, wife of Hollywood kingpin Clinton (**James Coburn**), is killed in a hit-and-run. One year later, Clinton invites six friends—some ex-lovers and all suspects in his mind—to his yacht, hoping to discover the culprit. There is a talent agent (Dyan Cannon); a has-been director (James Mason); the daughter of a studio executive (Joan Hackett) and her husband; a second-rate screenwriter (Richard Benjamin); a celebrity leech (Ian McShane); and a beauty queen, Alice (Raquel Welch). Obsessed with unmasking his wife's killer, Clinton has devised a game for his guests involving nasty secrets and Mediterranean ports-of-call as an exotic chessboard. In the ruins of a French monastery, Clinton, disguised as Alice (**photo**), is murdered and the action suddenly takes a vicious new twist. After another crime is committed among the guests, the five survivors, including the murderer, decide to bring their adventure to the screen.

◀ DAVID CARRADINE
SONNY BOY (1990, TransWorld)
Powerful tale of abject child abuse in rural America directed by Robert Martin Carroll ● New Mexico, 1970. The town of Harmony is ruled by Slue (**Paul L. Smith**, left), a sadistic fence who lives with his cross-dressing mate Pearl (**David Carradine**) in the desert. When one of his crew, Weasel (Brad Dourif), kills a couple of tourists, a baby boy is found in their car among the spoils. Pearl convinces Slue to keep the child, whereupon Slue cuts out the baby's tongue. When Sonny Boy is older, Slue houses him in an empty water tank where he feeds him live chickens and periodically drags him behind a truck. Now a teenager who ambles like an animal, Sonny Boy (Michael Griffin) is sent to slaughter Slue's enemies. One day, Weasel uses him to kill a prospector for his gold, prompting the townsfolk to hunt down Sonny Boy. When he takes refuge at Slue's, the crowd sets the place on fire. Pearl begs her son to escape and he reluctantly obeys before his "parents" perish in an apocalyptic battle. Welcomed by a physician (Conrad Janis) who knows his story, Sonny Boy has his tongue rebuilt using a graft from a monkey.

► ANTHONY PERKINS
CRIMES OF PASSION
(1984, New World)

Thriller delivering mixed messages about sex and salvation directed by Ken Russell ● Joanna Crane (Kathleen Turner), is a Los Angeles fashion designer by day and a hooker named China Blue by night. She is stalked by Peter Shayne (**Anthony Perkins**), a street evangelist haunted by sin and redemption, who has rented a room next door to observe her through a peephole having sex with weirdoes. Bobby Grady (John Laughlin) also trails China Blue. When he falls in lust with her, she is moved by his "normal" approach to life. When he leaves his wife (Annie Potts), she tells him China Blue is a fantasy and that life with Joanna will be much less thrilling. Rev. Shayne feels her relationship with Bobby is an obstacle to her salvation. Bursting into her apartment brandishing a knife-shaped dildo, he claims he is going to save her once and for all. Bobby, who had come to see Joanna, breaks down the door. He sees Joanna in her China Blue guise and witnesses her murder. But then he discovers that Rev. Shayne had exchanged clothes and a wig with China Blue and that she had killed the minister dressed as the sinner he wanted to save (**photo**).

◄ CHRISTOPHER MORLEY
FREEBIE AND THE BEAN
(1974, Warner)

Testosterone-fueled action flick directed by Richard Rush ● Freebie (James Caan) is a reckless San Francisco cop whose partner, Bean (Alan Arkin), is a cuckolded family man. For over a year, the bickering buddies have been rummaging through gangster Red Meyers' garbage to find evidence. When the police learn that rival mobsters have put out a contract on Meyers, Freebie and Bean are assigned to protect him. On Super bowl Sunday, Meyers (Jack Krushen) is accosted by a woman who forces him at gunpoint to drive to the stadium where the game is in progress. Freebie and Bean follow the car to the entrance, but the woman shoots Bean and flees with Meyers in tow. Running up the crowded escalators, the blonde kills Meyers who is slowing her down. She then takes refuge in a ladies room with a child as hostage (**photo**). Freebie soon realizes the killer is a karate expert and a handsome young man (**Christopher Morley**). He does not hesitate to execute him.

◄ MICHAEL CAINE
DRESSED TO KILL
(1980, Filmways)

Erotic psychological thriller directed by Brian De Palma ● Dr. Robert Elliott (**Michael Caine**), a psychiatrist specializing in sexual disorders, is treating Kate Miller (Angie Dickinson). One night, after having had steamy sex with a stranger, Kate is slashed to death in an elevator. A witness, call girl Liz Blake (Nancy Allen), describes the killer to the police as a tall blonde female (**photo**). Fearing for her life, Liz bonds with the victim's son, Pete (Keith Gordon), and decides to check if one of Dr. Elliott's patients could be the murderer. During her appointment, she seduces the psychiatrist while Pete watches the doctor's office windows with binoculars. When she undresses and asks Elliott to do the same, she rifles through his files but is suddenly attacked by the blonde slasher. Pete shoots the woman who, after losing her wig, is revealed to be Dr. Elliott. Later, another psychiatrist discloses he had been analyzing a patient in drag who resembled Dr. Elliott, a man named Bobbi who wanted to become a transsexual.

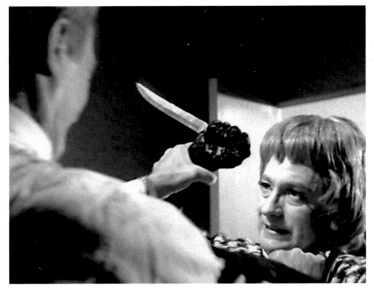

◀ **CLIFF FIELDS**
DAY OF THE NIGHTMARE (1969, Governor Films)
Thriller with weak psychology and a weaker budget directed by John Bushelman ● While his wife Barbara (Beverly Bain) waits for him at home, artist Jonathan Crane (Cliff Fields) sketches naked models in his Los Angeles studio. Next door lives Doris Mays, a private woman who wears a pageboy hairstyle. One afternoon, loud noises coming from her apartment surprise a neighbor who, seeing a man carrying a trunk to a car, informs the police. Unable to find Ms. Mays, Detective Harmon (John Ireland) is convinced she has been murdered and suspects Jonathan. When Barbara seeks advice from her father-in-law, Dr. Philip Crane (**John Hart,** left), she learns that as a boy Jonathan witnessed his mother having sex with strangers, incidents that could have triggered schizophrenia. Soon, a woman that Barbara identifies as Doris Mays bursts into her house and chases her with a knife. She escapes, but Dr. Crane, back at his office and realizing Doris Mays is his son Jonathan in drag, is stabbed to death by him (**photo**). Cornered by Harmon in an amusement park, Jonathan/Doris falls into the sea and dies when hit by a yacht.

▲ **VINCE VAUGHN**
PSYCHO (1998, Universal)
Slavish color remake of the classic Hitchcock thriller directed by Gus Van Sant ● Marion Crane's (Anne Heche) affair with Sam Loomis (Viggo Mortensen) is cramped by lack of money. When her boss at the real estate agency asks her to deposit $400,000 in the bank, Marion takes the cash and drives toward California and Sam. Arriving at the Bates Motel, she is greeted by Norman Bates (**Vince Vaughn**), an amateur taxidermist whose arguments with his unseen mother up at their adjacent house hint at a disturbed relationship. While taking a shower, Marion is stabbed to death, ostensibly by Mrs. Bates. Meanwhile, Marion's sister, Lila Crane (Julianne Moore), is upset about her sister's disappearance. She and Sam team up with private investigator Milton Arbogast (William H. Macy) who learns from the sheriff that Mrs. Bates has been deceased for years. But when the suspicious detective returns to the house, Mrs. Bates dispatches him with her knife. Tracing Arbogast to the motel, Lila finds the taxidermically preserved Mrs. Bates in the basement and is attacked by Norman dressed as his mother (**photo**). Sam disarms the creature in the nick of time. Alone in his mental ward cell, Norman speaks to himself in his mother's voice. *(Contrary to popular belief, Anthony Perkins does not appear in drag in Alfred Hitchcock's* Psycho.*)*

▶ **BILLY ZANE**
I WOKE UP EARLY THE DAY I DIED
(1998, Cinequanon)
Wordless movie based on an unfilmed Ed Woods, Jr. script directed by Aris Iliopolous ● In a sanitarium, a psychotic thief (**Billy Zane**) knocks down a female nurse and escapes wearing her outfit (**photo**). After stealing men's clothes, a gun and a car, he holds up a loan office, grabs $15,000 and kills the manager. Possibly remorseful, he goes to a burial that he mistakes as the loan officer's. When the mourners are gone, he hides the money in the coffin. The next morning the cash is gone. Obsessed with getting it back, he obtains a list of the funeral attendees and kills them one by one, including a stripper (Sandra Bernhardt) and the widow (Tippi Hedren). Returning to the cemetery, the penniless thief, in a terrifying rage, destroys the gravedigger's bagpipes and realizes the money is hidden inside. But when he opens it, a strong wind scatters the bills and pushes him into an open grave.

BABES BEHIND BARS

Beautiful belles in the big house

MICHAEL GREER
FORTUNE
AND MEN'S EYES
(1971, Cinemax)
Gritty depiction of life in the slammer directed by Harvey Hart ● In Canada, young and naïve Smitty (Wendell Burton) receives six months for pot possession and is sent to jail where he discovers a world in which brute force is a daily reality. To avoid gang rape, he is forced to submit to sodomization by a "protector," a cellmate named Rocky (Zooey Hall), who intimidates even the strongest prisoners. The violence that reigns within the prison walls is witnessed silently by sadistic guards and commented on by jailbird Queenie (**Michael Greer**), an amusing but cunning transvestite. At Christmastime, during a talent show authorized by the warden, Queenie puts on a drag act (**photo opposite**). His flamboyantly tantalizing song-and-dance number, enjoyed by his fellow inmates, infuriates prison officials, who put him in solitary confinement. In the meantime, pulled inexorably into the ugliness of the environment, a hardened Smitty rebels against Rocky, knocking him out during a fight. The nice youngster who entered the prison a few months before is now ready to become a "protector" himself. *(Based on a play written by John Herbert.)*

▶ CHARLES HAWTREY & ALBERT BURDON
JAIL BIRDS (1939, Butchers)

Hilariously lowbrow comedy based on a Fred Karno stage sketch directed by **Oswald Mitchell** ● Sent to the big house for contempt of court, Bill Smith (**Albert Burdon**, left) forges a friendship with two jailbirds, Spike Nelson (Charles Farrell) and a sweet man named Nick (**Charles Hawtrey**, left). During a show organized by the prison warden, Governor Pepper (**Shaun Glenville**, center), Bill and Nick borrow the clothes of two female artists and perform a routine. The illusion is so perfect that Pepper invites the girls to a restaurant (**photo**), but after an argument with the owner, the duo leaves abruptly. Free and back in male clothing, they find a job in a bakery. Meantime, their buddy Spike, who has escaped from prison, contacts Nick and gives him temporary custody of a stolen necklace that the nincompoop hides in a loaf of bread. Confusing events convince Bill and Nick to go back to jail to finish their time. But Governor Pepper, who doesn't want his superiors to discover how the jailbirds escaped, kicks them out.

▶ ARTHUR TREACHER & PRESTON FOSTER
UP THE RIVER (1938, Fox)

Jail-meets-football comedy drama directed by **Alfred Werker** ● (**Center photo**): Darly Randall (**Arthur Treacher**, second from left) and Chipper Morgan (**Preston Foster**, second from right), specialists in fixing poker games, are sent up the river. First assigned to sweeping detail, they are later offered a position on the football team by the coach, Slim (**Slim Summerville**, far left). Chipper and Darly excel at the sport and liking their soon-to-be-paroled cellmate Tommy Grant (**Tony Martin**, right), are concerned when they hear his mother is on the verge of being conned by a couple of crooks. When Tommy tells them he is going to break out to defend his mother, Chipper and Darly decide to do the job for him. They get their chance at the inmates' Frolics Show where the two buddies impersonate female characters. (**Bottom photos**): Escaping at the finale still dressed as women, they hitchhike to the town of Tommy's mother. On the way they resist the advances of a lusty driver (**William Irving**, left photo, right) and an inebriated passenger (**Irving Bacon**, right photo, left). In the meantime, the warden is up in arms because a big game is coming up and he has bet a fortune on his jail's team. When their mission is accomplished, Chipper and Darly return to prison just before the game's last play, coming up with a devious strategy to win.

▼ GEORG STANFORD BROWN
STIR CRAZY (1980, Columbia)

Enjoyable but strained comedy directed by Sidney Poitier ● In order to restart their careers, unproduced playwright Skip Donohue (Gene Wilder), convinces his unemployed actor buddy, Harry Monroe (**Richard Pryor,** right), to set out for Hollywood. After their van dies in Arizona, they find jobs as singing and dancing woodpeckers for a savings and loan. When thieves steal their feathered costumes and rob the bank, they are sent to jail. At the Glenboro State Prison, Skip is asked by warden Beatty (Barry Corbin) to ride a mechanical bull. To Beatty's surprise, Skip shows potential as a cowboy and he asks him to take part in the pen's rodeo. Skip agrees after an inmate claims the location is ideal for an escape and incorporates in his team Harry, posing as a clown, and a few other inmates, notably a gay man with a lisp (**Georg Stanford Brown, photo**). On rodeo day, each member escapes. The last man out, Skip learns that the real robbers have been caught.

▼ MICKEY ROURKE
ANIMAL FACTORY (2000, Silver Nitrate-Franchise Pictures)

Harrowing and richly textured prison tale directed by Steve Buscemi ● Ron Decker (Edward Furlong) is sentenced to two years for marijuana possession. He first shares a cell with a toothless transvestite nicknamed Jan the Actress (**Mickey Rourke**), who warns him that his boyishness makes him a target for sexual predators. Earl Copen (Willem Dafoe), a tough inmate who is respected for his work as a legal aid, notices that Ron doesn't fit the usual derelict image. Using his influence to get him in his cell block, Earl takes Ron under his wing. After a psychotic convict (Tom Arnold) tries to rape Ron, he seeks vengeance and knifes his aggressor. When a new trial adds more years to his original sentence, Ron agrees with Earl that they should escape. Their plan to sneak out aboard the jail's garbage truck works only for Ron. Unable to join him, Earl continues to serve his time as the "King of the Yard."

▲ RALF HAROLDE
JAIL HOUSE BLUES (1942, Universal)

Unpretentious musical action film directed by Albert S. Rogell ● Convict Sonny McGann (**Nat Pendleton** pointing a finger at cross-dressed Charlie-the-Chopper, played by **Ralph Harolde, photo**) has been pardoned but he wants to stay in jail so he can put on *Stick 'Em Up*, his dual-gender musical comedy played by an all-male cast. When Charlie-the-Chopper escapes, Sonny gets permission from the warden to go out and look for his star. During the search, he sees his mother, a small-time crook who has unionized her neighborhood's panhandlers, and helps her fight a rival association. After meeting a charming girl, Doris (Anne Gwynne), he finds the Chopper. When Sonny has all his ducks in a row, he asks former cohorts to deliver theatre critics to the big house for the dress rehearsal of his show. The day after, he gets rave reviews: obviously, his first post-prison show will premiere on Broadway.

▶ **JIM BAILEY**
PENITENTIARY III
(1987, Cannon)
Gritty action-fantasy directed by Jamaa Fanaka ● Cellblock kingpin Serenghetti (**Anthony Geary,** right) shares quarters with murderer and transvestite Cleopatra (**Jim Bailey,** left). Though she is Serenghetti's girlfriend, her sequined get-ups—befitting the Queen of the Nile—are frequently stripped away before the inmates. But beside romance, Cleo's boyfriend is also interested in finagling a return trip to the slammer for wiry prizefighter Martel "Too Sweet" Gordone (Leon Isaac Kennedy) so he can enter the champ in an upcoming prison bout. Serenghetti has Too Sweet drugged, a scheme that causes him to punch his opponent to death. Now in jail, he becomes part of a battle for supremacy between the warden's team and Serenghetti's. Driven to fight again when a friend is beaten to a pulp in the ring, Too Sweet is trained in the martial arts by a midget called Midnight Thud and lined up to slug it out with another challenger. In spite of the fact that the fighter is drugged, Too Sweet beats him, thus ending Serenghetti's chokehold on his fellow prisoners.

▼ JAMES BELUSHI
TAKING CARE OF BUSINESS
(1990, Buena Vista)

Frantically-paced comedy about stolen identity directed by Arthur Hiller ● Two days before being released from jail, car thief Jimmy Dworski (**James Belushi**) escapes in order to attend a game between the Cubs and the Angels. Later, he stumbles upon a Filofax lost by adman Spencer Barnes (Charles Grodin). Thanks to Barnes' credit cards and his Malibu villa keys, Jimmy impersonates the executive who, unable to prove his identity, is in trouble with the police, his wife and his boss. Barnes finally corners the usurper but at the end of an altercation the men realize the mess they are in and decide to straighten things out together. The most urgent move is to have Dworski break back into prison, where his fellow inmates have staged a protest to cover for his absence. With Barnes posing as a priest, Dworski, masquerading as his own mother (**photo**), fakes his way back into the slammer just in time to be officially freed. Barnes reunites with his wife and gets a new job with Dworski as a partner.

◀ RICKY SUMMERS
RIOT (1969, Paramount)

True-to-life escape drama directed by Buzz Kulik ● At Arizona State Penitentiary, Red Fletcher (Gene Hackman) and a group of inmates capture several guards and start a cellblock uprising. Prisoner Cully Briston (Jim Brown), more levelheaded than the others, moves the hostages to a secret location to protect them. Meanwhile, Fletcher's cronies are digging a tunnel that heads out beyond the pen walls. Stalling, he tells the warden that the prisoners are preparing a list of grievances. Elsewhere, while transvestite Gertie (**Ricky Summers**) is in Queen's Row (**photo**) performing a striptease that entrances fellow homosexuals, some men drunk on moonshine are brutalizing stool pigeons. When Fletcher and his crew are ready to break out, Briston joins them. As soon as they exit the underground shaft, a volley of bullets mows most of them down. Some retreat into the tunnel but Briston, Fletcher and psychopath Joe Surefoot (Ben Carruthers) try to reach the motor pool. In a murderous rage, Surefoot suddenly knifes a guard and then slits Fletcher's throat. Only Briston escapes.

▶ ROBERT CHRISTIAN
AND JUSTICE FOR ALL (1979, Columbia)

Crusading law-and-order downer directed by Norman Jewison ● Baltimore lawyer Arthur Kirkland (Al Pacino) realizes he is working in a sinkhole of injustice where corrupt magistrates often rule with impunity. One such court officer is the overbearing Judge Fleming (John Forsythe) who has sentenced Kirkland to jail for contempt. While in a holding cell, he witnesses another abuse when an African-American transvestite named Ralph Agee (**Robert Christian**) is forced by prison guards to strip to his underwear in front of jeering inmates (**photo**). The victim of a botched probationary hearing, Agee later hangs himself. Judge Fleming, meanwhile, has been arrested for a vicious rape. To avoid being destroyed by his enemies, Kirkland agrees to defend Fleming—although he is convinced of his guilt. At the trial, when it appears Kirkland will offer a convincing defense, he vehemently turns on his client and is physically removed from the courtroom, ranting about the system.

▶ RODRIGO SANTORO
CARANDIRU (2003, Sony Pictures Classic)

Metaphor about the social conundrum facing contemporary Brazil directed by Hector Babenco ● An oncologist (Luis Carlos Vasconcelos) arrives at São Paulo's Casa de Detenção–nicknamed Carandiru–to start an AIDS prevention program. Living in an overcrowded world rife with brutality, fear and, occasionally, humor, many of the 7,000 inmates, while submitting to the doctor's care, begin unburdening themselves of their most intimate secrets. Through their haunting tales, the physician vicariously experiences both the dark underbelly of crime and his patients' passion to live. Among his confidants are a professional killer named Dagger (Milhem Cortaz) who experiences a religious conversion, and a thinker, No Way (**Gero Camilo,** right), who fantasizes about his love affair with Lady Di (**Rodrigo Santoro**) and marries "her" in a mock wedding ceremony (**photo**). After 12 years of service, the doctor witnesses the Carandiru massacre of October 2nd 1992, an actual event that causes the deaths of 111 inmates. *(Based on the best-seller* Carandiru Station *by Drauzio Varella.)*

▲ JOHNNY DEPP
BEFORE NIGHT FALLS (2000, Fine Line)

Life story of Cuban poet Reinaldo Arenas directed by Julian Schnabel ● Raised in pre-Castro Cuba, Reinaldo Arenas (Javier Bardem) moves at age 14 from a deprived rural life to an existence marked by a strong involvement in the revolution. As an adult, his first novel, *Singing from the Well,* wins the attention of one of Havana's intelligentsia. Besotted with writing and, increasingly, other men, Arenas, now somewhat of a literary lion, becomes prey to *El Jefe*'s persecution of homosexuals. After an attempt to survive in hiding, he is sent to the concentration camp of El Morro. There, he sneaks out his new manuscript with the help of Bon Bon (**Johnny Depp**), a flashy transvestite and talented rectal smuggler. Broken by solitary confinement and his forced confession, Arenas takes advantage of Cuba's 1980 amnesty for deviants and criminals and becomes part of the Mariel Harbor Boatlift. New York, however, is not the culmination of his dreams and the disabused writer, dying of AIDS, commits suicide in 1990.

▶ WILLIAM HURT
KISS OF THE SPIDER WOMAN
(1985, Island Alive)

Drama about personal liberation directed by Hector Babenco ● In a South American jail, homosexual Molina (**William Hurt**) and Marxist journalist Valentin (Raul Julia), co-exist in the destructive monotony of their filthy cell. Repulsed by Molina's effeminate ways (**photo**), Valentin is won over as his cell-mate, day by day, acts out scenes from his favorite films—in one, a spider woman (Sonia Braga) weaves dangerous webs. Responding to Molina's kindness, Valentin confesses his politically incorrect passion for Marta (Sonia Braga also), an upper-class woman. Molina, in turn, admits he is a stooge of the warden who wants information about his cellmate's leftist cadre. The night before Molina's release, he and Valentin make love. The next day, Molina agrees to pass along a secret telephone number to Valentin's comrades. Followed by the police, he attempts to deliver the information but is mistakenly shot to death by Valentin's friends. Valentin, meanwhile, is tortured again, but with the help of a kind intern's morphine injections, fantasizes some blissful moments at the beach with Marta.

SLEUTHS IN SLIPS

Crime fighters as femmes fatales

◄ CLIVE BROOK
SHERLOCK HOLMES (1932, Fox)

Romantic Holmes adventure dramatically directed by William K. Howard ● Sentenced to the gallows, Professor Moriarty (Ernest Torrence) escapes. His plans to import American protection-style racketeering to England horrifies Sherlock Holmes (**Clive Brook**). He also learns that Moriarty plots to rob a bank owned by Mr. Faulkner (Ivan Simpson), the father of Holmes' fiancée, Alice (Miriam Jordan). To inform the old man without being spotted by Moriarty's spies, Holmes morphs into Aunt Matilda, a spry, bespectacled matron with a taste for feathered hats (**photo**), and crashes an exclusive party at the Faulkner home. He then tells Faulkner that Moriarty's men are digging a tunnel leading to his bank. When Moriarty has the nerve to show up at Mr. Faulkner's to inform him that he has abducted his daughter to facilitate the heist, Holmes, now in his usual clothes, speculates that Alice has been hidden in the tunnel. He rushes to rescue her and calls the police while the gang robs the bank. During the ensuing shootout, Moriarty tries to flee using Alice as a shield but Holmes guns him down. That done, a triumphant Holmes marries Alice, deeply upsetting his loyal comrade Dr. Watson (Reginald Owen).

▲ THORLEY WALTERS & DOUGLAS WILMER
THE ADVENTURES OF SHERLOCK HOLMES' SMARTER BROTHER (1975, Fox)

Exuberant spoof of all Holmes films aptly directed by Gene Wilder ● London, 1891. Entrusted by Queen Victoria with the "fate of England" contained in a single document, Foreign Secretary Ripley hides the scroll in his apartment, which is promptly burglarized. To save his country, Sherlock Holmes (**Douglas Wilmer,** right) decides to use his unsuspecting detective brother Sigerson (Gene Wilder) as a decoy to foil Professor Moriarty (Leo McKern), who is also after the manuscript. To do so, Sherlock Holmes and Dr. Watson (**Thorley Walters,** left) make a fuss about leaving London by train. But, once in their compartment, they exchange clothes with two women, emerging in frills and feathers (**photo**) under the eyes of a clueless Moriarty thug. In Scotland Yard, Sgt. Sacker (Marty Feldman) tells Sigerson Holmes—who is insanely jealous of his brother's fame—of his pseudo-mission. Sigerson investigates and creates more pandemonium than necessary by confronting Moriarty and falling for ditzy singer Jenny Hill (Madeline Kahn), not knowing that his ever-present big brother is preventing disasters. In the end, the scroll is back in a safe place, thanks to Sigerson Holmes—or perhaps his older brother.

◄ MELVYN DOUGLAS
THE AMAZING MR. WILLIAMS
(1939, Columbia)

Lighthearted police comedy directed by Alexander Hall ● Debonair homicide detective Kenny Williams (**Melvyn Douglas**) cannot seem to keep his job from interfering with his private life: every time he has a date with girlfriend Maxine Carroll (Joan Blondell), the mayor's executive secretary, he is forced to cancel or to bring a handcuffed prisoner (Edwards Brophy) before taking him to jail. When he is ordered by Captain McGovern (Clarence Kolb) to impersonate a woman (**photo**) in order to catch a serial lady-killer nicknamed "the phantom slugger," an exasperated Maxine roams the streets to track down her boyfriend. Attacked by the psychopath, she is saved in the nick of time by Kenny in drag. At the hospital, pretending to be sicker that she is, she convinces Kenny to resign from the police force. But Capt. McGovern, banking on the young detective's professionalism, cons him into investigating a murder that occurred during a bank robbery. Maxine then decides to break up with him for good. But when she obliquely helps Kenny arrest the bank robber-murderer, she is awarded the title of special deputy by Capt. McConnell and decides to accept the lot of a cop's wife.

▲ EDMUND LOWE
MURDER IN TIMES SQUARE
(1943, Columbia)

Adequate backstage whodunit directed by Lew Landers ● Cory Williams (**Edmund Lowe**), a self-absorbed Broadway thespian, is the main suspect in a series of murders where the victims are injected with rattlesnake venom. Fingered by Longacre Lil (Esther Dale), a panhandler he has always ridiculed, he is arrested by the police but escapes with the help of a cute press agent (**Marguerite Chapman**, left). Williams starts to investigate and disguised as Longacre Lil (**photo**) succeeds in prompting a confession from the serial killer. It is Dr. Blaine (John Litel), an insanely jealous man who has been murdering all the lovers of his actress idol–a former college sweetheart.

► GEORGE E. STONE & CHESTER MORRIS
THE CHANCE OF A LIFETIME
(1943, Columbia)

Convicts-for-Uncle-Sam wartime flick directed by William Castle ● In 1943, Boston Blackie (**Chester Morris,** right) sponsors the parole of 10 jailbirds who, able to operate heavy machinery, can contribute to the war effort. One of the cons, Dooley Watson, disappears on his first parole day to unearth $60,000 worth of loot from a previous robbery. When one of his former accomplices is killed, the police confiscate the money and link Boston Blackie to the murder. Before they can arrest him, however, Blackie and his loyal sidekick, the Runt (**George E. Stone,** left), dress as cleaning women so they can pay a discreet visit to the police station's stolen property room (**photo**). There they crack the safe and remove the $60,000. Later, Blackie proves his innocence and delivers the real culprit to Inspector Faraday (Richard Lane).

► GEORGE E. STONE & CHESTER MORRIS
BOSTON BLACKIE'S RENDEZVOUS
(1945, Columbia)

Routine psycho-thriller directed by Arthur Dreifuss ● Psychopath James Cook (Steve Cochran) escapes the insane asylum and impersonating Boston Blackie goes on a strangling excursion through the city. To extricate himself from this untenable situation, Blackie (**Chester Morris,** right) launches a full-fledged investigation with the help of his close friend the Runt (**George E. Stone,** center). When their sleuthing leads them to the Park Madison Hotel, they don chambermaid garb and in outrageous blackface makeup convince the receptionist (**Dan Stowell,** left) that they are two new hires, Sapphire and Prunella (**photo**). That done, they are able to save the life of a credulous taxi girl (Nina Foch) a few seconds before the strangler tries to choke her. Consequently, Blackie's name is cleared—temporarily.

► GEORGE E. STONE
TRAPPED BY BOSTON BLACKIE
(1948, Columbia)

Light drama with intriguing suspense directed by Seymour Friedman ● Reformed thief-turned-private detective, Boston Blackie (**Chester Morris,** left) and his buddy the Runt (**George E. Stone**) are hired as jewelry guards for an exclusive costume party given by Mrs. Carter. When the wealthy socialite's highly valuable pearl necklace is stolen, Inspector Farraday (Richard Lane) assumes Blackie and Runt are guilty. The two succeed in avoiding arrest, however, and decide to investigate the crime in order to clear themselves of the charges. Using several disguises, at one point they dress as an elderly couple with Runt aptly playing the part of a charming straight-laced lady (**photo**). After a series of setbacks, the sleuths find the necklace and identify the thief who is none other than Mr. Carter (William Forrest), the victim's husband, who had been denied access to his wife's fortune. When Farraday shows up, Carter tries to escape but the

◀ FRANKIE THOMAS
NANCY DREW & THE HIDDEN STAIRCASE (1939, Warner)

Girl sleuth comic drama about the paranorma directed by William Clemens ● A gang of crooks drives two spinsters who plan to donate their mansion to a children's hospital insane. Nancy Drew (**Bonita Granville,** second from left) comes to their rescue bringing along her boyfriend, Ted Nickerson (**Frankie Thomas**). To reveal the fakery behind the spooky phe nomena experienced by the old ladies, Nancy convinces Ted to spend a night in the mansion. When he falls asleep, an unidentified man steals his clothes. Forced to wear female garb the following morning, Ted's explanations (**photo**) are listened to dubiously by Nancy's father (**John Litel,** second from right) and police captain Tweedy (**Frank Orth,** far right). Back a the house, Nancy and Ted find a hidden underground tunnel leading to the estate next door. Nancy unmasks the neighbor as the originator of the threats to the women and the leader of a consortium trying to take control of their home for construction of a racetrack.

▲ FRANKIE THOMAS
NANCY DREW, DETECTIVE (1938, Warner)

First film based on a Carolyn Keene book directed by William Clemens ● Mrs. Eldridge decides to donate $250,000 to Brinwood, the school where perky Nancy Drew (**Bonita Granville,** left) is a student. But before signing the papers, the benefactress is spirited away by her business associates who, in order to keep the money for themselves, try to show she is insane. After some daring sleuthing, Nancy coerces her beau, Ted Nickerson (**Frankie Thomas**), into disguising himself as a female nurse (**photo**) in order to gain access to the sanitarium where the dowager is detained. After freeing her, Nancy proves that Mrs. Eldridge is

▲ OLIN HOWLAND
NANCY DREW, REPORTER (1939, Warner)

Girl sleuth whodunit comedy-drama directed by William Clemens ● Nancy Drew (**Bonita Granville,** right) takes part in a newspaper contes with her schoolmates and gets a chance to play the reporter. With the help of boyfriend Ted Nickerson (**Frankie Thomas,** center), she tries to prove that a young woman who has been jailed for the murder of Kate Lambert, her legal guardian, is blameless. Nancy and Ted engage the cooperation of Sgt. Entwhistle (**Olin Howland**), who dresses as a granny in order not to be recognized as a policeman tailing the suspects (**photo**) In the end, Nancy reveals Kate Lambert's nephew as the villain and the

▼ BENNY HILL
WHO DONE IT?
(1956, Ealing Studios)

Screwy spy chase directed by Basil Dearden ● Modest ice-rink sweeper and avid pulp fiction reader Hugo Dill (**Benny Hill**) wins a contest organized by a crime magazine. The prize is £100, which he uses to open his own investigation agency. His first job as a private eye, a simple case of marital infidelity, turns out to be a cold war plot fomented by evil conspirators from Uralia who, hoping to take over the world, are planning the assassination of several British scientists. Pitted against inept but nevertheless lethal spies, Hugo tries to involve Inspector Hancock (**Garry Marsh,** right) who, unfortunately, dismisses him as a defective detective. After unwittingly escaping death, Hugo enrolls the help of his secretary Frankie (Belinda Lee) and disguises himself as a frumpy woman (**photo**) who is scheduled to participate in a radio game show. Once on stage, Hugo triggers a chain of events leading to the annihilation of the villainous ring.

► WILL HAY
THE BLACK SHEEP OF WHITEHALL
(1941, Ealing Studios)

Fish-out-of-water wartime yarn directed by Will Hay & Basil Dearden ● Professor Davis (**Will Hay**), a correspondence course teacher, becomes embroiled in a plot in which Nazi sympathizers have abducted an economist extremely valuable to the Allied cause. Asked by British officials to investigate, Davis uses a variety of guises, notably when checking the Claremont Nursing Home where he thinks the kidnapped victim has been secreted away. Dressed as a female nurse and introducing himself as Sister Plunkett (**photo**), he obtains precious information from Sister Spooner (**Barbara Valerie,** right). He then succeeds in making off with the expert by means of a daring car chase and safely delivers him to the Ministry of International Commerce. When he also manages to have Scotland Yard arrest the Nazi ring, he is rewarded with a hot new job: air raid warden.

▼ LEE J. COBB
IN LIKE FLINT (1967, Fox)
Overcomplicated send-up of the James Bond series directed by Gordon Douglas ● The U.S. is preparing its next space launch from the Virgin Islands. Nearby, a troika of female tycoons led by Ms. Elizabeth (Anna Lee), runs a beauty salon staffed with karate-trained amazons. Their secret society has devised a technology capable of brainwashing women using salon hair dryers. Envisioning women everywhere under their spell, the powerhungry trio expects to rule the universe by taking control of orbiting space stations. When Pentagon official Lloyd Cramden (**Lee J. Cobb**) discovers the plot, he puts agent Derek Flint (James Coburn) in charge of the investigation. He himself flies to the spa to pose as a customer, but when he arrives in veiled hat and conservative dress (**photo**), he is captured. As renegade General Carter and his men invade the spa, Flint comes to Cramden's rescue. While Carter tries to transform the American rocket into a nuclear device to annihilate the world, Flint escapes and thanks to his intricate gadgets saves humanity.

▼ PAT HENRY
LADY IN CEMENT (1968, Fox)
Tony Rome's second action-adventure film directed by Gordon Douglas ● While hunting gold in the ocean, gumshoe Tony Rome (**Frank Sinatra**, left) comes upon the corpse of a blonde who was stabbed and anchored in cement. Soon after, a Herculean man named Gronski (Dan Blocker) hires Rome to determine if the lady is his former girlfriend. Rome's investigation leads him to heiress Kit Forrest (Raquel Welch), who knew the dead woman, and to her neighbor Al Mungar (Martin Gabel), a retired crime lord. The detective visits Rubin (**Pat Henry**), a cop who works undercover in drag (**photo**) in Miami's seediest hangouts, and realizes that everyone he talks to winds up dead or tries to rub him out. After finding out the dead girl was Gronski's girlfriend, Rome is framed for the murder of a gay man. Arrested, he escapes and snags the killer, Paul Mungar (Steve Peck), the crime lord's son, just when he tries to stab Kit Forrest. Delivering young Mungar to the cops, Rome goes back to his boat for more treasure hunting, now sharing his hobby with Kit.

◄ JACKIE COOGAN
THE BEAT GENERATION (1959, MGM)
Un-thrilling thriller with an exploitive slant directed by Charles Haas ● Misogynistic LAPD Detective Dave Culloran (**Steve Cochran**, right) is assigned to the case of the Aspirin Man, a burglar-rapist who pretends to have a headache to gain entry into married women's homes. The case becomes more personal for Culloran when the criminal rapes his wife, Francee (Fay Spain). The investigation next moves to lover's lane where he and his partner, Detective Jake Baron (**Jackie Coogan** in woman's garb, **photo**) wait for the suspect. Afterward the cops visit poetry-cum-bongos coffeehouses where pot-addled beatniks act ridiculously. The chase soon becomes a quest for vengeance when Culloran learns that his wife is pregnant—possibly by the rapist, a man named Jerry Hess (Ray Danton). An enraged Culloran finally catches Hess and, having become a better man through the nerve-shattering experience, abandons his thirst for revenge. He spares the criminal's life.

◀**BUBBA SMITH**
POLICE ACADEMY 3: BACK IN TRAINING
(1986, Warner)
Third installment of a low-humor comedy series directed by Jerry Paris ● Due to budgetary cutbacks, Governor Neilson announces that only one of the two state police academies can survive. Will it be the one shepherded by lovable Comdt. Lassard (George Gaynes)? Or the other one run by devious Comdt. Mauser (Art Metrano)? A committee of citizens will decide. When they hear the threatening news, former graduates— like unusually clever Mahoney (Steve Guttenberg) and vocal wiseacre Jones (Michael Winslow)— join forces to help Lassard, their former loony mentor. Even Hightower (**Bubba Smith**), at the time of the call posing as a sultry blonde trying to lure purse snatchers (**photo**), agrees to reunite with his buddies to save their alma mater. This bunch of veterans trains some of the most inept recruits while the Mauser group of nasty goofballs tries to sabotage Lassard's team efforts. But when Mahoney and his unit free the governor, who had been taken hostage at an elegant fund-raiser, the boys and the girls of Lassard's academy win the competition.

▶ ROBERT CARRADINE
NUMBER ONE WITH A BULLET
(1987, Cannon)
Cops vs. drug lords action flick directed by Jack Smight ● Cops in the LAPD, high-strung Nick Berzak (**Robert Carradine**) and suave womanizer Frank Hazeltine (Billy Dee Williams) could not be more different. But both agree on borderline investigative practices. To make a drug bust at a Latino fair, Hazeltine poses as a blind man while mini-skirted Berzak impersonates a hot blonde (**photo**). Their masquerade results in the arrest of a gunslinger who is killed by his cohorts. Forcing a couple of low-life pushers to cough up information, Berzak and Hazeltine realize that the drug kingpin they are after is Harry Da Costa, a seemingly upstanding citizen. Surprised that someone is always one step ahead of them, they start suspecting their boss, Capt. Ferris (Peter Graves), of colluding with Da Costa. After some bloody pedal-to-the metal antics result in the drug lord's arrest, they discover that the mole in their department is not their boss, but a buddy, Lt. Kaminski (Ray Girardin).

▶ KURT RUSSELL
TANGO & CASH (1990, Warner)
Tongue-in-cheek buddy-cop movie directed by Andrei Konchalovsky ● Elegant Beverly Hills detective Ray Tango (Sylvester Stallone) and scruffy downtown L.A. cop Gabe Cash (**Kurt Russell**) are pitted as rivals by the press although both are obsessed by fighting against the drug trade. When they separately inflict financial losses on crime lord Yves Perret (Jack Palance), they are framed together and sent to jail for 18 months. Often beaten by goons paid by Perret, they break out in audacious style, planning to meet at Cleopatra's, a nightclub where Tango's sister, Kiki (**Teri Hatcher,** right), is an exotic dancer. When the place is raided, Gabe eludes the police by dressing as one of the club's mini-skirted sexpots (**photos**). After reuniting, Tango and Cash borrow the prototype of a high-powered, abundantly armed RV they use to trash Perret's fortress-like headquarters. They eliminate an army of thugs and kill the drug kingpin who had used Kiki as a shield in an attempt to escape.

▶ JOHN CANDY
ARMED AND DANGEROUS (1986, Columbia)
Innocuous in the extreme SCTV's alumni vehicle directed by Mark Lester ● Frank Dooley (**John Candy**), a policeman who has lost his job because of a frame-up, and Norman Kane (**Eugene Levy,** right), a lawyer disbarred for incompetence, wind up together at the Guard Dog Security Company. After minimal training, they are assigned the graveyard shift at Carlex Pharmaceuticals. When a burglary occurs under their watch, they figure out that Carlex is in cahoots with Carlino (Robert Loggia), their union's president. Frank's instincts bring the pair to an exclusive party in Bel Air where they witness Carlino's thugs murder the union's treasurer. Chased by crooked cops, they dash into a porn shop: Norman comes out in a biker outfit and Frank emerges looking like female impersonator Divine (**photo**). Later the duo rounds up mobsters and dirty cops after an epic chase through L.A.'s streets. Afterwards, Frank re-enters the force and convinces Norman to join him.

◄**SYLVESTER STALLONE**
NIGHTHAWKS
(1981, Universal)
Slam-bang police pot-boiler directed by Bruce Malmuth ● Tough New York cop Deke Silva (**Sylvester Stallone**), who works as a decoy in women's clothes (**photo**), and his partner Matthew Fox (Billy Dee Williams), are transferred to a newly created anti-terrorist unit. Their first assignment is to find and arrest Wulfgar (Rutger Hauer), a European terrorist who planted a bomb in a London department store that killed many children, has moved to the States. When Wulfgar hijacks a group of tourists in the Roosevelt Island tram, Silva and Fox succeed in saving the lives of some hostages but fail to capture the mass murderer. After several vain attempts at cornering their prey, Silva sets the stage for a final confrontation at his home, where he uses his decoy trick. Dressed as his own wife, whom Wulfgar wants to kill as revenge, Silva confronts the bewildered terrorist, removes his wig and shoots him to death.

▶**WILLEM DAFOE**
THE BOONDOCK SAINTS
(1999, Franchise Entertainment)
Moralistic and confusing bloody thriller directed by Troy Duffy ● Fraternal Irish twins Connor (Sean Patrick Flanery) and Murphy (Norman Reedus) McManus believe that God has ordained them as special deputies to rid Boston's neighborhoods of crime. Originally targeting the local Russian and Italian mafias, they end up including low-lifes like prostitution johns in their web of death. From the start they are tracked by Paul Smecker (**Willem Dafoe**), an extremely clever and openly gay FBI agent who though repulsed by the growing body count is secretly drawn to the moralistic goal of the twins, whom the public are now calling saints. At one point, when the McManus duo is captured by the Italian mafia, Smecker dresses up as a blond femme fatale (**photo**) and after flirting his way into the house where the boys are being tortured helps them escape. Desperate, the Italian hierarchy arranges for the release from prison of the feared Il Duce to whack the brothers. Not only does the legendary assassin fail, but he also turns out to be the boys' father. As a final show of their dedication to *veritas* and *aequitas,* the three interrupt the trial of a don and promptly dispatch him, leaving the populace to debate the ethics of their actions.

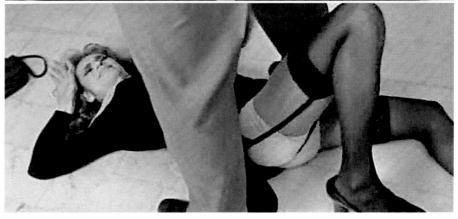

◄ **PETER SELLERS**
THE REVENGE OF
THE PINK PANTHER
(1978, United Artists)
**Third adventure of the
master bumbler directed
by Blake Edwards ●**
After escaping an attempt
on his life while trying on
a Toulouse-Lautrec outfit,
Inspector Clouseau
(**Peter Sellers**) gives a
ride to a female hitchhiker
(Sue Lloyd). She quickly
steals his car and
exchanges clothes with
him. The hijacking proves to
be a blessing: after a few
miles, the car explodes.
While news of Clouseau's
death reaches the *Sûreté,*
the inspector, who has put
on the dress and wig of his
assailant, is picked up by
the police for "special
vagrancy" (**photo**). At
Clouseau's funeral, Chief
Inspector Dreyfus (Herbert
Lom) reluctantly eulogizes
his former subordinate who,
taking advantage of his
reported demise, decides
to derail a multimillion dollar
heroin transaction. Dressed
as a Godfather, Clouseau
travels to Hong Kong
with his sidekick Cato
(Burt Kwouk) and after
unwillingly triggering
massive destruction
arrests drug lord Douvier
(Robert Webber) and
seizes the narcotics.

▶ **PAUL LYNDE**
THE GLASS BOTTOM BOAT (1966, MGM)
Romantic spy spoof directed by Frank Tashlin ● Handsome scientist Bruce Templeton (Rod Taylor), the boss of
a California space laboratory, falls for employee Jennifer
Nelson (Doris Day). To be close to her, he asks her to write
his biography. Jennifer accepts but the flattery quickly
wears thin when she finds herself engulfed in a world
where wiretapping is a way of life. Suspected of being a
Soviet mole trying to steal the plans of a breakthrough
invention (code name: GISMO), she is trailed by security
agent Homer Cripps (**Paul Lynde**), who disguises himself
as a woman in order to follow her into the powder room.
Exasperated, Jennifer strikes back. First, she confuses
Julius Pritter (**Dom DeLuise,** left), an inept KGB spy. Then
she establishes her innocence—a fact Bruce never
doubted—and finally discovers the identity of the real
double agent. All that done, the supercapable Jennifer is
off to Catalina Island to become Mrs. Templeton.

◄ COLUCHE
INSPECTOR LA BAVURE (1982, Renn Productions)

Slapdash yet funny French police film directed by Claude Zidi ● Son of a fuzzy-headed cop killed in action, nebbish Michel Clément (**Coluche**) follows in his father's footsteps and soon becomes his colleagues' laughing stock. One day, he encounters a mystery writer seeking cops-and-robbers tips for his next book. The friendly author is in reality France's public enemy number one, Roger Morzini (**Gérard Depardieu**, right). What Morzini wants from Clément is inside information that would facilitate future crimes. But nosy journalist Marie-Anne (Dominique Lavanant), who yearns for an interview with Morzini, makes fun of the gangster's manhood on television. The irate Morzini takes advantage of Clément's naïveté and abducts the newshound. Now suspected by his peers of being in league with the gangster, Clément suits up in a trampy dress and wig (**photo**) to slip away from them and starts investigating Morzini's whereabouts himself. The gullible cop becomes a hero who frees Anne-Marie and lets his coworkers capture the bandit.

◄ JEAN-CLAUDE BRIALY
LEVY AND GOLIATH (1986, Gaumont)

Comedy-drama about Jewishness and gangsterism directed by Gérard Oury ● The Levy brothers, Moise (Richard Anconina) and Albert (Michel Boujenah), have been raised in the strict tradition of Antwerp's Hassidic community. Moise, a diamond cutter who wears the attire of his faith, has stayed with his family while Albert has left for France to manage a bistro. When Moise travels to Paris by train to deliver three kilos of diamond powder, a trafficker substitutes cocaine. Realizing he is involved in a smuggling operation, Moise calls Albert who agrees to help him on the condition that he cut his locks to blend with the city's population. While the authorities look for Moise, drug kingpin Goliath (Maxime Leroux) hunts down the brothers. During a police raid in a seedy hotel, they are arrested along with Bijou (**Jean-Claude Brialy**), the madam of a transvestite boîte. When the pursuers finally catch them, Bijou (**photo**), a narc in drag, mows the gangsters down after Moise wounds Goliath in the head with a bolt catapulted by a sling.

◄ JOHN CANDY
WHO'S HARRY CRUMB? (1989, TriStar)

Good cast lost in a stumbling slapstick farce directed by Paul Flaherty ● Harry Crumb (**John Candy**), son and grandson of the deceased founders of the detective agency Crumb & Crumb, is so inept that the company has put him in charge of the Tulsa office. Fumbling case after case, it is a surprise to everyone when the big boss, Eliot Draisen (Jeffrey Jones), summons him to Los Angeles to solve the kidnapping of wealthy P.J. Downing's teenage daughter. After disguising himself as a Eurotrash mogul and an Indian air-conditioning technician—and recklessly driving a brake-busted sports car—Harry frees the victim, recoups the $10 million ransom and discovers the instigator of the abduction is his boss, Mr. Draisen. Named chief executive of the agency, Crumb continues to personally investigate the most interesting cases, like a murder at the Bottoms Up, a San Francisco club where he goes inconspicuously dressed in women's garb (**photos**).

▶ MARTIN LAWRENCE
BIG MOMMA'S HOUSE (2000, Fox)

Heavyweight crime comedy directed by Raja Gosnell ● FBI agent Malcolm Turner (**Martin Lawrence**) is staking out the Georgia home of the oversized grandmother of Sherry (Nia Long), ex-girlfriend of a recently escaped murderous bank robber (Terrence Howard), in hopes that the young lady will eventually lead him to the criminal. When the 300-pound sassy matriarch (Ella Mitchell) leaves her home unexpectedly, Malcolm impersonates her with phony fat face and limbs, a pair of grapefruit-sized falsies and a *really* baggy dress (**photo**). He does it so successfully that Sherry falls for the charade. Sensitive to her sensual zest, Malcolm is soon smitten, but he remains suspicious about her role in the robbery. His investigation, mainly in heavyweight drag, is rife with humorous incidents but ends with a dramatic confrontation: the killer appears to threaten Sherry just as the real Big Momma arrives home. Malcolm arrests the criminal, discovers that the flummoxed Sherry is innocent and sweeps her off her feet in front of Big Momma's congregation.

▲ SHAWN WAYANS & MARLON WAYANS
WHITE CHICKS (2004, Sony Pictures)

Stereotype-reversing buddy cop comedy directed by Keenan Ivory Wayans ● FBI Section Chief Gordon (**Frankie Faison**, right) assigns African-American agents Kevin (**Shawn Wayans**, left) and Marcus Copeland (**Marlon Wayans**, center) to the protection of teen socialites Brittany and Tiffany Wilson who have been targeted by kidnappers. On their way to the Hamptons, an accident leaves the girls with minor facial bruises. Fearing they will damage their beauty, the girls cancel their appearance at a benefit organized by the father (John Heard) of their nemeses, the snotty Vandergeld sisters. To pursue the case, Kevin and Marcus ask friends who specialize in latex disguise to make them look like the Wilson girls. Embosomed and blond-wigged, the agents check in at the Hampton Palace and are identified by friends and foes alike as the real thing. The ultraglamorous babes-du-jour untangle yuppie plots and derail unwanted male advances. Finally, they unmask the abduction plan's mastermind: broke millionaire Warren Vandergeld who wanted ransom money from the Wilson girls' father to keep his daughters happy.

SIRENS OF THE SAGEBRUSH
Back in the sidesaddle again

▲ IGGY POP
DEAD MAN (1997, Pandora Films-Miramax)

Offbeat tale of survival and death in the Wild West directed by Jim Jarmush ● In the 1880s, accountant William Blake (**Johnny Depp,** right) arrives in the western city of Machine to learn that the job he had been offered is filled. He accepts the invitation of pretty Thel (Mili Avital) to spend the night at her place. When her ex-fiancé finds the couple in bed, he shoots Thel to death and wounds William, who kills the jealous man. William then steals a horse and disappears. Pursued by three bounty hunters led by Cole Wilson (Lance Henriksen), William meets Nobody (Gary Farmer), a Native American who nurses his wounds and marvels when he learns that his patient is, in spite of his denials, the deceased poet William Blake. During their eventful journey to Nobody's hometown, Makah, they meet three trappers, the weirdest of whom is Salvatore Jenko (**Iggy Pop**), a Bible-reading cook in drag nicknamed Sally (**photo**). The other two fight to know who will "have" William, but a fusillade of gunshots leave all three trappers dead. When William and Nobody finally reach Makah, Cole Wilson shoots and wounds William. Nobody, still thinking that the dying William is poet Blake, sends him in a canoe to return to the world of spirits. Then, after being mortally shot by Wilson, he kills the gunslinger before dying.

▶ ROBERT MITCHUM
THE GIRL RUSH (1944, RKO)

Well-paced way-out-west comedy directed by Gordon Douglas ● In San Francisco, Mike Strager (Alan Carney) and Jerry Miles (Wally Brown) manage a thriving music hall until the 1849 Sutter's Mill gold strike draws away the majority of their patrons. Unable to pay their showgirls, Mike and Jerry become prospectors themselves. After six unsuccessful weeks, they land in the womanless town of Red Creek where they easily find enough gold to bring their dancers back from San Francisco. Accompanied by local cowboy Jimmy Smith (**Robert Mitchum**), Mike and Jerry leave Red Creek to fulfill their mission but soon learn that thieves are planning an ambush. To save their gold, the three dress as bonneted women and return to town where they are welcomed with enthusiasm—until Mike's wig falls off. Eventually, with promoters and performers reunited, the *Frisco Follies* reaches Red Creek to the great satisfaction of everyone, until word comes of another gold strike.

▼ JIMMY DURANTE
MELODY RANCH (1940, Republic)

Flat-footed horse opera directed by Joseph Santley ● Singing cowboy radio star Gene Autry (Gene Autry) comes back to his hometown of Torpedo, Arizona, to serve as honorary sheriff in the Frontier Day celebration. Arriving with his band, singing sensation Julie Shelton (Ann Miller), broadcast announcer Cornelius J. Courtney (**Jimmy Durante**) and old friend Pop Laramie (George "Gabby" Hayes), he soon finds out that the Wildhack brothers, his childhood foes, have been terrorizing the townspeople. Forced to become a real lawman, Gene experiences several humiliating contretemps but eventually brings the no-good siblings to justice. In the interim, girl crazy Cornelius Courtney has fallen for schoolteacher Veronica Whipple (**Barbara Jo Allen,** right), who asks him to act "wolfish" in an improv performance of *Little Red Riding Hood* for her pupils (**photo**).

▶ HARRY CAREY
THE TEXAS TRAIL
(1925, PDC)

Iron-hand-in-velvet-glove action adventure directed by Scott R. Dunlap ● Ranch foreman Pete Grainger (**Harry Carey**) is an unassuming loner. When his boss sends him to the bank to deposit $10,000, three men ambush him and steal the money without a struggle. Observing the scene is the visiting nurse of Pete's boss, Betty (Ethel Shannon), who is appalled by the foreman's lack of courage, a quality she expected to find in a western town "where men are men." By chance, she overhears who the ruffians are and where their loot is. Deciding to impersonate a bandit and recover the money herself, she brings back a box of apples where she thought the cash was hidden. When Dan Merrill (Claude Payton), the main scalawag, abducts her, Pete goes after him using a cross-dressing ruse (**photo**). He then dispatches the culprit over a cliff at the end of a vigorous fight that, witnessed by Betty, invokes her love.

▼ HOOT GIBSON
A TRICK OF HEARTS
(1928, Universal)

Tongue-in-cheek action-adventure comedy directed by B. Reeves Eason ● A western town has elected its new sheriff, a woman named Carrie Patience (Rosa Gore). Young rancher Ben Tully (**Hoot Gibson**), however, smells a rat. Impersonating a woman (**photo**), he stages phony holdups in order to discredit the new lawperson. But his strategy backfires when an authentic outlaw (**Joe Rickman,** right) kidnaps Ben's girlfriend (Georgia Hale). In the end, justice is served.

◀ CHARLES SULLIVAN
THE WILD FRONTIER (1948, Republic)
Surprisingly well-plotted low-budget drama directed by Philip Ford ● Legendary marshal Frank Lane (Pierre Watkin) has agreed to restore law and order in Clayton City with his son, Alan "Rocky" Lane (himself), accompanying him. Upon arrival, gunsmith Charles Barton (Jack Holt) and other concerned citizens greet them warmly. Frank then realizes that Barton engineers the town's criminal activities and arrests the gunsmith who, tragically, kills him. Revengeful, Rocky takes over his father's job and devises a trap he thinks will be irresistible for Barton: he leaks the news that $50,000 in insurance money is stashed in the jail's safe. He then asks deputy Tucker (**Reed Harper,** left) to hold the fort, but two gang members, Morgan (**Stanley Blystone,** right) and Baker (**Charles Sullivan**)—who disguises himself as a woman— steal the money (**photo**). The trail leads Rocky to Barton who gets his comeuppance from the young marshal's fists.

◀ GEORGE "GABBY" HAYES
THE LUCKY TEXAN
(1934, Monogram)
Basic tale of good versus evil in gold-rush country directed by Robert Bradbury ● College graduate Jerry Mason (**John Wayne,** left photo, center) goes west to mine gold with one of his deceased father's friends, an old-timer named Jake Benson (**George "Gabby" Hayes**). After finding a nugget, the two locate the vein, striking it rich. They sell their first take to two assayers, Harris and Cole who trick the naïve Benson into signing over the deed to his ranch. Shooting him, they pin the crime on Jerry, unaware the old man is not dead. Desperate to prove Jerry's innocence, Benson knows he cannot reach the trial alive if Harris and Cole recognize him. So he masquerades for his court testimony as a harmless granny in widow's weeds. While addressing the court, however, his dress catches in a chair, revealing his long johns (**right photo**). The comic event leads to Benson identifying the real criminals, the return of his property and even the marriage of lucky Texan Jerry Mason to Betty (Barbara Sheldon), his old buddy's granddaughter.

◀ FUZZY KNIGHT
STAGECOACH BUCKAROO (1942, Universal)
Modest action-filled yarn directed by Ray Taylor ● In Cottonwood, Molly Denton (**Nell O'Day,** third from left) hires Steve (**Johnny Mack Brown,** second from right) as a stagecoach driver. To protect a large gold shipment, Steve has his sidekick Clem (**Fuzzy Knight,** right) and two cowpokes masquerade as female passengers. When a band of highwaymen attack the coach, the aggressive "ladies" rout them. Steve soon discovers that saloon owner Kincaid, father of Nina (**Anne Nagel,** second from left), heads up the gang. Using his daughter's friendship with Molly, Kincaid learns Steve's next ruse: while Steve and Clem drive an empty coach, the girls, pretending to go on a picnic, will transport the gold shipment to Redwood City. When Kincaid's bandits take over Nina's wagon, she realizes her dad is a crook. In the meantime, Steve and Clem find Kincaid furiously trying to escape in Nina's gold-filled wagon and after a brutal scuffle capture him.

▲ WEST OF SONORA (1948, Columbia)
Haphazard but at times amusing film directed by Ray Nazarro ●
While his friend Steve Rollins (Charles Starrett) is busy solving the kidnapping of little Penny Clinton by bandit Black Murphy (Steve Darrell), small-time promoter **Smiley Burnette** (himself) arrives in Sonora with his company. Madame Fifi Latour, a French singer billed as the Toast of Europe, is supposed to join them. When she fails to show up, Burnette impersonates her, wearing an ill-fitting blond wig

and a cheesy dance-hall ensemble (**photo**). The chunky impresario does not fool any man in this isolated western town where the seductive charms of real women—though rarely experienced by these lonely miners—have not been forgotten. In the meantime, Steve Rollins has donned the mask of his alter ego, the Durango Kid, and soon discovers that Murphy is not a bandit after all. The man who really needs to be eliminated is the sheriff's treacherous brother, Sandy Clinton (Hal Taliaferro).

◀ CAROLINA MOON
(1940, Republic)

Southbound routine ride directed by Frank McDonald ● At a Wyoming rodeo **Gene Autry** (as himself, second from right) and his pal Frog Millhouse (**Smiley Burnette**) meet swindle victim Colonel Stanhope (Eddy Waller) and his granddaughter Caroline (**June Storey,** left). Because the old man has been defrauded out of $1,000, Gene steps in and to help him pay his debt buys his horse Betsy. Caroline, thinking Gene is one of the conmen, loads Betsy into her trailer and goes back to South Carolina. In order to claim the horse, Gene and Frog follow her. Once in South Carolina, they discover that the Stanhopes are good people, and after observing unethical landowner Henry Wheeler (Hardie Albright) scheming to ruin them and their neighbors, decide to intervene. To gain entry to Wheeler's house, Frog successfully impersonates a black maid (**photo**). Later, with fists and guns, songster Gene prevents Wheeler and his crew from hoodwinking the plantation owners out of their woodland properties, thereby convincing Caroline that he is eminently lovable.

▲ OH, SUSANNA (1936, Republic)

Ballads 'n' bullets action film directed by Joseph Kane ● While traveling by train to collect $10,000 loaned to old pal Jefferson Lee (Carl Stockdale), Gene Autry (as himself) is brutally thrown out by escaped convict Wolf Benson (Boothe Howard). Professor Daniels (**Earle Hodgins,** left) and Frog Millhouse (**Smiley Burnette**), two itinerant entertainers who earn a meager living in a variety of guises (**photo**), rescue Autry and decide to help the cowboy find his assailants. Meanwhile, assuming that Autry is dead, Benson impersonates him to collect the borrowed money. When Lee, knowing he is an impostor, refuses, the gunslinger shoots him and robs his safe. But the identity switch engineered by Benson pays off when the sheriff charges Autry for murdering Lee. It takes several fistfights and a handful of songs to exonerate Autry and eliminate Benson and his sidekicks.

▲ THE KID FROM AMARILLO (1951, Columbia)

Treasury-men-in-action yarn directed by Ray Nazarro ● It is the 1890s and Jonathan Cole (Fred Sears) heads up a silver bullion smuggling ring. Treasury agent Steve Ransom, alias the Durango Kid (Charles Starrett), is put on the case along with Tom Mallory (Harry Lauter) who, undercover, joins the Cole gang as a bandit nicknamed the Kid from Amarillo. Along for the ride is his deputy and master of disguise **Smiley Burnette** (as himself, second from left). After a lot of shoot-'em-up action, Ransom hones in on the fact that Cole's private penal colony transports prisoners in chains that are never worn on the return trip. When the gang discovers that Mallory and Burnette (**photo**) are agents, they hide them out in Mexico while Ransom learns that silver ingots are melted into chains painted in black. After rescuing Mallory and Smiley, Ransom dismantles the gang.

◀ DICK WESSON
THE MAN BEHIND THE GUN (1952, Warner)

California-here-we-come potboiler directed by Felix Feist ● A few years before the Civil War, Major Callicut (**Randolph Scott,** second from left) is secretly investigating all military administrations in Southern California. During a stagecoach trip to Los Angeles, he travels with prim schoolteacher Lora Roberts (**Patrice Wymore**), Senator Sheldon (**Roy Roberts**) and some unsavory characters. Upon arrival, Callicut meets a saloon owner, his star singer and several gunslingers. He figures out that these people are part of a conspiracy led by the senator to make the area a separate—and slave—state. Major Callicut wises up the garrison commander, clueless Capt. Giles (**Philip Carey,** far left) and to capture the senator and his men asks his longtime civilian sidekicks, Olaf (**Alan Hale Jr.,** far right) and "Monk" (**Dick Wesson** in drag), to impersonate a couple of settlers (**photo**). He then follows the seemingly inoffensive wagon, and after a bloody gunfight neutralizes the senator's guards. The conspirators surrender and the schoolteacher falls into Callicut's arms.

◀ DON KNOTTS
THE SHAKIEST GUN IN THE WEST
(1968, Universal)

Pale remake of Bob Hope's *Paleface* directed by Alan Rafkin ● In 1870, shy Philadelphia dentist Jesse Heywood (**Don Knotts**) leaves a comfortable existence to move to the primitive west. His misadventures start when he is duped into marrying Penelope "Bad Penny" Cushings (**Barbara Rhoades**), an alluring redhead and ex-highwaywoman. In exchange for a pardon, Bad Penny has made a deal with the sheriff: she will identify the men who sell rifles to the natives. When Bad Penny is involved in shootouts with renegade Indians, Jesse's cowardice is flagrant. But when challenged to a duel he can't refuse by the town's bad guy (**Robert Yuro**), he manages to kill him. It is his wife, however, who unbeknownst to Jesse has killed the ruffian from a window. Now, feeling secure in his newfound marksmanship, Jesse redeems himself by rescuing his captive mate after many perils—one of which involves him dressing as an Indian woman who attracts the lust of a tribal warrior (**Joseph Perry, photo**).

◀ FUZZY KNIGHT & KIRBY GRANT
GUNMAN'S CODE (1946, Universal)

Gunfights-cum-romance action film directed by Wallace Fox ● After witnessing a stagecoach robbery and a murder, two riders, Jack Douglas (**Kirby Grant,** right) and Boscoe O'Toole (**Fuzzy Knight,** left), "confiscate" the hijacked trunk which belongs to the Bank of Calliope. Later, Jack recognizes local businessman Lee Fayne (**Danny Morton**) as the killer and meets Laura Burton (**Jane Adams**), the daughter of the city's bank owner. At a party during which he romances Laura, Jack identifies her brother, Danny (**Bernard Thomas**), as one of the stagecoach robbers. Jack then informs Laura and her father that he and Boscoe are Wells Fargo detectives in charge of solving highway robberies. After Danny is asked by Fayne to help him kill Jack, he cooperates with Boscoe and Jack who then trick the killer into attacking another stagecoach. Dressed as harmless women (**photo**), they bring Fayne's outlaws to justice.

▲ DON KNOTTS & TIM CONWAY
THE APPLE DUMPLING GANG RIDES AGAIN (1979, Buena Vista)

By-the-numbers Western farce directed by Vincent McEveety ● Dull-witted outlaws Amos (**Tim Conway**, right) and Theodore (**Don Knotts**, left) decide to go straight. Trying to make a deposit in the Junction City bank, they are, by an unanticipated turn of events, accused of robbing it. The two hide in a U.S. Cavalry wagon that brings them to Fort Concho where their brainlessness results in the place blowing up. Put in a stockade, they find a tunnel that leads to a room full of conspirators cooking up an attack on the train carrying the soldiers' wages. The leader, Big Mac (Jack Elam), sees that the boys are military prisoners and hires them. Amos and Theodore escape, taking refuge in Junction City's saloon where they impersonate two *belles de jour* (**photo**). Later, dressed as Indian women, they help Captain Harris (Tim Mattheson) turn the tables on the train robbers.

◀ DICK WESSON
CALAMITY JANE (1953, Warner)

Déja-vu but charming horse operetta directed by David Butler ● In Dakota Territory's Deadwood City, the local saloon is promoting the arrival of Frances Fryer, a sexy vaudeville star from the East. Unfortunately, the stagecoach delivers a male ham (**Dick Wesson**) whose moniker happens to be Francis Fryer. Panicked, the saloon owner begs Francis to impersonate the female singer. An eyeful in a green dress and make up, he sings "I've Got a Hive Full of Honey" (**photo**) to an enthralled audience, until the trombonist inadvertently removes her wig. To quell the wrath of the audience, up steps stagecoach guard Calamity Jane (Doris Day). A hot-headed cowgirl who can outride and outdraw any man, she shoots her gun in the air and promises that she will go to Chicago herself to bring back Adelaid Hall, one of the country's most famous entertainers. Wild Bill Hicock (Howard Keel), with whom "Calam" has a love-hate relationship, challenges her to succeed. In almost fulfilling her goal, she is finally tamed by the famous gunslinger who makes "a real woman"—and a bride—of her.

▲ GEORGE HAMILTON
ZORRO THE GAY BLADE (1981, Fox)

Zany parody of a popular movie legend directed by Peter Medak ● Don Diego Vega (**George Hamilton**), son of Zorro, carries on his father's mission as a swashbuckler who rights the wrongs committed by the local oppressor, El Alcalade Esteban (Ron Liebman). When Diego injures himself, his long-lost identical twin Ramon—now a foppish Englishman named Bunny Wigglesworth (George Hamilton also)—takes over. Substituting the bullwhip for the sword, Bunny decimates Esteban's goons while displaying an outrageous sense of fashion. At the masked ball organized by Esteban to trap Zorro, Diego is accompanied by his cousin, Margarita Wigglesworth, a charming lady who is, in fact, Bunny in full drag (**photo**). When Esteban finally discerns that Margarita is Zorro, the exotic blonde has already fled. The chase is on until the twins, surrounded by Esteban's mercenaries, fight side by side with the peasants who have joined forces in a popular uprising that triggers Esteban's surrender.

▶ CHRIS HUERTA

HIS NAME IS HOLY GHOST
(Italian title "Uomo avvisato
mezzo ammazzatto...Parola di
Spirito Santo," 1971, Lea Films)
**Routine spaghetti western directed
by Giuliano Carnimeo (as Anthony
Ascott)** ● General Ubarte (Poldo Ben-
dandi) has seized power in the State.
Now he wants his mercenaries to kill
President Don Firmino (Georges
Rigaud) and his daughter Juana (Pilar
Velazquez). They are saved by a famous
pistolero nicknamed Spirito Santo
(Gianni Garko), who is not there to take
sides but to find the person who can
confirm his ownership of a gold mine
won at gambling. Don Firmino promises
to assist him when he is back in power.
Spirito Santo agrees to help him and
enrolls his old friend Chuck (**Chris
Huerta**). Joining forces with a bunch of
Don Firmino's loyalists, the two men use
unorthodox guerilla warfare methods—as
when Chuck, in order to take over the
garrison defending General Ubarte's
encampment, dresses as a woman
(**photo**). Ubarte eventually flees and
Spirito Santo gets his mine, sharing the
booty with buddy Chuck.

▶ KEVIN KLINE

WILD WILD WEST (1999, Warner)
**Expensive retooling of the '60s televi-
sion series directed by Barry Sonnen-
feld** ● In the wake of the Civil War, two
government agents meet while tracking
down the murderous General McGrath
(Ted Levine). The encounter takes place
in a saloon where Artemus Gordon
(**Kevin Kline**), an inventor masquerading
as a prostitute (**photo**), tries to hypnotize
the general while James West (Will
Smith), attempts to overpower him.
While the agents are arguing, McGrath
escapes and the two men go their separate ways. The president, Ulysses Grant
(also Kevin Kline), orders them to work
together again to neutralize McGrath.
They soon discover that McGrath is
the henchman of Dr. Arliss Loveless
(Kenneth Branagh), an ex-Confederate
general who has abducted scientists to
develop the weaponry he needs to
create the De-United States. West and
Gordon face Loveless' most daring
machine, an eight-story-high steel-and-
steam tarantula in which Grant and the
scientists are held prisoners. Gordon
builds a flying machine that allows him
and West to penetrate the tarantula
after which they make fast work of the
abominable Dr. Loveless.

◀ **MARLON BRANDO**
THE MISSOURI BREAKS
(1976, United Artists)
Violent and unusually messy high-priced drama directed by Arthur Penn ● A rancher (John McLiam) who has transformed a parcel of the Montana Badlands into a thriving operation through blood, sweat and tears, sees his empire threatened by a gang of horse thieves headed by Tom Logan (**Jack Nicholson,** right). To defend his property and reinstate law and order, the landowner hires "regulator" Lee Clayton (**Marlon Brando**). But Clayton, who owns a strangely flamboyant wardrobe for the rugged terrain, is a psychotic killer. Bringing savagery and sadism with him, he incessantly provokes Logan into cat-and-mouse fights until the moment when, dressed as a bonneted frontier woman (**photo**), he sets fire to a shack where Logan is supposed to spend the night.

Jackie Coogan

Mickey Rooney

Tommy Kelly

George du Fresne

BOYS JUST WANT TO HAVE FUN

Carl "Alfalfa" Switzer

Mickey Daniels

George "Spanky" McFarland

Allan "Farina" Hoskins

From the Little Rascals to La Vie en Rose

Alex D. Linz

Elijah Wood

THE LITTLE RASCALS

IN THE HIERARCHY of comedy, one of the most popular and ageless series continues to be *The Little Rascals* or, as originally titled, the *Our Gang* comedies. Between 1922 and 1944, 221 two-reel segments were produced, creating an impressive record. Originated by legendary producer Hal Roach, the films were based on his unique notion that, unlike the plastic child stars of the early '30s who mimicked adults, kids could be more appealing just being kids. Roach further developed this concept by creating a believable, down-at-the-heels neighborhood of underdogs who were intent on enjoying themselves no matter what. Disadvantaged, they encountered not only class issues by facing down wealthier children, but also issues involving disapproving elders. The popularity of the early *Our Gang* silent films was as quick as casting was easy. Ernie "Sunshine Sammy" Morrison, a young African American boy who had shone in the comedies of Harold Lloyd, was the first to sign on. ▶▶

▲ ALLEN HOSKINS
ELECTION DAY
(1929, Hal Roach)
Two-reel comedy directed by Anthony Mack ● It is election day for the gang and until the polls are closed neither African-American Farina (**Allen Hoskins,** second from left) nor his little sister Pleurisy (unidentified child, second from right) can leave the farmyard to do their chores. They use diverse disguises to escape —Farina masquerading as a girl (**photo**)—but Joe (**Joe Cobb,** far left) and Jay (**Jay R. Smith,** third from left), for no clear reason, keep them prisoner with help from Mary Ann (Mary Ann Jackson) and the diminutive Wheezer (**Bobby Hutchins,** far right). But Farina and Pleurisy will triumph when they find missing ballots hidden by crooks in their laundry wagon.

▲ MICKEY DANIELS
BABY CLOTHES (1926, Hal Roach)
Two-reel comedy directed by Robert F. McGowan ● For years, a couple has been extorting a weekly stipend from a rich out-of-town uncle for the support of their two imaginary children. When the old man announces an imminent visit, the couple panics at the challenge of presenting their family of four. Fortunately, their eight-year old neighbor Mickey (**Mickey Daniels**) is happy to pose as their daughter, wearing a dress, a wig with ringlets and a huge bow to help fool the relative. He is not too happy, however, when his friends, Mary (**Mary Kornman,** center) and Johnny (**Johnny Downs,** right), make fun of him (**photo**).

He was followed by Jackie
Condon (the feisty rascal), Peggy
Cartwright (the cute girl), Mary
Kornman (the blonde beauty),
Jackie Davis (the vulnerable
toughie), Allen "Farina" Hoskins
(another African American
tyke), Mickey Daniels (the
freckled Huck Finn type) and,
eventually super-chubby Joe
Cobb. Oh, and yes, Pete the
Pet. Critics judge the earlier
two-reelers, like *The Champeen*
(1923) and *Ask Grandma*
(1925), to be among the series'
best silents, a fact that had
much to do with Roach's full
participation and the talent of
his director, Robert McGowan.
When lodestar Mickey Daniels
left and McGowan began
playing less of a hands-on role,
the series stumbled but then
recovered with the talkies.
McGowan then made such
classics as *Love Business* (1931)
and *Bedtime Worries* (1933).
From the mid-'30s till 1937,
the studio turned out its best,
thanks to the arrival of naturals
such as Jackie Cooper, Carl
"Alfalfa" Switzer and George
"Spanky" McFarland. The final
two-reeler, 1944's *Tale of a Dog,*
was produced by MGM, which
had purchased the series rights
from Hal Roach and made some
52 *Our Gang* comedies. A
decade later the child troupe
became a television sensation.
For youngsters who were
seeing Spanky and Darla and
Buckwheat for the first time,
it was levity at first sight. For
those who had seen the gang's
shenanigans as children, it was
as if time had stood still. •

▼ GEORGE MCFARLAND
ALADDIN'S LANTERN (1938, Hal Roach)

Two-reel comedy directed by Gordon Douglas ● Puting on a show for their peers, the gang organizes a kiddy version of the legend of Aladdin's lamp. Alfalfa (**Carl Switzer,** left) takes the eponymous plum part and with Darla (Darla Hood) as his partner sings "Your Broadway and Mine." Unfortunately, Buckwheat (Billie Thomas) and Porky (Eugene Lee) inter-

rupt the goings on, a prank that prompts Darla to leave the show. Ever resourceful, Spanky (**George McFarland,** right) borrows Darla's harem outfit and steps onto Alfalfa's rope-rigged magic carpet (**photo**). While singing "I'll Take You Home Darleen to Spanky," Alfalfa fails to notice that a monkey has pulled the carpet over the flaming lantern, which is directly below his bottom. His backside baked, Alfalfa exits the stage to cool it in a nearby washing machine.

◄ GEORGE MCFARLAND & SCOTTY BECKETT
OUR GANG FOLLIES OF 1936 (1935, Hal Roach)

Two-reel comedy directed by Gus Meins ● Inspired by MGM's *Broadway Melody of 1936,* the gang, under the direction of Spanky (**George McFarland,** right), is putting on a show in their kid-rigged theatre. Alfalfa (Carl Switzer), in cowboy attire, spoofs Gene Autry's "Comin' Round the Mountain," followed by an ensemble of moppets doing the hula and by Darla (Darla Hood) crooning "I'll Never Say 'Never Again' Again." But the highlight of the Follies is the Flory-Dory Sixtette—a tot version of the then Broadway famous Flora Dora Sextette—featuring Spanky, Scotty (**Scotty Beckett,** left) and other boys struggling in ill-fitting dresses while butchering a tightly choreographed routine.

► BILLIE THOMAS
PAY AS YOU EXIT (1936, Hal Roach)

One-reel comedy directed by Gordon Douglas ● The gang stars in a performance of *Romeo and Juliet* with Alfalfa (**Carl Switzer,** left) and Darla as the leads. Repulsed by Alfalfa's onion breath, Darla walks out in the middle of the show. Buckwheat (**Billie Thomas**) replaces her wearing frills and a wig much to the delight of the audience.

► TRAVIS TEDFORD & BUG HALL
THE LITTLE RASCALS
(1995, King World-
Universal)

Pale attempt to resurrect the classic series directed by Penelope Spheeris ● Meeting in their shack, the members of the juvenile He-Man Woman Haters Club find Alfalfa (**Bug Hall,** right) romancing Darla (Brittany Ashton Holmes). Spanky (**Travis Tedford,** left) sabotages the courtship and Alfalfa, judged for having betrayed the club's policy, is sentenced to guard the Blur, a prized go-cart coveted by two bullies, Butch (Sam Saletta) and Woim (Blake Jeremy Collins). Chased by this irksome pair, Spanky and Alfalfa take shelter at Darla's ballet school and to avoid being caught dress as ballerinas (**photo**). They then reluctantly participate in a recital, which greatly amuses the audience. To make matters worse, Butch and Woim steal the Blur before the big event. But the Rascals build a new go-cart and win the race with the help of a local rich kid, Waldo. At the finish line, they discover that it was actually Darla driving Waldo's cart and that A.J. Ferguson, their racing idol, is a woman (Reba McEntire)! That is enough for Spanky to admit girls to the club.

► GEORGE MCFARLAND & CARL SWITZER
RUSHIN' BALLET
(1937, Hal Roach)

One-reel comedy directed by Gordon Douglas ● Chased by a pair of bullies (**Tommy Bond,** far left and **Sidney Kibrick,** second from left), Spanky (**George McFarland,** second from right) and Alfalfa (**Carl Switzer,** far right) retreat into a chic dancing school during a kids' recital. Finding wigs and tutus and posing as ballet dancers to the bewilderment of the teacher and the hilarity of the audience the boys foil their pursuers.

► BILLIE THOMAS
SPRUCIN' UP
(1935, Hal Roach)

Two-reel comedy directed by Gus Meins ● After agreeing that pretty young things will not break up their friendship, Alfalfa (Carl Switzer) and Spanky (**George McFarland,** right) have their heads turned by the back of an elegantly attired girl sauntering along the street. It is Buckwheat (**Billie Thomas**) in drag!

MICKEY ROONEY
(as Mickey McGuire)

EVERYONE KNOWS Mickey Rooney, the energetic youngster who sang and danced with Judy Garland in several musical hits of the early '40s and starred as the fast-talking teen in a queue of Andy Hardy movies. But few remember his earlier cinematic alter ego, Mickey "Himself" McGuire, the seven-year-old wisecracking street tough of the eponymous series, who had legally changed his birth name, Joe Yule, Jr., to adopt his character's. Based on the newspaper comic strip *Toonerville Trolley,* the low-budget two-reelers were produced to capitalize on the success of Hal Roach's *Our Gang* comedies. And, as in these "classics," there were drag scenes, notably in *Mickey's Tent Show* (1929), directed by Albert Herman, in which Mickey—then nine years old—mimics Mae West (**photo**). When the series of over 50 short subjects ended, Mickey—born in 1920 in Brooklyn—was 13. Upon signing a long-term contract with MGM, he then adopted Rooney as his legal name. His father, vaudevillian Joe Yule, who had started Mickey on stage at 18 months, appeared in the '40s as Jiggs in two films based on George McManus' comic strip. Pint-sized Mickey eventually filled his professional life with some 100 films and his private life with eight wives. ●

MORE BOYS HAVING MORE (OR LESS) FUN

▲ **JACKIE COOGAN**
A BOY OF FLANDERS
(1924, MGM)
Feel-good tear-jerker aptly directed by Victor Schertzinger ● Nello (**Jackie Coogan**), a young Flemish boy who courageously saves the life of a dog, returns to the home of his grandfather, his last surviving relative, only to find him dead. Now without a home, he lives with the dog in a haystack until he is accused of starting a fire. Ostracized by most adults, he dresses up as a girl in lace hat and clogs in order to attend a party given by the *demoiselle* of his dreams. Unmasked, he is to be sent away. But just before he leaves, he enters a drawing contest organized by a local artist, Jan van Dullan (Joseph Swickard). Nello wins the first prize—and the affection of van Dullan, who adopts him.

▲ **JACKIE COOGAN**
CIRCUS DAYS (1923, First National)
Teary-eyed melodrama directed by Eddie Cline ● After his father's death, sweet-faced Toby Tyler (**Jackie Coogan**) lives with his mother, Ann, on the farm of his miserly uncle, Eben (Russell Simpson). Beaten by the mean-spirited farmer for the slightest mistake, the boy, on one occasion, pluckily takes a whipping to deflect his uncle's anger at his mom. Later, when Toby attends a performance of Daly's Mammoth Circus, he gets so excited that he joins the troupe as a dollar-a-week lemonade boy, sending his salary to his mom every week. His willingness to learn allows him to graduate quickly from soda jerk to performer. One day, donning the clothes of the world-famous ailing bareback rider Jeannette (**Peaches Jackson,** left), Toby takes her place in the center ring. A stunning success, he is invited to continue his act as a boy and quickly becomes a star in the bigtop world. After having saved enough money, he returns to his uncle's home and takes his mother away.

▲ **TOMMY KELLY**
PECK'S BAD BOY
WITH THE CIRCUS
(1939, RKO)
Juvenile film based on a familiar story directed by Eddie Cline ● When a circus comes to town, prank-prone teenager Bill Peck (**Tommy Kelly**) and his buddies ruin the lion tamer's performance by giving sleeping pills to his big cats. Bill soon develops a crush on juvenile bareback rider Fleurette De Cava (Anne Gillis). Attending one of her rehearsals, he observes jealous coworker Myrna instigate an accident that will prevent Fleurette from performing her act for several days. After Bill learns that her contract stipulates she'll lose her job if she misses a performance, he volunteers to replace her. Wearing her costume and a curly wig (**photo**), and helped by the lion tamer (**Edgar Kennedy,** right), who clumsily manipulates invisible wires, Bill performs Fleurette's routine, fooling almost everybody and saving his paramour's career.

◀ MICKEY ROONEY
THE ADVENTURES OF HUCKLEBERRY FINN (1937, MGM)

Second filmed adaptation of Mark Twain's classic adroitly directed by Richard Thorpe ● Huckleberry Finn (**Mickey Rooney**) lives comfortably in St. Petersburg, Missouri, with motherly Widow Douglas (**Elizabeth Risdon**) and home slave and best friend Jim (Rex Ingram). When Buck's no-good dad (Victor Killian) asks the widow for $800 if she wants to keep his son, Huck and Jim flee to Jackson Island. They raft down the Mississippi River and bring aboard Duke (William Frawley) and King (**Walter Connelly,** right), two men who have been thrown off a steamboat. Soon the con men take over the raft. Arriving in a small town, the scoundrels stage a performance of *Romeo and Juliet* to bankroll their next scheme. When the audience realizes that the part of Romeo is played by King–and not by famous actor David Garrick–and that Huck, masquerading as Juliet in a straw bonnet and makeshift toga (**photo**), is only a stand-in for a well-known actress, they are furious. The motley crew escapes from the bamboozled crowd in the nick of time. After being involved in some major scams perpetrated by King and Duke, Huck and Jim escape, but the slave is captured and sent back to St. Petersburg to stand trial for Huck's murder. Arriving just in time to prevent his black friend's lynching, Huck makes a plea with Widow Douglas to obtain the slave's freedom. In exchange, Huck will resume his life with the old woman, go to school, wear shoes and learn how to become a Southern gent. (*With* **Sarah Padden,** *center.*)

▲ EDDIE HODGES
THE ADVENTURES OF HUCKLEBERRY FINN (1960, MGM)

Uninspired rehash directed by Michael Curtiz ● Huck (**Eddie Hodges**) escapes from his father's shack, leaving bloodstains that indicate he might have been killed. Huck joins Jim (Archie Moore) aboard a makeshift raft on which he plans to travel the Mississippi to reach an abolitionist state. The perils are multiple for the kid and his black friend and when a sheriff (**Royal Dano,** left) arrests Jim, Huck dresses as a girl (**photo**) and succeeds in lifting his friend's cell keys. When Jim reaches a slavery-free state, Huck catches a boat to New Orleans hoping to reach South America.

◀ ELIJAH WOOD
THE ADVENTURES OF HUCK FINN (1993, Disney)

The classic tale adapted once more and directed by Stephen Sommer ● After being kidnapped by his feckless father, Huck Finn (**Elijah Wood**) burns their hideout cabin so it appears he has perished. He canoes out to Jackson Island and meets up with his friend Jim (Courtney B. Vance) who is on the run to the slavery-free state of Ohio. Huck then sneaks into town disguised as a girl (**photo**) to find out how his father feels about his death, but he only learns that Jim has been accused of his murder. Preventing his lynching, Huck facilitates his access to freedom.

◀ JIMMY FAY
MILLION DOLLAR BABY (1934, Monogram)

Hollywood wannabes melodrama directed by Joseph Santley ● Grace (**Arline Judge,** left) and Terry Sweeney (**Ray Walker,** right) are a vaudeville team desperate to find a job. When they learn that Colossal Pictures, a Hollywood studio, is holding auditions in New York to find another Shirley Temple, they disguise their son Pat (**Jimmy Fay,** center) as a curly-topped girl. Pat, now named Patricia, wins the contest and the trio goes to Los Angeles. Uncomfortable in his girl's outfit, however, and perturbed by the control of the studio's scouts, Pat jumps off the train. Soon after meeting a sympathetic hobo, he is held by a gang of thugs who, having discovered his identity, plan to extort a ransom from the studio. Saved by the police, Pat reveals to the press that he is a boy. The brass of Colossal Pictures sees the ensuing publicity as a great opportunity: Pat will be a child star—as a boy.

◀ DENIS GILMORE
ALMOST ANGELS (1962, Buena Vista)

Sweet general audience Austrian choir boy film directed by Steve Previn ● During an audition, 13-year old Toni Fiala (Vincent Winter) is selected to become a member of the Vienna Boys Choir. His mother is elated but his railroad engineer father, Herr Fiala, is unhappy at the thought of his son embracing an artistic career. Encouraged by choirmaster Max Heller (Peter Weck), a rivalry surfaces between Toni and the oldest member of the group, Peter (Sean Scully). At first Peter tries to sabotage Toni's popularity but later gives a grudging nod to the new competition and even helps the young recruit. The atmosphere improves before the vocal ensemble leaves on an important tour: Friedel Schmidt (**Denis Gilmore**), for example, takes the kidding of his choir mates in good spirits when he tries on his costume for the role of Mitzi in a Strauss operetta (**photo**). But the good humor fades when the boys realize that Peter's voice has cracked. Fortunately, Toni replaces him as the lead and Peter, gifted at composing, goes on tour with his friends as assistant conductor.

◀ ALEX D. LINZ
THE DRESS CODE (2000, Lions Gate)

Likeable comedy about a kid's quest for self-expression directed by Shirley MacLaine ● In Long Island, eight-year old spelling prodigy Bruno Battaglia (**Alex D. Linz**) lives with his mother (Stacey Halprin), a flamboyant 450-pounder who still carries a torch for her cop husband (Gary Sinise). At the catholic school he attends, Bruno is a gifted student bullied by his classmates, except for Shanique (**Kiami Devael,** left), an unconventional African American tomboy. When an angel in holy vestments appears in one of his dreams, Bruno thinks he should adopt his look and like the angel wear a dress. Shanique playfully helps him (**photo**) but when a car hits Bruno while he is dressed in a woman's wig and a skirt, his mother has a mild heart attack and his ashamed father refuses to look after him. Bruno's atypical grandmother, Helen (Shirley MacLaine), takes him home and sides with him. During the rounds of the National Catholic Spelling Championship, Helen orders the nuns to let Bruno perform in drag. The diminutive genius wins the tournament and with his mom and grandmom departs for Rome to meet the Pope—another man who favors dresses!

▶ GEORGES DU FRESNE
MY LIFE IN PINK
(Belgian title "Ma vie en rose,"
1996, Sony Classics)

Poignant children's identity crisis tale directed by Alain Berliner ● Despite rejection and loneliness, confident seven-year old Ludovic Fabre (**Georges du Fresne**) has faith in a miracle: eventually, he will be accepted as the little girl he feels he was born to be. In contrast, his middle-class suburban parents can think of nothing worse. When Ludo shows up at the family's housewarming party in a frilly dress (**photo**), father Pierre (Jean-Philippe Ecoffey), mother Hanna (Michèle Laroque) and the neighbors are mildly entertained, never dreaming that what appears to be a lark is the innocent boy's quiet obsession. Emotions intensify when Ludo announces to his parents his plans to marry the boy next door—who is none other than the son of Pierre's new boss. Increasingly isolated from his three siblings and his schoolmates, Ludo refuses to waver, even when his father loses his job and the family must move. Happily, he strikes up a friendship with a tomboy, Chris (Raphaelle Santini), whose mother's loving acceptance of her daughter's unfeminine ways forces Hanna—and ultimately the entire family—to treat Ludo with the tolerance he craves.

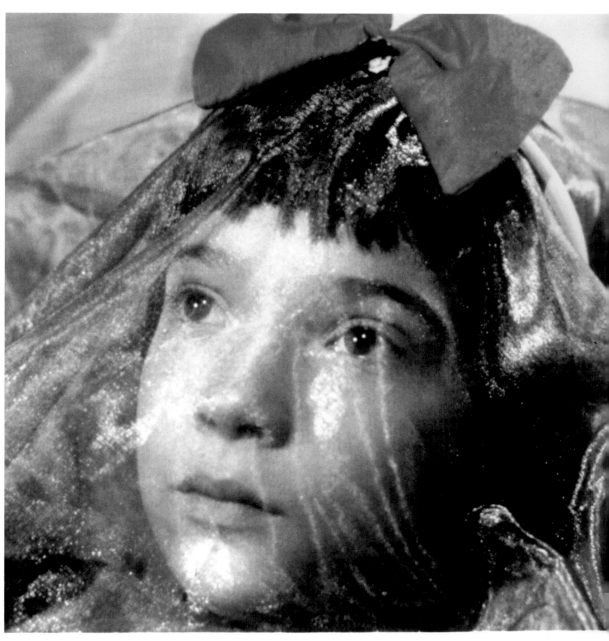

◀ NED BIRKIN
THE CEMENT GARDEN (1992, Neue Constantin)

Disturbing tale of teenage incest in a moral wasteland directed by Andrew Birkin ● In a desolate British suburb, the strict father of four dies of a coronary while covering the garden of his plain-looking house with cement. Several weeks later, the compassionate mother dies of a debilitating illness. Fearful of being separated from his teenage sister Julie (Charlotte Gainsbourg), on whom he has confusedly fixated a sexual infatuation, 15-year old son Jack (**Andrew Robertson,** right) suggests they bury their mother in a locker sealed with their father's remaining cement. Together in the basement, Jack and Julie fulfill the gruesome task. Preteens Sue (Alice Coultard) and Tom (**Ned Birkin**), now evolving in a moral vacuum, retreat into a fantasy world: Sue, frustrated with Jack's narcissism, confides her thoughts to a diary while gender-confused Tom dreams of becoming a girl (**photo**). Before summer's end Julie begins dating Derek, a businessman 15 years her senior. Jealous, Jack rejects this intrusion into the family circle and fights it as a real man, a move that impresses Julie so deeply that she initiates the consummation of their mutual attraction. Soon, the rotating light of a police car illuminates their naked, entangled bodies.

TEENAGE TRICKS & FRATHOUSE FOOLERY

From the Bowery Boys' streets to college dorms

Huntz Hall

Johnny Downs

Matthew Modine

Harland Williams

Dwayne Hickman

Frankie Avalon

Leo Gorcey

Andrew McCarthy

THE BOWERY BOYS

IN 1937, SIX YOUNG actors who played toughs from the slums in the hit Broadway play *Dead End* were brought to Hollywood by producer Samuel Goldwyn to star in the movie version. The performers were Billy Halop, the group's heartthrob; Leo Gorcey, a wild teenager who spoke tortured English; Bobby Jordan; Gabriel Dell; Bernard Punsly; and funnyman Huntz Hall, who had made his stage debut at the age of one. First known as the Dead End Kids, these wisecracking roughnecks would subsequently morph—with themselves and other actors continually moving in and out of the core group—into the Little Tough Guys, the Eastside Kids and then, finally, the Bowery Boys. The Dead End Kids' second film was *Crime School* (1938), the story of life in a gritty reformatory, which starred Humphrey Bogart. Before its release, Warner let Dell, Halop, Punsly and Hall go, but the four succeeded in doubling their salary at Universal under the moniker of the Little Tough Guys. While these films were being churned out, Warner continued to shoot six more Dead End Kids movies, the most celebrated being *Angels with Dirty Faces* (1938) directed by Michael Curtiz and starring Pat O'Brien as a thief-turned-priest and James Cagney as his unreformed partner in crime. Unrelentingly realistic, it places the kids, who are tempted by a fast buck, in the position of having to choose between good and evil. The following year, after appearing with Ronald Reagan in the reform school flop *Hell's Kitchen,* Warner let them go. Between 1940 and

1943, a new series featuring Bobby Jordan and Leo Gorcey was produced by Monogram under the name of the East Side Kids, and about the same time, Universal relaunched its Little Tough Guys series with Punsley, Halop and Jordan. In 1946, the Bowery Boys were born, with Leo Gorcey still the pugilistic punk he had been for over 15 years and Hall, his dumbbell foil. The engaging pack of slum boys continued to crank out films until 1958, the number finally raising to a total of 90. Today, in the wee hours of cable television, the Kids live on, examples of the toughness and humor it takes for deprived teens to survive on the wrong side of the tracks—and the darker side of life. ●

▲ HUNTZ HALL, LEO GORCEY, BENNIE BARTLETT, BERNARD GORCEY & GIL STRATTON, JR.
HOLD THAT LINE (1952, Monogram)
College football fantasy romp directed by William Beaudine ● The Bowery Boys are sent to Ivy University by two trustees who are curious to learn what effect the zany teenagers will have on the school's upperclass students. Considered vulgar morons, the Boys gain some respect after Sach (**Huntz Hall,** left) invents a potion that makes him an astonishing football player. As a result, quarterback Biff Wallace (**John Bromfield,** second from left) asks the Boys to join his fraternity. Led by Slip (**Leo Gorcey,** center) and followed by Butch (**Bennie Bartlett,** third from right), Morris (**Bernard Gorcey,** second from right) and Junior (**Gil Stratton, Jr.,** far right), the Boys dress as floozies as part of their hazing, enduring public humiliation (**photo**). As the big game nears, moll Candy (Veda Ann Borg) informs Biff that two bookies, hoping to make a fortune if Ivy League loses, plan to abduct Sach. Confident that he can win without him, Biff does not report the scheme. But, after being injured, he tells Slip where to find Sach. When Sach shows up at the game, Slip, who has prepared a concoction for his buddy, realizes that the mixture is no good. So Slip scores the decisive touchdown himself.

▲ HUNTZ HALL
HOLD THAT BABY!
(1949, Monogram)
Five-men-and-a-baby comedy directed by Reginald Le Borg ● When Slip (Leo Gorcey) and the Bowery Boys open a laundromat, they find a baby boy abandoned with a note asking them to take care of him. Elsewhere in town, widowed mother Laura Andrews (Anabel Shaw) is committed to a psychiatric hospital by her late husband's greedy aunts who want to cheat the infant out of his inheritance. The Boys wait, even after reading a newspaper story revealing the child's identity. Patrolman Burton (**Edward Gargan,** right) begins snooping around, but Sach (**Huntz Hall**), while pushing the baby in a carriage, fools him by dressing as a hausfrau (**photo**). To free Laura, Slip sneaks into the Midvale Sanitarium by posing as a shrink. A scuffle with gangsters ensues but the Boys are able to get both tiny tot and mother to the reading of the will. The conspiring aunts are arrested, the baby inherits $3 million and the Bowery Boys go back to their laundromat.

◀ BILLY BENEDICT
BOWERY CHAMPS
(1943, Monogram)
Tyro-reporter-solves-murder comedy directed by William Beaudine ● *Evening Express* copy boy Muggs (**Leo Gorcey,** second from left) dreams of becoming a crime journalist. Opportunity calls when a reporter is unable to cover the murder of the Pussy Cat Club's owner. With newsboy Glimpy (**Huntz Hall,** far right), Muggs sneaks into the crime scene and learns that the dead man's ex-wife, Gypsy (Evelyn Brent), was seen running out of his house wearing a fuzzy coat and a veiled hat. Muggs and Glimpy, aided by Shorty (**Bud Gorman,** far left), locate Gypsy and after questioning her are convinced she is innocent. When they hear the cops coming, Muggs asks Skinny (**Billy Benedict**) to wear the fuzzy coat and the veiled hat (**photo**) so the police will chase him. Skinny looses his pursuers and learns that the victim's lawyer, Ken Duncan, is the new manager of the Pussy Cat. He sneaks into the joint and overhears evidence incriminating Duncan. The Eastside Kids storm in and let the cops do their job.

◄ HUNTZ HALL
CLANCY STREET BOYS
(1943, Monogram)

Liars-meet-their-redemption comedy directed by William Beaudine ● Uncle Pete Monahan (Noah Berry, Sr.), a Texas cattleman, comes to New York to visit Muggs McGinnis (**Leo Gorcey,** right) and his supposedly many siblings. Muggs' late father, to take advantage of his wealthy relative, had let him think he had seven kids when, in fact, Muggs was his only child. To maintain the fiction—and to help his mother continue to receive Pete's stipend—Muggs inveigles the East Side Kids into being his five brothers and Glimpy (**Huntz Hall**), his sister Annabelle (**photo**). The charade works until the day when small-time hoodlum George Mooney (Rick Valin) spills the beans. Furious, Uncle Pete tells Muggs to forget about his generosity. Later, feeling guilty, the Kids go to Uncle Pete's hotel to return his gifts. Once there, they find out he is being abducted for ransom. The Kids overpower the kidnappers and a grateful Pete invites everybody to his ranch.

► HUNTZ HALL
PRIVATE EYES
(1953, Allied Artists)

Fast-paced comedy about detective wannabes directed by Edward Bernds ● When Sach (**Huntz Hall**) is hit in the nose by a kid named Herbie (Rudy Lee), he acquires mind-reading abilities. To exploit this gift, his pal Slip Mahoney (Leo Gorcey) opens the Eagle Detective Agency. Its first client is a moll named Myra Hagen (Joyce Holden) who is trying to sever ties with a gang of thieves. Relying on the neophyte private eyes, she gives them an envelope that if delivered to the police could dismantle the criminal organization. Myra is kidnapped and brought to the Rose Hill Health Farm, where she tells the ringleader, Dr. Damon (Robert Osterloh), about the letter. When Slip gets a phone call from Herbie the kid who is also locked up at Rose Hill, Slip and Sach hatch a plan. Sach, dolled up as a ringleted rich woman named Mrs. Abernathy (**photo**), and Slip, masquerading as her elegantly turned-out Viennese physician, infiltrate the sanitarium's security. In a steam room, after several falls and fistfights, the Boys free Myra and Herbie and subdue the ring of swindlers.

MORE TRICKS,
MORE FOOLERY

◄ SAMMY COHEN
THE CRADLE SNATCHERS (1927, Fox)

Cheating-husbands-get-their-just-deserts light comedy directed by Howard Hawks ● Three married women, frequently left alone by their husbands who are always off on business trips, are wondering about their mates' loyalty. When one of the wives, Susan Martin (Louise Fazenda), obtains proof that the spouses have been unfaithful, she decides to hire a college boy whose mission is to flirt with her to make her husband (J. Farrell MacDonald) jealous. When the two other women meet the young man, Joe Valley (**Joseph Stryker,** right), they ask to get their own. Joe secures two of his college chums and an evening at one of the ladies' homes is arranged. With alcohol flowing freely, the visit becomes a party, and boys being boys, pranks are played, notably by Oscar (Arthur Lake) and by Ike (**Sammy Cohen**) who dresses in full drag and tries to vamp Joe (**photo**). When the husbands arrive, they are incensed at what they see and confront their wives. But tired of waiting in the car the husband's flapper dates show up, exposing the philanderers. Now in control of the situation, Mrs. Martin and her two friends exit with their boyfriends, leaving their spouses speechless.

► JOHNNY DOWNS
ALL AMERICAN CO-ED (1941, Hal Roach)

Sassy teen flick directed by Hal Roach Jr. and Leroy Prinz ● When the Mar Bryn Horticultural School for Girls criticizes the Zeta Fraternity at Quincetown University for showing bad taste in their all-male ballet spoofs, the boys decide to strike back. Their opportunity arises when the girls school organizes a beauty contest and the frat chooses one of the brothers, wrestling champion Bob Sheppard (**Johnny Downs**), to enter the competition in drag under the name of Bobbie De Wolf. Chaperoned by press agent Hap Holden (**Harry Langdon,** left), Bob boards a train headed for Mar Brynn (**photo**) hoping to carry out Zeta's plans for humiliating its president, Mrs. Coolige (Esther Dale). But because Bob falls in love with Mrs. Coolige's daughter, Virginia (Frances Langford), he cannot push the stunt too far. He does manage, however, to present a great show for the girls school and win Virginia's affection.

◄ RAYMOND GALLE
CLUB DE FEMMES (1936, Films Jacques Deval)

Engaging French melocomedy directed by Jacques Deval ● Paris' Club for Girls offers material comforts and moral security at affordable prices for 150 twenty-something women who are far from home and living alone. Because men are not allowed in this plush-but-strict shelter, Claire Rivier (**Danielle Darrieux,** left) must sneak in her boyfriend, music student Robert (**Raymond Galle**), for visits. Elegantly dressed and impersonating Claire's cousin Suzanne (**photo**), he fools the club's disciplinarian director. Unfortunately, Robert is unmasked when a fire breaks out and he must join the girls' bucket brigade to put it out. Claire's transgression and her subsequent pregnancy, however, are minor events compared to the murder of the establishment's switchboard operator (Junie Astor), who has been using her job to procure naïve girls for a male friend.

▶ DWAYNE HICKMAN & FRANKIE AVALON

SKI PARTY (1965, American International)

Unapologetically by-the-numbers juvenile comedy directed by Alan Rafkin ● Two college students, Craig (**Dwayne Hickman,** left) and Todd (**Frankie Avalon,** right), are envious of the attention their favorite girls, Linda (Deborah Walley) and Barbara (Yvonne Craig), are lavishing on Freddie (Aron Kincaide), a nebbish but suave classmate. During a ski vacation in Sun Valley, the boys dress like girls and, thus masquerading as Jane and Nora (**photo**), flirt with Freddie in order to learn what women find attractive about him. Between drag sessions, Todd catches the eye of Swedish ski instructor Nita (Bobbi Shaw), a fact that makes Barbara jealous. Meanwhile, when Freddie, now totally smitten with Nora, makes serious advances, she flees the resort with Todd in a car while Freddie chases them on a motorcycle. Reaching Malibu, Linda and Barbara realize Todd and Craig's imposture and are immediately head-over-heels in love with them.

▶ CHRISTOPHER MORLEY

BACHELOR PARTY (1984, Fox)

Shamelessly prurient romp directed by Neal Israel ● Young hunk Rick Gassko (Tom Hanks) is set to tie the knot with his girlfriend Debbie Thompson (Tawny Kitaen), but not before his bachelor party. Coincidentally, the bash is scheduled for the same day as Debbie's shower. But while Rick is assuring his fiancée that his party will have no hookers, his chum Gary (**Gary Grossman,** left) is busy negotiating with a pimp. When the two prostitutes show up at Debbie's shower and proceed with their S&M performance, she and her outraged friends pay a visit to Chippendales and later tart themselves up as whores for a visit to Rick's party. In the meantime, Gary gets it on with a beautiful blonde (**Christopher Morley**), who turns out to be a guy named Tim (**photo**). Both get arrested along with all the other revelers, but not before Debbie's suspicions are laid to rest.

▶ JONATHAN PRINCE, MICHAEL ZOREK & MATTHEW MODINE

PRIVATE SCHOOL (1983, Universal)

Thin teenage sexploitation farce directed by Noel Black ● While Ms. Dutchbock (Fran Ryan), Cherrydale Academy for Women's headmistress, raises funds for a new wing, the students are only interested in the boys at nearby Freemount Academy for Men. And vice versa. Three of the teenagers—Roy (**Jonathan Prince,** left), Bubba (**Michael Zorek,** second from left) and Jim (**Matthew Modine,** second from right)—are more daring than their peers and dressing as co-eds disguise their way into the girls' dorm. But Jordan (**Betsy Russell,** right) is not tricked (**photo**). Inviting Jim to her room, she kicks him out just when Chris (Phoebe Cates), the girl Jim is mad about, crosses the hallway. In spite of the students' moronic pranks, Chris and Jim are oblivious to the surroundings but not to the pains and joys of first love. In a final graduation day stunt, the Cherryvale girls moon Ms. Dutchbok much to the glee of the Freemount boys.

▲ MARTIN WEST, STEVEN ROGERS & ARON KINCAID

THE GIRLS ON THE BEACH (1965, Paramount)

Bubble gum comedy with bikinis and songs directed by William Witney ● In 1964, Selma (Noreen Corcoran), Cynthia (Linda Marshall) and Arlene (Anna Capri) are spending Easter vacation in their sorority's California beach house. They have fun in the sun and in clubs where the Beach Boys and the Crickets perform. Learning that their housemother, Ms. Winters (Sheila Bromley), is unable to make her next house payment, the trio devises ways to bail her out. Three young men with eyes for the three co-eds—Duke (**Martin West,** left), Brian (**Steve Rogers,** center) and Wayne (**Aron Kincaid,** right)—tell them that as Ringo Starr is Duke's pal, they can get the Beatles for a free concert. As tickets sell like hotcakes, the telegraph man tells the boys that he has just delivered a cable to Selma from the Beatles threatening to sue for fraudulent misrepresentation. The boys sneak into Selma's room to get the telegram before she can read it, but the ladder they use to gain entry falls and they have to escape through the crowded living room wearing borrowed dresses and wigs (**photo**). Finding out they have been hoodwinked, the girls impersonate the Beatles and come up with the money to save Ms. Winters.

SORORITY BOYS
(2001, Touchstone)
**Frisky R-rated frat-house comedy
directed by Wally Wolodarsky** ●
Party-hearty fraternity KOK is holding
one of its keggers while feminist co-
ed Leah (Melissa Sagemiller) is out
front picketing against the brothers'
objectification of women. She has
her reasons. As a member of Delta
Omicron Gamma–a DOG–she is
considered too unattractive to be
rushed by the other sororities. Meanwhile, Doofer (**Harland Williams,**
left), Dave (**Barry Watson,** center)
and Adam (**Michael Rosenbaum,**
right), panty-chasing brothers all, are
accused of stealing the house's cash
and forced to leave. Leah and her sisters give the trio refuge next door in
the DOG's house and thus begins a
series of misshaps as the absurdly
disguised men (**photo**) try to survive
in a woman's world. Adam/Adina
fends off clumsy male come-ons,
Dave/Daisy falls for Leah and
Doofer/Roberta mostly just battles
slipping falsies. One and all become
gender sensitive.

◀ **ROB LOWE &
ANDREW MCCARTHY**
CLASS
(1983, Orion)
**Barely credible inter-generational
romance directed by Lewis John
Carlino** ● When Jonathan Ogner
(**Andrew McCarthy,** right) joins
Vernon Academy prep school, roommate Skip Burroughs (**Rob Lowe,**
left) strips to reveal a red bra and
matching panties. As a prank, he
explains that it is a tradition to
wear women's lingerie on the first
day. So he lends Jonathan some
undies and sends him out the door.
But once Jonathan is out on the
quad alone, Skip locks him out
(**photo**), causing much hilarity among
the undergraduates. When Jonathan
goes to Chicago, he encounters
Ellen (Jacqueline Bisset), a woman in
her early '40s who seduces him in
an elevator. They begin a steamy
affair that goes up in smoke when
Skip surprises the couple in a hotel
room and realizes the woman is his
mother. But the roommates decide
to remain friends…while Ellen will
seek psychiatric help.

▼ TONY GANIOS
PORKY'S II: THE NEXT DAY (1982, Fox)

Gross-out sequel with a social conscience directed by Bob Clark ●
In '50s Florida, six boys from Angel Beach High destroy the strip joint
Porky's as vengeance against some rednecks who had ridiculed them.
The day after, Pee Wee (Dan Monahan) and his buddies, who include
Billy (**Mark Herrier,** left) and Tommy (**Wyatt Knight,** center), are ready for
more girl chasing. When the school's drama teacher enrolls them in a
Shakespearean production, local evangelist Reverend Bubba Flavel (Bill
Wiley) brands it as obscene. Principal Carter (Eric Christmas) argues
that, compared to the bible, the Bard's texts are inoffensive. The local
chapter of the Klan comes to Flavel's help because the boy playing the
part of Romeo is a Seminole. After the Klan beats him severely, Pee Wee
and his friends decide to strike back. They reveal the racist side of the so-
called moral majority and the hypocrisy of the local politicians. Later, a
lively audience welcomes the show in which Meat (**Tony Ganios**) plays
the part of *Hamlet's* Ophelia (**photo**).

▶ CHAD LOWE
NOBODY'S PERFECT (1989, Moviestore)

**Comedy about women's tennis with a male twist directed by Robert
Kaylor** ● At Bramson College, freshman Stephen Parker (**Chad Lowe**) is
a low-ranking member of the tennis team. His game is suffering because
his eyes are always drawn to the nearby women's court—and sweet
co-ed Shelly Anderson (Grail O'Grady). When his coach cuts him from
the team, Stephen's friend, Andy (Patrick Breen), cons him into adopting
a female identity so he can join the women's team, be near Shelly and
help the girls win the league championship—all so Andy can clean up by
betting on them. As Stephanie Brown, Stephen is a dunce at first, but the
ruse begins to work when "she" ends up rooming with Shelly. Stephanie
also gets an earful when Shelly admits that the private time spent with her
boyfriend is nothing less than coerced sex. When Shelly surprises
Stephanie using her decidedly non-female equipment in their bathroom,
Stephen argues that his love for Shelly is what enabled him to put up with
the humiliation of wearing a skirt. He later dons it again and, as Stephanie,
aces the championship (**photo**).

NUNS ON THE RUN

Oh brother, it's a sister!

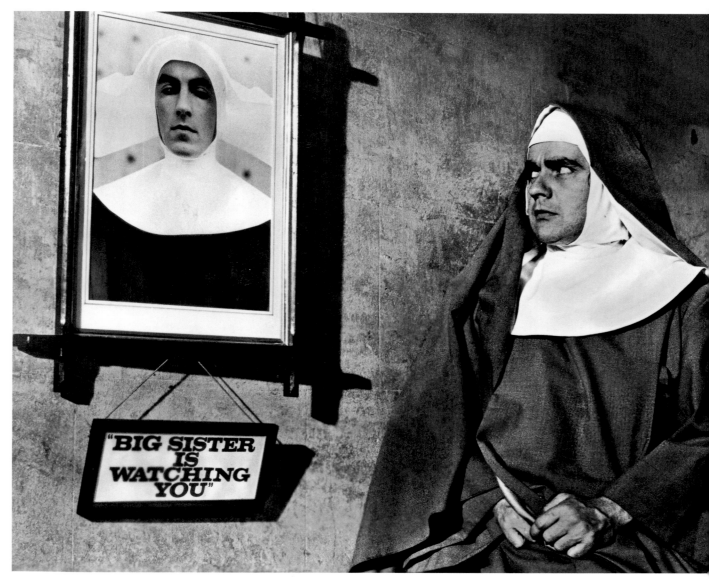

"BIG SISTER IS WATCHING YOU"

**DUDLEY MOORE
& PETER COOK**

BEDAZZLED (1968, Fox)

Oddball update of the Faust legend directed by Stanley Donen ● Meek short order cook Stanley Moon (**Dudley Moore**) is mad about sexy waitress Margaret Spencer (Eleanor Bron), but too shy to ask her for a date. Desperate, he tries to hang himself and, when thinking of what to do next, is interrupted by a stranger, George Spigott (**Peter Cook**), who identifies himself as the Devil. In the Faustian tradition, he offers Stanley the fulfillment of his dreams in exchange for his soul. Stanley accepts the bargain and six of his first seven wishes are granted—all with disastrous consequences. In frustration, Stanley wishes for a perfect love with Margaret in "serene surroundings." The Devil accepts and transforms Margaret and Stanley into silent nuns (**photo**) of the Order of the Leaping Berelians who to atone for their sins must bounce on trampolines. Finally, the Devil, who needs to do a good deed in order to be welcomed back into heaven, grants an eighth wish: Stanley finds himself in the same fast food joint where he and Margaret worked before. But this time he has the courage to ask her out.

**Above:
Peter Cook
and Dudley
Moore.**

▶ JEAN TISSIER
ONE STRANGE PARISHIONER
(French title "Un drôle de paroissien," 1963, Film d'Art)
Wickedly ironic comedy directed by Jean-Pierre Mocky ● An aristocratic Parisian family is now nearing abject poverty. Georges (Bourvil), the only son, tries to find a solution by praying devoutly in the church of his *arrondissement*. One day he interprets a parishioner's donation into the poor box as a sign from God encouraging him to rob such *troncs des pauvres*. He devises several techniques to deftly tease *francs* through the boxes' narrow slots: from the Sacré

Cœur to Notre Dame, he becomes a plunderer extraordinaire and a wonderful provider. Not surprisingly, his secret exploits soon attract the attention of the police's Church Crime Unit. After several attempts to catch him in the act, Inspector Cucherat (**Francis Blanche**, left) asks Inspector Bridoux (**Jean Tissier**) to clothe himself in a nun and investigate (**photo**), but Georges, himself masquerading as a priest, thwarts their plans. When cornered by the police, the remorseful thief fills up the poor boxes with some of his ill-gained fortune and escapes with his family to a foreign country—and to their former idle life.

▲ MAURICE CHEVALIER
PANIC BUTTON (1964, Yankee Productions)
Slightly shabby movie about the making of a bad film directed by George Sherman ● To create a $500,000 tax writeoff for his father, investment banker Frank Pagano (Michael Connors) goes to Rome to produce the worst television program possible, a show so bad that it will never been picked up by a network. For his version of *Romeo and Juliet*, Frank recruits a washed-up movie star, Philippe Fontaine (**Maurice Chevalier**), and a voluptuous but neophyte starlet, Angela (Jayne Mansfield), for the leads. When production is completed, Fontaine learns it will never be released, thereby annihilating his hopes of a comeback. With the help of his former wife and agent Louise (**Eleanor Parker,** right), he steals the print and, disguised as nuns (**photo**), the two drive to Venice where the International Television Film Festival is taking place. They succeed in having the tragedy screened in front of an audience that laughs hysterically. Philippe, at first miffed, swallows his pride when the jury awards the top comedy prize to *Romeo and Juliet*. Philippe becomes a major comic star in a series of films produced by Frank and costarring lovely Angela.

◄ **ENRICO MONTESANO**
I DON'T BUST... I BREAK
(Italian title "Io non spezzo... rompo," 1971)
**Italian all-action cops-in-trouble comedy directed
by Bruno Corbucci** ● In the Piazza di Spagna, two
Roman hippies are about to conclude a drug transaction.
But when money and dope are about to change hands,
each man handcuffs the other: this is how two decoy
cops, Attilio (**Enrico Montesano**) and Riccardo
(Alghiero Noschese), meet for the first time. Their boss
transfers the losers to another unit where they come
across three important drug lords. To trail the gangsters
while remaining anonymous, they disguise themselves.
As a nun, Attilio is particularly credible (**photo**) and
arrests are imminent. Unfortunately, during the bust a
hard-blowing fan bursts the packets of heroin open and
spreads the narcotics in the air, resulting in cops and
traffickers becoming friends and deciding to run away
together. At the airport, the police apprehend the
would-be fugitives. Guilty mainly of brainlessness, Riccardo and Attilio share the destiny of the real bad guys.

▲ **TONEY BREALOND**
COME BACK CHARLESTON BLUE
(1972, Warner)
Sequel to *Cotton Comes to Harlem* **directed by
Mark Warren** ● At a charity ball, fashion photographer
Joe Pinter (Peter De Anda) states that he plans to rid
Harlem of its dope dealers. When a few are murdered,
Joe claims that the ghost of Charleston Blue, a gang-
ster laid to rest in the '30s, has returned to clean up
the neighborhood. The small-time hoodlums believe
the charade because Charleston Blue's trademark, a
blue steel razor, has been found near each victim.
Some flee the city, others plead to be arrested, but
Detectives Gravedigger Jones (Godfrey Cambridge)
and Coffin Ed Johnson (Raymond St. Jacques) figure
out that Joe wants to carve out his own dope territory.
The two veterans investigate with such an ardor that
they are disciplined for using excessive force. Faking
their own death, they are able to freely chase a group
of criminals that includes a nimble killer dressed as a
nun (**Toney Brealond, photo**). In the mortuary chapel
where Charleston Blue is interred, Coffin Ed gives Joe
a severe beating before the deceased gangster's
widow (Minnie Gentry) slashes his throat.

◄ VINCENT PRICE
DR. GOLDFOOT AND THE GIRL BOMBS
(1966, American International)

Bargain-basement spy spoof directed by Mario Bava ● Wicked scientist Dr. Goldfoot (**Vincent Price**) devises a type of bomb which upon insertion in the navels of his gorgeous robot girls explodes while they are seducing their male targets—seven NATO generals attending a conference in Rome. The callipygian clones are part of an ambitious plan to start a war between the United States and the USSR for the benefit of China and Goldfoot himself. Fortunately, cherubic American secret agent Bill Dexter (Fabian) is on the trail of the evil plotter. At the Country School for Girls where Goldfoot's lab is situated, the scientist deflects an investigation by dressing as a nun (**photo**) and giving a gymnastic's class to the undetectable robot girls. Later, Dexter takes control of the B-52 carrying an H-bomb programmed to hit the States and throws Goldfoot from the plane.

► MAX JULIEN
THOMASINE AND BUSHROD
(1974, Columbia)

Tale of the rise and fall of two folk heroes directed by Gordon Parks, Jr. ● It is southwest America in 1911. Fearless bounty hunter Thomasine (Vonetta McGee) learns that her former lover Bushrod (**Max Julien**) has been accused of bank robbery and is on the lam. After she joins him, the two embark on a life of crime, taunting the authorities and sharing their loot with the poor. But while their generosity makes them folk heroes, they take the time between bank robberies to enjoy a life they know will end tragically. Trailed relentlessly by Sheriff Bogardie (George Murdock), they once avoid capture when they flee dressed as nuns (**photo**). After Thomasine tells Bushrod she is pregnant, they dream of the day when they can put down their guns and settle in Mexico as a family. But soon death catches up with Thomasine and a grieving Bushrod, enacting vengeance on his tormentor, dies as a legendary outlaw.

◄ PETER SELLERS
THE MAGIC CHRISTIAN
(1970, Artisan Pictures)

Satire of human nature directed by Joseph McGrath ● Sir Guy Grand (**Peter Sellers**), a rich and cynical man, meets a vagrant (Ringo Starr) and adopts him. Introducing him as Youngman Grand to his employees, the billionaire takes his new heir on a train ride. On the trip, Sir Guy induces a passenger into a psychedelic dream where he himself appears dressed up as a nun (**photo**). He then initiates a series of outrageous schemes aimed at demonstrating to Youngman that anybody will do anything for money. Inviting a group of London socialites to sail on the maiden voyage of a cruise ship, the *Magic Christian,* he mortifies his guests—who all take the abuse expecting future largesse. To prove irrevocably that human nature is despicable, Sir Guy dumps several million pounds of banknotes into a tank filled with a broth of blood, urine and fecal matter. The passing crowd, after some initial reluctance, dives into the ghastly mixture to retrieve the bills—making Sir Grand's point.

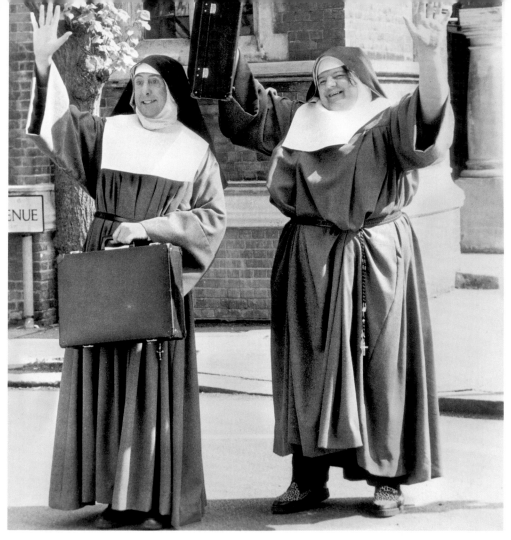

◄ ERIC IDLE & ROBBIE COLTRANE
NUNS ON THE RUN (1990, Fox)

Non-blasphemous change-of-habits comedy directed by Jonathan Lynn ● After bilking their gangster employer of a million pounds of drug money, two middle-aged hoodlums yearning for retirement in Rio —Brian Hope (**Eric Idle**, left) and Charlie McManus (**Robbie Coltrane**, right)—escape. Chased by fuming thugs, they run out of gas in front of a priory. Inside, they trade their clothes for religious habits and convince the sister superior (Janet Suzman) that they are visiting nurses from a different order. Charlie uses his Catholic upbringing to coach atheist Brian on the proper way to cross oneself: "spectacles, testicles, wallet, watch," he explains. Asked to teach theology to the convent's teens, they resist temptation and circumvent the inevitable cross-dressing traps when mingling with other nuns. Forced to lock up the two suitcases containing the stolen cash, Brian and Charlie are unmasked by the superior when they retrieve the loot. Escaping again, they head for the airport chased by the nuns, the goons and the police. They lose one valise, which is quickly snatched by sister superior, but succeed in boarding the plane to Rio.

◄ KEITH MOON
TWO HUNDRED MOTELS
(1971, United Artists)

Psychedelic musical comedy directed by Frank Zappa and Tony Palmer ● Predating MTV rock videos is Frank Zappa's visual homage to his wild-and-crazy "daze" on the road with his infamous rock band, the Mothers of Invention. A confused and rudimentary mélange of supposedly psychedelic color and imagery, this musical "trip film" is composed of an incoherent series of animation, sight gags, groupie primping and general all around road-musician high jinks. It features ex-Beatle Ringo Starr as the goateed Zappa himself, folk performer Theodore Bikel in various unidentifiable guises and **Keith Moon (photo)** as a nun—shown here with affectionate groupie **Janet Ferguson**. The central theme, if there is one, swirls around the berserk wasting of a typical American town called Centerville, with its Cheesy Hotel, Fake Nightclub and Redneck's Eat Café. In hodgepodge fashion, the action turns around such world-shaking dilemmas as to whether or not the group's members should rise up against their tyrannical master—that would be the real-world rock genius Frank Zappa—or whether they should just generally run amok while making goofy faces and cracking inside jokes about their so-very-cool life as turned-on rock rebels.

▼ JEFF GOLDBLUM & ROWAN ATKINSON
THE TALL GUY
(1989, Virgin Vision)

Cleverly whimsical romantic comedy directed by Mel Smith ● American Dexter King (**Jeff Goldblum,** right) is the straight man to a self-centered comedian named Ron Anderson (**Rowan Atkinson,** left) whose Rubberface Review forces him to partner in tasteless skits–like the one where they perform as singing nuns (**photo**). Dexter, who hates his role but needs to eat, is troubled by hay fever. He visits a hospital and taking a shine to nurse Kate Lemon (Emma Thompson) keeps going in for allergy shots even though he dreads injections. Dexter finally asks her out and they end up living together. Fired by his irascible boss for trying to upstage him, he lands the eponymous role in a musical production of *The Elephant Man.* Kate's intuition leads her to correctly suspect that Dexter has been shagging his leading lady and packs her bags. Shattered, he becomes furious when he sees her on the tube sitting with Anderson at a comedy award show. He rushes to the hospital and after helping Kate administer CPR to one of the patients declares his love in front of the approving ward.

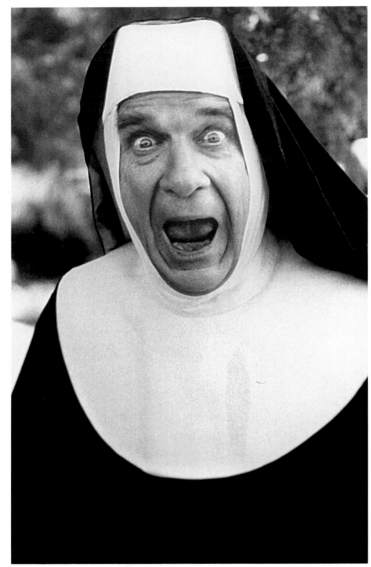

◀ LESLIE NIELSEN
SPY HARD
(1996, Buena Vista)

Bond-meets-Clouseau attempt at comedy directed by Rick Friedberg ● In order to thwart a lethal scheme devised by megalomaniac criminal General Rancor (Andy Griffith), secret agent Dick Steele (**Leslie Nielsen**) blows up his helicopter. Fifteen years later, a patched-up Rancor kidnaps Professor Urinsky, the inventor of a microchip with dangerous potential for the free world. Sent to Los Angeles to investigate, Steele meets Urinsky's sultry daughter, Veronique (Nicollette Sheridan) and together they try to find her father. But Rancor's thugs abduct her, too. Steele, however, succeeds in rescuing the professor and he finds him a safe house. After learning that Veronique is being detained in a convent, he dresses up as a nun (**photo**). Impersonating the new choir director, Steele spirits Veronique away only to learn that Professor Urinsky has been kidnapped again and moved to Kikiree Island, General Rancor's tropical hideout. Steele and Veronique infiltrate the general's fortress, annihilate the microchip in the nick of time, and after strapping the evil man to a missile launch him into space.

◀ **BURT REYNOLDS & JACK WESTON**
FUZZ
(1972, Filmways)
Treacherous cat and mouse game directed by Richard A. Colla ● The cops of Boston's 87th Precinct are on the trail of the Deaf Man (Yul Brynner), an elusive criminal who has threatened to kill several city officials if he doesn't get paid off. When the police accept his blackmail demands, the money transfer is arranged to take place in a park. Detectives Steve Carella (**Burt Reynolds,** top) and Meyer Meyer (**Jack Weston,** bottom), disguised as inoffensive nuns (**photo**), keep a sharp eye on the lunch box in which the pay-off money is supposedly stashed. But the trap is another fruitless attempt to catch the sly con artist, who immediately raises the blackmail amount and threatens to bomb the mayor's mansion. It is during a routine stakeout that the Deaf Man, for once an innocent bystander, is caught in the crossfire. Carella and Meyer are unable to catch him, but two teenage hooligans are more successful: thinking the Deaf Man is a bum, they soak him with gasoline and torch him.

ROLE REVERSALS

When the best woman for the part is a man

The Klumps family: Ernie Jr. (Jamal Nixon) and Granny, Papa, Sherman, Ernie and Mama, all played by Eddie Murphy.

◄ EDDIE MURPHY
THE NUTTY PROFESSOR
(1996, Universal)

Comical revisit to the Jekyll-and-Hyde horror tale directed by Tom Shadyak ● Seriously obese science professor Sherman Klump (Eddie Murphy) conducts weight-loss experiments on hamsters. When charming Carla Purty (Jada Pinkett) joins the faculty, Sherman becomes sweet on her. Convinced he needs to shed pounds to win Carla, he comes up with a testosterone-rich fat-reducing serum that transforms him into Buddy Love (Eddie Murphy without makeup), an alter ego who is everything he is not—witty, self-assured and thin. Carla finds Buddy interesting, but she is puzzled by his mean-spirited humor. When Sherman fails to show up for a presentation of his research to a potential benefactor (James Coburn), Buddy plots to present Sherman's findings as his own. The elixir having worn off, Sherman takes Carla home for dinner to meet his mother (**Eddie Murphy** in drag, opposite **photo**) and the rest of the family. Later, the monomaniacal Buddy reemerges and at the presentation, struggles with Sherman for preeminence in front of an aghast audience. Fortunately, Sherman's goodness, and roundness, win out, the college gets the donation and Sherman takes a spin on the dance floor with Carla. *(Inspired by an eponymous Jerry Lewis film.)*

▲ EDDIE MURPHY
THE NUTTY PROFESSOR II:
THE KLUMPS (2000, Universal)

Multi-identity comedy of coarse humor and latex prosthetics directed by Peter Segal ● Brilliant and blimpy, Wellman College scientist Sherman Klump (Eddie Murphy) has finally succeeded in ridding himself of his internal nemesis, Buddy Love (Eddie Murphy), by extracting Buddy's errant gene sequence from his own. The professor has also won the affections of fellow teacher Denise Gaines (Janet Jackson). It is quite a victory, considering Sherman's R-rated family (four of them played by **Eddie Murphy,** above), which excels at raunchiness and noisy bodily functions. Meanwhile, the dog on which Sherman has tested his new youth formula knocks over the beaker and sheds a hair onto the puddle. As a result, Buddy is reconstituted with canine tendencies. When Phleer Pharmaceuticals offers Wellman $150 million for Sherman's discovery, Dean Richmond (Larry Miller) is ecstatic—as is Buddy, who wants in on the deal. Unfortunately, by jettisoning Buddy's DNA, the professor has begun to lose brain capacity and is fired. But he reingests the strand and throws Buddy a ball injected with an improved formula. Buddy turns into a toddler and then a gooey blob that evaporates at the edge of the fountain. After Denise encourages Sherman to drink the water, the two are next seen sipping wedding champagne.

▶ VICTOR MOORE
CAROLINA BLUES (1944, Columbia)

Wartime show biz musical comedy directed by Leigh Jason ● Kay Kyser (himself) and his band have been booked at the Carver shipyards. There, Phineas Carver (Victor Moore), an impecunious parent of the plant's owners, summons five of his wealthy relatives—including Aunts Martha and Minerva Carver (both played by **Victor Moore, photos**)—to impress Kyser so he will hire his daughter Julie (Ann Miller) as the band's vocalist. Later, a childhood friend convinces Kyser to hold a bond rally in New York so their hometown of Rocky Mount, N.C., can buy a warship bearing its name. But Kyser learns that the money he has raised in New York cannot be allocated to his town. Crushed, he thinks he can persuade Phineas to make up for the loss. But Julie tells Kyser how poor they are and the two succumb to love. Phineas, meanwhile, blackmails his rich relatives—Aunts Martha and Minerva included—into making Kay's hometown project a reality.

▶ DUDLEY MOORE
THE HOUND OF THE BASKERVILLES (1978, Hemdale)

Sarcastic mockery of Conan Doyle's characters directed by Paul Morrissey ● Obsessed with the legend of a killer hound that roams the nearby moors, Sir Charles Baskerville has been murdered. His heir apparent, the unhinged Sir Henry (Kenneth Williams), contacts Sherlock Holmes (Peter Cook), but the detective delegates the case to his inept aide, Dr. Watson (Dudley Moore). Accompanied by Sir Henry, Watson goes to the Baskerville estate and meets a series of eccentric locals, each more unbalanced than the next. Unable to conclude the case, Watson asks Holmes for help. Joined by his dotty mother (**Dudley Moore** again, left), Holmes uncovers a complex conspiracy involving all of Sir Charles' daffy neighbors. When his will is read, it is revealed that the infamous hound, who turns out to be totally harmless, is to inherit the estate under the management of Sir Henry.

▶ ALASTAIR SIM
THE BELLES OF ST. TRINIAN'S (1954, London Film)

Ronald Searle's cartoon characters transposed to film and cleverly directed by Frank Launder ● St. Trinian's is a shabby British girls school where the hell-raising pupils brew homemade gin in the lab while the muddle-minded headmistress, Millicent Fritton (**Alastair Sim** in drag), fights for the institution's financial survival. Her twin brother (**Alastair Sim** also), a bookie, convinces her to readmit his daughter Arabella (Vivian Martin) into the school's Sixth form. But he does not tell his sister he wants the girl to relay to him information about Arab Boy, a racehorse owned by the Sultan of Makyad, father of student Princess Fatima. The girls of the Fourth form want to bet on him with Fatima's £100 of pin money. But, to get the school out of debt, the headmistress wages it on Arab Boy herself. When the Sixth form kidnaps the horse before the race, Sgt. Ruby Gates (Joyce Grenfell)—brought in undercover as a gym teacher—can do nothing. The feisty Fourth, however, hiding the horse, gets him to the track just in time to run and win.

◄ **ALEC GUINESS**
KIND HEARTS &
CORONETS
(1949, Ealing Studios)
Brilliant blend of social satire and black comedy directed by Robert Hamer ● Louis Mazzini (Dennis Price) is an arrogant cad in early 1900s London who is ninth in line to the dukedom D'Ascoyne. Impatient, he decides to eliminate the eight relatives who obstruct his path. Interestingly, all eight bear an uncanny resemblance to each other (all are played by **Alec Guiness**). Methodically, Mazzini knocks off his adversaries—from a senile general to eccentric suffragette Lady Agatha (**photo**), who is dispatched in a hot air balloon. With every heir except himself now history, Mazzini becomes the duke. Unfortunately, he is unable to enjoy his victory: accused by his scorned lover Sibella (Joan Greenwood) of a murder he didn't commit—her husband's—he is sentenced to death. A suicide note, however, written by Sibella's husband, exonerates him. As he exits the prison, the duke, who had written his life story in jail to impress the world after his hanging, realizes he has left the manuscript in his cell.

▶ **WILFRID BRAMBELL &
BERNARD CRIBBINS**
THE ADVENTURES OF PICASSO
(1978, Svensk Filmindustri)
Fictitious biographical farce ingeniously directed by Tage Danielsson ● Born in Malaga at the end of the 19th century, Picasso (Gösta Eckman) studies art in Madrid and then decamps to Paris. When American writer Gertrude Stein (**Bernard Cribbins** in drag, right) and her companion Alice B. Toklas (**Wilfrid Brambell** also in drag, left) buy one of his paintings, he is welcomed by the city's avant-guardists. During WWI, he triggers a stir in London with his decors for the Diaghilev ballets. His affair with Finnish torch singer Sirkka, who knows only one song, leads to boredom and to the States where he encounters the obscenely rich Ingrid Svensson-Guggenheim (Birgitta Andersson). Back to Paris at the start of WWII, Picasso joins the Résistance and in the '50s moves to the Riviera where he reencounters an old flame, Dolores (Lena Olin). Depressed by the commerce surrounding his art, Picasso vanishes, causing collectors everywhere to throw themselves off skyscrapers.

◀ **PETER SELLERS**
THE MOUSE THAT ROARED
(1959, Columbia)

Ingenious political satire directed by Jack Arnold ● Grand Fenwick, Europe's tiniest country, is on the verge of bankruptcy because its only export, a type of wine selling briskly in America, has been imitated by a California winery. The Prime Minister, Count Mountjoy (Peter Sellers), comes up with a plan to keep the country from going broke—declare war on the United States with the intention of losing quickly and then benefiting from American aid. The Grand Duchess Gloriana XII (**Peter Sellers** again, **photo**) puts the Grand Constable of the Armed Forces, Tully Bascombe (Peter Sellers also), in charge of the invasion. Soon after, 30 of Grand Fenwick's archers land in New York during an air raid drill, come upon empty streets and find nobody to surrender to. Capturing a scientist (David Kossoff), his daughter (Jean Seberg) and a powerful new weapon, the Q-bomb, the Duchy unwittingly forces the U.S. to surrender. The two countries negotiate the dissolution of the California winery and the inception of a League of Little Nations that will dictate to big nations a new order—peace forever.

▶ **PIERRE PIÉRAL**
LE VOYAGE SURPRISE
(1946, Pathé)

Well-orchestrated Gallic lunacy directed by Pierre Prévert ● Mr. Piuff (Sinoël), the owner of an almost defunct travel agency based in Fleurville, organizes a mystery tour of the region by bus. Enrolling the help of grandson Teddy (Maurice Baquet) and his pal Philippe (Jacques-Henri Duval), he lures many intrigued customers. This irritates his competitor, Mr. Grosbois, whose daughter Isabelle (Martine Carol) joins the trip to sabotage it. After enjoying several surprises, the adventurous zanies become involved in a revolution at the palace of the diminutive Grand Duchess of Stromboli (midget actor **Pierre Piéral**). They think the dangerous action is part of the tour and unwittingly risking their lives revel in the mayhem. Especially enthusiastic is Isabelle, who has traded her nefarious plans for the charms of Philippe. On his return to Fleurville, Mr. Piuff is given a hero's welcome.

▶ **PETER SELLERS**
THE GREAT McGONAGALL
(1974, Dartlan-Scotia)

Wacky portrayal of the lousiest Victorian poet directed by Joseph McGrath ● In 1890 Scotsman William McGonagall (Spike Milligan) sees Queen Victoria in a theatre (**Peter Sellers**) in the Royal Box and thwarts an attempt on her life. After this encounter with the monarch, McGonagall, who yearns for literary glory, decides to abandon his job as an out-of-work handloom weaver and give himself completely to his muse. Spouting ridiculous verse in mostly mediocre music halls, the poet's epic journey leads to Balmoral Castle. There he hopes to meet the Queen again and receive the coveted Poet Laureate award, but he is turned away. His quest for recognition, however, is almost realized when Lord Tennyson, representing the Crown, has Zulu King Theebaw decorate him with the Order of the White Mountain. The honor is so overwhelming that McGonagall dies a few weeks later, leaving a widow, two children and the reputation of being the greatest bad verse writer of his era.

◀ **ALBERTO LIONELLO &
MAX VON SYDOW**
THE BIG STEW (Italian title "Gran Bollito,"
1977, aka "Black Journal," Triangolo)
**Macabre tale of absolute madness directed by
Mauro Bolognini** ● Lea (Shelley Winters) has had 12
pregnancies in her life. Some have ended in miscar-
riages, some in premature deaths. This is why she is
obsessively attached to her only living son, Michele
(Antonio Marsina), and will do anything to prevent him
from marrying anybody – including dance teacher Sandra
(Laura Antonelli). When her husband is paralyzed by a
stroke, Lea slaughters three women who she thinks do
not have the right to live because they are childless. The
first is Berta (**Alberto Lionello** in drag, left) who, having
won the lottery, plans to move to America. The second is
Stella (Renato Pozzetto in drag), a singer proud of her
jewelry earned though sex. The third is Stella (**Max von
Sydow** in drag, right) who feels men are beasts and has
securities in the bank. The three spinsters die the same
way: decapitated with a hatchet, dismembered and
boiled in a caustic soda stew to make soap. The remaining bones are ground up to bake cookies that Lea serves
to her friends. When Michele is sent to the army, she
invites Sandra to stay with her and readies another stew.
Fortunately, the police stop her. In a daze, Lea tells her
paralyzed husband to finish the cookies.

▲ **VITTORIO GASSMAN**
THE MONSTERS (Italian title "I Mostri," 1963, Fair Films)
**Series of hilarious vignettes about human shortcomings directed
by Dino Risi** ● *Sketch "La musa" (The Muse):* During the lengthy delib-
erations of a literary jury in charge of awarding a novel first prize, one of
the members, Elisa (**Vittorio Gassman**), pushes a book that nobody
really cares for. Her aggressiveness finally rallies the tired jury to her
cause. Later, Elisa welcomes the flabbergasted winner (Salvatore
Borgese) at her apartment and promptly indicates to the naïve young
man that the time to pay his debt has come.

◀JOHN CANDY
NOTHING BUT TROUBLE (1991, Warner)
Sadly flawed comedy directed by Dan Aykroyd ● A self-satisfied New York book publisher, Chris Thorne (Chevy Chase), agrees to drive lawyer Diane Lightston (Demi Moore) to Atlantic City. One wrong turn off the New Jersey turnpike forces them to follow a cop into the backwoods town of Valkenvania, where they appear before dotty 106-year old judge J.P. (Dan Aykroyd). Sentenced to spend the night in his mansion, Chris and Diane discover that he has executed thousands for traffic violations. When the judge tells Chris that he will overlook all charges if he marries his mute and obese granddaughter Eldona (**John Candy, photo**), the ceremony is performed immediately. But Chris and Diane, who have fallen in love, try to escape—a difficult feat as Valkenvania is a sort of amusement park full of deadly traps, all operated by J.P. and Eldona. Free, the lovers see J.P. on the tube announcing he is going to New York to live with his new grandson-in-law.

▶ DOM DELUISE
HAUNTED HONEYMOON (1986, Orion)
Flawed send-up of '30s horror films directed by Gene Wilder ● Two mystery theatre radio stars of the '30s, Larry Abbot (**Gene Wilder,** right) and Vickie Pearle (**Gilda Radner,** left), plan to get married in the spooky mansion of Larry's Aunt Kate (**Dom DeLuise**). Unexpectedly, Larry is the victim of a series of phobias triggered, according to his psychiatrist uncle, Paul Abbot (Paul L. Smith), by fear of marriage. The shrink asserts that if Larry is scared almost to death his fears will vanish. To reach this goal, Dr. Abbot, enlists the help of Larry's family and plans a weekend that turns into a nightmare when Aunt Kate announces she has designated Larry as her sole heir. If he should die, the money will be divided among the family members, all of them weirdoes who now want Larry dead. After a night of gothic horror—complete with meowing doors and a scruffy werewolf—Larry is cured and the lovebirds get hitched. But was the scary adventure real or simply an episode of their radio program "Haunted Honeymoon"?

▶ MILTON BERLE
CRACKING UP (aka "Smorgasbord," 1983, Warner Bros)
Hodgepodge of recycled sight gags directed by Jerry Lewis ● Depressive Warren Nefron (**Jerry Lewis,** right) is such a screw-up that he fails at several attempts to take his own life. Conscious of his ineptitude, he shuffles into the office of Dr. Jonas Pletchick (Herb Edelman) and tells stories of his life as a clumsy carpet layer and an unfit hotel doorman. One day, while waiting for his appointment, he meets another patient, a sex-starved blonde (**Milton Berle**) who makes a pass at him but to no avail (**photo**). Dr. Pletchick diagnoses Warren's sickness as the Dingle Syndrome and prescribes a cure called post-hypnotic suggestion that will give him total control of his moves. After being hypnotized, Warren becomes a man at ease with himself, while the shrink turns into an insecure bumbler, the victim of psychiatric transference.

◀MICHAEL J. FOX
BACK TO THE FUTURE PART II (1989, Universal)
Ingenious time-travel fantasy directed by Robert Zemeckis ● It is 1985 and time-traveling teenager Marty McFly (Michael J. Fox) is settling down to quotidian routine. But life in Hill Valley is interrupted for the second time by the arrival of crazed scientist Dr. Emmett Brown (Christopher Lloyd) who whisks Marty away in his DeLorean time machine. Marty, Brown explains, must thwart a crime perpetrated in 2015 by the son of the then-adult Marty—who at that juncture also has a teenage daughter, Marlene (also played by **Michael J. Fox**)—that would dishonor his family down the road. After going back and forth in time, they return to 1985 and then, to bring the future back to normal, to 1955, when the trouble began.

▶ TYLER PERRY
DIARY OF A MAD BLACK WOMAN
(2005, Lions Gate)

Blend of romance, revenge and faith in a funny melodramatic comedy directed by Darren Grant ● Madea (**Tyler Perry**), a feisty, overweight matriarch, is not the mad black woman. It is her granddaughter, Helen McCarter (Kimberly Elise). Supplanted after 18 years of marriage by the mistress of her successful but nasty lawyer husband Charles (Steve Harris), Helen shows up at Madea's. The gun-toting granny encourages her to return to her mansion where the two wreak havoc. But Helen is still not really angry, even though she must now work, pretend to endure the attentions of an Adonis named Orlando (Shemar Moore) and put up with Madea's older over-sexed brother (also Tyler Perry). When Charles becomes crippled in a shooting, Helen rushes to his side and torments him. But Christian mores win out and she rushes to Orlando's side.

▶ ARSENIO HALL
COMING TO AMERICA
(1988, Paramount)

Pleasurable contemporary fairy tale directed by John Landis ● In the African country of Zamunda, Prince Akeem (**Eddie Murphy,** left) lives a pampered life. On his 21st birthday, he tells his father, King Joffer (James Earl Jones), that he wants to find his own queen in America. The king gives him 40 days, after which, if unsuccessful, he must marry the court's candidate. Excited, Akeem asks his confidant Semmi (Arsenio Hall) to accompany him. Posing as students, they begin their search. In local singles' bars, they encounter a disappointing assortment of ladies that includes a sexually aggressive redhead (**Arsenio Hall, photo**). Later, Liza McDowell (Shari Headley), daughter of a fast food restaurateur (John Amos), piques Akeem's interest and to be close to her he and Semmi get jobs as janitors at McDowell's. Displaying courage during a hold up, Akeem wins Liza's heart and marries his American love.

▶ PAUL MAZURSKY
MOON OVER PARADOR (1988, Universal)

Spoof about life in a Banana Republic directed by Paul Mazursky ● B-actor Jack Noah (Richard Dreyfuss) is shooting a film in the Caribbean country of Parador when the local dictator dies of a heart attack. Interior Minister Straussmann (Raul Julia), who notices that the actor is a dead-ringer for the deceased, coerces Jack into impersonating him. Among the people Jack must convince are his mistress, the spunky Madonna (Sonia Braga), and his strong-willed mother (director **Paul Mazursky** in haute-couture drag, **photo**). Jack enjoys the role until rebels try to kill him during one of his speeches. The ensuing repression opens Jack's eyes to the evil nature of the regime, so he fakes his own assassination and, before "dying," publicly names Straussmann as the culprit. When an uprising brings Madonna to power, she promises free elections. Jack returns to New York after having played the part of a lifetime.

▶ STEVE MARTIN
DEAD MEN DON'T WEAR PLAID
(1982, Universal)

Ingenious tribute to *film noir* directed by Carl Reiner ● Rigby Reardon (**Steve Martin**), an inept L.A. private eye of the '40s, is hired by femme fatale Juliet Forrest (Rachel Ward) to track down her father's killer, a noted scientist. During the investigation, Rigby interacts with characters from *films noirs* of the era (Alan Ladd, Burt Lancaster, Ava Gardner), and to approach a witness (Fred MacMurray), dresses up as blond bombshell Barbara Stanwyck in *Double Indemnity* (**photo**). On a tip from Philip Marlowe (Humphrey Bogart), Rigby then goes to a South American island where he discovers that the murder is connected to a ring of Nazi conspirators. In a secret lab, Marshall Von Kluck (Carl Reiner) is planning to annihilate the U.S. using an invention stolen from Juliet's dad. After a struggle, Rigby kills Von Kluck, saves his country and gets carnal compensation from Juliet.

Identity thieves & daring impersonators
THE GREAT PRETENDERS

ROBIN WILLIAMS
MRS. DOUBTFIRE (1993, Fox)

Family charmer with a preposterous plot directed by Chris Columbus ● Daniel Hillard (**Robin Williams**) is facing a divorce from Miranda (Sally Field), the mother of his three adored children, Lydia (Lisa Jakub), Chris (Matthew Lawrence) and Nathalie (Mara Wilson). When Daniel gives an out-of-control birthday party for his son, Miranda loses it and the couple ends up in court. Because Daniel is a sporadically employed actor, his successful interior decorator spouse gains custody of the kids, a decision that deeply wounds him. So when Miranda advertises for a housekeeper, Daniel gets his makeup expert brother (Harvey Fierstein) to turn him into the redoubtable Iphegenia Doubtfire. Miranda hires the plump Scotswoman to be the children's nanny and Mrs. Doubtfire soon endears herself to both them and his wife, who confides to him intimacies about her beau, Stu (Pierce Brosnan). Eventually Daniel's two older children catch on to their father's deception and all unravels at a restaurant when he must pitch a show to a TV big wig while participating in a family birthday party. When Stu chokes on a shrimp, Daniel saves him with the Heimlich maneuver—but dislodges his makeup thus revealing his identity. At sea without her precious nanny, Miranda approaches Daniel—who as Mrs. Doubtfire now has a popular children's television program—and brings him back into the family fold on a part-time basis.

► **TIM MOORE**
BOY! WHAT A GIRL!
(1947, Herald Pictures)
Stereotype-driven comedy directed by Arthur Leonard ● In Harlem, a pair of would-be producers, Jim (Elwood Smith) and Harry (Duke Williams) are expecting two potential backers for their jazz-and-dance variety show. As planned, Mr. Cummings (**Al Jackson,** left) comes from Chicago. However, Madame Deborah, an investor due from Paris, is unexplainably late. In order to keep Mr. Cummings interested, Jim and Harry ask one of their performers, Bumpsie (**Tim Moore**), to impersonate the wealthy Parisian beauty (**photo**). Against all odds, the ruse succeeds. Then, Madame Deborah herself (Sybil Lewis) arrives and after seducing Mr. Cummings secures the financing of the show.

◄ **"LITTLE BILLY" FITZGERALD**
OH BABY (1926, Universal)
Boisterous family-friendly comedy directed by Harley Knoles ● Midget "Little Billy" (**Billy Fitzgerald**) and his partner Charley Burns (Creighton Hale) are in the fight game. In the midst of preparing Jim Stone for the heavyweight title, Charley announces he has been filling his aunt Phoebe (Flora Finch) with stories about his imaginary family. When Phoebe announces that she is coming to town, Burns inveighs his tiny chum Billy to be a stand-in for the little girl (**photo**) and asks another friend, a magazine writer (**Madge Kennedy,** right), to pose as his wife. Barely avoiding being tucked into bed by the aunt's friend (**Ethel Shannon,** left), Billy, still in his frilly dress, races to the big bout at Madison Square Garden and shouts out advice to his champ from beyond the ropes. After Stone wins and Billy removes his disguise, Aunt Phoebe discovers that her nephew Charley has been deceiving her. No matter: she forgives him and it is all one happy family.

► **SYDNEY HOWARD**
GIRLS PLEASE!
(1934, British & Dominions)
Likeable but lackluster farce directed by Jack Raymond ● "Tram" Trampleasure (**Sydney Howard**), the gymnastics instructor at Highleigh Girls School, is left in charge when the headmistress suddenly leaves. His first visitor, Mr. Van Hoffenheim (Peter Gawthorne), introduces his daughter, Renée (Jane Baxter), and demands that Trampleasure keep her away from Jim Arundel (Edward Underdown), a boy with whom she might elope. When Tram learns that an academic inspector is arriving, he impersonates the headmistress, donning a prim-looking dress, spit-curled wig and pillbox hat (**photo**). But the inspector is Jane (Neva Carr-Glyn), a friend of Jim's who has come to tell Renée to get ready to run away the following morning. Tram succeeds in countering this attempt planned by the school's *enfants terribles* but he is unable to prevent one last try. When he finds Jim and Renée at the local hotel, he is so impressed with their commitment that he convinces Mr. Van Hoffenheim to consent to their union.

▼ SID SILVERS
BROADWAY MELODY OF 1936
(1935, MGM)

Sprightly satire of the hoity-toity set directed by Roy Del Ruth ● To ridicule Broadway producer Bob Gordon (Robert Taylor), who is desperately looking for a female dancing star to headline his next show, muckraking columnist Bert Keeler (**Jack Benny,** right) plants items about the arrival of a marvelous, but fictitious, new French star, La Belle Arlette. To give substance to his phony stories, Keeler has his sidekick, Snoop (**Sid Silvers**), dress as Mlle Arlette and register in an elegant Manhattan hotel. A frantic Bob Gordon tries to reach the performer to no avail, while Keeler continues to mock the producer's ineptitude. But when Irene Foster (Eleanor Powell), a former high school sweetheart of Gordon's who has since become a talented dancer, learns that Mlle Arlette does not exist, she adopts the French woman's identity and shows up at the producer's office. Bob Gordon fails to recognize her but at an impromptu audition he is impressed by the "French" dancer's special kind of magic. Later, at a lavish press party where Irene performs as herself, he finally realizes her identity and watches as a Broadway star is born.

◀ WILLIAM POWELL
LOVE CRAZY (1941, MGM)

Superbly ingenious screwball comedy directed by Jack Conway ● For their fourth anniversary, the Irelands—architect *farceur* Steven (**William Powell**) and socialite Susan (Myrna Loy)—have arranged an exquisite evening. But when Susan's mother, Mrs. Cooper (Florence Bates), shows up unexpectedly, their romantic plans evaporate. Prompted by her husband's strange behavior, Susan suspects he is having an affair with their neighbor, old flame Isobel Grayson (**Gail Patrick,** right), and decides to make Steven jealous by flirting with Isobel's husband. When her mother convinces her that Steven is indeed guilty of infidelity, Susan files for divorce. Steven agrees with his lawyer's scheme of feigning insanity, but he is not, as he hoped, released into the custody of his wife: he is interned in a sanitarium where he unwittingly convinces Dr. Wuthering (Sig Ruman) that he is crazy. Planning to arrange an appeasing tête-à-tête with Susan, Steven escapes the institution and rushes to his apartment where the police are on the lookout for him. Shaving his moustache, he dresses up convincingly as a woman and pretends to be his own sister (**photos**). Though he fools his mother-in-law and Susan's fervent suitor, Ward Willoughby (**Jack Carson,** center), Steven fails to deceive his wife who comes to her senses.

◀ LESLIE HENSON & ALBERT BURDON
IT'S A BOY! (1933, Gainsborough)

Delightfully oddball comedy directed by Tim Whelan ● On his wedding day, Dudley Leake (**Edward Everett Horton,** right) is confronted by a young man, Joe Piper (**Albert Burdon,** center), who claims to be his son. While Dudley and his best man, James Skippett (**Leslie Henson,** left), try to get rid of the lad, the father of the bride, waiting with his daughter in church, cancels the wedding. Desperate to justify their lateness, Dudley and James come up with an identical idea but do not communicate their stratagem to one another. Each planning a cross-dressing scheme, Dudley bribes his "son" Joe to borrow the maid's civilian clothes while James quickly finds his own female outfit. When the two women show up at the bride-to-be's house, immense confusion occurs (**photo**). Fortunately, the police intervene, revealing that Joe Piper is a notorious blackmailer who has made a profession out of posing as a long-lost son. Immediately, everything is forgiven and Dudley's fiancée agrees to marry him.

► **STIG JÄRREL**
LITTLE MARTA RETURNS
(Swedish title "Lille Märta
kommer tilbaka," 1948)
**WWII Scandinavian wild goose
chase directed by Hasse Ekman**
● On a train to Knättarp, a German
agent hides a sensitive document
in the coat of gentleman farmer
Pontus Bruzell (Hugo Jacobsson).
Upon his arrival, Mr. Bruzell discovers that a section of his property is
occupied by a Swedish army unit
under the command of Lt. Curt
Svensson (Hasse Eckman), who
has taken a shine to his daughter
Inga (Brita Borg). When a couple
of children inform Lt. Svensson
about a secret Nazi meeting, he
enrolls the help of the unit's cook,
Stig Lettström (**Stig Järrell**). Masquerading as Nazi officers, they
learn that the task of retrieving the
document from Mr. Bruzell's coat
has fallen on fascist lawyer Peter
Sonne (Douglas Hage) who as a
young man had gotten Mr. Bruzell's
wife pregnant, but has never laid
eyes on his illegitimate daughter. In
the ensuing pandemonium, Stig
Lettström dresses up as a female
journalist named Little Märta
(**photo**), while Svensson impersonates Sonne's daughter. When
pro-Nazi Sonne gets hold of the
coveted papers, the pursuit is on:
the Swedes are happy to have
contributed to the war effort.

◀ MANTAN MORELAND
UP JUMPED THE DEVIL (1941, Toddy Pictures)

Comic tale of petty crime and redemption directed by William Xavier Crowley ● Two recent parolees, Jefferson (**Shelton Brooks**, left) and Washington (**Mantan Moreland**), are afraid of being picked up for vagrancy. Excited about a job at the Aid to Abyssinia bazaar on the estate of wealthy Mrs. Wendell Brown, they are disappointed to learn that she has advertised for a couple. That is when Jefferson decides to pose as a butler and asks Washington to impersonate a maid. As the couple (**photo**) hitchhikes to Mrs. Brown's, they meet Bad News Johnson (**Maceo Sheffield**), a crook they knew in jail. He suggests they cooperate in a scam he wants to put over on their future employer but, aspiring to an honest life, they decline. Bad News, however, shows up at the bazaar dressed as a soothsayer named Swamee River and steals Mrs. Brown's necklace while reading her fortune. Knowing where Bad News has hidden the jewels, Jefferson and Washington trick him into restitution.

◀ LEE BENNETT
SCARED TO DEATH (1947, Screen Guild)

Incoherent cult horror film directed by Christy Cabanne ● The corpse of Laura Van Ee tells her tragic story: Married to the son of psychiatrist Joseph Van Ee (**George Zucco**), she is being driven insane by threatening letters and haunting memories. When hypnotist Leonide (**Bela Lugosi**) shows up at Van Ee's mansion, the shrink foretells problems, but his son Ward (**Roland Varno**) is interested in the psychic's powers. Showing Leonide the photo of couple René and Laurette, performers in a Parisian club before WWII, Ward tells him he suspects Laurette to be his wife Laura. A mute and mean dwarf and a box containing a mannequin's head generate more terror in Laura's mind. She admits that during the war she accused René of being a spy and turned him in to the Nazis. Now the fear of his return drives her crazy. When a ghastly green mask appears at the window, Laura is literally frightened to death. House detective Bill Raymond (**Nat Pendleton**, left) finds a woman outside who is René (**Lee Bennett**) in drag (**photos**). He says he only wanted to scare his former partner. Leonide, who had met him in a concentration camp, validates this version. *(With Douglas Fowley.)*

◀ LESLIE FULLER
FRONT LINE KIDS (1942, Signet-Butchers)

Endearing blitz-time comedy directed by Maclean Rogers ● In WWII London, the police arrest a pack of teenage boys who disturb their neighborhood with pranks and pilfering. The diminutive leaders, Bert and Ginger, are rescued by adult friend Nobby Clarkson (**Leslie Fuller**) who offers them jobs as pageboys at the Paramount Hotel where he works as head porter. The other street urchins are sent to the country. At the hotel, Bert and Ginger discover that the manager (**Anthony Holles**) and a client (**Marion Gerth**, right) plan to double-cross a gang of jewel thieves. Excited, the "front line" kids investigate with Nobby's help, but the suspicious manager fires him. Then, to return to the scene of the future crime, Nobby masquerades as Mrs. Ida Down (**photo**) and with Bert and Ginger rounds up the swindlers of both gangs.

◀ JOE YULE
JIGGS AND MAGGIE IN COURT
(1948, Monogram)

Adequate cinematic version of comic strip *Bringing Up Father* directed by Eddie Cline & William Beaudine ● Maggie (Renie Riano), a wealthy New Yorker who yearns to be a social butterfly, is so enraged when she hears herself compared to the comic-strip character Maggie, created by George McManus, that she sues him. While she fights for respect and A-list status, her husband Jiggs (**Joe Yule**) is considerably less hoity-toity. Throwing a party one night, he dons woman's clothing and convinces Dinty Moore (**Tim Ryan,** left), the owner of his favorite watering hole, that she is his long lost love (**photo**). The practical joke upsets Maggie who goes berserk, giving her husband a contemptuous dressing-down. When the lawsuit against McManus goes to trial, the cartoonist (played by himself) wins by proving that Maggie is too young to have inspired him. Flattered but still incorrigible, Maggie continues to annoy her down-to-earth husband in her attempt to climb Manhattan's social ladder. *(Joe Yule, who plays Jiggs, was Mickey Rooney's father.)*

◀ RICHARD LEGRAND
GILDERSLEEVE ON BROADWAY
(1943, RKO)

Convoluted romp based on radio characters directed by Gordon Douglas ● Summerville's pharmacist, J.W. Peavy (**Richard LeGrand**), goes to a druggist's convention in New York to convince his main supplier, Sun Drugs, to stay in business. He takes with him a chubby friend, the bass-voiced Throckmorton P. Gildersleeve, aka Gildy (**Harold Peary,** left). On the train, Gildy meets scatterbrained Laura Chandler (Billie Burke), the recently widowed and current owner of Sun Drugs. She immediately falls for Gildy and invites him to a party in her Broadway hotel's penthouse. Mr. Peavy and his fellow druggists hope that Gildy's charm will influence Ms.Chandler to keep her company alive. At the party, when Gildy asks her to sign the crucial deal with the Druggists Association, she agrees, thinking it is a marriage proposal. To get his friend off the hook, Mr. Peavy disguises himself as a woman (**photo**) and introduces "herself" to Laura as Gildy's current wife, all the while alluding to his bouts with amnesia. Laura takes the news graciously and signs the agreement.

◀ ROBERT LIVINGSTON
GOODNIGHT SWEETHEART (1944, Republic)

Tale of love and redemption directed by Joseph Santley ● Johnny Newsome (**Robert Livingston**), a big-city reporter, moves to a small town to take over a newspaper he half owns. Bringing his tough and arrogant anything-for-a-scoop style of journalism with him, he stirs up trouble during the mayoral election by accusing the main candidate, Judge Rutherford (**Henry Hull,** right), of having an illicit affair. Unable to find any romantic liaison in the judge's past or present, Newsome disguises himself as "Marie Stevens" and checks into a local hotel claiming that she will reveal everything about the judge's private life. When he cannot sustain his scheme, Johnny makes Marie disappear, but some evidence indicates that he killed her. Arrested and jailed, Johnny proves his innocence by appearing at the trial dressed as Marie (**photo**).

◄ HANNS LOTHAR
ONE, TWO, THREE
(1961, United Artists)

Hyperactive Cold War comedy directed by Billy Wilder ● C.R. McNamara (James Cagney), a mid-level Coca-Cola executive based in West Berlin, is asked by his boss, Mr. Hazeltine (Howard St. John), to keep an eye on his 17-year old daughter, Scarlett (Pamela Tiffin), during her vacation in Germany. Mr. Hazeltine indicates that if all goes well C.R. will become a top contender for the CEO position in Europe. Unfortunately, Scarlett spends her evenings partying in East Berlin and marries a Communist, Otto Piffl (Horst Buchholtz). To remedy this catastrophe, C.R. proposes to three lecherous Soviet diplomats who want to hire his curvaceous secretary, Ingeborg (Lilo Pulver), that in exchange they free Otto. During the swap, C.R. substitutes his heel-clicking assistant, Schlemmer (**Hanns Lothar, photo**), for the blonde, thus double-crossing the Russians. Soon after, Mr. Hazeltine realizes that his son-in-law has a great business sense and gives him, not C.R., the CEO position. Disappointed C.R. is "rewarded" with the vice-presidency of procurement at the company's headquarters in Altanta.

◄ PETER ALEXANDER
THE ADVENTURES
OF COUNT BOBBY
(Austrian title "Die Abenteuer des Grafen Bobby," 1961, Constantin)

Musical-cum-slapstick farce based on a comic-book character directed by Geza von Cziffra ● Count Bobby Pinelski (**Peter Alexander**) is in need of cash, and his financially strapped aunt asks him to take a job chaperoning a young American named Mary Piper (Vivi Bach) around Europe. Mary's mother has been forced to return stateside because of divorce proceedings but her daughter wants to continue on her trip from Paris to Vienna. Obviously the job calls for a woman, so Bobby dolls up as a fairly fashionable lady and gets the much-needed $50-a-day job. Warming up to the attractive Mary, he woos her during the evenings as himself, while still maintaining his female identity during the day. At one point Mary's father (**Oskar Sima,** right) finds Bobby's disguise so convincing (**photo**) that he attempts to court her. But love will prevail when Bobby and Mary happily unite.

▲ PHIL SILVERS & JACK GILFORD
A FUNNY THING HAPPENED ON THE WAY
TO THE FORUM (1966, United Artists)

Reprisal of Sondheim's Tony-winning stage hit directed by Richard Lester ● A slave named Pseudolus (**Zero Mostel**, right) plots his way to freedom by helping Hero (Michael Crawford), the son of his owners, meet his heart's desire. Hero lives next door to the whorehouse of Lycus (**Phil Silvers**, left), where his innamorata, Philia (Annette Andre), is staying. Because she is a virgin, she has been pledged under contract to Cpt. Gloriosus (Leon Greene) who is on his way to marry her. To prevent the wedding from happening and to make Philia available to Hero, Pseudolus impersonates Lycus and tells Gloriosus that his bride-to-be is dead. To convince him, slave Hysterium (**Jack Gilford**, second from right) poses as the deceased. Meanwhile, Erronius (**Buster Keaton**, second from left) arrives after a 20-year search for his twins who were kidnapped at birth. Nobody cares about his quest, especially Lycus, who is obsessed with honoring his contract with Gloriosus. Opting for diaphanous robes from his whorehouse's closet (**photo**) to get access to Gloriosus, he tells him that Philia is alive. Then it is discovered that Gloriosus and Philia are Erronius' long lost twins and therefore cannot marry. This leaves the way open for Hero and Philia to wed—and for Pseudolus to be freed.

▶ WOJCIECH POKORA
WANTED: THIEF OR MAID
(Polish title "Poszukiwany, poszukiwana," 1972)

Satire of an upside down job market directed by Stanislaw Bareja ● The only employment college graduate Stanislaw Rechowicz (**Wojciech Pokora**) can find is that of museum guard, a job notorious for low wages. Consequently, he and his wife live in a one-bedroom apartment. When he is accused of having stolen a valuable painting from the museum and is fired, Stanislaw transforms himself into a cleaning woman (**photo**). Moving from job to job to avoid the sexual overtures of some of his male employers who are attracted by his feminine magnetism, Stanislaw, now known as Marie, discovers that his new occupation is fairly lucrative. After relocating with his spouse to bigger digs, he learns he has been found innocent. But instead of going back to his museum job, he continues to toil as a freelance housekeeper.

▲ TONY CURTIS
CASANOVA AND COMPANY
(aka "Some Like It Cool," 1977, Panther Films)

Bawdy period farcetta directed by François Legrand ● In 1756, legendary lover Giacomo Casanova (Tony Curtis) is rotting in the Republic of Venice jail. Escaping, he takes refuge in a nunnery where three scantily clad novices volunteer to be deflowered by him. However, Casanova, much to his dismay, realizes that he has become impotent. At the same time, minor league crapshooter Giacomino (also **Tony Curtis**), a dead ringer for the famous stud, is also on the lam. He finds sanctuary in the bedroom of the Prefect of Venice's wife, Gelsomina (**Sylva Koscina,** left), a doe-eyed stunner who, believing him to be the real deal, enjoys a languorous afternoon with Giacomino. When her husband unexpectedly returns home, Giacomino dresses as a chambermaid and is introduced to the cuckold as Rosetta (**photo**). From that moment on, from boudoirs to *auberges*, from Gelsomina to Contessa Trivulzi (Britt Ekland), the adventures of the sexually charged look-alike help the real Casanova keep up his amorous façade.

▶ JOHN RITTER
STAY TUNED
(1992, Morgan Creek-Warner)
Cleverly plotted but ultimately bland fantasy-comedy directed by Peter Hyams ● While his wife Helen (Pam Dawber) is a star advertising executive, Roy Knable (**John Ritter**), a charisma-impaired salesman, seeks escape from her success in intensive TV watching. When a brash talker named Spike (Jeffrey Jones) offers him a chance to try a 666-channel television set, Roy cannot resist: he signs a contract with Hell Vision, unaware that this firm has turned soul-acquiring into an entertainment extravaganza for the benefit of Satan. Sucked into a huge satellite dish installed in their backyard, Roy and Helen are trapped in the electronic network and propelled from an asinine quiz show (*You Can't Win*) to a hellish version of *Driving Over Miss Daisy* and a terrifying miniseries about the French Revolution (*Off With His Head*) in which Roy is the Marquis de Knable, an enemy of the people who escapes the guillotine by wearing a female disguise (**photo**). Roy and Helen finally find their way back to their Seattle suburban house with the ingenious help of an electronics whiz—their down-to-earth son.

▶ PEE-WEE HERMAN
PEE-WEE'S BIG ADVENTURE
(1985, Warner)
Fantasy-anchored and breezily original comedy directed by Tim Burton ● A problem-free individual, Pee-wee (**Paul Rubens**, aka Pee-wee Herman) enjoys a childlike existence in a fantasy-filled house where every appliance is a toy that satisfies his innocent lifestyle. When his most cherished possession, a one-of-a-kind bicycle, is stolen, he consults a soothsayer who tells him that it is in the Alamo's basement. Determined to recover it, Pee-wee hitchhikes to Texas. Picked up by a convict on the lam (**Judd Omen**, left), he helps him evade a roadblock by masquerading as his girlfriend (**photo**). When in San Antonio, Pee-wee learns that the Alamo has no basement. But then he sees his beloved bicycle on television: it is to be featured in an upcoming film! In Hollywood, Pee-wee bluffs his way onto the Warner lot, steals his bike and leads security guards on a merry chase. Once caught, Pee-wee lands a movie deal based on his odyssey and gleefully learns that James Brolin will play the lead.

◀ T.K. CARTER
HE'S MY GIRL
(aka "Pulling It Off," 1987, Scotti)
Inoffensive musical comedy directed by Gabrielle Beaumont ● In a Missouri town, singer/composer Bryan Peters (David Hallyday) dreams of becoming a rock star. His personal manager, gas station attendant Reggie (**T.K. Carter**), shares his hopes. One day, Reggie mails Bryan's demo tape to Video LaLa, a cable channel running a contest which offers as first prize a trip to Los Angeles for two. Bryan wins but, realizing the companion invitation is valid only for a female, thinks of canceling the trip. Reggie, however, has the bright idea of becoming Regina, a black beauty of earthy allure (**photo**). Mason Morgan, the boss of Video LaLa, shocked by the biracial couple, minimizes their access to the press. But a cascade of events unfolds, which includes higgledy-piggledy gender switches for Reggie, who has fallen for P.R. beauty Tasha (Misha McK) while David has been swept away by sculptress and biker Lisa (Jennifer Tilly). In the end, Regina reveals his real gender and David performs in celebrity rocker Simon Sledge's show, producing instant fans.

◀ DABNEY COLEMAN
MEET THE APPLEGATES (aka "The Applegates," 1991, Triton Pictures)
Satire of middle-class shallowness directed by Michael Lehman ● Dick Applegate (Ed Begley, Jr.), his wife Jane (Stockard Channing) and their two children compose a normal suburban family. But in fact, they are giant Brazilian bugs that have mutated into humans. Dick, who has landed a job at a nuclear facility, plans to trigger a meltdown to make Earth habitable for insects only. The operation's leader, known as Aunt Bea (**Dabney Coleman**), manages his people in drag to avoid suspicion (**photo**). But the Applegates succumb to consumerism: Jane becomes a shopaholic and Dick begins an affair with his hot-to-trot secretary. This does not stop Bea whose vermin soldiers are digging a tunnel beyond the plant's walls: he dynamites the place, but Dick intervenes and saves the world. The Applegates return to Brazil and keeping their human appearance organize the pacifist Bug Liberation Army.

▶ JOHN HURT
EVEN COWGIRLS GET THE BLUES (1993, Fine Line)

Adaptation of Tom Robbins' cult novel directed by Gus Van Sant ● Model for a feminine hygiene company owned by an outlandish transvestite known as the Countess (**John Hurt**), Sissy (Uma Thurman), born with unusually large thumbs, has become the world's greatest hitchhiker. To shoot a new commercial, the Countess sends Sissy to her Oregon ranch managed by Miss Adrian (**Angie Dickinson,** right). The compound has been attracting a group of cowgirls whose volatile craziness meshes well with Sissy's psyche, but badly with the Countess and Miss Adrian. Torn between her loyalty to the Countess and her affection with the cowgirls, Sissy sides with them when they attempt to prevent the last surviving flock of whooping cranes from migrating by feeding them peyote. During a showdown with the FBI, Bonanza Jellybean (Rain Phoenix), the girls' leader, is shot to death. A saddened Sissy, to whom the Countess has deeded the ranch, abandons her insouciant life on the road.

▶ ROBERT STEPHENS
BRITNEY, BABY, ONE MORE TIME (2002, Republic Films)

Freewheeling mockumentary centered on the adventures of a Britney Spears-obsessed-fan directed by Ludi Boeken ● After winning a Britney Spears look alike contest in Milwaukee, young transvestite **Robert Stephens** (himself) can't wait for the first prize: a meeting with the teen icon. But when her road manager realizes the winner is not a girl, she kicks Robert out. Meanwhile, a local television station offers logistical support to indie filmmaker and major geek Dude Schmitz (Mark Borchardt) for an interview with Spears. After being ejected upon asking MTV's well-endowed singer if "they are for real," he finds Robert weeping in a diner. Realizing she is a fake, Dude promises her a meeting with Britney. Grateful, Robert allows Dude and his motley crew of three, to shoot her pig-tailed impersonation, so long as he can reveal his identity at the end. But Dude has other plans: selling the interview for big money. After a lively journey to New Orleans involving everything from dancing with gay truck drivers to warbling with hospitalized kiddies (**photo**), Robert accidentally sees the film's final edit—without his confession. All ends well, however, when Britney's agent arranges for Robert to hug the pop idol and finds in Dude the kind of genius needed for the star's next project.

▶ MIGUEL A. NUÑEZ, JR.
JUWANNA MANN (2002, Morgan Creek)

Bearable hoopster-in-a-bra farce directed by Jesse Vaughan ● No one in pro basketball has a worse case of "big head" than hugely talented Jamal Jefferies (**Miguel A. Nuñez, Jr.**). But when he moons the TV cameras during a game, he is ejected from the league. Now penniless, the athlete gets a brainstorm while observing a teenage girl working on her moves on a homemade court: he'll shoot hoops as a gal. Making it onto the Charlotte Banshees of the Women's National League, Juwanna Mann (**photo**) hogs all the action—and all the pretty girls. In this case, the loveliest is the team's captain, Michelle (**Vivica A. Fox,** left), who is sweet on a two-timing R&B singer. Meanwhile rap biggie Puff Smokey Smoke (Tommy Davidson) has taken a shine to Juwanna, which translates into awkwardness when Juwanna and Puff double date with Michelle and her man. After Michelle and Juwanna start chalking up victories, Jamal's real identity is exposed in the early minutes of a playoff. Now chastened, he returns at the half to deliver a let's-go-girls speech, cheering his teammates and showcasing his newfound sincerity.

HIDE & CHIC Lovelies on the lam

◀ EDDIE CANTOR
PALMY DAYS (1931, United Artists)

Fizzy musical farce directed by A. Edward Sutherland
● Eddie Simpson (**Eddie Cantor**) works for Yolando (Charles Middleton), a crackpot psychic who soon becomes the force behind several mishaps in his life. First Yolando sets him up with one of his lonely followers, Helen Martin (Charlotte Greenwood). Then he "divines" for an ardent supporter, baker A.B. Clark (Spencer Charters), that an efficiency expert will cross his path. But before Yolando can send an accomplice to defraud A.B., Eddie, assumed to be the expert by the baker, shows up and soon gains his trust. When two musclemen sent by Yolando, prey on Eddie to obtain A.B.'s safe combination, he escapes by masquerading as one of the salesgirls (**photo**). Undetected, he then hides the weekly payroll in a loaf of unbaked bread. Accused of having stolen the money, he rushes back to the ovens and with Helen's help locates the loaf and fingers Yolando as a thief.

▲ EDDIE CANTOR
ALI BABA GOES TO TOWN (1937, Fox)

Charming Arabian Nights-style spoof directed by David Butler ● During his vacation in Hollywood, modest autograph hound Alyosius Babson (**Eddie Cantor**) gets a job as an extra in an Arabian Nights production. Falling asleep on the set, he dreams he is in Baghdad in the year 937. When he reveals his name, Al Babson, he is mistaken for Ali Baba's son and is made prime minister by the sultan. Implementing social measures inspired by FDR's New Deal, Al angers the country's rich and powerful. Their leader, impenetrable Prince Musah (**Douglass Dumbrille,** right) soon takes over the kingdom, but Al fights back. As a woman swathed in diaphanous veils (**photo**), he mesmerizes Musah with a seductive dance, thereby neutralizing him. After a duel on a flying magic carpet, Al pushes Musah off. But it is he who falls…into present time. Awakened, he is promptly fired by the film's director.

▶ NED SPARKS
FOR BEAUTY'S SAKE (1941, Fox)

Blend of mystery, comedy and romance directed by Shepard Traube ●
A handsome astronomy professor, Bertram Dillsome (Ted North), inherits a swank New York beauty parlor, but soon realizes that something is amiss in his new business: after being sued by an actress, a customer leaps from a window to her death. Even his sourpuss press agent, Jonathan Sweet (**Ned Sparks**), is attacked and hospitalized. Beautician Dottie Nickerson (Joan Davis), after observing employee Anna Kuo (Lotus Long) making a suspicious call, learns that a blackmail ring has been operating on information picked up at the salon. She informs Sweet who escapes from the hospital in bedraggled female garb (**photo**) and takes a taxi (driven by **Matt McHugh**, right) to Ms. Kuo's flat. Once there, he tries to get into the apartment via the dumbwaiter, but Kuo and her partner-in-crime try to asphyxiate him. Dillsome comes to the rescue, however, and has everybody arrested, including the ringleader—his own lawyer.

▲ GORDON HARKER
LOVE ON WHEELS (1932, Gainsborough)

Corny but likeable musical comedy directed by Victor Saville ● Sales clerk at Gallop, London's leading department store, Fred Hopkins (Jack Hulbert), rides the bus every day with music student Jane Russell (**Leonora Corbett,** left) and, on the advice of the conductor (**Gordon Harker**), he tells her he is the general manager. The ploy works but, when he is fired, Jane dumps him because he lied. Getting a job in a women's clothing shop as a window dresser, Fred is so successful he is rehired by Gallop as ad director. Meanwhile, Jane has disappeared. When Fred learns that she is playing piano in a club, he and his bus conductor mate go from bar to bar looking for her. Getting drunk in the process, they find themselves at Gallop's the morning after. When the conductor is caught trying to change from a borrowed tuxedo into his uniform in the store window, a wild goose chase corners him in the women's dressing room. There he "borrows" a fur coat and a cloche hat (**photo**) from a female customer and flees while Fred and Jane are reunited.

▲ GEORGE FORMBY
COME ON, GEORGE! (1939, U.I.)

Comedy mixing risqué songs and horse racing directed by Anthony Kimmins ● George (**George Formby**), a cuddly pipsqueak who sells ice cream at racetracks while dressed as a jockey, is accused of stealing a wallet found in his cart. Though innocent, he jumps on a train and hides in the stall of a psychotic thoroughbred named Maneater. When they both arrive at the stables of its owner, the trainers are so surprised to see Maneater's calm behavior in George's hands that they ask him to ride the mount in the upcoming Bargrave Stakes. Despite his delight, George is still paranoid about the wallet theft, so when the local police sergeant (**George Carney,** right) shows up at the residence of Maneater's owner, George dresses up as a maid (**photo**). Later charmed by the sergeant's daughter, Anne (Pat Kirkwood), he rents a room—a recently refurbished jail cell—at their home. Training for the race, George learns the truth about Maneater and becomes terrified but a shrink renews his self-confidence: even a gang of conmen cannot prevent him from winning the race—and Anne's hand.

◀ **EDWARD EVERETT HORTON**
THE WHOLE TOWN'S TALKING
(1926, Universal)
Retro-kitsch comedy directed by Edward Laemmle ● After being wounded in WWI, Chester Binney (**Edward Everett Horton**) returns to his hometown with a weak heart. Surprisingly, his former employer, George Simmons (Otis Harlan), wants him to marry his daughter Ethel (Virginia Lee Corbin). Behind the idea, there is only greed: Chester is to collect a fortune in the near future. To counteract Ethel's negative feelings, her father fabricates a torrid past for Chester that includes an affair with movie star Rita Renault (Dolores Del Rio). Chester goes along with the plan but, when Ms. Renault comes to town, her suspicious husband zeros in on Chester. To disappear from the bully's field of vision, he dresses up as a middle-aged woman (**photo**). But when he learns that his heart condition had been misdiagnosed, Chester acquires a new male assurance. His thrashing of the movie star's irascible husband so impresses Ethel that she falls for the now macho veteran.

▲ DICK POWELL
HARD TO GET (1938, Warner)

Door-slamming romantic comedy straight-forwardly directed by Ray Enright ● Gas station attendant Bill Davis (**Dick Powell**), a persistent but rather naïve entrepreneur, dresses as a cleaning woman (**photo**) in a last desperate attempt to explain to a potential investor his plans for a cross-country chain of motor courts. His perseverance finally pays off when eccentric millionaire Big Ben Richards (Charles Winninger) agrees to finance the ambitious project. As frosting on the cake, Bill wins the tycoon's pretty daughter Margaret (Olivia de Havilland) as his wife. A fairly bratty minx, she comes to love Bill mainly because he refuses to acquiesce to her whims.

◀ STURE LAGERWALL
ADVENTURES AT THE HOTEL
(Swedish title "Äventyr på hotel,"
1934, Europa Films)

Pleasingly plotted comedy-adventure directed by Gösta Rodin ● Scion of a steelwork empire, Gunnar Berg (**Sture Lagerwall**) is an unemployed actor who lives at the Carlsson Hotel in Stockholm. One day at the hotel he sees the consul of Costa Banana, Mr. Svensson, a notorious bamboozler. When Gunnar realizes that the diplomat stays not only at the Carlsson but also at the Esplanad Hotel, he becomes suspicious. After a short investigation conducted with the help of an ex-flame, opera diva Elly (Isa Quensel), Gunnar discovers the nature of Svensson's con game: a kickback from an industrialist named Bandini. At a masquerade ball where the consul and Bandini are supposed to show up, Gunnar, impersonating a stunning blonde in the Mae West style (**photo**), brings to light the fraudulent Svensson's plot. Satisfied with his successful imitation, Gunnar realizes that even though acting is easy, there is no money in the theater. So he joins his father's business—with Elly at his side.

◄ LEON ERROL
SLIGHTLY TERRIFIC
(1944, Universal)

Double identity musical comedy directed by Eddie Cline ● Penniless car salesman James P. Tuttle (**Leon Errol**) foolishly agrees to finance *The Stars of Tomorrow,* a variety revue produced by Charlie Young (Eddie Quillan). Over his head, James P. calls his twin brother, steel tycoon John P. Tuttle (Leon Errol, also), hoping he will also invest in the show. John P. refuses and orders his brother to come back to their hometown to attend a Czechoslovakian folk festival. Seeing this as a golden opportunity, James P. brings the troupe to the event and impersonates his twin. Creating extreme confusion, he then devises a scheme to open his brother's wallet: disguised in the traditional costume for Czech women, he pretends to be John P.'s lost love, Hilda. John P. sees through the charade but lets *The Stars of Tomorrow* perform anyway. Despite the unwigging of the ill-at-ease Hilda (**photo**) by show stars Marie (**Betty Kean,** left) and Julie (**Anne Rooney,** right), John P. loves the revue and decides to be its angel.

► WILLIAM BENDIX
KILL THE UMPIRE
(1950, Columbia)

Crowd-pleasing baseball comedy directed by Lloyd Bacon ● Baseball fan Bill Johnson (**William Bendix**) is so obsessed with the game that he loses job after job. When his father-in-law suggests that he combine his passion with a career, Bill enters umpire school. Assigned to the Texas league after graduation, he becomes well liked—until the day when he makes a difficult call against the home team and, brutalized by an irate fan, forfeits the game. A threatening crowd surrounds Bill's hotel, but he refuses to be intimidated and decides to arbitrate the next game. Disguising himself as a woman (**photo**) with the help of a bandana, an oversized woman's suit and his colleague Roscoe's tailoring (**Tom D'Andrea,** right), Bill makes his way back to the field. There, the catcher who has recovered from the injuries that had prevented him from speaking in Bill's favor validates the call. Exonerated, Bill's simple comment is "play ball!"

◄ FRANK ORTH
GREENWICH VILLAGE (1944, Fox)

Affectionate tribute to the '20s music hall directed by Walter Lang ● Danny O'Mara (William Bendix) owns Danny's Den, a speakeasy in Greenwich Village where his sister, Bonnie (Vivian Blaine), is a singer on the rise. While Danny dreams of raising money to stage a Broadway show, Kenneth Harvey (Don Ameche), a composer who has written his first piano concerto, falls for Bonnie. Cadway (**Frank Orth**), a talent scout for Ziegfield, is constantly lurking around Danny's Den trying to lure Bonnie away but is regularly ejected by bouncers. In order to round up funds for his Broadway musical, Danny throws a costume party uptown where Cadway-the-spy shows up dressed as a female society swell from Vienna (**photo**). Promptly identified, he is ousted by Danny himself. The fundraiser is a big success and Danny's dream becomes reality—with music composed by Ken Harvey.

BLONDIE GOES LATIN (1941, Columbia)

Dagwood-gets-a-beat comedy directed by Frank R. Strayer ● Mr. Dithers (Jonathan Hale), the boss of Dagwood Bumstead (**Arthur Lake**), invites him, his wife Blondie (Penny Singleton) and their son Baby Dumpling to accompany him on a South American cruise. Once aboard, Mr. Dithers learns that an important deal must be signed immediately. Expressing his apologies, he asks Dagwood to go back to the office. But when Dagwood attempts to disembark, he gets trapped on the boat that a few minutes after sails away. Afraid of telling anyone, including his wife, that he is still on board, he plans to hide by replacing the no-show drummer of the ship's band (**photo**), and to be unidentifiable borrows a dress and wig from the singer. Dagwood's fear of retribution if Blondie recognizes him dissolves when he learns that his not signing the deal actually benefits Mr. Dithers.

◀ARTHUR LAKE
BLONDIE HITS THE JACKPOT
(1949, Columbia)

Dagwood-blows-the-whistle comedy directed by Edward Bernds ● A case of mistaken identity is the cause of an altercation between Dagwood Bumstead (**Arthur Lake**) and one of his firm's potential clients, J. B. Hutchins (**Lloyd Corrigan,** center). The morning after, Dagwood, afraid of being discharged, temporarily trades desk and clothes with the switchboard girl (**photo**) so he can eavesdrop on his boss. When Mr. Radcliffe (**Jerome Cowan,** right) discovers Dagwood's ruse, he fires him on the spot. After a string of short-term jobs, Dagwood finds work in construction where he discovers that his supervisor is using defective steel on Mr. Hutchins' building. He reports the felony to the owner and is swiftly rehired by Mr. Radcliffe. Dagwood is even more elated when his wife Blondie (Penny Singleton) wins the consolation prize at a radio contest—a dog.

▶ ANDY DEVINE
ALI BABA AND THE FORTY
THIEVES (1943, Universal)

Middle Eastern romantic adventure directed by Arthur Lubin ● After killing the Caliph of Baghdad, the Mongols pursue his son, Prince Ali, who finds shelter in the cave of a band of 40 thieves. Their leader, Old Baba (Fortunio Bonanova), adopts him. Ten years later and grown to manhood, Ali (Jon Hall) returns to Baghdad to avenge his father's murder. But the Mongols capture him and sentence him to death. The 40 thieves, having become freedom fighters, decide to liberate him. One of them, Abdul (**Andy Devine**), is ridiculed by his companions and so abandons his impersonation of a woman (**photo**) to confuse the enemy. A better ruse involving 40 gigantic oil jars allows the thieves to enter Baghdad, free Prince Ali and help him reclaim the throne. That done, he reunites with his childhood sweetheart, Amara (Maria Montez).

▶ CESAR ROMERO
WINTERTIME (1943, Fox)

Light but charming comedy-on-ice directed by John Brahm ● When a Norwegian skating star named Nora (Sonja Henie) and her uncle, Hjalmar Ostgaard (**S.Z. Sakall,** right), arrive at Canada's Château Promenade, they are welcomed by two men: owner Freddy Austin (Cornel Wilde) and fortune hunter Brad Barton (**Cesar Romero**). The Château's press agent, Skip Hutton (Jack Oakie), thinks that a romance between Nora and Freddie would help the resort and tries to ridicule Brad by stealing his clothes while he is taking a shower. Forced to swipe female garb to get back to his room, Brad is caught by Nora's uncle (**photo**), thereby squashing his chances of marrying the Nordic celebrity. Meanwhile, Germany has invaded Norway, resulting in a freeze of Mr. Ostgaard's assets. Unable to pay his bills, he is desperate until he meets a New York ice skating promoter who has come to check out Nora's talent. Thrilled by her artistry, the impresario brings her to Broadway where she triumphs in *Wintertime: A Musical Icestravaganza.*

▼ JAMES HAYTER & BURT LANCASTER
THE CRIMSON PIRATE (1952, Warner)

Action-packed parody of pirate movies directed by Robert Siodmak ● Late in the 18th century, a band of barbarous seadogs led by skipper Vallo (**Burt Lancaster**) attack a Spanish galleon and discover an eminent passenger, Baron Gruda (Leslie Bradley). When the Crimson Pirate, as the captain is known, learns that the baron has been sent by the king to a Caribbean island in order to crush a revolution fomented by El Libre (Frederick Leicester), he sets in motion a fiendish double cross. After selling El Libre the guns and cannons stolen from the Crown's vessel, Vallo plans to disclose the location of the freedom fighters for a reward of 50,000 gold florins. His stratagem evaporates when he catches his first glimpse of Consuelo (Eva Bartok), El Libre's daughter. To please the lady, he impersonates Baron Gruda, foils a mutiny and joins the rebels. Assisted by his deaf-mute sidekick, Ojo (Nick Cravat), and Professor Prudence (**James Hayter,** left), inventor of a potent new explosive, he even masquerades as a flower girl (**photo**) to thwart Consuelo's forced marriage to the governor. Finally, thanks to Vallo, the island is freed from colonialist tyranny.

▶ ANTHONY PERKINS & ROBERT MORSE
THE MATCHMAKER
(1958, Paramount)

Farcical precursor to *Hello Dolly* **directed by Joseph Anthony** ● Dolly Levi (**Shirley Booth,** left), a 1880s matchmaker, is determined to land a wealthy bachelor for herself. Luring rich but cranky Yonkers shop owner Horace Vandergelder (Paul Ford) to New York, she lets him think he is going to meet a gorgeous young prospect. Meanwhile, his two naive clerks, Cornelius (**Anthony Perkins**, center) and Barnaby (**Robert Morse**, right), have decided to venture secretly to New York as well. When they all inadvertently end up at the same posh restaurant, Cornelius and Barnaby panic. In order to escape detection by their irascible boss, they borrow the lengthy coats and veiled hats of their dates (**photo**), Irene (Shirley MacLaine) and Perry (Minnie Fay). Back in Yonkers, Dolly and the boys open their own emporium across from Mr. Vandergelder's, forcing the dyspeptic man to give them a share of his business and propose marriage to the conniving but adorable Dolly.

◀ BOB CRANE
THE WICKED DREAMS OF PAULA SCHULTZ
(1968, United Artists)

Cold War escapist comedy directed by George Marshall ● Paula Schultz (**Elke Sommer**, center), a babelicious East German athlete training for the Olympic Games, defects to the West by pole-vaulting over the Berlin Wall. Bill Mason (**Bob Crane**), a broke American black marketeer living in the western zone, agrees to help Communist Propaganda Minister Klaus (Werner Klemperer) retrieve their champion in exchange for $75,000. After spending an enchanting evening with Paula, Bill reneges on the deal. But when she learns what the suave Yankee had intended, Paula voluntarily returns to East Berlin. In order to get her back, Bill clandestinely enters the Soviet-controlled sector dressed as a female athlete (**photo**), finds Paula and after fighting off local not-so-secret agents, Weber (John Banner) and Oscar (Leon Askin), convinces his love to defect again—this time for marriage.

▼ LANDO BUZZANCA
LA CALANDRIA (1972, Filmes Cin.ca)

Ribald Renaissance-era romp about illicit sex directed by Pasquale Festa Campanile ● Fulvia (Agostina Belli) is the naïve and graceful wife of an old man named Calandro (Salvo Randone)—hence her nickname La Calandria. Outside of Calandro's mansion, a young stud, Lidio (**Lando Buzzanca**), who considers himself the township's Don Juan, dreams of seducing the beautiful bride. When, in order to develop her son's knowledge in the art of love, Calandro's mother looks for an experienced female teacher, Lidio sees an opportunity to further his libidinous plan. Disguised as the expected woman (**photo**), he is able to approach La Calandria with the assistance of her gullible husband who, not surprisingly, falls for him. Lidio however succeeds in deflecting Calandro's senile attraction while enjoying the carnal pleasures of adultery with the superb Calandria. Unfortunately, Lidio's luck is not everlasting: he will pay dearly for his misdeeds by being castrated. *(With **Barbara Bouchet** as Lucrezia, left.)*

▲ FRANCIS HUSTER
COLINOT
(French title "L'histoire très bonne et très joyeuse de Colinot trousse-chemise," 1973, Warner)

Tale of a medieval rite of passage directed by Nina Companeez ● In 15th century northern France, a young and innocent country girl named Bergamotte (Ottavia Piccolo), the betrothed of Colinot (**Francis Huster**), a randy 20-year-old farmhand nicknamed Skirtlifter, is abducted by miscreants on their engagement day. Bravely, Colinot sets out on a desperate search for his innamorata in the company of his friend Tourneboeuf. During his north-to-south quest, he crosses paths with many of the fair sex: châtelaine Rosemonde (Bernadette Lafont), who forces him to don wig and wimple (**photo**) when her suspicious husband (**Julien Guiomar**, right) comes back home; an unhappily married boatwoman, Bertrade (Nathalie Delon); and courtly Arabelle (Brigitte Bardot), a comely maiden who travels surrounded by troubadours celebrating ad infinitum her astonishing physical charms. When Colinot finally finds Bergamotte, he is crushed to learn that she is happily united in wedlock with handsome noblemen Mesnil-Plessis (Jean-Claude Drouot). Fortunately, Colinot reconnects with the adorable Arabelle, who gives him the most instructive—and sweetest—lesson in lovemaking, thereby helping him find himself.

▲ ALBERTO SORDI
I VITELLONI (1953, Api Productions)
Nostalgia-tinged tale of feckless youth directed by Federico Fellini ● It is the summer's end in a small Italian seaport after WWII and five friends, all living off their respective families, have nothing to do all day but try to amuse themselves. When these *vitelloni,* or "overgrown calves," are not lazing about in cafés, they speak to each other of dreams that, because they involve effort, they hope will never come true. Fausto (Franco Fabrizi)

has gotten Sandra (Leonora Ruffo), the sister of his chum Moraldo (Franco Interlenghi) pregnant and he is the only one of the little group who by marrying succeeds in leaving town—if only for his honeymoon. He is also the only to get a job because he is pushed by his father-in-law. Another *vitellone,* Leopoldo (Leopoldo Trieste), who each night writes till dawn, is the only semi-disciplined one, and Riccardo (Ricardo Fellini) sings in public but only once a year. Alberto (**Alberto Sordi**), whose sister gives him spending

money, rouses himself only during Mardi Gras and then masquerades as a caricatural woman (**photo**). Meanwhile, Fausto, an unrepentant ladies man, makes a pass at the boss' wife and gets fired. When Sandra learns of this and disappears, the five friends search for her. After they find her, Fausto returns home with her. Moraldo, the most restless little "calf," soon boards the train for where…he does not even care. *(Released in the U.S. in 1957 under the inadequate title* The Young and the Restless*.)*

▲ JAMES FOX
THOROUGHLY MODERN MILLIE
(1967, Universal)

Roaring '20s musical about flapper feminism directed by George Roy Hill ● Millie Dilmount (**Julie Andrews,** right) moves to the big city to get a job as a "stenog." Staying with new arrival Dorothy Brown (Mary Tyler Moore) in a hotel for single young ladies, she notices that residents have been disappearing with frequency. Millie soon finds a chum in swell paper clip salesman Jimmy (**James Fox**), lands a job working for wealthy potential catch Trevor Gordon (John Gavin) and makes friends with merry widow Muzzy (Carol Channing). To Millie's disappointment, Trevor falls for Dorothy, but when Dorothy mysteriously disappears, she suspects that rooming house owner Mrs. Meers (Beatrice Lillie) is running a white slavery ring for Chinese customers. To investigate Dorothy's abduction, Jimmy dresses as a lonely flapper (**photo**) and checks into the hotel. Sensing another victim, Mrs. Meers contaminates her room with a sleeping potion so she passes out. Millie follows Mrs. Meers to Chinatown where she finds and frees the female slaves—and Jimmy. Back at Muzzy's grandiose estate, Millie realizes that Jimmy is her half-brother and that both are multimillionaires. A double wedding unites Trevor to Dorothy and Jimmy to thoroughly modern Millie.

▲ JEAN-PAUL BELMONDO
UP TO HIS EARS (French title "Les tribulations d'un Chinois en Chine," 1966, Films Ariane)
Unpretentious action-adventure film directed by Philippe de Broca ● After experiencing all the pleasures of life, billionaire Arthur Lempereur (**Jean-Paul Belmondo**) wants to die. In Hong Kong, family friend Mr. Goh (Valery Inkijinov) offers to arrange his demise. Arthur accepts but when he sees two men trailing him, he thinks they are hired guns and takes shelter in the dressing room of a gorgeous stripper, Alexandrine (Ursula Andress). She helps him escape and because Arthur is now in love, he decides to live. So, he must find Mr. Goh who is in Nepal. Arthur's journey leads to the slopes of the Himalayas where, taken prisoner by Tibetan bandits, he escapes in a hot air balloon only to be captured by Chinase pirates. When Arthur reaches Mr. Goh, the old man tells him the men following him were charged with his protection. Relieved and happily reconnected with Alexandrine, Arthur becomes the target of scoundrel Charley Follinster (Joe Saïd) who sends his goons after him. Taking refuge in Alexandrine's club, he goes on stage in one of her costumes and improvises a strip act (**photos**) to avoid discovery. After derailing Follinster's plans, Arthur learns that Alexandrine has been stripping to subsidize her studies in archeology.

◀ **BING CROSBY**
HIGH TIME
(1960, Fox)

Flimsy and predictable back-to-college comedy directed by Blake Edwards ● Owner of a chain of fast food restaurants, 50-year old widower Harvey Howard (**Bing Crosby**) decides to go back to college. In spite of his children's protests, he enrolls in an East Coast university where his cool demeanor helps him gain the respect of his roommates Gil (Fabian) and Bob (Richard Beymer). But the real test comes with his initiation, which requires him to attend a society ball dressed as a hoop-skirted Southern Belle (**photo**) and to sweet talk the local gout-suffering judge into dancing with him. Harvey succeeds on all accounts, becoming a hero among the students. He also develops into an object of desire for the French teacher, Hélène Gauthier (Nicole Maurey), a beautifully accented thirty-something charmer. After a discrete courtship, Harvey gives his valedictorian speech and accepts Hélène's offer of marriage.

▶ ALEC GUINESS
THE COMEDIANS (1967, MGM)

Graham Greene saga about repression and romance directed by Peter Glenville

● In Haiti, under the regime of Papa Doc Duvalier, each foreigner needs to be a "comedian" in order to avoid arrest and torture at the hands of the despot's Tontons Macoute. In Port-au-Prince, cynical hotelier Mr. Brown (**Richard Burton,** right) is the lover of Martha (Elizabeth Taylor), the wife of a South American ambassador, Manuel Pineda (Peter Ustinov). Major Jones (**Alec Guiness**), a hotel guest who brags about his military exploits, is an arms dealer selling weapons to the Haitian army. When the transactions turn sour, Brown suggests to Jones that he ask Ambassador Pineda for political asylum, and in order to elude the cops watching the hotel disguises him as his black female cook (**photo**). At the embassy where Jones now resides, Martha is so sensitive to his charms that Brown wants to break the relationship. To do so, he challenges Jones to lead a group of rebels in overthrowing Duvalier's iron rule. Major Jones, seeking redemption, accepts. Predictably, the Tontons Macoute kill him before he can reach the rebels. Remorseful, Brown takes his place while the Ambassador and his wife flee the country.

▶ NINO MANFREDI
ADULTERY ITALIAN STYLE
(Italian title "Adulterio all'italiana," 1966, Titanus)

Boisterously bouncy farce directed by Pasquale Festa Campanile ● Marta (Catherine Spaak), the spirited wife of Franco, a macho Roman executive (**Nino Manfredi**), discovers that her husband is cheating on her with her best friend. Revengeful, Marta remains calm: instead of creating a scandal she simply informs Franco that in fairness she may now reciprocate and sleep with whomever she wants—whenever she wants. This threat makes Franco intensely jealous. Marta feeds this paranoia with multiple false hints, thus derailing her husband's attempts at discovering who his rivals are. Becoming unstable, he does the craziest things to unmask his once scorned mate's potential lovers: he pretends to have ingested poison, and later masquerades as a woman (**photo**) to divert the attention of another possible lover (**Akim Tamiroff,** right) away from his wife. After this series of humiliations, Franco, forgiven, is allowed back in Marta's bed. He learns then that she has remained faithful the whole time.

▲ PHILIPPE NOIRET
JUSTINE (1969, Fox)

One-quarter of Lawrence Durrell's exotic *Quartet* elegantly directed by George Cukor

● In 1938 Alexandria, Justine (Anouk Aimée), a Frenchwoman married to powerful banker Nessim (John Vernon), is a free spirit who seduces a variety of men to serve her politics. Among her lovers is Darley (**Michael York,** left), an English writer captivated by her sensuality. At a masquerade ball, Pombal (**Philippe Noiret**), a French consular attaché who is being harassed by his boss (Marcel Dalio), appears dressed as a well-endowed woman (**photo**). Luring his superior into a compromising situation, Pombal exposes him as a lecher. Meanwhile, Darley realizes that Justine has used him as an amorous diversion and that she and her Coptic Christian husband are the nexus of a group of conspirators supplying guns to Jews in Palestine to help them overthrow the British rule and create an Israeli state. After one of Justine's paramours, a diplomat (Dirk Bogarde) who knew about the scheme, poisons himself, the Egyptian police place Justine and her husband under house arrest. A heartbroken Darley leaves Alexandria forever.

◄ WOODY ALLEN
BANANAS (1971, United Artists)

Slapdash satire of greed, power and naïve New Yorkers directed by Woody Allen ● Neurotic product-tester Fielding Mellish (**Woody Allen**), in love with an activist (Louise Lasser) whose cause is the uprooting of the dictatorial regime ruling the Caribbean state of San Marcos, wings his way to the tiny country. Upon arrival, he is invited to dinner by San Marcos' strong man, General Vargas, who, in order to pin a murder on the Communist rebels and get the CIA to send money, plans to kill the New York nebbish. When Vargas' men botch the mission, rebel leader Esposito saves Fielding and seizes power. After he declares the official language of San Marcos to be Swedish, the insurgents decide to name Fielding president of the banana republic. (*The scene in which Allen appears as a dueña during the dinner with General Vargas was edited out of the final print.*)

▼ MICHAEL PALIN
JABBERWOCKY (1977, Columbia-TriStar)

Bloody but merry medieval fairy tale inspired by Lewis Carroll and directed by Terry Gilliam ● The kingdom of Bruno the Questionable is gripped by fear: a monster they call Jabberwocky is roaming the land, devouring peasants and villagers. Meanwhile, simple-minded cooper apprentice Dennis Cooper (**Michael Palin**), who loves the porcine Griselda Fishfinger, leaves his hamlet to look for job opportunities in the capital. His perilous quest leads him to the castle apartments of King Bruno's daughter (**Deborah Fallender**, left). Thinking Dennis is her prince charming, the princess helps him escape the fortress disguised as a nun (**photo**). Her father, meanwhile, calls for a tournament to select the knight able to slay Jabberwocky. As the chosen man's valet, Dennis witnesses the savage duel between the creature and the designated champion. Jabberwocky kills the brave knight but endures his own death when he impales himself on Dennis' sword. Now a hero, the coppersmith is given the princess's hand, a rude disappointment for a peasant who wanted to marry the zaftig Griselda.

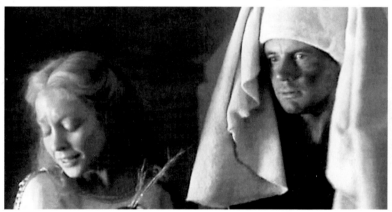

► NINO MANFREDI
KILL ME WITH KISSES
(Italian title "Straziami, ma di baci saziami," 1968, Fida Productions)

Cynical comedy about jealousy, suicide and murder directed by Dino Risi ● Barber Marino Balestrini (**Nino Manfredi**) becomes so enamored of beautiful Marisa Di Giovanni (Pamela Tiffin) that he gets a job in her hometown. Unfortunately, Marisa's father opposes their marriage. After the lovebirds fail at a suicide attempt, the old man dies and the couple decides to tie the knot. But a jealous innkeeper tells Mario that his intended has led a low-life past. The story is apocryphal but Marisa is so upset by Marino's reaction that she escapes to Rome, eventually marrying Umberto Ciceri (**Ugo Tognazzi**, left), a deaf-mute tailor. When Marisa reads in the papers of Marino's survival from a jump into the Tiber, she rushes to his side. Recovered, Marino tries to gain the favor of Marisa's husband by attending a costume party. There, dressed as an Andalusian belle, he meets Umberto, who has donned an Indian chief's outfit (**photo**). Enraptured with each other again, Marino and Marisa plan Umberto's death. But the cuckolded husband survives the plot and thanks to it gains back his speech and hearing. Grateful, he annuls his wedding vows, blesses the marriage of his wife to Marino and enters a monastery.

▶ JAMES HAAKE
TO BE OR NOT TO BE (1983, Fox)
Slapsticky remake of the '42 Lubitsch classic directed by Alan Johnson ● During the German occupation of Poland, self-important Frederick Bronski (**Mel Brooks**, left) and his sensuous wife Anna (**Anne Bancroft**) are the stars of a rinky-dink theatre company. Suspected by the Nazis of being members of the Resistance, the couple and their cast and crew bring into play ingenious deceptions to avoid arrest. Anna feigns to be attracted to the rotund Gestapo chief, Colonel Ehrardt (**Charles Durning**), and Frederick aptly impersonates Adolf Hitler. Meanwhile, Sasha (**James Haake**), Ms. Bronski's personal dresser, disguises himself as a woman to play a female role and passes out on stage (**photo**) when the Germans show up. Eventually, they all help the real Resistance, save their own lives and continue to perform risible plays such as *Highlights From Hamlet*, during which Bronski haughtily spouts "To be or not to be."

▶ GENE WILDER
HANKY PANKY (1982, Columbia)
Thin Hitchcock-style suspense spoof directed by Sidney Poitier ● While high-strung Kate Hellman (**Gilda Radner**, left) looks desperately for her brother's killers, architect Michael Jordon (**Gene Wilder**) is the innocent witness of the beating to death of a young woman (**Kathleen Quinlan**) whom he met that very day. Suspected of murder, Michael goes on the lam and fortuitously hooks up with Kate. Caught in an international intrigue concerning the most advanced defense system ever devised, Michael and Kate are chased by an enigmatic criminal named Ranson (**Richard Widmark**). Forced to hide from government agents and the police (**Madison Arnold**, right), often in ridiculous disguises (**photo**), the two run in tandem through New York, Connecticut and the Grand Canyon. With all this proximity, Michael and Kate fall in love. When an Arizona desert showdown with Ranson and his thugs takes place, Michael turns the tables on his pursuers and proves his innocence.

◀ MICHEL PICCOLI
RENÉ LA CANNE (1977, Amlf)
Gallic-charmed cat-and-mouse comedy directed by Francis Girod ● In 1942 Paris, swindler René Bornier, aka René la Canne (**Gérard Depardieu**) and anti-Nazi traffic cop Marchand (**Michel Piccoli**) meet in a hospital where they have been sequestered after their unrelated arrests. They escape together and join the "voluntary work" program created by the occupying forces. Toiling in Germany, they have a series of pleasant sexual encounters with a set of swinging twins but they irritate the Germans so much that they are forced to escape again. René la Canne manages with the help of a Dutch girlfriend (**Sylvia Kristel**), and Marchand by joining, in drag (**photo**), a troupe of French female entertainers on their way back to Paris. After the liberation of France, Marchand is promoted to police inspector and René becomes a flamboyant jewel thief in Marseille. On opposite sides of the law now, the two meet again, and after a series of chases Marchand catches René. But instead of arresting him he joyously takes off with him—and his loot—to Switzerland.

◀ **SEAN CONNERY**
ZARDOZ
(1974, Fox)
Muddled sci-fi fizzler directed by John Boorman ● In 2293, the primitive Brutals live in the Outlands and the more sophisticated Eternals in the Vortex. Zed (**Sean Connery**), of the Exterminators, helps this elite cadre oversee the Brutals. Losing his faith in the Exterminator god Zardoz, who takes the form of an enormous stone, he explores inside. He discovers and shoots Buggy (Arthur Frayne) who has been the string-puller behind the fake divinity. The god-vehicle finally lands in the Vortex where the inhabitants are ruled by a supercomputer known as the Tabernacle. When the Eternals imprison Zed, genetic engineer May (Sara Kestelman) wants to use him as a stud to reinvigorate the race. Consuella (Charlotte Rampling), a sexy Eternal, is tantalized by him but still wants to kill him. As she and some Eternals search for Zed, members of the Renegades, a sub-race, hide him by dressing him as a bride (**photo**). Consuella falls in love with Zed before he destroys the Tabernacle. Time recedes and after the Exterminators annihilate the now mortal Eternals, Zed says goodbye to the many he has impregnated and settles down with Consuella to raise their son. (**Photo** at left comes from a production costume trial.)

345

▼ BURT REYNOLDS, SAMMY DAVIS JR. & DOM DELUISE
CANNONBALL RUN II (1984, Fox)

Vapid sequel to an earlier vapid farce directed by Hal Needham ● The Cannonball Run, a cross-country race from California to Connecticut, draws car enthusiasts and oddball flunkies attracted by the prize: one million bucks. Among the latter are the daredevil team of J.J. McClure (**Burt Reynolds,** left) and Victor (**Dom DeLuise,** right); a duo of hoods with medium-to-loose morals, Blake (Dean Martin), Fenderbaum (**Sammy Davis, Jr.,** center) and Sheik El Falafel (Jamie Farr) who carries the prize money in his limo. Nearing Las Vegas, the sheik is kidnapped and the cash stolen by a mafia family. When J.J., Victor and Fenderbaum consult Frank Sinatra (as himself), he suggests that the three disguise themselves as exotic dancers (**photo**) in order to participate in a casting call at the mob's compound. The audition is a disaster but with the help of a bunch of ragtag drivers J.J. and his pals free the sheik and get the money back. A few days later, a chimpanzee wins the race.

► PAT MCCORMICK & PAUL WILLIAMS
SMOKEY & THE BANDIT PART 3 (1983, Universal)

Crass warp-speed comedy directed by Dick Lowry ● Texas Sheriff Buford T. Justice (Jackie Gleason) is contemplating retirement in Florida. It is there that two entrepreneurs, Big Enis (**Pat McCormick,** left) and Little Enis (**Paul Williams,** right), offer him a chance to publicize their new restaurant franchise, Fish & Chips. If Buford can deliver a plastic shark from Miami in less than 24 hours, he will collect $250,000. If he fails, the lawman must retire. Considering the relatively short distance, Buford accepts the dare. The Enises, however, hire Cledus "The Bandit" Snow (Jerry Reed) to prevent the sheriff from arriving on time. What follows is a series of road chases, sliced-off doors, cut-off tops and pulverized cars. In the hopes of distracting Buford, the Enises arrive in lamé gowns (**photo**) at a motel where he stays. The move is ineffective: the sheriff crosses the finish line with the shark just before the deadline.

◀ GARY BUSEY
DIARY OF A SERIAL KILLER (1998, Goldbar)

Well-acted but psychologically shallow thriller directed by Joshua Wallace ● Author of an award-winning article titled *Through the Eyes of an Alcoholic*, Los Angeles journalist Nelson Keece (**Gary Busey**) starts to research the transvestites' milieu. In a nightclub, dressed as a blonde siren (**photo**), he notices a man named Stefan (Arnold Vosloo) who seems at ease with the entourage. Following him, he witnesses a woman's murder. Horrified, his instincts take over when the psychopath offers to tell him his story for publication. Keece agrees on the condition that Stefan refrains from knifing anybody until the interviews are over. But the killer nabs two more victims. Now he is after Juliette (Julia Campbell), the writer's girlfriend. Keece prevents her murder by killing Stefan who dies a satisfied man: his future biographer has enough material to reveal that his game of pursuing a prey and destroying it was pure euphoria.

◀ JOHNNY DEPP
DON JUAN DEMARCO (1995, New Line)

Charming tale of romantic delusion directed by Jeremy Leven ● Psychiatrist Jack Mickler (Marlon Brando) is attempting to discover why a handsome youth (**Johnny Depp**), who dresses like Zorro and speaks like Fernando Lamas, is pretending to be Don Juan, the legendary lover. Dr. Mickler is soon engrossed in DeMarco's life, involving invented or potentially real tales that begin with his birth in a Mexican village and continue with a duel with his inamorata's father, the resulting death of his own father and his own sale—disguised as a female slave (**photo**)—to a harem where he learns love's secrets from the sultan's beauties. Later, escaping to the island of Eros, the caballero finds, and loses, his one true love, Dona Ana (Géraldine Pailhas). As Dr. Mickler is increasingly drawn into DeMarco's fantasy world, he himself experiences a rebirth of a romanticism whose beneficiary is his wife Marilyn (Faye Dunaway). After releasing his amorous patient from the hospital, he takes him along with Marilyn back to Eros where Dona Ana awaits her Don Juan.

◀ OLIVER PLATT
THE IMPOSTORS (1998, Fox Searchlight)

Slight but charming comedy-mystery directed by Stanley Tucci ● In 1930s New York, Arthur (**Stanley Tucci**, left) and Maurice (**Oliver Platt**), two unemployed actors caught in a brawl, are chased by the police. They find refuge on a cruise ship and become stowaways when the liner lifts anchor. Masquerading as porters—and always on the move in order not to be detected—they overhear the ship's First Mate (Tony Shalhoub) confide to a telephone correspondent that he plans to kill a passenger, the deposed queen (Isabella Rossellini) of a Mediterranean country. The anarchist intends to detonate a bomb that will rub out not only the ex-queen but also all the boat's "bourgeois" voyagers. To foil the plot, Arthur and Maurice disguise themselves as an aging couple (**photo**), attend the Captain's ball and with the help of a stewardess (Lilli Taylor) save the day.

▶ JACKIE CHAN & STEVE COOGAN
AROUND THE WORLD IN 80 DAYS (2004, Disney)

Martial-arts-infused version of Jules Verne's classic directed by Frank Coraci ● A Chinese man (**Jackie Chan**) steals a jade Buddha from the Bank of London, and to avoid the constables becomes, under the sobriquet of Passe-partout, the valet of inventor Phileas Fogg (**Steve Coogan,** center). When Fogg, who tinkers with experimental machines, explains to the Royal Academy that it is possible to circumnavigate the planet in 80 days, Lord Kelvin (Jim Broadbent) offers this wager: if Fogg can accomplish the feat, he will replace him, Lord Kelvin, as Minister of Science; if Fogg fails, he will be banned from working in his profession. Soon en route to the starting point of their world tour, Fogg and Passepartout realize that a detective hired by Lord Kelvin is trying to slow them down. In Paris, vivacious damsel Monique (**Cecile de France,** right) joins them, facilitating their escape in a hot air balloon. In Turkey, they are held in Prince Hapi's (Arnold Schwarzenegger) harem; in Calcutta, they disguise themselves as Indian women (**photo**) to evade British soldiers; in China, Passepartout—whose real name is Lau Xing—returns to his village the Buddha he repossessed in London; and in San Francisco the threesome fights off a Chinese warlord and her goons. After constructing a flying contraption that carries them across the Atlantic, Fogg and his friends crash at the Academy's steps in time to win his wager—and the Queen's appointment to Minister of Science.

◀ **JOSEPH FIENNES**
SHAKESPEARE IN LOVE
(1998, Miramax-Universal)

Enchanting fictional account of the genesis of *Romeo and Juliet* **directed by John Madden** ● London 1593. Playwright William Shakespeare (**Joseph Fiennes**) is unable to complete *Romeo and Ethel, the Pirate's Daughter,* a work commissioned by the cash-strapped owner of The Rose theatre, Philip Henslowe (Geoffrey Rush). During casting, Will notices a graceful lad. When the chap runs away, Will follows him and meets Lady Viola de Lesseps (**Gwyneth Paltrow,** right), a delicate beauty for whom he falls hard. He realizes he has found his muse and the fact that his love is returned unleashes his imagination: he begins writing again while romancing his new flame. Realizing that Viola had auditioned as a man to bypass the law preventing women from acting, Will learns that she has been promised in marriage to Lord Wessex (Colin Firth), an obnoxious noble approved by Queen Elizabeth (Judi Dench). Will and Viola's secret affair is almost uncovered when Wessex shows up at his fiancée's house while the couple is in bed. Will fools Wessex, however, by masquerading as Viola's female cousin (**photo**). His hopeless love causing him to transform his original comedy into a drama called *Romeo and Juliet,* Will continues rehearsals with a mustachioed Viola as Romeo and a boy dressed and made up as Juliet. But when Viola marries Wessex and there is no one to play Romeo at the premiere, Will decides to take the part himself. To his elation, Viola appears at the last minute and, replacing the boy in drag who was supposed to be Juliet, plays the role herself. The lover's suicide at the play's end moves the crowd, and the queen—who has recognized Viola—applauds both "male" actors. Nevertheless she orders Viola to join her husband who is sailing for America.

HELLO DOLLIES!

Mascaraed mam'zelles strut their stuff

◄ **PATRICK SWAYZE,**
JOHN LEGUIZAMO & WESLEY SNIPES
TO WONG FOO, THANKS FOR
EVERYTHING! JULIE NEWMAR
(1995, Universal)

Big-time Hollywood take on the world of drag directed by Beeban Kidron ● New York drag divas Vida Boheme (**Patrick Swayze,** left) and Noxeema Jackson (**Wesley Snipes,** right) win a trip to Los Angeles where they tie for first place in a transvestite beauty contest. Their friend, Chi Chi Rodriguez (**John Leguizamo,** center), is left out, but Vida and Noxeema decide to make the journey a threesome. They set off in a 1967 Cadillac, placing the poster "To Wong Foo, thanks for everything" on the dash as a sort of guiding star. In mid-mid-America, Officer Dollard (Chris Penn) stops them and after coming on strong is kayoed by Vida. Running for their lives, they end up in Snyderville where their car dies. At first, they set the burg on its ear with their outrageous behavior, but soon they work magic in the lives of several locals: Noxeema urges a mute woman to speak by playing movie trivia; Vida knocks a wife beater on the jaw and forces him out of town; Chi Chi, meanwhile, lets his hormones take over and teases an innocent male teen. When Officer Dollar locates them, he realizes they have become Snyderville's darlings and abandons the chase while Chi Chi wins the National Drag Queen Championship.

▲ **HUGO WEAVING,**
TERENCE STAMP & GUY PEARCE
THE ADVENTURES OF PRISCILLA,
QUEEN OF THE DESERT
(1994, Gramercy Pictures)

Glitzy "fish-out-of-water" road movie directed by Stephan Elliott ● Tick (**Hugo Weaving,** left), who as Mitzy is a lip-synching drag performer in Sydney, has contracted for a gig in Alice Springs, a resort town in Australia's northern territories. He joins up with two other cross-dressing entertainers: Bernadette (**Terence Stamp,** center), a sharp-tongued, motherly type, and Adam, aka Felicia (**Guy Pearce,** right), another biting wit who is less secure in his gayness. Taking them across the desert outback is Priscilla, a run-down bus that the group transforms into an outlandishly decorated home. When it breaks down in the middle of nowhere, Bernadette gets help from Bob (Bill Hunter), a local who fixes the bus and eventually decides to come along. Covering their pain with wisecracks, the trio gradually reveals their longing to be loved in a society that largely rejects them. Tick's ex-wife, it turns out, owns the casino where they are scheduled to do their show—and Tick has a son, Benji (Mark Holmes). He plans on revealing his sexual identity, only to discover that the adolescent is already accepting of it. After the three help Adam fulfill his dream of being the first queen to climb King's Canyon, Tick takes his son to Sydney and Bernadette stays in Alice Springs, taking another chance on love—this time with Bob.

► **REG VARNEY**
**BEST PAIR
OF LEGS IN THE
BUSINESS**
(1972, Sunny Productions)
**Comedy about broken—
and repaired—family ties
directed by Christopher
Hodson** ● "Sherry" Sheridan
(**Reg Varney**), a drag artist
and burnt-out comedian
(**photo**) who lives with his
wife Mary (Diana Coupland)
at a vacation caravan camp,
is concerned about employment when the summer ends.
Unbeknownst to him, the
camp's owner, Charlie (Lee
Montague), is carrying on
with Sherry's spouse. Meanwhile, Alan (Michael Hadley),
the Sheridans' son, arrives
from boarding school and
informs his parents that he is
marrying a vicar's daughter.
He then takes them for tea at
the vicarage where Sherry
makes a complete fool of
himself. After this embarrassment, Sherry learns about his
wife's affair and following a
confrontation with her tries to
find Alan. While searching the
grounds, Sherry, mistakenly
looking into the caravan of
two girls getting ready for
bed, is caught in the act by
their boyfriends and after
being tossed into the pool is
saved by his son. Sherry then
makes amends with both
Alan and Mary.

◄JEAN-PIERRE MARIELLE
HOW TO SUCCEED IN LIFE WHEN
YOU ARE A STUPID CRYBABY
(French title "Comment réussir dans la vie quand on est
con et pleurnichard," 1974, Gaumont)

**Jubilantly uninhibited French comedy directed by Michel
Audiard ●** Antoine Robineau (Jean Carmet) sells adulterated vermouth to bistros with cheesy chiming clocks as a come-on premium. When in trouble, he sheds tears to make people feel sorry
for him. His tactics often work, especially with women like Jane
(**Jane Birkin,** right), a sexy stripper. Marie-Josée (Evelyne Buyle),
the receptionist of a Parisian hotel and the mistress of its general
manager, Gérard (**Jean-Pierre Marielle**), is the only woman who
resists him. But when he is wounded during one of Marie-Josée's
attempts to commit suicide, Antoine is molly-coddled by Gérard's
wife, Cécile (Stéphane Audran). Gérard, in the meantime, falls so
hard for Jane that he follows her everywhere, eventually impersonating a transvestite (**photo**) in a low-rent strip joint. But Antoine-
the-weeper, realizing the love of his life is Marie-Josée, goes back
to his door-to-door trade, this time selling his clocks with cases of
fake vermouth as a premium.

◄PAUL B. PRICE, JACK WESTON &
F. MURRAY ABRAHAM
THE RITZ (1976, Warner)

**Adaptation of Terrence McNally's Broadway hit directed by
Richard Lester ●** More than the typical New York all-male bathhouse, the Ritz is an entertainment complex and the ideal hideout
for Cleveland executive Gaetano Proclo (**Jack Weston,** center),
whose gangster brother-in-law, Carmine Vespucci (Jerry Stiller),
has decided to rub him out. Gaetano plays the gay game and is
hit on by singer Googie Gomez (Rita Moreno). Convinced he is
a theatre producer, she suggests he try a woman once in his life,
but Gaetano turns her down because he thinks she is a drag
queen. Terrorized by the thought of Vespucci, Gaetano accepts
the advances of Claude (**Paul B. Price,** left) and participates in a
talent contest with him and another patron, Chris (**F. Murray
Abraham,** right), as member of a trio that lip-synchs the Andrews
Sisters' *Three Caballeros*. After Vespucci interrupts the performance and asks all the "fairies" to jump into the pool, he shoots
Gaetano but is overpowered by some Ritz habitués. With nothing to wear but a dress, he is taken to the police station.

◄HARVEY FIERSTEIN
TORCH SONG TRILOGY (1989, New Line)

**A gay man's quest for love and respect in '70s New York
directed by Paul Bogart ●** Mother-dominated Arnold Beckoff
(**Harvey Fierstein**), a Jewish homosexual who performs in
drag as Virginia Hamm (**photo**), falls for schoolteacher Ed
(Brian Kerwin). Arnold's bliss evaporates when he discovers
that Ed has been dating a woman. Then Arnold finds himself
pursued by Alan (Matthew Broderick), a handsome hustler/
model touched by the drag artist's gentleness. The couple
plans to become foster parents to a gay teenager but Alan
dies at the hands of a gang of gay-bashers. After Arnold and
ex-lover Ed get back together, Arnold's mother (Anne Bancroft), who knows her son is a homosexual, arrives from
Florida. But when she learns what his lifestyle really entails,
she is incensed and at the cemetery where his father is buried
screams at her son she wishes he had never been born.
Arnold, however, now comfortable with his gayness, makes
peace with his mother. (*Adapted from Harvey Fierstein's
1982 long-running off-Broadway play.*)

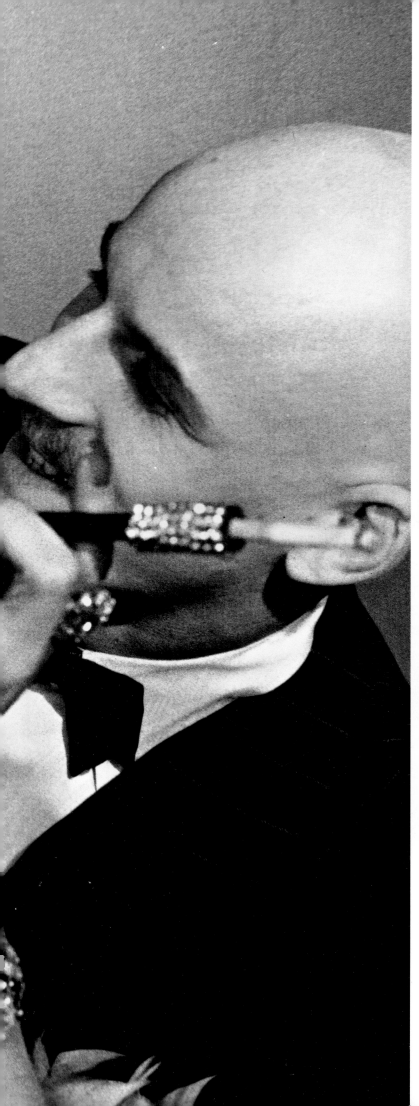

▼ JOEL GREY
CABARET (1972, ABC Pictures-Allied Artists)

Insightful musical drama about the fall of a decadent democracy and the rise of Nazism directed by Bob Fosse ● In 1931, Cambridge graduate Brian Roberts (Michael York) arrives in Berlin to finish his doctorate in philosophy. In his boardinghouse, he meets American singer Sally Bowles (Liza Minelli), a radiant performer at the Kit Kat. Also headlining at the cabaret is a gender-bending emcee (**Joel Grey**) whose songs and choreography satirize the Weimar Republic's decadent sexual mores and mock the nation's growing anti-Semitism. Sally, moved by Brian's sexual ambiguousness, initiates him into the

joys of carnal love. They are happy until they meet Maximilian von Heune (Helmut Griem), a wealthy and dissolute charmer who after spoiling the penny pinchers not only seduces Sally but also forces Brian to confront his bisexuality. The result of this ménage-à-trois is a pregnancy and a paternity question. Maximilian having left, good-hearted Brian asks Sally to marry him, but Sally, fearing they will regret their decision, makes it for them. After her abortion, Brian goes back to England and Sally to the Kit Kat where more and more of the audience wears the swastika.

Left: Ricky Renée as transvestite Elke with an unidentified bald actor.

▼ RICARDO MONTALBAN
SAYONARA (1957, Warner)

Tragic tale of interracial marriage and miscegenation directed by Joshua Logan ● During the Korean War, Maj. Lloyd Gruver (Marlon Brando) is assigned to an air base in Japan where his fiancée Eileen (Patricia Owens) lives with her father, General Webster. One evening the couple goes to a Kabuki theatre featuring a famous oyama (female impersonator) named Nakamura (**Ricardo Montalban**) and after being introduced Lloyd and Eileen argue about her attraction to him. Lloyd, despite encountering prejudice, agrees to be best man at the wedding of chum Joe Kelly (Red Buttons) to Katsumi (Miyoshi Umeki). Meanwhile, Lloyd finds himself entranced with Hana-ogi (Miiko Taka), a dancer of the elite Matsubayashi troupe. When Kelly realizes servicemen with Japanese wives must return to the U.S. without their spouses, he kills himself with Katsumi. But Lloyd, learning that military rules on interracial marriage will soon change, asks Hana-ogi to marry.

▼ KAZUO HASEGAWA
AN ACTOR'S REVENGE (1963, Toho)

Stunning film about an obsessive thirst for revenge directed by Kon Ichikawa ● In 1630s Edo, Yukinojo Nakamura (**Kazuo Hasegawa**) is a famous oyama (female impersonator) performing with the Ichimura kabuki troupe. One evening, he spots in the audience Sansai Dobe, the magistrate who was responsible for the suicide of his father and the death of his mother. Obsessed with revenge, Yukinjo weaves a complex plot to punish not only Dobe but also Kawaguchiya and Kikaiya, two merchants who were implicated. First he seduces Dobe's daughter, Namiji (Ayako Wakao), who despite being the shogun's mistress is mesmerized by Yukinojo's cross-dressing performance and falls in love. Then, knowing that Kawaguchiya and Kikaiya are competing to corner the rice market, Yukinojo uses their rivalry to wreak havoc in their lives. Finally, he watches Dobe's favored position with the shogun destroyed when Namiji is kidnapped. Yukinojo's revenge is complete but short-lived as she is murdered.

▶ LESLIE CHEUNG
FAREWELL MY CONCUBINE (1992, Miramax)

Tragic love triangle in a brutally unpleasant situation directed by Chen Kaige ● In the '20s, delicate Cheng Dieyi (**Leslie Cheung**) is admitted to the prestigious Peking Opera Academy. Cheng is ideal for female roles, while his friend Duan (**Zhang Fengyi**, right), the focus of his homoeroticism, is given masculine roles. Their chemistry makes them famous—especially starring in the classic *Farewell My Concubine*—but it is dissolved by Duan's marriage to prostitute Juxian (Gong Li). In 1937, when Japan invades China, Juxian implores Cheng to entertain the occupants so they will free Duan. When Duan is released, he severs ties with Cheng for collaboration and rejoins Juxian. At the beginning of the Cultural Revolution, Duan denounces Cheng for his homosexuality and Cheng attacks Duan for wedding a whore, after which Juxian kills herself. Considered "reeducated," the two are rehearsing for their signature roles when Cheng, playing the concubine (**photo**), pulls the saber from his partner's sheath and commits suicide.

◄**GEORGE SANDERS**
THE KREMLIN LETTER
(1970, Fox)
Cold War tale of intrigue and mystery directed by John Huston ● A letter from the Kremlin approved by an ill-advised American official threatens war on China. To retrieve the document before delivery, master spy Ward (Richard Boone) recruits an elite team. He selects Naval Officer Rone (Patrick O'Neal) to head the unit; safecracker ace B.A. (Barbara Parkins); and nightclub pianist and female impersonator the Warlock (**George Sanders, photo**). The group succeeds in bugging the residence of Secret Police Chief Kosnov (Max von Sydow), who is in the midst of a political struggle with high-ranking Bresnavitch (Orson Welles). A string of events, including the abduction of B.A., who had become Rone's lover, reveals that the Kremlin letter never existed. It was probably a hoax devised by Ward, a revenge-minded double agent operating in cahoots with Bresnavitch. After killing Kosnov, Ward drives Rone, leaving for New York, to the Moscow airport. Once there, he opens the door of an ambulance where B.A. lies, still alive. Before boarding, he gives Rone a letter to be read after takeoff: it states that B.A. will be freed if Rone assassinates a U.S.-based Soviet spy, his wife and daughter.

◀ **MICHAEL JETER**
THE FISHER KING
(1991, TriStar)

Loony New Age tale of guilt and redemption directed by Terry Gilliam ● Shock D.J. Jack Lucas (Jeff Bridges) hits the skids after one of his on-air ravings triggers fatal shootings at Babbitts, a chic Manhattan club. Despite the affections of video storeowner Anne (Mercedes Ruehl), he is unable to shake his depression and tries to jump off a bridge. Parry (Robin Williams), a vagrant with a mystical vision of possessing the Holy Grail, stops him. When Jack learns that his ragged acquaintance was a medieval history professor and his insanity is the result of his wife's death at Babbitts, he tries to help him connect with Lydia (Amanda Plummer), a shy woman with whom Parry is obsessed. He gets a homeless man (**Michael Jeter**), who imitates Ethel Merman, to dress as a flapper (**photo**) and go to Lydia's office to tell her she has won a year's free videos at Anne's store. Parry and Lydia click, but beaten by young thugs, he ends up in a mental ward. Jack steals the "grail"—actually a silver trophy—thereby bringing Parry out of his catatonic state. Lydia is overjoyed and Anne finally receives Jack's declaration of love.

▶ TIPPI, GINGER QUEST, DORIS FISH & MISS X

VEGAS IN SPACE (1994, Troma)

50's-style sci-fi drag spoof directed by Phillip R. Ford ● It is the 23rd century and the crewmen of spaceship *USS Intercourse* are off to Clitoris, a planet in the Beaver galaxy inhabited only by women. The three need to change sex to avoid being noticed so each pop a pill: Capt. Daniel Tracy (**Doris Fish**, bottom row, center) becomes Tracy Daniels as his sidekicks Mike and Steve (real women **Ramona Fisher** and **Lori Naslund**, bottom row left and right) morph into Debbie and Sheila, respectively. Upon landing, they discover a spa-like capital devoted to beauty and shopping. Princess Angel (**Tippi**, top row, left) introduces the trio to Empress Nueva Gabor (**Ginger Quest,** center) who asks them to get back the crown jewels stolen by Queen Veneer (**Miss X,** right). An earthquake complicates the mission of the astronauts who must resolve the theft and squelch an outbreak of shoplifting and fashion no-nos. To investigate, the three present a drag act from the 20th century's lounge history. It is a success, as is Tracy's attempt to find the jewels: she is rewarded with total control over the population's personal appearance.

▼ STEPHEN BOGARDUS, JOHN BENJAMIN HICKEY, JASON ALEXANDER & JUSTIN KIRK
LOVE! VALOUR! COMPASSION! (1997, Fine Line)

The Big Chill meets *La cage aux folles* ensemble film directed by Joe Mantello ● For each of the three long summer weekends, aging choreographer Gregory Mitchell (**Stephen Bogardus,** far left) and his blind lover Bobby (**Justin Kirk,** far right) host a house party at their New York country home for their gay friends: the yuppie couple of Arthur (**John Benjamin Hickey,** second from left) and Perry (Stephen Spinella); the contentious Brit John Jeckyll (John Glover) and his Latin "hottie," Ramon (Randy Becker); Broadway musical buff Buzz Hauser (**Jason Alexander,** second from right) who is HIV positive; and John's queen-like twin, James (also played by Glover), who is dying of AIDS. During the Memorial Day fest, Ramon seduces Bobby while Gregory is sleeping. Fourth of July is dedicated to the 14th anniversary of Arthur and Perry. While Buzz and James are drawn together, Gregory's and Bobby's relationship is threatened when Bobby confesses his one-nighter. Labor Day weekend climaxes after James collapses during the group's rehearsal for *Swan Lake,* a drag performance Gregory has organized for an AIDS benefit (**photo**). To release tensions, all the men, except for cold-hearted John, bond in a moonlit skinny dip.

◄ CRAIG RUSSELL
OUTRAGEOUS (1977, Almi Cinema 5)

Tale of schizophrenia and female impersonation directed by Richard Benner ● One evening in Toronto, Liza Connors (Hollis McLaren) shows up at gay hairdresser Robin Turner's doorstep, explaining she has escaped from a mental institution. Convinced she can make it on her own, Robin (**Craig Russell**) takes her in and protects her against her mother who wants her back. His faith is returned when Liza persuades him he has the talent to become a female impersonator. After performing in several seedy clubs where his impressions of Tallulah Bankhead and Bette Davis draw thunderous applause, Robin moves to New York. At the Jack Rabbit Lounge, he is a hit when his parody of Mae West (**photo**) brings down the house. Meanwhile, Liza, who has remained in Toronto and become pregnant, is devastated when the child is stillborn. To cheer her up, Robin invites her to New York to build a life of loving mutual support.

▲ CRAIG RUSSELL
TOO OUTRAGEOUS! (1987, Specta Films)

Drag-to-riches sequel to a sleeper hit directed by Richard Benner ● Female impersonator Robin Turner (**Craig Russell**) performs in the Village's gay nightclubs. Living with straight girlfriend Liza Connors (Hollis McLaren), who has used her chemically controlled schizophrenia to develop as a writer, Robin dreams beyond his gig of aptly vamping Garland, Streisand and other "glamour" queens. When talent agent Betty Treisman (Lynne Cormack) discovers him, she insists he abandon his raunchiness and reject his gay identity. In his hometown of Toronto preparing his new show with his manager Bob (**David McIlwraith,** left) and his accompanist Luke (Ron White), Robin learns that Luke has contracted AIDS. Depressed, Robin soon finds solace in an affair, but it ends unhappily. Finally, after intentionally alienating some influential Broadway angels, he scotches his big chance at success in favor of being true to himself.

◄ ALEC MAPA, ROBERT KAISER, STEPHEN SPINELLA & CHRIS LOGAN
CONNIE AND CARLA
(2004, Spyglass-Universal)

Feel-good musical comedy following familiar paths directed by Michael Lembeck ● Chicago cabaret singers Connie (Nia Vardalos) and Carla (Toni Collette) witness a murder and, terrified, hit the road. In Hollywood, they pretend to be men dressed as women to land a job. Donning wigs and flashy make up, they audition at the Handlebar Club were, because they do not lip-synch like the other drag queens (**Alec Mapa**, far left; **Robert Kaiser**, second from left; **Chris Logan**, far right), they find the recognition they had been craving. But then Connie falls for Jeff (David Duchovny), the brother of bartender Peaches (**Stephen Spinella**, second from right). But Jeff is freaked by his own attraction to Carla, whom he believes is a male transvestite. When the Chicago murderer who has tracked the girls down bursts onto the stage, the troupe lays him low. Connie and Carla then decide to reveal their real identity to the crowd. After a moment of hostile bemusement, Connie reignites the show, winning the hearts of everyone in the audience, including Jeff.

◄ MICK JAGGER
BENT (1997, MGM)

Fascinating "coming out" film set during WWII directed by Sean Mathias ● In Nazi Berlin, the gay population comes alive at night in an over-the-top *boîte* run by transvestite Greta (**Mick Jagger**). One of the customers is erotically magnetic Max (Clive Owen) whose sexual encounter with a Nazi gets him—and his lover Rudy (Brian Webber)—thrown into a concentration camp. While Max hides his sexual identity by wearing the yellow Jewish star, Rudy is left exposed to the brutality of the train guards, who beat him to death. Taking the advice of fellow detainee Horst (Lothaire Bluteau), Max fakes apathy and survives the trip to Dachau where he and Horst fall in love. When Horst becomes dangerously ill, Max turns tricks with his captors to obtain medicine. Uncovering the couple's affection, the Nazis murder Horst. Max then takes his love's pink star, which denotes his homosexuality, pins it to his shirt and throws himself against the prison's fence.

► YUL BRYNNER
THE MAGIC CHRISTIAN
(1970, Artisan Pictures)

Satire of human nature directed by Joseph McGrath ● Cynical billionaire Sir Guy Grand (Peter Sellers) adopts a vagrant (Ringo Starr). In order to demonstrate to his new son that anybody will do anything for money, he invites London socialites to the maiden voyage of *The Magic Christian*. There a handful of performers play scary tricks and gender-bending pranks—like the one delivered by a ravishing blonde woman who, after singing "Mad About the Boy" for **Roman Polanski** (right), removes her wig to reveal that she is **Yul Brynner** (photos). Later, watching people dive into a tank full of blood, urine and feces to retrieve millions of banknotes Sir Grand has placed in it, he concludes he has made his point and becomes a hobo. *(Another photo of this film, with Peter Sellers in drag, can be found in the chapter "Nuns on the Run.")*

It's a mad mad mad world
CROSS-DRESSING LIFESTYLES

▶ **MIGUEL BOSÉ**
HIGH HEELS
(Spanish title "Tacones lejanos," 1991, Miramax)

Psychodrama about love, murder and drag directed by Pedro Almodóvar ● Rebecca (Victoria Abril), an anchor on Spanish TV, and Becky (Maria Paredes), the singer mother she worships, are nervously awaiting their reunion. Rebecca is so adoring she has married one of her mother's ex-boyfriends, Manuel (Feodor Atkine). When he tries to rekindle his romance with Becky, Rebecca visits a transvestite cabaret where she is so turned on by the lead act, Letal (**Miguel Bosé, photo**), that she has sex with him. Manuel is found slain and though Rebecca admits to the act on live television, the judge (also Miguel Bosé) is loath to believe her. Becky, who has re-achieved stardom despite a bad heart condition, visits the jail-bound Rebecca, who now rescinds her confession. She admits, however, having killed her stepfather years ago so her mother could follow her dreams. When the judge realizes Rebecca is pregnant, he unaccountably releases her, encountering her next in the drag club—where he reveals himself to be Letal, the father of their child. Learning of Becky's heart attack on television, they hurry to her side. At the hospital, in a burst of maternal love, Becky confesses having killed Manuel and dies.

◀ **JAVIER CAMARA & GAEL GARCIA BERNAL**
BAD EDUCATION
(Spanish title "La mala educacion," 2004, Sony Classics)

Labyrinthine *film noir* about passion and murder directed by Pedro Almodóvar ● In 1980 Madrid, a man (**Gael Garcia Bernal**) forces his way into the office of a young film director, Enrique Goded (Fele Martinez), stating he is his old school friend Ignacio. Enrique remembers Ignacio who adds he is now an actor named Angel and has written an autobiographical script. Intrigued, Enrique reads the tale that starts in a Catholic school where he and Ignacio were two 10-year-olds in love separated by the jealous Father Manolo (Daniel Gimenez-Cacho) who was molesting Ignacio. The tale continuing, Enrique learns that his friend had later morphed into Zahara, a drug-addled homosexual transvestite who perpetrated petty crime in the company of another *maricón* named Paquito or, when in drag, Paca (**Javier Cámara, left**). He also reads about—and visualizes—a tough confrontation between Zahara, who came to church with blackmail in mind, and Father Manolo, who barely recognizes Ignacio. When Enrique decides to make this story his next film, an elated Ignacio/Angel says he wants to play the part of Zahara. After several nightly "auditions" during which they renew their love, Enrique reluctantly agrees. To better understand his main characters, he visits Ignacio's mother and realizes that the manuscript's author is dead and that the pretender awaiting him in Madrid is in reality

Ignacio's younger brother Juan, a revelation Enrique keeps to himself. At the end of shooting, a man waiting for the director identifies himself as Manuel Berenguer. He is the defrocked Father Manolo who chronicles events involving the real Ignacio (Francisco Boira), a junkie who had undergone a sex-change operation and died of an overdose when lovers Berenguer and Juan knowingly gave him pure heroine. Angry and depressed Enrique kicks Juan/Angel out of his home. A few months later, Enrique's movie is such a success that it makes Angel the new Hispanic heartthrob.

▶ EDWARD D. WOOD, JR.

GLEN OR GLENDA
(1952, Screen Classics)

Low-budget comment about sexual confusion directed by Edward D. Wood, Jr. ● Inspector Warren (Lyle Talbot) is investigating the suicide of a transvestite. To better understand cross-dressing, he consults well-known psychiatrist Dr. Alton (Timothy Farrell), who tells him the story of patient Glen (**Edward D. Wood, Jr.**). A heterosexual, Glen has occasionally worn women's clothes since his childhood to become Glenda, a fictitious character he invented when his parents denied him love. Now an adult engaged to Barbara (**Dolores Fuller,** on floor), Glen is reluctant to tell her his secret. At night, he is haunted by dreams, all witnessed by "the Spirit" (Bela Lugosi), a scientist who insists "the story must be told." During the visits of "Morpheus, God of sleep," Barbara rejects Glen for being a transvestite and, during a dreamed wedding scene, his unloving father appears as a demonic figure. In another nightmare, Glen (in Glenda's outfit) cannot lift the branches of a tree that has fallen on Barbara (**photo**). When he tells her his particularity, she is shocked and indecisive, but finally, in acceptance, gives him the angora sweater he always lusted after. During a joint session Dr. Alton tells the couple that Glen can be cured by therapy and understanding, a combination that will transfer Glenda's persona to Barbara.

▶ JOHNNY DEPP

ED WOOD (1995, Touchstone)

Biopic of Hollywood's wackiest filmmaker directed by Tim Burton ● Edward D. Wood, Jr. (**Johnny Depp**) comes to post-WWII Hollywood with a passion for moviemaking. A charismatic lad, he is quickly surrounded by losers, including girlfriend Dolores Fuller (Sarah Jessica Parker). When Ed learns that producer George Weiss (**Mike Starr,** right) intends to make a movie about transsexual Christine Jorgensen, he asks for the director's job, telling Weiss that despite the fact he is a strict heterosexual he loves to dress as a woman. Weiss has in the meantime lost the rights to the Jorgensen story, but agrees to finance a Wood film in the same genre: *Glen or Glenda.* A chance encounter with Bela Lugosi (Martin Landau) gives Ed the idea of casting the ex-Dracula star in the film, which is a flop. Later, Ed—often wearing a wig and an angora sweater on the set (**photo**)—directs Lugosi in another turkey, *The Bride of the Monster.* When Lugosi, a 74-year-old junkie, is hospitalized, Ed does not abandon him and, on the occasion of his friend's release shoots a few minutes of film with Lugosi in front of his Baldwin Hills home. Unfortunately, the old horrormeister dies soon after, but Ed, unfazed, uses the meager footage and gives Lugosi top billing in his following opus, *Plan 9 From Outer Space.* An unmitigated disaster, critics later brand *Plan 9* the worst piece of fiction cinema ever produced.

◄ UGO TOGNAZZI
SPLENDOR AND MISERY OF MADAME ROYALE
(Italian title "Splendori e miserie di Madame Royale," 1970, Mega Films)
Charmed-gay-life-turned-tragic tale directed by Vittorio Caprioli ● Alessio (**Ugo Tognazzi**), a homosexual living in Rome, owns a framing shop. Every Saturday night he transforms himself into Madame Royale, the carefree host(ess) of a wild drag party (**photo**). An ex-dancer, he has brought up the daughter of one of his friends but despite her careful upbringing Mimmina (Jenny Tamburi) is accused of an attempted abortion. To get the charges dropped, Alessio agrees to become a snitch. When aware of his indiscretions, his chums abandon him one by one. Unable to stand the isolation, Alessio organizes a party to celebrate his plans to leave the city. When no one shows up, he falls asleep, only to be awakened by a stranger who wants to take him to another party Alessio's *amici* have planned. The stranger, however, is a killer. Ironically, Mme Royale's costume is pulled out of Lake Albano the next day by the one person guilty of turning the kind-hearted soul into a stool pigeon: the police commissioner.

► CHRISTOPHER HEWETT
THE PRODUCERS (1968, Embassy)
Deliciously tasteless Broadway-based farce directed by Mel Brooks ● When neurotic accountant Leo Blum (**Gene Wilder**, second from left) audits Broadway producer Max Bialistock (**Zero Mostel**, far left), a man who has not had a hit in decades, it dawns on him that a producer could become rich by staging a sure-fire flop if he sold more than 100% of its shares to investors. Max loves the idea and asks Leo to help him produce the worst show ever. They unearth a play—*Springtime for Hitler*—by one Franz Liebkind (Kenneth Mars), a deranged admirer of the Fürher, and sign up the world's worst director, transvestite Roger De Bris (**Christopher Hewett**), coifed by his dresser Carmen (**Andreas Voutsinas**, second from right). Max then raises money from the older women he has been sexually servicing in order to survive, selling 25,000 percent of his future bomb. When *Springtime* premieres, the audience is first treated to a number featuring chorines in skimpy Nazi costumes. Exiting in disgust, the crowd returns when Lorenzo St. Dubois (Dick Shawn) takes the stage as a hippie Hitler. They interpret his hammy performance as inspired satire and laugh uproariously. With a hit in their hands, Max, Leo and Franz blow up the theatre and are promptly jailed. Their first production behind bars is *Prisoners of Love,* the percentage of which they oversell to their fellow inmates.

▲ ROMAN POLANSKI
THE TENANT
(French title "Le locataire",
1976, Marianne Productions-Paramount)

Exceedingly creepy psychological study directed by Roman Polanski ● A shy, inconspicuous office clerk, Polish expatriate Trelkovsky (**Roman Polanski**), is trying to rent an apartment from an austere owner, Mr. Zy (Melvyn Douglas) in what appears to be a respectable building in his adopted Paris. He learns from the surly concierge (Shelley Winters) that the former tenant, Simone, had recently tried unsuccessfully to end her life by jumping out of her window. With uncertain motive, Trelkovsky goes to the hospital where Simone is swathed head-to-toe in bandages. At her bedside he meets Simone's attractive friend, Stella (Isabelle Adjani), and bonds with her after the dreadful shock of Simone's death in their presence. Gradually, strangely, the apartment building's residents begin to wrongly accuse Trelkovsky of minor transgressions. He becomes convinced they are plotting to make him suicidal, just as they had the former tenant, and he eventually starts taking on her traits. After renewing his relationship with Stella, he has sex with her.

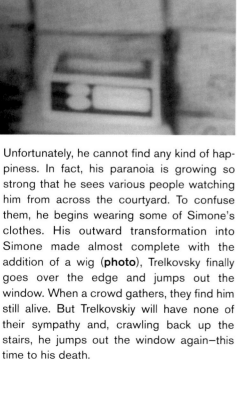

Unfortunately, he cannot find any kind of happiness. In fact, his paranoia is growing so strong that he sees various people watching him from across the courtyard. To confuse them, he begins wearing some of Simone's clothes. His outward transformation into Simone made almost complete with the addition of a wig (**photo**), Trelkovsky finally goes over the edge and jumps out the window. When a crowd gathers, they find him still alive. But Trelkovskiy will have none of their sympathy and, crawling back up the stairs, he jumps out the window again—this time to his death.

▲ DONALD PLEASENCE
CUL-DE-SAC (1966, Compton-Tekli Films)
Gripping chiller about three lost souls in a dead-end situation directed by Roman Polanski ● Middle-aged hermit George (**Donald Pleasence**) and his nymphet wife Teresa (**Françoise Dorléac**, right) live in a dank 11th-century castle on a small island off Britain. Two thugs who have bungled a heist job shatter their twisted, hermetic world. Dickie (Lionel Stander), who has left his wounded partner Albie (Jack MacGowan) in their car, arrives at the castle to find George and Teresa playing a giggly game of dress-up (**photo**). To save his

cohort, Dickie takes them to the causeway where Albie is still stuck in the vehicle. Though the trio gets the injured man to the castle, he lasts only a short while. Holding the couple hostage and awaiting the arrival of his boss, Dickie ups the psychological ante by humiliating and terrorizing George and his provocative spouse. Just when everyone seems to get strangely comfortable with one another, some snobbish friends of George's burst onto the scene, all of whom he eventually kicks out. His pent-up emotions then erupt and he kills Dickie, his tormentor. Teresa leaves him, alone and on the verge of insanity.

WARHOL'S "WOMEN"

▶ **HOLLY WOODLAWN**
TRASH (1970, Andy Warhol)
Contercultural tale of drugs, sex and indigence directed by Paul Morrissey ● It is the '70s on the Lower East side and big time junkie Joe (Joe Dallesandro) is living in the squalid basement apartment of a whiskey-voiced nymphomaniac named Holly (**Holly Woodlawn,** right). Restless and impotent because of his habit, he visits his ex-girlfriend Gerri (Gerri Miller), a go-go dancer who offers him cash if he will go to bed with her—which, of course, he cannot. Joe's encounter with a rich young woman looking to score LSD leads to some quick, rough sex, and needing to get off, his asking for money again. Holly, meanwhile, is growing impatient with Joe's lack of both performance and pocket change and encourages him to break into an uptown apartment. Jane (Jane Forth), the tenant, takes a shine to Joe and, while he takes a bath asks if he will sleep with her and her husband (Bruce Pecheur) who has just returned. They watch Joe shoot up, but the husband gets disgusted and throws him, naked and half-high out onto the street. Then Holly takes in her pregnant sister (Diane Podlewski), who has offered to let her use the baby so Holly and Joe can get on welfare, but Holly kicks her out. When the welfare worker arrives, Holly uses a pillow to show she is pregnant. But the investigator catches on and Joe and Holly are left to their own devious devices.

▶ **STEPHEN DORFF**
I SHOT ANDY WARHOL
(1996, Sam Goldwyn Co.)
Artful portrait of a radical feminist directed by Mary Harron ● Educated in Maryland, lesbian writer Valerie Solanas (Lili Taylor) moves to New York in 1966, to sell her feminist manifesto, SCUM (Society for Cutting Up Men), using prostitution, begging and petty theft to survive. One day she runs into a crew shooting a scene for an Andy Warhol film. Desperate for help and attention, Valerie infiltrates the pop artist's sex-and-drug-drenched Factory. Warhol (Jared Harris) takes a slight interest in Valerie, but another groupie of his entourage, glamorous transvestite Candy Darling (**Stephen Dorff**), is more in tune with the Factory's vibes. Warhol's lack of interest in Valerie's writings and the jeering of the artist's sycophants exacerbate her madness. Enraged at not being recognized as a great thinker by her idol, Solanas steals a gun from a wannabe anarchist and on June 3, 1968, shoots her idol. Warhol survives and Solanas serves three years in a psychiatric hospital before dying in San Francisco in 1989.

◀ **JACKIE CURTIS**
▶ **CANDY DARLING**
WOMEN IN REVOLT
(1972, Score Movies)
Andy Warhol's low-budget satire of the feminist movement enacted by three transvestites and directed by Paul Morrissey ● Three women from diverse social milieus are fed up with men's oppression, albeit for different reasons. Candy (**Candy Darling, photo** opposite) is a socialite who is sexually involved with her brother; Jackie (**Jackie Curtis, left photo**) is a frigid middle-class former schoolteacher; and Holly (**Holly Woodlawn**), who comes from the gutter, is an insatiable nymphomaniac. Together, they decide to swear off men, join the feminist group PIG (Politically Involved Girls) and start a career. Unfortunately, their newfound sexual freedom peters out. In order to enter show business, Candy is forced to agree to a session on the casting couch; trampy, alcoholic Holly returns to the gutter; and Jackie, after sleeping with a male hustler, conceives an unwanted child. In spite of their valiant efforts, the three women end up badly—exploited and brutalized (Candy), abandoned and depressed (Jackie), and wasted and down-and-out on the Bowery (Holly).

▲ JOSÉ SACRISTAN
A MAN CALLED AUTUMN FLOWER
(Spanish title "Un hombre llamado Flor de Otoño," 1978, J.F. Films)
Unusual mix of cross-dressing and politics directed by Pedro Olea ●
It is the '20s and Lluis de Serracant (**José Sacristan**), a prominent young
Catalonian, is living a dual existence. By day he is an upright attorney, by
night a transvestite named Autumn Flower (**photo**) who performs in a gay
cabaret. To complicate matters further, he is an anarchist. When another
transvestite is killed, Lluis falls under suspicion as the two had quarreled
the previous night. Because the deceased had threatened to expose
Lluis's political activities, the dead man's friend, Armengol (Roberto
Camardiel), is so certain that Lluis is the murderer that he and some
toughs give him a bloody trouncing and dump him at his door dressed in
woman's clothing. It is such a cruel shock to his mother that to retaliate
Lluis hides stolen drugs in Armengol's pool hall and succeeds in having
him viewed as a suspect. After Luis' anarchism comes to light, he tries to
blow up a train during the visit of Dictator Primo de Rivera to Barcelona
and receives the death sentence.

► JOHN LONE
M. BUTTERFLY
(1993, Warner Bros)
**Unbelievable story of espi-
onage and passion directed by
David Cronenberg ●** In Beijing
in 1946, French diplomat René
Gallimard (Jeremy Irons) attends
a performance of *Madame Butterfly*. Unaware that a man plays
the female lead, he becomes
intoxicated with the singer's
delicate charms. Song Liling
(**John Lone**) keeps a shy dis-
tance, but when Gallimard's passion requires intimacy, the clever
beauty offers him superb sexual
gratification. Gallimard also inno-
cently reveals tidbits of classified
information, not knowing Song
is a Maoist spy. The illicit affair
takes on a deeper meaning when
Song tells him she is expecting.
Leaving Beijing during her pregnancy, she comes back with a
baby boy—procured by a Communist cell. But the meeting is
short: the singer is sent to a work
camp and Gallimard to France.
Some years later, the couple
reunites in Paris, at which point
the once incorruptible bureaucrat begins dabbling in espionage to send funds to China for
his child. At Gallimard's trial,
Song's gender is revealed, as is,
for the first time, "her" naked
body when they are alone at last
in a paddy wagon. His illusions of
the perfect Asian woman in
tatters, Gallimard plays out his
own finale in prison where he
reenacts *Madame Butterfly's*
tragic ending for fellow inmates.

◀LOU JACOBI
EVERYTHING YOU WANTED TO KNOW ABOUT SEX
(1972, United Artists)

Patchwork of risqué vignettes directed by Woody Allen ● Sketch *"Are Transvestites Homosexuals?"* Sam (**Lou Jacobi**) and his wife visit their daughter's future in-laws. Bored with the luncheon conversation, Sam goes to the bathroom, a mere ruse to snoop around the master bedroom where he changes into one of the hostess' outfits (**photo**). He is having the time of his life—until the husband comes upstairs. Sam escapes but falls into the front yard. A boy steals his purse, creating some commotion and bringing the two families outside. A patrolman joins the ruckus causing Sam to strip off his outfit. Back at home he is gently reprimanded by his wife and promises to see a shrink.

◀JAMES FOX & MICK JAGGER
PERFORMANCE (1970, Goodtimes Enterprises Productions)

Brutally decadent drama directed by Donald Cammell & Nicolas Roeg ● Chas Devlin (**James Fox,** left), a "performer" in gang parlance, is a vicious bloke who does the dirty work of protections racketeer Harry Flowers (Johnny Shannon). No form of sadistic violence seems beneath Devlin as he roams about terrorizing those he does not kill. One of his victims is Joey Maddocks, whom he is supposed to be protecting but murders instead after Maddocks has the audacity to give him more than a few bruises in a fight. Furious, Flowers goes after Devlin with a vengeance. The young hood finds shelter in the gothic townhouse of Turner (**Mick Jagger,** right), a sybaritic rock star who has become a recluse—except for two lusty female bedmates, Pherber (Anita Pallenberg) and Lucy (Michèle Breton). The three lovers are attracted to Devlin's harsh edges and turn their houseguest on with hallucinogenic mushrooms, cross-gender dress-up (**photo**) and outlandish sex play. In a kind of climax, Turner gives his final musical performance. Just as the appearance—and identities—of the four begin to mingle, Flowers locates Devlin's hideout and sends thugs to fetch him. When they arrive, Devlin becomes enraged and shoots Turner in the head. As he is dragged off, Devlin oddly resembles Turner, making the identity switch complete.

371

▲ ROBERT VAUGHN
S.O.B.
(1981, Lorimar-Warner)
Hilarious *film-à-clef* **about Hollywood's standard operating bullshit directed by Blake Edwards ●** Felix Farmer (Richard Mulligan) is a successful movie producer married to star Sally Miles (Julie Andrews). Their last big budgeter, *Night Wind,* is such a failure that Felix decides to take his life. An impromptu orgy organized unbeknownst to him at his Malibu residence gives him the idea of reshooting the film as a musical about sex, and of drastically altering his wife's wholesome image. To realize his vision, Felix buys *Night Winds'* rights from studio honcho David Blackman (**Robert Vaughn**), a tyrant who dresses in female lingerie when having kinky sex (top left **photo**, with **Marisa Berenson**). By convincing his wife Sally to bear her breasts in the reshoot, Felix creates a positive buzz for the film. So positive that conniving Blackman signs a distribution deal with Sally who owns 50% of the property. Enraged, Felix arms himself with a water pistol and rushes to Blackman's office where the police kill him. To prevent Felix's body from appearing at a funeral attended by hypocrites, his grieving buddies–Ben Coogan (Robert Webber), unapologetic quack Dr. Finegarten (Robert Preston) and director Tim Culley (William Holden)–steal his corpse and bury him privately at sea. A couple of months later, *Variety* announces that *Night Winds* is a smash hit.

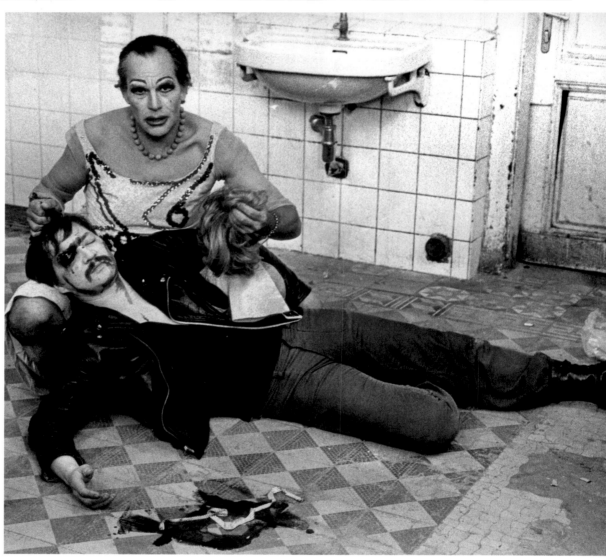

▲ ADRIAN HOVEN
SHADOW OF ANGELS
(German title "Schatten der Engel,"
1975, Albatros-Artco)
Inexorable descent into madness directed by Daniel Schmid ● In a sinister German city, Lily Brest (Ingrid Caven), a beautiful prostitute plagued with sadness, has trouble finding clients. Her impotent husband, Raoul (**Rainer Werner Fassbinder,** on floor), shows only contempt for the submissive Lily and lives off her rare tricks. One night, thanks to her gift for listening to existential woes, she piques the attention of a real estate broker (Klaus Löwitsch). Well

compensated, she transforms herself into a glamorous woman. But this new affluence does not help her mental state, which is shattered by the discovery that her own father (**Adrian Hoven**), who had abused her when a little girl, now performs as a transvestite torch singer. When Raoul—who has left her to go with a man able to restore his virility—is beaten in a gay bar and taken care of by her father (**photo**), Lily wants to die and asks the broker to end her hopeless life. He strangles her in a mercy killing that will go unpunished: to protect the prominent citizen, the police pin the murder on Raoul. *(Film based on R.W. Fassbinder's play Garbage, the City and Death.)*

◀ **ROBERTO COBO**
PLACE WITHOUT LIMITS
(Mexican title "Lugar sin limites," 1977, Conacito)
Poignant tale about desire, fear, machismo and murder directed by Arturo Ripstein ●
El Olivo is a dying Mexican village owned by old politician Don Alejo Cruz. The only piece of real estate that has escaped his greed is the local whorehouse lost some years back in a bet with Japonesa (Ana Martin), the village madam. Now deceased, she has been replaced by Japonesita (Lucha Villa), the daughter she had with the current co-owner, a transvestite dancer who calls himself Manuela (**Roberto Cobo**). One of the brothel's patrons, hunky Pancho (**Gonzalo Vega,** left), is attracted to Manuela but represses his homosexuality through anger. One evening, when Pancho comes to the bordello, Manuela hides in the chicken coop, fearing Pancho's fists. Yet concerned about his daughter, Manuela peeks through the window and sees that she is refusing to strip for the tough. To protect her, Manuela dons a tight-fitting dress and interrupts the altercation. Sitting Pancho on a chair, Manuela dances and sings for him "The Legend of the Kiss," mercilessly teasing the young man (**photo**). While they exchange a sensuous kiss, Pancho's brother-in-law breaks up the embrace. Furious at himself, Pancho turns on Manuela, chases her through the streets in his truck and finally beats her to death.

► CHRISTIAN CLAVIER
LE PÈRE NÖEL
EST UNE ORDURE
("Santa Claus is a Piece of
Crap,"1982, Le Splendid Prods.)
**Outrageous pitch-black comedy
directed by Jean-Marie Poiré** ● It is
Christmas Eve in the Paris branch of
SOS Distress, a hot line that helps people who are on the verge of a nervous
breakdown. While the director, Mme.
Muscat (Josiane Balasko), is stuck in
the elevator, empathetic phone volun-
teers Thérèse (Anémone) and nebbishy
Pierre (Thierry Lhermitte) are unable to
prevent a group of lost souls from congregating in their office. Among them
are ex-convict Félix (**Gérard Jugnot,**
left), who works a Santa Claus hustle
on the street, and Katia (**Christian
Clavier**), a transvestite in suicidal
despair (**photo**). Around midnight,
Félix's ditzy pregnant girlfriend, Josette
(Marie-Anne Chazel), accidentally
shoots the elevator repairman to death.
All of a sudden, the madcap evening
mutates into a repulsive nightmare
when Félix, completely freaked out
and still in his Santa costume, starts to
dismember the corpse.

► LIEV SCHREIBER
MIXED NUTS (1995, TriStar)
**Misfired remake of *Le Père Noël est
une ordure* directed by Nora Ephron**
● While the Seaside Strangler terror-
izes Venice Beach, daffy Philip (**Steve
Martin**, left) operates with mousy
Catherine (Rita Wilson) a suicide prevention hotline called Lifesavers. The
day before Christmas, the office per-
colates in an uncontrollable fashion:
Catherine's pregnant friend Gracie
(Juliette Lewis) breaks up with her
sad sack boyfriend Felix (Anthony
LaPaglia) and Philip allows a despon-
dent woman—who turns out to be a
transvestite (**Liev Schreiber**)—to visit
the office (**photo**). By Christmas Eve,
Gracie has taken shelter at Lifesavers
where Felix joins her with a gun. When
the group tries to disarm him, Gracie
unloads the pistol into the walls, killing
the landlord (Garry Shandling) who
was ringing the doorbell. The event
has unexpected effects: Philip admits
to Catherine that he is in love with her
while Gracie and Felix disguise the
corpse as a Christmas tree and dump
it on the boardwalk. When the cops
discover that the landlord was the
Seaside Strangler, they inform Gracie
she has won a $250,000 reward.

► LADY CHABLIS
MIDNIGHT IN THE GARDEN
OF GOOD AND EVIL
(1997, Warner)
**Puzzling crime in a Southern clime
directed by Clint Eastwood** ● Free-
lancer John Kelso (John Cusack) visits
Savannah, Georgia, to write a piece
about the genteel city's most important
holiday event, socialite Jim Williams'
(Kevin Spacey) Christmas *soirée*. Mysterious yet affable, the wealthy bon
vivant is an inveterate collector, not
only of valuable paintings and objects
but also of eccentric chums—including
his low-class boyfriend Billy Hanson
(Jude Law). Just when Kelso seems to
be fitting into the bourbon-soaked
milieu, he is jolted back to journalistic
objectivism when Williams shoots
Hanson to death. Kelso, convincing
Williams that he should write a book
about the self-defense case, begins to
wade into deeper waters. He makes
the acquaintance of The Lady Chablis
(**as herself, photo**), a transvestite
whose sizzling hip-swinging slices
through the city's social scene like a
hot knife through butter and who eventually testifies on Williams's behalf. Just
when Kelso comes across a detail that
may exonerate his friend, Williams
confesses to him that he shot Hanson
even though his lover's gun jammed.
Kelso, involved with a local singer,
Mandy (Alison Eastwood), sticks
around Savannah to finish his book.
*(Based on John Berendt's best-
selling novel.)*

FOUR FLAMING DRAGUMENTARIES

▲ THE QUEEN
(1968, First Run Features)

Pioneering *cinéma-vérité* documentary about a drag queen contest directed by Frank Simon ● A 24-year-old man named Jack Doroshow, also known as Sabrina, is one of the organizers of the 1967 "Miss All-America Camp Beauty Pageant." After finding a theater and a Manhattan hotel with 28 empty rooms and hip enough to let "his guys" in, he briefs candidates about contest rules and the show during which they will participate in a chorus line. Coming from diverse states where most of them have won local events, the men bond amicably when putting together their competition outfits and applying their makeup. Most of them—except Richard, a loner from Philadelphia known as Harlow—exchange beauty tips and opinions about gay life, the draft board and sex change operations. During the rehearsals of "It's a Grand Old Flag," in which the boys try out their fishnets and stilettos, everyone prepares for the big night. After introducing the contestants, Jack emcees the pageant as Sabrina. At the end of the evening, the judges have selected five finalists—**photo** from left to right: Misses **Sonia** (Boston), **Harlow** (Philadelphia), **Emory** (New Jersey), **Alfonso** (Chicago) and **Crystal** (Manhattan). They award the Queen's crown to Harlow. Outside the building, Crystal goes berserk, accusing the judges of favoritism and threatening to sue Sabrina and the organizers. The morning after, the lonely Harlow boards a bus, her tinsel crown in hand.

▲ PARIS IS BURNING
(1990, Miramax)

Graphic portrayal of the '80s Harlem drag balls and their queen culture directed by Jennie Livingston ● In the late '80s, a series of drag balls—one named *Paris Is Burning*—were staged in rundown Harlem venues. Elaborate and highly organized, they reflected the impossible dreams of Afro-American and Latino gay transvestites whose heroines were successful white women—the best example of these intense competitors being **Octavia Saint Laurent** (above, **left photo**) who idolized Paulina Porizkova and dreamed of fame and fortune. A non-violent response to the racism and homophobia of the white heterosexual mainstream, the balls are described—in interviews with legendary queens such as **Dorian Corey** (left on **right photo**) and **Angie Xtravaganza** (right on **right photo**)—as demanding perfect illusion, a "realness" from each performer when compared to their counterpart's appearance in the straight world. Costuming themselves according to categories, the challengers "vogue" between cheering spectators like runway models. Each entrant belonged to a "house"—Ninja, Adonis, Xtravaganza—which provides unconditional acceptance. Headed by an older drag performer "mother," it functions as a family, as their sexuality had alienated their biological parents. The intense irony of the whole subculture depicted is that its members imitate the very people who exclude them.

▲ WIGSTOCK: THE MOVIE
(1996, Samuel Goldwyn Company)

Relevant and amusing document about Manhattan's Super Bowl of drag directed by Barry Shils ● Manhattan's annual Labor Day Cross-Dress-A-Thon offers lots of genuine talent, naked ambition and exposed cheeks. Part concert film—hence the title's reference to Woodstock—part documentary combining footage from the Wigstocks of both 1993 and 1994, the movie bounces like its hand-held camera from interviews of festival goers to rehearsals, behind-the-stage preparations and actual performances. Here, in makeup thicker than molasses and finery more over-the-top than any Hollywood fantasy, the flamboyant holds sway, with the Tennessee-accented repartee of founder and mistress of ceremonies **The Lady Bunny** (top right **photo**) trying to focus the crowd on the harmony and love to be found in donning a wig and heels. Other performers include the chain-smoking Dueling (Tallulah) Bankheads, whose flailing purses keep time to their hoarse-voiced rendition of "Born to Be Wild"; amazingly believable and funny **John Epperson** (aka **Lypsinka,** top center **photo**) who sings an electric version of "I'm Alive," and "supermodel of the world" **RuPaul** (top left **photo**) who urges the crowd to hold on to their dreams. The thousands roar with approval when she says: "look at the bitch now!"

▲ THE COCKETTES
(2002, GranDelusion Productions)

Nostalgic documentary about San Francisco's "Fairy Tale Extravagandists" directed by Bill Weber and David Weissman ● Legendary for their outlandish drag lifestyle and theatrical performances, the Cockettes were born and nurtured in nonconformist San Francisco just as the pot-puffing '60s morphed into the LSD-soaked '70s. Boasting both men and women—gay, straight and androgynous with heroic doses of hair, feathers, lamé, flowers and nude appendages flaunted everywhere—the campy group epitomized a freewheeling, nonprofessional aesthetic that was at once charming and appalling. But known for love-ins, the city took it and its self-proclaimed she-freaks, such as Scrumbly,

Kreemah Ritz and Goldie Glitters, to its heart. So did later fringe-to-center entertainers like Bette Midler and David Bowie, as well as others, like Divine, who joined the hippie troupe but never made it to the mainstream. Started by a compelling young bohemian called Hibiscus, the Cockette's chaotic history began on New Year's Eve '69-'70 with an impromptu theater piece before an unsuspecting audience of old movies at the Palace Theater. Soon complete, albeit wacky, shows such as *Tinsel Tarts in a Hot Coma* and *Hollywood Babylon* were on the boards. But after Hibiscus formed a splinter group and the Cockettes bombed in the Big Apple, the organization made its final bow in 1972. Can anyone say the creators of *The Rocky Horror Picture Show* did not remember the Cockettes?

◀ JAYE DAVIDSON
THE CRYING GAME
(1991, Miramax)

Unconventionally romantic shocker directed by Neil Jordan ● A radical cell of the IRA has captured black British soldier Jody (Forest Whitaker) and is holding him hostage in exchange for the release of a group of prisoners. Extremists Jude (Miranda Richardson) and Maguire (Adrian Dunbar) lead the cadre, but Jody is watched over by a more sympathetic underling, Fergus (Stephen Rea). The situation turns critical when Maguire orders Fergus to execute his charge. Jody makes a run for it, but when he reaches the road, a passing vehicle kills him: it is an armored truck that disgorges British soldiers, who, in turn, destroy the hideout. Fergus escapes and goes to London where he looks for Jody's lover whose picture his prisoner had shown him earlier. Fergus finds Dil (**Jaye Davidson**) singing in a working-class bar. She is strangely enchanting though he finds it impossible to pin down what makes her so intriguing. He is also haunted by the secrets he cannot share. To Fergus' amazement, the discovery that "she" is a he does not diminish his attraction. When out of the blue Maguire and Jude appear and demand one more assassination, Fergus agrees only because they threaten Dil. The mission fails and Jude, with blood in her eye, shows up at Dil's. Dil, who has been devastated by Fergus' confessions, guns her down, but it is Fergus who takes the rap and goes to prison. His regular visitor will be Dil.

▼ GÉRARD DEPARDIEU & MICHEL BLANC
MÉNAGE
(French title "Tenue de soirée," 1986, Hachette-Première)

Off-putting yet brilliantly darker-than-dark social comedy-drama directed by Bertrand Blier ● Bob (**Gérard Depardieu**, left), a macho burglar, meets dorky Antoine (**Michel Blanc**, center), a loser with an amorphous personality and his dissolute wife Monique (**Miou-Miou**, right). Hiring the mediocre couple as partners, he, and his criminal audacity, turn their miserable existence into lives of luxury. But Bob falls for Antoine who resists his strong sexual overtures in spite of Monique's avarice-based encouragement. Finally, Antoine succumbs to Bob's intoxicating personality and ceases to be sexually attracted to Monique, thereby creating a strange ménage-à-trois in which love, self-loathing and vile insults co-exist routinely. Monique finally leaves the two lovers and becomes a prostitute. Later, Antoine, who has dressed as a woman to please Bob, sees his former wife in a popular ballroom being beaten by her pimp and knifes the man to death. The unholy trio reunites and, plunging into total depravity, end their lives in the gutter as low-rent whores (**photo**).

◀ NICO VAN DER KNAAP & JOACHIM KRÓL
MAYBE…MAYBE NOT (Original German title "Der bewegte Mann," 1993, Bernd Eichinger Prod.)

Wickedly droll gender-twisting comedy directed by Sonke Wörtmann ● Caught with his pants down, hunky Axel Feldheim (Til Schweiger) is dumped by his fiancée Doro (Katja Raimann). Looking for a place to live, he follows a gay acquaintance, Walter (Rufus Beck), to a party. In the car on the way to the club, Axel is introduced to two men in drag, Fräzehen (**Nico van der Knaap**, left) and Norbert (**Joachim Król**, right), and learns they are going to a queens ball. Accepting shelter from Norbert, who seems to be the nicest, Axel fends off his timid advances. One evening, Doro searches for Axel to tell him she is expecting their baby. She surprises him half naked in her bedroom—where he had come to get his slide projector—with a fully undressed Norbert hiding in the closet. Outraged, Doro rejects reconciliation. The couple eventually marries, however, and it is Norbert who helps Doro deliver the baby—while Axel is having sex with an ex-girlfriend at Norbert's apartment.

◄ DANNY AIELLO
READY TO WEAR
(French title "Prêt-à-porter," 1994, Miramax)

Soft satire of the international fashion scene directed by Robert Altman ● In France, a country that has a minister of fashion, the mysterious death of that office holder during Paris' couture week should be a showstopper. But because designers, models, editors, writers, photographers and buyers and sellers congregating for the show are so self-involved, it's business as usual. This ritualistic dance involves a group of strange bedfellows that includes sportswriter Joe Flynn (Tim Robbins), who is forced to share a room with reporter Anne Eisenhower (Julia Roberts); design star Simone Lowenthal (Anouk Aimée), who is betrayed by her devious son Jack (Rupert Everett); and brainless television interviewer Kitty Potter (Kim Basinger). There is also Louise Hamilton (**Teri Garr,** left), who is frantically shopping for large-sized women's clothes. The purchases turn out to be for her husband, Major Hamilton (**Danny Aiello**), the fashion director of Marshall Field's who loves to dine incognito in restaurants dressed as a lady (**photo**).

▲ WOODY HARRELSON
ANGER MANAGEMENT
(2003, Sony Pictures)

Average comedy about inner rage directed by Peter Segal ● Cool-tempered Dave Busnik (**Adam Sandler,** left) is embroiled in a series of mishaps on an airplane. Charged with committing an "act of rage," he is sentenced to 20 hours of group therapy run by anger management specialist Dr. Buddy Rydell (**Jack Nicholson,** right). At the end of a session, Dave convinces the doctor to let him off. Unfortunately, additional contretemps force him to undergo a more concentrated treatment. This program includes a "walk on the wild side" during which the shrink takes Dave to a seedy New York area and introduces him to a German transvestite prostitute (**Woody Harrelson**) who offers him "discipline." The treatment also involves Rydell actually moving in with Busnik, a step that encompasses the irritating shrink's sharing his patient's bed—and eventually his girlfriend Linda (Marisa Tomei). When Dave follows Rydell and Linda to Yankee Stadium, he understands through interaction with the crowd why the good doctor has decamped with his girlfriend. It was to see if his patient was worthy of her.

◄ PATRICK TIMSIT
WHAT A DRAG
(French title "Pédale douce," 1996, Pathé)

Flashy seriocomic gay film directed by Gabriel Aghion ● Adrien Aimard (**Patrick Timsit**) leads a double life: a successful advertising executive by day, he is an outrageous transvestite by night (**photo**). When invited by prospective client Alexandre Agutte (Richard Berry), president of the European Bank, to join him and his family for dinner at his house, Adrien feels that he must hide his homosexuality by bringing along a wife. Friend and confidante Eva (Fanny Ardant), an aging beauty who is a little bit cracked and owner of the best gay restaurant in Paris, agrees to play the part of his imaginary kids' mother. At dinner, Eva creates a scandal that triggers a series of events in which certain sexual relationships are born while others crumble. In the end, Adrien, for whom Eva is simultaneously the woman he would like to love and the woman he would like to be, becomes the father of Eva's son, a child sired in reality by Alexandre. The three happily decide to confront life together.

◀ CANDIS CAYNE
MOB QUEEN
(1999, First Run Features)

Low-budget mob-and-sex comedy directed by Jon Carnoy ● In 1957 Brooklyn, George Gianfranco (David Proval) works his way up the mob hierarchy by pleasing his boss, Joey Aorta (Tony Sirico). To celebrate Aorta's birthday, George finds a sexy prostitute, Glorise (**Candis Cayne**) and hires her as a present. When introduced to Aorta, Glorise throws a plate of pasta onto his head, but the boss loves this insolence—and the subsequent fellatio. Relieved, George sees Glorise a few hours later peeing in an upright position. Trying to prevent Aorta from discovering her true gender, George contacts a "problem solver" (Jerry Grayson) to rub out the transvestite. But the girl recognizes the hit man and identifies herself as his nephew Gary. After Aorta decides to marry Glorise, George interferes: he too wants to marry her. To convince the boss she is not whom he thinks, Glorise lifts her wedding dress for a vision that gives Aorta a massive coronary. George becomes the capo and finds happiness with Glorise and their four kids—all adopted.

▲ BLANCA LI
PIGALLE
(1995, Koch-Lorber)

Chilling trip to Paris' violent underbelly directed by Karim Dridi ● Pigalle is a magnet for individuals in pursuit of sex and drugs. There, junkies, perverts and lost souls hoping to get high rub elbows with pimps, dealers and criminals looking for opportunities to swindle them. In this seedy environment, bisexual hustler Fifi (Francis Renaud) has a casual affair with good-hearted drag queen Divine (**Blanca Li**) but then falls for peep show stripper Vera (Vera Briole). After Divine is savagely killed, the couple realizes they are embroiled in a war between two drug gangs. When Vera finds the dead body of her manager, Jésus the Gypsy, in her bed, she goes crazy. Her boss, Pacha, takes advantage of the situation to coerce Fifi into executing Malfait, the thug responsible for both murders. Given instructions and a gun, Fifi heads up to an opium den but is taken aback when he sees a drugged up Vera lying on a couch. Malfait shoots him but dies in a fiery exchange of bullets. Wounded, Fifi is sent to the hospital and Vera goes back to the peep show.

PARTY MONSTER
(2003, Strand Releasing)

Chilly depiction of the '90s gay glam club scene directed by Fenton Bailey & Randy Barbato ● After moving to New York, Midwest gay teen Michael Alig (**Macaulay Culkin**, right) gloms onto James St. James (**Seth Green**, left), the queen of the city's club scene and begs to be clued in to the secrets of his success. Soon the Peter Pan–like Alig outpaces his mentor. He hustles Peter Gatien (Dylan McDermott), the owner of Limelight, which is fading as the epicenter of the era's hot sex-and-drugs club scene, into letting him throw outrageously themed costume parties (**photo**) for teens. Initially anti-drug, Alig thrives as an ab-fab ringleader, but soon becomes a poster child for bad behavior. Now an inveterate junkie, his life spins out of control. Abandoned by Gatien and unable to pay for his drugs, he is threatened by his boyfriend-cum-dealer, Angel (Wilson Cruz), whom he kills with a Drano injection. While Alig serves his time in jail, St. James writes *Disco Bloodbath,* a book recounting their story.

► JACK PLOTNICK, CLINTON LEUPP & JEFFERY ROBERSON
GIRLS WILL BE GIRLS
(2003, SRO Pictures)

Scathing soap-opera about Hollywood's shadowy side, starring three cross-dressing men, directed by Richard Day ● Nasty actress Evie Harris (**Jack Plotnick**, top photo) keeps her career dreams alive by drenching them in alcohol and watching the tape of her only starring film *Asteroid!* Meanwhile her companion-cum-maid Coco (**Clinton Leupp**, center photo) survives hoping to reconnect with Dr. Perfect, a physician who performed her first abortion. In need of money, the aging star takes in Varla (**Jeffery Roberson, bottom photo**), an up-and-coming thespian whose deceased mother knew Evie when the two were starlets. After Coco is assaulted in the ER, she discovers that the rapist is none other than Dr. Perfect. She nevertheless embarks on an affair with him that is briefly thwarted when she finds him having sex with Evie. Varla, meanwhile, has taken up with Evie's genitally challenged son and finances a cable special called *All About Evie.* When Coco slips some hallucinogens into Evie's drink, the taping turns into a disaster. The actress' babble reveals that her campaign to steal the lead of *Asteroid!* had prompted the suicide of Varla's mother. When Evie apologizes, her redemption is assured. Meanwhile, Dr. Perfect impregnates Coco, and Varla gets hitched to Evie's son and signs on for *Tarantula!*

▲ GAD ELMALEH
CHOUCHOU
(2003, Films Christian Fechner)

Eager-to-please comedy about cross-cultural love and values directed by Merzak Allouache ● Sneaking into Paris, a North African man nicknamed Chouchou (**Gad Elmaleh**) because of his effeminate manners, looks for a job. In a suburb, Father Léon (Claude Brasseur) gives him shelter and finds him a position as a manservant in the office of Dr. Milovavich (Catherine Frot). The female psychoanalyst detects Chouchou's sexual ambiguity and when she learns that he hopes to change his gender one day, she suggests that he dress as a woman and become her personal assistant. Jubilant, Chouchou toils arduously, surprising everyone with his arsenal of French malapropisms. At the suggestion of a childhood friend, he accepts employment as a nighttime waitress in a Pigalle transvestite cabaret. Shimmying out of an alluring uniform with girlish grace, Chouchou piques the curiosity of Stanislas de la Tour-Maubourg (**Alain Chabat,** left), a sexually adventurous heterosexual man. When Chouchou becomes the club's lip-synching star, Stanislas is swept off his feet. The feeling is mutual and the couple (**photo**) is soon en route to marital bliss.

Gender reassignment surgery:
SNIP & TUCK pre-op boys & post-op girls

◀ **JOHN HANSEN**
THE CHRISTINE JORGENSEN STORY
(1970, United Artists)

Biographical sex-change melodrama directed by Irving Rapper ● George Jorgensen (**John Hansen**), born with a severe hormonal imbalance, is unhappy with his gender as early as age seven when his preference for dolls provokes sneering from his playmates. His discomfort only increases: in the Army the violence of the training appalls him and later, his experience with a prostitute is even more unsavory. Things seem to look up when George becomes a fashion photographer, but a homosexual advertising executive's attempt to rape him drives him to try and jump off a bridge. Thwarted, he goes to Denmark and begins a series of hormone treatments. Soon after, he undergoes the world's first sex-change operation, a procedure performed by leading Danish surgeon Dr. Victor Dahlman (Oscar Beregi). Staying at the home of his Aunt Thora (Joan Tompkins), George recuperates successfully and adopts the name of Thora's deceased daughter, Christine. The press hounds the surgical curiosity, but one reporter makes it through the frenzy: magazine writer Tom Crawford (Quinn Redeker) takes Christine to a remote cabin in the mountains for an extended interview. There the two fall in love, making plans to rebuild Christine's life.

▲ **JOHN CAMERON MITCHELL**
HEDWIG AND THE ANGRY INCH
(2001, New Line)

Rock opera about salvation through art directed by John Cameron Mitchell ● Hedwig Schmidt (**John Cameron Mitchell**), a transsexual punk rocker of minimal repute, tells her harrowing life story through her music. In glam outfits and huge golden Farrah Fawcett wigs, she sings about her early years of conflicted sexuality in East Berlin and of how a botched surgery to turn her into a woman—so she could emigrate to the U.S. as the bride of her black lover—left her with an "angry inch." She also sings of love, the saving power of artistic creation and how her songs were stolen by her teenage lover, international rock star Tommy Gnosis (**Michael Pitt,** right). Trailing her protégé's tour, Hedwig and her pan-Slavic band perform in sad little diners, growing more disaffected with each other. The tragic but caustically witty odyssey ends with a brief reunion between Hedwig and Tommy and Hedwig's decision to pass along her creative power again, this time to Yitzak (Miriam Shor), her talented sideman. *(Adaptation of the off-Broadway rock odyssey written by John Cameron Mitchell with lyrics and music by Stephen Trask.)*

► **VOLKER SPENGLER**
IN A YEAR WITH
13 MOONS (German title
"In einen Jahr mit 13 Monden,"
1978, Argos Films)
Poignant fish-out-of-water tale directed by Rainer Werner Fassbinder ● A year with 13 moons is a malefic one for hypersensitive beings. In 1978 (the fifth year of the 20th century's 13 moons), angst-ridden and love-starved transsexual Elvira Weishaupt (**Volker Spengler**) revisits her life's journey: a child-hood spent by little boy Erwin in a convent, teenage years in a slaugh-terhouse where he was a butcher, and the surgery that transformed him forever into a woman. Her life has been consumed by a constant search for love, but now Elvira real-izes that the quest was illusory. Teaming up with empathetic prosti-tute, Zora the Red (Ingrid Caven), she cruises the desolate streets of Frankfort and encounters Anton Saitz (**Gottfried John,** left), the man for whom she became a woman. Anton does not understand her aim-lessness. In fact, in this loveless city, nobody does.

► **ANTONY SHER**
SHADEY (1987, Skouras)
Surrealistic espionage spoof directed by Philip Saville ● Curly-haired Oliver Shadey (**Anthony Sher**) is gifted with unusual talents: he can read people's minds, witness current events without being present and print his findings on 8mm film. Confiding his clairvoyance to Sir Cyril Landau (Patrick McNee), Shadey hopes to milk him for the £12,000 needed for a sex change operation. Sir Cyril alerts British Intelligence, which orders its lead scientist, Dr. Cloud (Billie Whitelaw), to force the pacifist-inclined Shadey to "mind-film" the current technolog-ical state of Soviet submarines. Various foreign spies try to contact Shadey but he avoids them all. Frustrated by Dr. Cloud's inability to finance his operation, he uses his telepathic powers to manipulate Sir Cyril's loony wife (Katherine Helmond) to cut off his penis. After his hospital stay, Shadey wrangles a restaurant meal from Dr. Cloud, who says nothing about his female attire (**photo**). Now, Shadey is a truly changed person.

◄ DANNY EDWARDS
HEAVEN (1998, Miramax)
Violent and cryptic thriller directed by Scott Reynolds ● Architect Robert Manning (**Martin Donovan**, left) is a gambler whose career and marriage are on the skids. His wife Jennifer (Joanna Going) is suing him for custody of their son and has an affair with his shrink, Dr. Melrose (Patrick Malahide). At The Paradise, the strip joint where he plays poker with sly owner Stanner (Richard Schiff), Robert meets exotic dancer Heaven (**Danny Edwards**), a transsexual clairvoyant (**photo**). After Heaven helps Robert in his custody case by handing over phone tapes incriminating Melrose, she also gives him a tip leading to a big win in a game with Stanner. Meanwhile, needing money, Stanner hires two thugs to burn down his club. The sinister duo torches The Paradise, kills its owner, kidnaps Heaven and brutally beats Robert who was trying to rescue her. Saved by an ex-bouncer friend, Heaven gives Robert a portion of the loot stolen from Stanner so he can sort out his life.

◄ STEVEN MACKINTOSH
DIFFERENT FOR GIRLS (1996, BBC Films)
Thought-provoking boy-meets-boy-turned-girl film directed by Richard Spence ● Twenty years after protecting a delicate boy named Karl Foyle from school bullies, London motorcycle messenger Paul Prentice (**Rupert Graves**, left) runs into him unexpectedly. He doesn't recognized him at first, simply because Karl has become Kim (**Steven Mackintosh**), a post-operative transsexual. Intrigued, Paul wants to understand what happened to Karl, but Kim deflects his curiosity. Pugnacious Paul and reserved Kim are worlds apart as far as their vision of life is concerned, but a physical attraction starts to develop. After an argument during which Paul shows his penis to Kim in public, both are arrested. Brutalized by a homophobic cop, Paul sues the police department. Kim, who has always avoided scandal in order to protect her privacy, is reluctant to testify at the trial, but at the last minute shows up, helping Paul win his case. When they meet at Kim's flat, Paul asks her to explain how the surgery made her a woman and insists that Kim show her body. It moves Paul so much that the two make love.

◄ HAROLD PERRINEAU, JR.
WOMAN ON TOP (2000, Fox Searchlight)
Exotic contemporary fairy tale directed by Fina Torres ● Isabella (**Penélope Cruz**, right), an incredibly gifted cook from Bahia, marries Toninho Oliveira (Murilo Benicio) and with her inventive chili pepper recipes turns his restaurant into a culinary hot spot. When she finds him in bed with another woman, she flees to San Francisco to start a new life with the help of childhood chum, Monica Jones (**Harold Perrineau, Jr.**), an exuberant transsexual. To get over her cheating husband, Isabella asks the Bahian sea goddess Yemanja to obliterate her love for him. Suddenly freed of his charms, every man she meets falls under hers—including a television producer who makes Isabella the star of her own cooking program, *Passion Food*. The heat is turned up when Toninho shows up to woo Isabella again.

◄ JEAN CARMET
MISS MONA (1986, CineVog Films)

Major downer about survival on the fringes directed by Mehdi Charef ● In one of the seediest suburbs of Paris, Miss Mona (**Jean Carmet**), a transvestite prostitute by night and a fortune teller by day, lives in a trailer with his catatonic father who, like him, dresses as a woman. Miss Mona dreams of having the operation that will transform him into the woman he has always felt he is. By chance, the pathetic streetwalker hooks up with Samir (**Ben Smail,** left), a young illegal alien from Algeria who has lost his unrewarding job in a sweatshop. Miss Mona shrewdly corrupts Samir, who hopes to obtain a fake French identity card, by forcing him to turn tricks as a gay hooker. Prey to illusion, the symbiotic misfits feed into each other's dreams and gradually slide down together into abject degradation and, ultimately, murder.

◄ JESSE BORREGO
I LIKE IT LIKE THAT (1994, Columbia)

Tender depiction of multiracial neighborhood life directed by Darnell Martin ● Lisette (**Lauren Vélez,** left) and Chino Linares (Jon Seda) are raising their three hyperactive children in a Bronx apartment where emotional crises are plenty. During a blackout, Chino steals a stereo system for his wife and is arrested. In order to bail him out, Lisette tries to borrow money from her cross-dressing brother Alexis (**Jesse Borrego**), who refuses, telling her he is keeping his savings for a sex-change operation. He advises his sister, however, on how to look like a model—lending her falsies and showing her how to "vogue"—in order to find a job. After a disastrous visit to a Times Square agency, Lisette serves as an escort to music producer Stephen Price (Griffin Dunne) who wants to bring some Latin vibes to a dinner with the Mendez brothers, a hip-hop singing duo. Looking for a deal with the Mendezes, Price hires fast-talking Lisette as his assistant. When he makes bail, Chino, prompted by rumormongers, accuses Lisette of straying. Crushed, she breaks up with him but soon discovers in herself talent for transferring her street smarts to pop music and reunites with her family.

◄ PETER OUTERBRIDGE
BETTER THAN CHOCOLATE (1999, Trimark)

Lesbian-themed film of self-discovery directed by Anne Wheeler ● In Vancouver, penniless gamine Maggie (Karyn Dwyer) lip-synchs standards at the Cat's Ass, sleeping nights on the couch at the Ten Percent Bookstore owned by a resolute lesbian (Anne-Marie McDonald) whose salesgirl, Carla (**Marya Delver,** left), is a wise-cracking bisexual. When semi-butch artist Kim (Chistina Cox) pulls into town in her Merry Prankster-type bus, she and Maggie become an item. But Maggie's brother, Paul (Kevin Mundy), and his naïve mom, Lila (Wendy Crewson), invade their cozy loft, forcing the lusty couple to put a lid on their sighs and giggles. Meanwhile, another affair blooms between the repressed owner of the bookshop and Judy (**Peter Outerbridge**), a pre-op transsexual (**photo**) who is depressed over his parents' rejection. Eventually, Maggie's mom discovers not only the romance between her daughter and Kim but also, after finding a box of hidden didos, a sexual awakening for herself. Having become chums with Judy, whom she now accepts for who she is, Lila comes with her to Maggie's rescue when some skinheads firebomb her bookstore.

▲ PHILIP SEYMOUR HOFFMAN
FLAWLESS (1999, MGM)

Better-than-average melodrama directed by Joel Schumacher ● In a Lower East Side building, retired security guard Walt Koontz (**Robert DeNiro**, right) lives alone with memories of his past heroism. When a punk steals money from Mr. Z (Luis Saguar) and hides in the building, the gangster sends his henchmen after him. Koontz comes to the rescue but suffers a partially paralyzing stroke. When his social worker urges him to take lessons to rehabilitate his speech, he reluctantly seeks the help of the singing teacher upstairs—drag queen Rusty (**Philip Seymour Hoffman**). As Mr. Z's minions ransack apartment after apartment with no success, Koontz and Rusty establish an uneasy alliance that includes many confidences (**photo**), not the least of which is that Rusty has the stolen money and is planning to use it for a sex-change operation. But the desk clerk alerts Mr. Z. Once in Rusty's apartment, he wounds Koontz but the drag queen comes to his rescue and tells the ambulance driver that he is Koontz' sister. His macho friend, with a rare smile, agrees.

◄ VINCENT PEREZ
THOSE WHO LOVE ME CAN TAKE THE TRAIN
(French title "Ceux qui m'aiment prendront le train," 1999, Fox World Cinema)

Sharply focused character study directed by Patrice Chéreau ● Having chosen to be buried in Limoges, larger-than-life Parisian painter Jean-Baptiste Emmerich (Jean-Louis Trintignant) had, before dying, mentioned to friends that those who really loved him would be forced to take the train if they wanted to attend his funeral. So it is on a train en route to Limoges, some 450 kilometers south of the French capital, that a sad, wild and revealing journey begins. It reunites the men and women with whom Jean-Baptiste had established a special connection: certain family members, old friends, former wives and ex-lovers of both sexes. Lucie (**Marie Daëms**, left) and Vivian (**Vincent Perez**)—who is in the midst of a sexual reassignment surgery—are two of the many people aboard the train. For them, as for all the others whose shared mourning has triggered jealousies and reignited rivalries, the cathartic trip brings a certain kind of closure.

▶ INGRID DE SOUZA
PRINCESA (2001, Strand Releasing)
Brutal modernization of the *Cinderella* fairy tale directed by Henrique Goldman ● Born Fernando Farias in the Amazon, 19-year old Fernanda (transsexual actor **Ingrid de Souza**) finds employment in Milan among Brazilian transvestite prostitutes. Working under the *nom de puta* of Princesa, she is picked up one night by a man who thinks she is a real woman. But when the man's hand goes south, he finds an unexpected surprise and kicks the girl out of his car. A few days later, the same man, Gianni (**Cesare Bocci, top photo**, left), invites Princesa to dinner. He tells her he is married and she confesses that she plans a sex-change operation. Gianni becomes so besotted with Princesa that he leaves his beautiful wife Lidia (Alessandra Acciai) to live with his new love and offers to pay for the surgery. Now discovering the day-to-day existence of a housewife, Fernanda consults a psychiatrist who warns her that the procedure is irreversible and gives her a hormone, Androcure, to make her mind and body feel like a woman's. But the medicine makes her feel tired and sad. So, when Lidia shows up and begs her rival to give up Gianni because she is pregnant, Fernanda decides to forgo the operation and goes back to the streets.

▶ JOHN LITHGOW
THE WORLD ACCORDING TO GARP (1982, Warner)
A writer's journey through a sex-heavy, violent and loopy life directed by George Roy Hill ● It is 1944 and nurse Jenny Fields (**Glenn Close**, right) is desperate to have a child–without a husband–and so has sex with a dying soldier. The result is Garp, a boy who will grow up in a cauldron of violence. As a teen, Garp (James McCall) and his mother live at a boys' prep school. His decision to join the wrestling team leads to meeting the coach's daughter, Helen Holm (Mary Beth Hurt), whom he will marry. When Garp (Robin Williams) returns from college, he is anxious for the debut of his novel, but it is his mother's feminist autobiography that becomes a best seller. As Garp and Helen raise their two sons, Jenny becomes the center of a movement spawned by a raped woman who had her tongue cut out. As more followers mutilate themselves, they find their way to Jenny's home. Into all this comes the calming influence of transsexual Roberta Muldoon (**John Lithgow**, center). Garp, who is having an affair, is shocked to learn his wife is having one too. While performing oral sex on her lover in his old Buick in her driveway, Helen unintentionally bites off his penis just as Garp and their sons arrive and hit the car. One dies, the other loses an eye. After Jenny is assassinated, Garp is also shot. He survives and is carried away in a helicopter, the answer to his childhood dream of flying. *(Based on John Irving's best-selling novel.)*

▲ CLARK GREGG
THE ADVENTURES OF SEBASTIAN COLE (1999, Paramount Classics)
Huck Finn-like tale of a teenager's quest for an exciting life directed by Tod Williams ● It is 1983 in upstate New York and 16-year-old Sebastian Cole (**Adrian Grenier**, left) is living a rather normal family life with his mother Joan (Margaret Colin) and his stepfather Hank Rossi (**Clark Gregg**)—until Hank announces he intends to undergo a sex-change operation. Unable to cope, Joan takes her son to her native England, but after a year there, sends Sebastian back to the U.S. to live with Hank, now a pre-op transvestite named Henrietta (**photo**). A supportive stepfather in skirts, Henrietta tries to help Sebastian deal with wounding local prejudice and navigate the traumas of his teenage years. As the surgery that will make Henrietta a real woman nears, Sebastian borrows her car and drives for a few days to ease his anxiety. Having arrived in a western state, he calls the hospital and learns that Henrietta has died earlier from surgery complications. Crushed, Sebastian hits the road again with tears in his eyes.

NEAR MISSES

Clothes encounters of the closet kind

◄ ROCK HUDSON
LOVER COME BACK (1961, Universal)

Slaphappy Madison Avenue romance directed by Delbert Mann ●
To please a starlet, charming but wily advertising executive Jerry Webster
(**Rock Hudson**) shoots a series of bogus commercials for a non-existent
product he calls Vip. When his distracted boss debuts it on the tube,
Webster is forced to create a product—any product—and selects wacky
scientist Linus Tyler (Jack Krushen) to do it. Ad rival Carol Templeton (Doris
Day), who only knows Jerry by reputation, decides to steal the Vip account
but mistakes Jerry for the inventor. She wines and dines him and falls in
love. Discovering that Jerry has played this charade only to bed her, she
proposes skinny-dipping at the beach and when he is naked drives off.
The next morning, a trucker who delivers furs picks up Jerry, who ends up
wearing one to enter his apartment (**photo**). Carol reports Jerry to the Ad
Council, but at the hearing he shows up with a candy named Vip. Since
each has the effect of three martinis, Jerry is exonerated when the testing
by the judges and Carol results in drunken hilarity. The next morning, Carol
awakes in Jerry's bed, the tipplers having gotten married. The wedding is
annulled but nine months later she remarries Jerry in the delivery room.

▲ CARY GRANT
BRINGING UP BABY (1938, RKO)

Quintessential screwball comedy directed by Howard Hawks ●
Dr. David Butler (**Cary Grant**) is a paleontologist who has been painstak-
ingly reconstructing the skeleton of a brontosaurus. While playing golf, he
meets ditzy heiress Susan Vance (**Katharine Hepburn,** second from left)
and is suddenly engulfed in catastrophic events. One of David's first mistakes is to help Susan bring her pet leopard, Baby, to her Connecticut
home. During the car trip, she rams into a truck full of chickens that are
eaten by Baby. At Susan's house, David takes a shower while the smitten
brat purposely sends his clothes to the cleaners. Discombobulated, David
reluctantly dons her feather-trimmed nightgown just when Aunt Elizabeth
(**May Robson,** second from right), a potential museum donor, shows up
(**photo**). More confusion occurs when Susan's dog, George (**Asta**), steals
the last bone necessary for the reconstruction of the brontosaurus. Weeks
later, Susan gets David the million he needs and goes to the exhibit hall to
give him the found missing fossil. Perched on a ladder that scales the pre-
historic animal, she professes her love and when David reciprocates in kind
her excitement causes the giant skeleton to collapse.

◀ MELVYN DOUGLAS
THEY ALL KISSED THE BRIDE
(1942, Columbia)

Light satire of Park Avenue gentry directed by Alexander Hall ● Michael Holmes (**Melvyn Douglas**) is writing a biography of M.J. Drew (Joan Crawford), the chairwoman of a trucking company she runs with an iron fist. To get close, Michael sneaks into her house on the occasion of her sister's wedding. When M.J. sees him, she experiences a sudden weakness in her knees, a symptom her physician diagnoses as "falling in love." When, at the Truck Drivers Ball, she wins a jitterbug competition thanks to her trucker dance partner, Johnny Johnson (Allen Jenkins), she is so elated that she invites Michael, who is now enamored with his subject, home. But the writer, slightly drunk, falls asleep. The next morning, he is in M.J.'s bed, dressed in a woman's nightgown, which the butler (**Frank Dawson,** left) identifies as the cook's (**photo**). After arguing with Michael—and more knee shaking—M.J. asks Johnny Johnson if "love is reserved only to the proletariat." When Johnny answers negatively, she decides to marry Michael.

◀ MELVYN DOUGLAS
HE STAYED FOR BREAKFAST
(1940, Columbia)

Politically incorrect screwball comedy directed by Alexander Hall ● Militant communist Paul Beliot (**Melvyn Douglas**) is working as a waiter in a Paris café when one day he takes out his distaste for capitalists on a rich banker, Maurice Duval (Eugene Pallette). Duval has made the error of holding his coffee cup with his pinkie extended and Beliot shoots it off his hand. Chased by *gendarmes*, he takes refuge in the apartment of Marianne (**Loretta Young,** right). Amused by Beliot's politics and agreeing to let him stay until he finds out a way to avoid the police, she reveals that she is Duval's soon-to-be-ex-wife and introduces the Marxist to the comforts of wealth. When the laundryman picks up Beliot's clothes that Doreta the maid (**Una O'Connor,** center) had left on the kitchen floor, Beliot is forced to wear Mme Duval's gown (**photo**). One night, to help Marianne escape the unwanted attentions of her husband, he is forced into putting on a tux, which makes him even more attractive to his hostess. When Duval realizes Beliot's identity, Marianne agrees to go back home with her husband if he lets him flee. But once ensconced in her velvet cage Marianne rebels—by shooting a coffee cup out of her husband's hand. Marianne reunites with Beliot, who has renounced the party.

◀ DON AMECHE
SO GOES MY LOVE
(1946, Universal)

Old-fashioned tale of an inventor and his muse directed by Frank Ryan ● In the late 18th century, country girl Jane Budden (Myrna Loy) moves to Brooklyn and meets Hiram Maxim (**Don Ameche**), a struggling inventor. Her perception of Hiram as a loser is confirmed when the scientist, after donning a wig to test out his revolutionary hair curler in front of his landlady (**Clara Blandick,** right on **photo**), sets his room on fire, an incident that brings firefighters to the rescue. The Captain, Josephus Ford (Richard Gaines), is a lawyer in whom Jane sees a potential husband. A wedding is planned but Josephus insists upon setting up strict rules for his future wife. Jane breaks up the engagement and asks Hiram to marry her. The inventor happily agrees but warns her of his diminished financials. Strong-willed Jane, however, knows that with understanding and encouragement, the eccentric inventor will grow into a successful one. He does and becomes the proud father of their son, Percy (Bobby Driscoll).

▲ JOHN HUBBARD
TURNABOUT
(1940, Hal Roach-United Artists)
Well-acted comic fantasy directed by Hal Roach ● Tim Willows (**John Hubbard**), the visionary behind a powerful ad agency, and his elegant wife Sally (**Carole Landis**, right), quarrel frequently in their bedroom in front of an Indian idol they call Mr. Ram. During one of their arguments, they wish to trade places. Surprisingly, the statue announces their desires will be granted. Next morning, Tim wakes up in Sally's négligé and Sally in Tim's pajamas. They are astonished to realize they have also switched personalities, mannerisms and even voices. Friends are also stunned by the suddenly feminized Tim and masculinized Sally. The situation creates confusion among Tim's clients as well as panic on the home front. The couple, sorry to have wanted to switch, begs the idol for a return to their former identities. Ram works his magic again but this time makes a slight mistake: it is Tim who will bear the couple's child.

▶ WALTER MATTHAU
HOUSE CALLS (1978, Universal)

Romantic midlife crisis romp directed by Howard Zieff ● After the demise of his wife, Dr. Charley Nichols (**Walter Matthau**) finds himself fending off young females. The saggy-faced surgeon plunges into his new life with gusto, until he encounters patient Ann Atkinson (Glenda Jackson). Despite the fact that Ann is 15 years older than most of his conquests, Charley is attracted to her feistiness. Romantically gun-shy, Ann wonders if Charley can remain faithful and asks for a two-week test. Meanwhile, senile chief-of-staff Dr. Amos Willoughby (Art Carney) demands that Charley woo the widow of a man who died in surgery so she will drop her lawsuit. To oblige, Charley stays out all night on the anniversary of his two-week trial. After sneaking into Ann's apartment, he takes a shower and she, furious, hides his clothes. Charley then goes to the hospital in the only item of Ann's that fits—a marabou-trimmed robe (**photo**). Influenced by her earlier tongue-lashing about his cowardice, Charley withdraws his support of Dr. Willoughby for a renewal of his position and begs Ann for a month-long test of their love.

▶ ROBERT MONTGOMERY
FORSAKING ALL OTHERS (1934, MGM)

Sophisticated comedy about love, loyalty and betrayal directed by W.S. Van Dyke ● Childhood chums Mary Clay (**Joan Crawford**, right), Jeff Williams (Clark Gable) and Dill Todd (**Robert Montgomery**) have remained close into adulthood. When Jeff comes back from Spain with plans to propose to Mary, he finds out that Dill is marring her. Dill lives up to his playboy reputation when he jilts Mary the day of the ceremony to wed his erstwhile girlfriend Connie (Frances Drake). Mary, ignorant of Jeff's affection for her, leans on him for support. Soon Mary finds herself drawn back into Dill's arms and, after a bike ride in the rain, into his country home for the evening. She manages to keep him at arm's length, which is easy to do after Dill has to change his wet clothes for drier, frillier apparel (**photo**). Planning to marry Dill again, Mary is shocked into realizing her love for Jeff when she learns that he—not Dill—filled her rooms with flowers on her last wedding day. Jeff has already left for Spain again, but Mary dashes off just in time to sail with him into the sunset.

◀ GREGORY PECK
THE YEARLING (1946, MGM)

Family fare about a wilderness boy's maturation directed by Clarence Brown ● It is the 1870s and Penny Baxter (**Gregory Peck**), his wife Orry (**Jane Wyman,** left) and son Jody (**Claude Jarman, Jr.,** right) are eking out a living in Florida's scrublands. When a rattlesnake bites Penny, Jody shoots a doe and cuts out his heart to treat the wound. As a reward, the boy is allowed to adopt the orphaned fawn which he names Flag. Tragedies ensue, beginning with the loss of the family's crop to rain. There is time for lightheartedness, though, as when Jody catches his embarrassed father serving as a model for Orry's dressmaking (**photo**). But Flag eats the new crop. Injured while planting a replacement, the bedridden Penny orders Jody, who has sowed yet another crop, to shoot Flag if he destroys it. Flag does and Jody disobeys, releasing the yearling into the wilderness. When the animal comes back, Orry then botches shooting him, forcing Jody to finish off his pet. The trauma drives him to run away, but he returns home to grateful parents.

▲ ROBERT NEWTON CYRIL CUSACK, & STEWART GRANGER
SOLDIERS THREE
(1951, MGM)

Kipling-inspired period military comedy directed by Tay Garnett ● In 1890 India, Colonel Brunswick (Walter Pidgeon) is overwhelmed by pugnacious rebels, demanding superiors and the annoying behavior of three undisciplined soldiers whose favorite activity is drunken brawling: Dennis Malloy (**Cyril Cusack,** far left), Jack Sykes (**Robert Newton,** third from left) and Archibald Ackroyd (**Stewart Granger,** far right). Their free, often destructive spirit, mutates at times into sheer resourcefulness. For example, when the clothes of a 10-man patrol are carried downstream at a river crossing, Archibald is encouraged by his two buddies to dash into the local saloon to borrow enough attire from the hostess—albeit feminine—to allow the pantless squad to return to camp with some dignity (**photo**).

▲ TIM DALY
DR. JEKYLL & MS. HYDE (1995, Savoy Pictures)

Retelling of the horror classic, with a post-feminist slant, directed by David Price ● Chemist Richard Jacks (**Tim Daly**) discovers he is the great-great-grandson of Dr. Henry Jekyll. In the notes bequeathed to him by his uncle, he finds the scientist's formula for genetic change and recreates the potion. Adding a few twists, he morphs into a seductive, evil woman (Sean Young). Introducing herself as Richard's new assistant, Helen Hyde sleeps her way to the top. But the potion is unstable and she reverts to the man she is, waking up one morning in female clothing (**photo**). From woman to man and man to woman, Richard tries to end the oscillating process. To defend her life, Helen attempts to destroy all traces of the formula, but during the introduction of his/her new fragrance, Richard's fiancée, Sarah, injects Helen with the modified serum. In front of stunned guests, Helen mutates into Richard who, still in female garb, explains that he had to get in touch with the womanly part of himself to create the ultimate female fragrance.

▲ W.C. FIELDS
MY LITTLE CHICKADEE
(1940, Universal)

Comedy of sexual innuendo and visual gags directed by Eddie Cline ● Flower Belle (Mae West), seen kissing a masked bandit, is condemned to leave town and never return until she is married. On the train she meets boozy conman Cuthbert J. Twillie (**W.C. Fields**) and thinking he is wealthy, weds him. Greasewood City, where they settle, is a lawless town. Its "boss," Jeff Badger (Joseph Calleia), notices Flower Belle and, intending to make Cuthbert's wife a widow, names him sheriff. One evening, hoping to consummate his marriage, Cuthbert makes his ablutions in his wife's bathroom and avails himself of her nightgown (**photo**). When he enters the bedroom, he finds a goat under the blanket instead of his wife. Undeterred, Cuthbert suits up as the masked bandit and is arrested. To prove her husband's innocence, Flower Belle requests Badger's help but upon embracing him recognizes the masked bandit's kiss. Before Cuthbert is to be hanged, Flower Belle shoots the rope off. Innocent, Cuthbert goes back East while Flower Belle will have to chose between Badger and a local journalist.

◄ **GEORGE SEGAL**
THE LAST
MARRIED COUPLE
IN AMERICA
(1980, Universal)
**Morality tale about
divorce American style
directed by Gilbert
Cates** ● Architect Jeff
Thompson (**George Segal**)
and his wife Mari (Natalie
Wood) live comfortably in
Beverly Hills. They are
concerned by the divorce
epidemic involving their
friends but all the freedom
they observe among their
neighbors tempts them.
After being hit on by
divorcée Barbara (Valerie
Harper), one of Mari's
aggressively sexy friends,
Jeff sleeps with her and
catches gonorrhea. He tries
to keep the fact secret but
Mari, when she contracts
the disease herself and
finds out the source,
decides to live her own life.
She has an affair with tennis
pro Rick (Robert Wahler),
while Jeff, cured, goes to
bed with Helena (Priscilla
Barnes), the former wife of
a close friend. Unable to
perform satisfactorily,
he dons Helena's frilly
nightgown (**photo**) and,
smoking a cigar, ruminates
about the emptiness of sex
without love. After rejecting
participation in a foursome,
Jeff and Mari reunite,
concluding that loyalty is
better than the alternative.

Otto Waalkes in *Otto–Der Katastrofenfilm* (2000, Rialto Films), directed by Edzard Onneken.

INDEX

Page references in italic refer to captions.

ABOUT THE PHOTOS

Most photos shown in this book have been taken for publicity purposes by photographers hired by producers and/or distributors to publicize their films. These companies are credited in the body of the book after the title of each movie and its year of release. It is the ambition of *Ladies or Gentlemen* to prolong these stills' mission by helping its readers discover or re-discover unknown or forgotten films and prompt them to go to their neighborhood video store to rent or purchase them. Videos and DVDs can also be purchased through mail order: two good sources are www.facets.org and www.moviesunlimited.com. By searching these sites, it is easy to know if a film is currently available in video or DVD formats in the United States.

Major studios and independent producers rarely acknowledged on the front or back of their stills the photographer's name. When they did so, we mention them (see below.) Efforts have been made to identify the copyright holders of all material published in *Ladies or Gentlemen*. We apologize for any error or omission and will insert appropriate credit in subsequent editions.

PHOTO CREDITS

Pages 6 Courtesy Carsey-Werner 14 (bottom right) Cinemateca Argentina 16 (center) Courtesy Hachette Filipacchi, Madrid (bottom right) Courtesy Fotogramas, Barcelona 23 Stiftung Deutsche Kinemathek, Berlin 25 (bottom) Everett Collection 28 Harry Gillard/The Kobal Collection 34 Brian Hamill for Columbia Pictures 41 Lorey Sebastian for United Artists 57 Simon Mein for MGM 63 Everett Collection 75 (bottom) Everett Collection 82 (top) Theatre Collection, Free Library of Philadelphia 83 (top) posters by Adrien Barrière, courtesy Maud Linder 84 (left) Richard W. Bann Collection 91 (bottom) Everett Collection 95 (left) Bert Anderson for Columbia 100 Courtesy Gérard Oury 112 (bottom left) Richard W. Bann Collection 119 Richard W. Bann Collection 128-131 Courtesy Suzanne Lloyd, the Harold Lloyd Estate and AMPAS 146 Courtesy Gente magazine, Milan 147 Reporters Associati, Rome 148 (top) Courtesy Gente magazine, Milan (center) Archivio Storico del Cinema, Rome 149 Reporters Associati, Rome 157 (top) Richard W. Bann Collection 158 Everett Collection 159 Corbis/painting by Joe Coscio 161 Everett Collection 163 (bottom left) Cronenweth for Columbia 164 Charley V. Martin for Columbia 174 (center) Joe Monte for Columbia 176 (top) Everett Collection (bottom) Clive Coote for Lions Gate 184 (top) Archivio Storico del Cinema, Rome 188 (top right) The Kobal Collection 198 (top) Photofest 202 (left) Richard W. Bann Collection 203 (top) Critt Davis Collection 210 (top) Photofest 212 (bottom) Everett Collection 213 Courtesy Danjaq S.A. 215 (bottom) Stiftung Deutsches Kinemathek, Berlin 216 (bottom) Reporters Associati, Roma 219 (top) Bob De Stolfe for Columbia 220 (top) Richard Blanshard for Miramax/The Koball Collection (bottom) E. Caro for Paramount Classics 225 (top) Francos Films 241 (bottom) Muki for Columbia/The Kobal Collection 242 (top) Marlene Bergamo for Sony Classics 247 (top) Tad Gillum for Columbia 252 (top) Photofest 255 (top, center) Courtesy Paris Match 256 Joe Lederer for Revolution Studios 258 Miramax/courtesy Paris Match 260 (bottom) Photofest 265 Max Julian for Warner Bros. 266 Courtesy Fox France 268-269

Mary Ellen Mark/Library 274 (top) Melissa Moseley for Universal 276 The Kobal Collection 281 Jean-Claude Lothar for Sony Pictures 290 (top) Doug Hyun for Touchstone (bottom) Jim Zenk for Orion 291 (center) Simon Films Production 295 (center) Reporters Associati, Rome 297 (top) Sophie Baker for HandMade Films 298 (top) Elliott Marks for Hollywood Picture Company 300 Everett Collection 301 Bruce McBroom for Universal 302 (top) Joe Walters for Columbia 305 (top) Courtesy Gente magazine, Milan 305 Archivio Storico del Cinema, Rome 306 Neal Peters Collection 307 (top) Ralph Nelson for Universal, (center) Graham Atwood for Orion 308 (top) Alfeo Dixon for Lions Gate (center) Bruce McBroom for Paramount 309 Neal Peters Collection 310 Arthur Grace for 20th Century Fox 311 Phil Bray for 20th Century Fox 313 Photofest 318 (top) Critt Davis Collection 320 (bottom) Courtesy Film magazine, Warsaw 324 (top) Abigayle Taraches for New Line 325 Kent Eanes for Morgan Creek/Warner 331 (top) Photofest 332 (top) M.B. Paul for Columbia 340 (bottom) Courtesy Paris Match 341 Courtesy Gente magazine, Milan 343 Reporters Associati, Rome 344 (top) Brookfilms Limited 347 (bottom) Bill Foley for Fox Searchlight 348-349 (top) David Appleby for Buena Vista 350 Gregory Heisler for Universal and Amblin 353 (top) Courtesy Paris Match 356 (top right) Courtesy Daiei 358 (bottom) Photofest 359 (bottom) Attila Dory for Fine Line 360 (top) Eike Schroter for Universal (bottom) Photofest 361 Courtesy Artisan Pictures 362 Lopez Calvin Diego for Sony Classics 363 Courtesy Fotogramas magazine, Barcelona 365 (top) Courtesy Gente magazine, Milan 370 (left) Courtesy Hachette Filipacchi, Madrid 371 (top left) Takashi Seida for Geffen Pictures 374 (bottom) Andy Schwartz for TriStar 375 Sam Emerson for Warner Bros. 376 (bottom left) Joseph Astor (bottom right) Michel Comte for Prestige/Miramax 377 Bud Lee for Strand Releasing 379 (top) Georges Pierre/Sygma 380 (center) Phillip Caruso, SMPSP for Columbia 383 IFC Films 387 (center) Sven Arnstein for First Look Pictures (bottom) Phil Bray for 20th Century Fox 385 Sophie Giraud for New Line Cinema 389 (top) Andrew Schwartz for MGM 386 (bottom) Film 4, London.

The national and private archives that have contributed enormously to the making of *Ladies or Gentlemen* are:

THE ACADEMY OF MOTION PICTURES ARTS & SCIENCES, MARGARET HERRICK LIBRARY, BEVERLY HILLS. Pages 1, 8, 44 (top) 45 (top, center) 65, 66, 67 (right) 68, 69, 70 (top) 71, 73, 75 (top) 80, 81, 82 (bottom) 106 (center) 112 (bottom right) 113 (bottom) 115, 117 (top) 121 (bottom) 126 (center) 138, 139 (top) 152, 155 (center, bottom) 157 (center, bottom) 160 (top) 161 (top right, bottom right) 163 (top left, bottom right) 165 (top) 166 (center, bottom left) 167, 168, 178, 182, 183 (bottom) 192 (top) 198 (bottom) 206, 211 (top) 224, 225 (bottom) 259, 277 (top left, bottom) 279 (top) 288 (top, center) 313 (bottom right) 318 (center) 323 (top) 334, 335 (top) 345, 375

LA BIBLIOTHÈQUE DU FILM (BIFI), ICONOCOTHÈQUE, PARIS. Pages 13, 96, 98, 99, 189, 190 (top) 210 (bottom) 304 (bottom) 337, 338 (top) 371 (top right) 319 (bottom)

THE BRITISH FILM INSTITUTE (BFI), STILLS COLLECTION, LONDON. Pages 14 (bottom left), 26, 27, 29, 30, 31, 45 (bottom), 46, 47, 48, 52, 53, 55, 60 (top), 79 (top), 83 (bottom) 135 (top) 151, 169, 171 (bottom) 180 (top) 188 (top left, bottom) 214 (left) 215 (right) 217, 226, 228, 238 (top) 248 (bottom left, right) 249, 280 (top) 298 (bottom) 303 (top) 305 (bottom left) 313 (bottom left) 315 (bottom) 328 (bottom) 330 (right) 352, 366, 370-371 (bottom)

LA CINÉMATHÈQUE SUISSE, PHOTOTHÈQUE, LAUSANNE. Pages 16 (top), 17, 97, 101, 102, 103, 104, 127, 148 (bottom) 173 (top) 174 (top, bottom), 196, 216 (top) 218, 229 (top) 249 (top right) 267 (top) 294 (top) 317 (bottom) 319 (bottom) 321, 328 (left) 336 (top) 353 (bottom) 356 (left) 372 (bottom) 373, 374 (top) 378, 382 (bottom) 386 (top) 400

THE MUSEUM OF MODERN ART, FILM STILLS ARCHIVES, NEW YORK. Pages 43, 44 (bottom), 70 (bottom), 72, 74, 76, 77, 78 (center), 85 (left), 86, 89 (bottom), 90 (top), 95 (right), 110, 111, 116, 117 (bottom) 121 (top) 183 (top) 187, 261 (top) 312, 326

THE SWEDISH FILM INSTITUTE, STOCKHOLM. Pages 12 (top) 15 (top right) 200 (bottom) 212 (top) 303 (bottom) 316, 330 (left)

EDDIE BRANDT'S SATURDAY MATINEE, NORTH HOLLYWOOD. Pages 14 (top), 24 (top), 84 (right), 49, 155 (top) 156 (bottom) 160 (bottom) 170, 172, 175, 190 (center) 193, 199, 200 (center) 203 (bottom) 247 (center) 260 (center) 261 (center, bottom) 262, 263, 264 (bottom) 272, 273 (top) 277 (right) 278, 280 (center) 317 (top) 328 (top) 336 (bottom) 384, 391, 392, 394, 396, 397, 398 (top left and right)

PREMIERE MAGAZINE, NEW YORK & PARIS. Pages 176 (bottom) 204 (bottom) 256, 257, 299 (top) 349, 362, 380 (center and bottom) 381 (bottom) 382 (top) 383, 387 (center and bottom) 388 (top and bottom) 389 (bottom)